A Golden Age Economy

A Golden Age Economy

"We can create an economy that will deliver unparalleled prosperity to ALL people on Earth"

KIM ANDREW LINCOLN

Copyright © 2013 Kim Andrew Lincoln

The moral right of the author has been asserted.

Apart from any fair dealing for the purposes of research or private study, or criticism or review, as permitted under the Copyright, Designs and Patents Act 1988, this publication may only be reproduced, stored or transmitted, in any form or by any means, with the prior permission in writing of the publishers, or in the case of reprographic reproduction in accordance with the terms of licences issued by the Copyright Licensing Agency. Enquiries concerning reproduction outside those terms should be sent to the publishers.

Matador
9 Priory Business Park,
Wistow Road, Kibworth Beauchamp,
Leicestershire. LE8 0RX
Tel: (+44) 116 279 2299
Fax: (+44) 116 279 2277
Email: books@troubador.co.uk
Web: www.troubador.co.uk/matador

ISBN 978 1780884 066

British Library Cataloguing in Publication Data.
A catalogue record for this book is available from the British Library.

Printed and bound in the UK by TJ International, Padstow, Cornwall
Typeset in 11pt Book Antiqua by Troubador Publishing Ltd, Leicester, UK

Matador is an imprint of Troubador Publishing Ltd

This book is dedicated to my dearest Mother, and all the Mother energies on Earth that have been subject to relentless and vicious attack by the forces of darkness since the Serpent tricked Eve into breaking God's Laws in the Garden of Eden.

And thus, the purpose of this book is to help restore God the Mother on Earth who brings forth her children and nurtures them, and who is the source of all the abundance that our Father/Mother God wants us to have.

This book honours the Mother energies and the Mother of the World, without whom there is no economy, and there can be no recovery.

The message of this book is that a Golden Age economy can only manifest when the Mother takes her rightful place at the side of the Father, and the balance in this world is finally restored.

About This Book

This book is the story of two economies: the one we have now that does not work, and the one that the 99% would like to have. In these chapters I explain how we can move from an age of enslavement, where the riches of this world are concentrated in the hands of a gilded few, to an Age of Freedom, where those of us who are prepared to 'multiply our talents' – can reap the abundance – material and otherwise – we are meant to have.

This book has been created for the benefit of those who say 'enough is enough', who are fed up with the way things are, and who want an honest, impartial and clearly stated explanation of what is wrong with our economy, and what can be done to put it right.

This book is not the work of an academic, but has been written by someone who has spent his working life helping businesses and private individuals to improve their financial position. But though this is no textbook, I hope that students of economics will be drawn to it, as I challenge accepted economic theories and practice and find them wanting.

What sets this book apart from others that have delved into the iniquities of our financial system is that it offers solutions based on the principles of 'Enlightened Free Enterprise'. Other points of difference are in the use of poetry and song lyrics as both a substitute and supplement to narrative, and the profuse use of quotations to explain and encapsulate complex concepts. Please, therefore, do not bypass a quotation, lyric or poem thinking that it is not pertinent – because it is. Indeed, I composed many of the quotes specifically for this book.

That this book is spiritual to its core, should not be a barrier to unbelievers, as this work is aimed at readers of all religious persuasions – but especially those of no persuasion. It is not my purpose to convert you, merely to convince you that there is a better

A GOLDEN AGE ECONOMY

way of running our economy, and that my way observes the Laws by which this Universe is made and sustained is incidental.

The material presented here is the minimum I consider necessary to appreciate the mind boggling scale of criminality and misrepresentation of the truth relating to the economy by the power elite. But please be assured that my intention is to raise awareness and provide solutions, not to spread fear and disillusion.

Although this book is called *A Golden Age Economy* it is concerned about much more than just money and economics. In fact, the underlying theme is how we can create more abundance, and this covers many interrelated subjects such as spirituality, science, health, history and music. Yes, music is important to the economy.

That this work is written from the perspective of a westerner is irrelevant, as most countries today operate their economies in accordance with the tenets of capitalism – the obvious exceptions being Islamic countries and closed/feudal societies like North Korea. But I say now, there is much that the West can learn from the Islamic model of finance. Indeed, had we heeded the original teachings on money and trade that Archangel Gabriel gave to the Prophet Muhammad fourteen centuries ago, I believe we would not be facing the challenging economic conditions that confront us now.

I expose the so-called 'free market', which is anything but free. And much of what has been hidden, I uncover, as I shine my spotlight into the dark and illusory world of those who have controlled economic life on this planet for too long. I turn the tables on the money changers and speculators in the City of London and Wall Street and consequently, the financial elite and the politicians who support them will not like what is written here. I open up the sick and dying patient that is our economy to show what lies beneath its outer appearances. I point to what is killing it from within. And I expose those cancers that must be excised if we are to create the conditions for abundance to flow.

Our most powerful weapon is to expose what is really going on, so if these words resonate with you please tell others about this work.

This book is divided into three interconnected sections, called episodes, as this story has a beginning, middle and end. And, as with

About This Book

any drama series, this book will only make sense if the episodes are viewed in ascending order. If you are tempted to read this historical drama from the end backwards, or from the middle outwards, or in any order other than starting with episode one, then your enjoyment of this work will be compromised, as the story will not make sense.

In Episode One – 'The LAW' – I identify and describe the Universal Laws that relate to the economy and explain how they operate in conjunction with the hierarchy in heaven. I examine those spiritual subjects that are essential to our understanding of how the economy works, but about which, the details were deliberately removed from the scriptures. This episode also contains practical examples of how the Ascended Master teachings can help us in our everyday lives.

In Episode Two – 'Disobedience of The LAW' – I analyse the devastating effect that the actions of power elite have had on the people and the economy, and how their policies have perverted all aspects of life on Earth. I also expose their secret plans, and reveal how they steal our money with their elaborate wealth transfer schemes.

Episode Three – 'Restoration of The LAW' – is my book of resolutions to the problems identified in episode two. The format is a series of student lectures that look back from a hundred years hence at what was done from 2013 onwards to bring about a Golden Age economy. I also outline what each one of us can do to assist the process of change that will make this vision a reality. My hope is that once you have read this book you will see the world through different eyes and that if you ever doubted that all things are possible, these words will give you the confidence to want to join me and countless others, in helping to establish a Golden Age economy on Earth.

EPISODE ONE

The LAW

"We cannot expect to win our victory in the game of life without first knowing the rules of the game"

– *Kim Andrew Lincoln*

CONTENTS

I Have Yet Many Things to Say unto Ye but Ye Cannot Bear Them Now	5
Multiplying Our Talents	13
The Universal Laws of Enlightened Free Enterprise	18
The Great Principle of MENTALISM	28
The Law of Divine Love	34
The Law of Hierarchy	36
The Law of Free Will	43
The Great Principle of CORRESPONDENCE	47
The Great Principle of VIBRATION	54
The Law of Attraction	57
The Law of Resistance	59
The Law of Fellowship	60
The Law of Forgiveness	61
The Law of Reflection	66
The Great Principle of POLARITY	67
The Great Principle of RHYTHM	73
The Great Principle of CAUSE & EFFECT	81
The Law of Action	83
The Laws of Inertia & Momentum	85
The Laws of Karma & Reincarnation	87
The Law of Relativity	99
The Laws of Abundance & Supply	105
The Law of Disintegration	111
The Law of Gratitude	113
The Great Principle of GENDER	114
Usury (Riba)	124
The Importance of GOLD	128
The Last Word from Jesus	131

I Have Yet Many Things to Say unto Ye but Ye Cannot Bear them Now

Some people think that there is nothing more that we can learn about God's Laws because everything that the great spiritual teachers wanted to say to us has already been said and recorded in the scriptures. But if this were true why did Jesus say:

> "I have yet many things to say unto ye but ye cannot bear them now."
>
> – **John 16:12**

What did he mean by this statement?

Well, one interpretation is simply that two thousand years ago Jesus said all that he could say that we were capable of understanding at that time, but that once our consciousness had been raised, by internalising his teachings he would bring forth further teachings that contain higher levels of truth as:

> "When the student is ready the teacher will appear."
>
> – **Jesus Christ,**
> (Through his former messenger, Kim Michaels)

What Jesus was talking about was the process of 'progressive revelation' whereby each new teaching given by Ascended Masters like Jesus is designed to help us step further up the ladder of enlightenment, so that by conquering our desires we can achieve mastery over the 'things of this world' and thus qualify to ascend permanently to heaven. This is what Jesus' parable of the talents is really about as is explained

A GOLDEN AGE ECONOMY

under the heading 'Multiplying Our Talents' that follows this section.

The official scriptures, however, are not the only way that the Ascended Host chose to impart spiritual knowledge to humankind.

The giving of dictations is one such method whereby a 'messenger' who maybe a chela (student) of a particular Ascended Master agrees to act as a channel through which the Master's thoughts are telepathically transferred. The messenger interprets these thoughts through the filter of their own consciousness and then transcribes them into words. Sometimes the messenger lends their voice to the Master, who literally speaks through the messenger, though their free will is never compromised as the messenger is always in control of the communication process.

Jesus gave his first public dictation (following his ascension) on 24th November 1932 in Chicago, Illinois, USA and continues to communicate by this method today. Indeed, all the spiritual teachings and associated information in this book are based upon what he and other Masters have released in the last hundred and fifty years or so through their various messengers – past and present. Our history books are full of evidence that the Masters have been actively helping us to raise our consciousness, for had this not been the case, Jesus would not be speaking to us today.

In his 'Great Principal of Vibration' Hermes states that all energy forms are constantly moving and that different energy forms vibrate at different frequencies. He also states that if the vibrational frequency of an energy form is altered it will be transformed into something else, so that if our own frequencies are raised, we become more like God, and vice versa.

And so it follows that as God's children it is our purpose in coming to the school room of Earth to learn how to raise the rate at which we vibrate. We do this by qualifying the energy (light) we are given by 'multiplying our talents', so that we will receive more of God's light to work with, and set in motion a virtuous ascending spiral whereby we are continually drawing down more and more light (abundance) from the spiritual realm so that eventually we become like Jesus whose energy field was so infused with the light of God that he could raise the dead and walk on water.

And it is the role of the Ascended Masters to help us to do just that.

This then is a scientific explanation for why we are here. But there is another side to this, which is what happens if we do not keep moving upwards by transcending ourselves, but instead stand still – or worse, go into reverse by disobeying God's Laws. Well, if this is our free will choice then we will lose even that which we have been given so that we start to decay physically and spiritually as the light is drained from our bodies. We will find that we will be able to do less and less both mentally and physically and this descending spiral of increasing loss will lead initially to premature physical death in this and subsequent embodiments and then ultimately – if we still refuse to bend the knee to our Father/Mother God – to our spiritual death where our individual identity is erased.

To illustrate what I mean by this process we all know of companies that have failed to invest in new technology and launch new products. What happens is they start to lose sales to their competitors so their profitability suffers and then they have less money to move the business forward. Gradually a spiral of decline develops that unless stopped will eventually force the company into bankruptcy.

The point I am making here is that the process of revelation is ongoing. It never stops because there is always something new to learn. No teaching by Jesus or any other Ascended Master is the final word because the word is like a river that is constantly flowing. It cannot be frozen in time nor set in stone. Once something is written down it is already out of date because the river has moved on. The Bible – though it contains many teachings that are relevant today – is not the definitive and final word of God because the work is incomplete, and always will be, as there is always a higher truth that can be told.

What Jesus taught in the New Testament has been added to by the wonderful examples of the lives of the Saints who followed in his footsteps. Here are just of few examples:

SAINT FRANCIS OF ASSISI conveyed the importance of being kind to animals. For in caring for them we are, in effect, caring for ourselves, as under the Law of One they are as much a part of us as we are a part of them. The story of this Saint is a metaphor for caring – not only for animals but for our planet because as Hermes explained, nothing is separate from anything else.

A GOLDEN AGE ECONOMY

By caring for and nurturing all life on Earth we are showing our love for God's creation, for God the Father, for God the Mother and for each other.

Saint Francis' message is that only by caring for all forms of life can we properly care for ourselves and each other. There is no other option because of the interconnectedness of all life.

We know from Genesis that we are co-creators with God and that we were given dominion over the Earth. But what Saint Francis is saying is that we must wield this power wisely. We must exercise care and consideration for all life forms and for everything under the sun over which we have dominion, because all life and all matter are important links in the greater chain of being. We must keep the balance in this world because only then can we fulfil our reason for being here.

> "The carbon argument is the wrong argument. What we should be focusing our attention on is caring for and conserving our planet. It is the level of our consciousness that counts not the amount of carbon we emit. If we love the Earth the Earth will love us back. When we love our planet we will not be minded to deplete its resources."
>
> **– Kim Andrew Lincoln**

Ascended Master Kuthumi ascended in 1889. One of his past embodiments was as Saint Francis of Assisi (1182 – 1226 AD)

MOTHER TERESA demonstrated the selfless path of service and surrender to God's Will. She urged us to "give until it hurts" – as Jesus did. She focused all her energy on ministering to the needs of the poor in Calcutta (Mumbai) and through her selflessness and devotion drew the attention of the world to their plight.

> "Verily I say unto you, Inasmuch as ye have done [it] unto one of the least of these my brethren, ye have done [it] unto me."
>
> **– Matthew 25:40**

By her magnificent example she helps us to see what our priorities should be in a world overflowing with wealth but where that wealth is in the hands of the few.

"It is the responsibility of the richest nations to help the poorest."
– **Kim Andrew Lincoln**

For me, the main message of Mother Teresa's mission is that we should focus our attention on helping the poor, for in doing so we will be laying the foundation stones for a Golden Age economy to manifest. It must be our first priority because under the Law of Karma abundance and poverty cannot co-exist indefinitely as unbalanced economies will eventually topple under the weight of their returning karma – as is happening now in the West.

"While there is poverty in the world no nation can truly prosper."
– **Kim Andrew Lincoln**

Only by first raising up the poor can we ever aspire to be truly wealthy for Jesus has recently said through his former messenger Kim Michaels that: "Whatever you chose for yourself you must give to another first."

Mother Teresa reminded us of this eternal truth. She ascended on 7th September 1997.

"The greatest among us are the servants of all."
– **Kim Andrew Lincoln**

MAHATMA GANDHI This spiritual giant of the twentieth century taught us that the road to self-determination does not have to overflow with the blood of our oppressors. He proved that peaceful resistance is a powerful weapon if people are prepared to stand together and not be moved by the forces of darkness. Through his dedication to non-violence and his policy of non-cooperation with the British power elite Gandhi demonstrated that ordinary people have real power when they work together for justice and freedom.

A GOLDEN AGE ECONOMY

> "The story of our recorded history is the cry for freedom from tyranny, oppression and slavery."
>
> **– Kim Andrew Lincoln**

His greatest achievement was to make the British Raj realise that when hundreds of millions of Indians refused to co-operate with the mechanisms of government there was nothing that that government could do to stop them. By the power of his will and an unwavering belief in natural justice Gandhi forced the British to confront this reality with the result that when they had, it was not long before India had been returned to the Indians.

> "When you envision the rulers and the ruled, as a driver and a coach and horses, you will see that the power behind a coach and horses is not the coach driver, it is the horses. It is only because the horses made a conscious decision to submit to the will of the driver – to surrender their power to him – that the coach goes where it is directed. If the horses decide that they do not like that direction, they can, at any time, exercise their free will, and choose not to co-operate with the driver. If this happens there is little the driver can do because it is the power of the horses that drives the coach forward."
>
> **– Kim Andrew Lincoln**

Gandhi showed us that it is not only our right under the Law of Free Will to seek to change unjust laws but that it is our duty to do so.

> "Every person can make a real difference. Doing nothing is not a viable option. Apathy and inaction are the engines of evil."
>
> **– Kim Andrew Lincoln**

He was a lawyer by profession and used the logic of the English legal system to win his arguments against the British Raj. But the real power of his leadership lay not in his belief in man's laws but in the absolute truth and justice of God's Laws in which he had total faith and to which he surrendered himself and the destiny of his country. Gandhi believed in God-Power, God-Justice and God-Victory, meaning that he knew that if he acted in total obedience to God's Laws, heaven would stand behind him and India's victory would be assured. And so it was to be.

Gandhi's achievements were colossal. He freed his country from a foreign invader without striking a single blow. He turned the other cheek but did not turn away from the task in hand. He stood up to injustice. He did everything right – in accordance with the Laws of God – and won a magnificent victory. No Son of God could have done more.

"My life is my message."

– Mahatma Gandhi

The Internet

The Ascended Host have been behind all human endeavours in the field of science and technology that have advanced our spiritual development. And one of the most significant inventions they inspired was the internet. It has brought freedom to billions of people who can now access the vast library of knowledge that exists in cyberspace. Information is power and the internet has empowered the ordinary people of the world.

In 297 BC it was again the Ascended Host who inspired the creation of the world's greatest library – the forerunner to the internet.

Demetrios of Phaleron – a graduate of the Lyceum (school) of Aristotle had been employed by the Pharaoh, Ptolemy Soter, to think brilliant thoughts. So the Ascended Host 'whispered in this scholar's ear' and suggested to him that it might be a good idea for the Pharaoh to found a library that would contain a copy of every 'book' that had ever been written, so that Alexandria would become the centre of learning in the ancient world. And so it was that when Ptolemy was presented with this idea he was so taken with it that he immediately gave the order for the work to begin and by the afternoon scrolls (books) began to arrive and the Great Library of Alexandria was founded.

A GOLDEN AGE ECONOMY

This is yet another example of how the Ascended Masters help us to move ever onwards and upwards, for they are the well-spring of all wisdom and knowledge.

To find out what the Ascended Masters are thinking and what messages they are conveying to us today, the internet is a good place to look, though we are advised to be wary because the false hierarchy use this medium to spread their half-truths and lies. Therefore, those who seek enlightenment must be careful to exercise discernment and learn to sort the wheat from the chaff, which is yet another lesson we are here to learn.

MULTIPLYING OUR TALENTS

Jesus' parable of the 'talents' is one of his most important teachings on the subject of manifesting abundance, but do we really know what it means? Well, now we do as Jesus has given an explanation of the true meaning in response to a question put to him on the 'Ask Jesus the Truth' website. I have printed a transcript of Jesus' answer after the parable below:

THE PARABLE OF THE TALENTS

14 For [the kingdom of heaven is] as a man travelling into a far country, [who] called his own servants, and delivered unto them his goods.
15 And unto one he gave five talents, to another two, and to another one; to every man according to his several ability; and straightway took his journey.
16 Then he that had received the five talents went and traded with the same, and made [them] other five talents.
17 And likewise he that [had received] two, he also gained other two.
18 But he that had received one went and digged in the earth, and hid his lord's money.
19 After a long time the lord of those servants cometh, and reckoneth with them.
20 And so he that had received five talents came and brought other five talents, saying, Lord, thou deliveredst unto me five talents: behold, I have gained beside them five talents more.

21 His lord said unto him, well done, [thou] good and faithful servant: thou hast been faithful over a few things, I will make thee ruler over many things: enter thou into the joy of thy lord.
22 He also that had received two talents came and said, Lord, thou deliveredst unto me two talents: behold, I have gained two other talents beside them.
23 His lord said unto him, well done, good and faithful servant; thou hast been faithful over a few things, I will make thee ruler over many things: enter thou into the joy of thy lord.
24 Then he which had received the one talent came and said, Lord, I knew thee that thou art a hard man, reaping where thou hast not sown, and gathering where thou hast not strawed:
25 And I was afraid, and went and hid thy talent in the earth: lo, [there] thou hast [that is] thine.
26 His lord answered and said unto him, [thou] wicked and slothful servant, thou knewest that I reap where I sowed not, and gather where I have not strawed:
27 Thou oughtest therefore to have put my money to the exchangers, and [then] at my coming I should have received mine own with usury.
28 Take therefore the talent from him, and give [it] unto him which hath ten talents.
29 For unto every one that hath shall be given, and he shall have abundance: but from him that hath not shall be taken away even that which he hath.

– Matthew 25:14-29

Jesus' Explanation of the True Meaning of the Parable of the Talents

"I am a spiritual teacher, and as such I follow God's law relating to the master-disciple or teacher-student relationship. I described this law in my parable about the three servants who received a number of talents from their master. The master then left, and when he came back he asked for an account of what the servants had done with the talents. Two of the servants had multiplied their talents, and they were rewarded. The third servant had projected his own consciousness upon the master and had used that as an excuse for not multiplying the talents, instead burying them in the ground. He had the talents taken away from him.

The symbolism is that the talents represent the understanding and the light that a spiritual teacher is allowed to give to the students. Multiplying your talents means that you take what is given and internalize it, so that you raise yourself above the state of consciousness you had when you received the gift. Burying your talents in the ground is a symbol for not being willing to raise your consciousness, instead finding an excuse for staying in your old state of consciousness. The point is that the teacher can give the student a certain amount of teaching. After that, more can be given only as the student multiplies the first offering."

– **Jesus Christ,**
(through his Messenger Lorraine Michaels, 2011)

Bible Interpretation

From Jesus' explanation of the true meaning of his own teaching we can see how easy it is to misinterpret his message if we look at the literal meaning of his words and ignore the 'symbolic' meaning.

The father of theology, Origen, who taught at the Catechetical School of Alexandria* believed that there were three levels of

---

*The Catechetical School of Alexandria (Egypt) was a world renowned institution where priests of Coptic Orthodox Church of Egypt were trained in the scriptures and where some of the greatest theologians of the Christian faith like Clement of Alexandria and Origen taught and interpreted the Bible. The school was said by St. Jerome to have been founded by the apostle St. Mark but other sources say that it began much later in about 190 AD.

understanding within scripture: the literal, the moral, and the allegorical or figurative. These meanings correspond to the body, soul and spirit, in ascending order of importance. The literal meaning of historical events is the least important for Christians in the same way that the body is less important than the soul or spirit. What are more important are the underlying meanings which can only be perceived allegorically. The divinely-inspired meaning may not lie in the literal meaning and be recognisable to everyone, but instead will be perceived by those gifted with the grace of the Holy Spirit in the word of wisdom and knowledge. For example, Origen was one of the first theologians to argue that the petition in the Lord's Prayer ought to read, not "Give us this day our daily bread" but "give us this day our spiritual bread".

Moreover, we also need to consider that for every teaching in the Bible there is a higher truth to be revealed that will be given to us when we are ready to receive it. And this is evident in the difference between the teachings of the Old Testament and the New Testament where the style of writing in the Old Testament is more aggressive and authoritarian than in the New Testament because people then needed to be told what to do. We move from the 'Thou Shall Not' style of the Ten Commandments to the much gentler and softer approach that Jesus uses in his parables. Jesus expands upon the basic teachings of the Ten Commandments because after fifteen hundred years people had had time to inwardly digest the old teachings and were thus ready to receive the higher truths that Jesus brought forth. Indeed we might say that what Jesus taught was not so much a New Testament but a 'Higher' Testament.

My last point concerning interpreting the written word is that words alone cannot always convey difficult concepts and thus the risk of misinterpretation can be high. They say "that a picture paints a thousand words" but where there is no picture to assist the process of understanding, difficulties in interpreting meaning arise. The following quotation from Jesus clarifies this point.

"There are no arguments you can construct by using words that cannot be counteracted by using words."

– Jesus Christ,
(through his former messenger, Kim Michaels)

Words are often inadequate for the task, which is why we have juries at criminal trials to intercede when the whirlwinds of words between advocates cancel themselves out. In the end we have to rely on our humanness, our intuition, our Christ discernment to sift the wheat from the chaff, to cleave the real from the unreal and the truth from the untruth.

THE UNIVERSAL LAWS OF ENLIGHTENED FREE ENTERPRISE

INTRODUCTION

The key to the door of illumination concerning the economy is to understand that the good life, the abundant life, the life of ever-increasing prosperity is not governed by whether or not we base our economic policies on the theories of John Maynard Keynes (Keynesianism); Milton Friedman (Monetarism); or the founders of the Austrian School of Economics or any other economic theory conceived in the minds of men – no matter how credible they may seem. Our economic success – indeed our success in all things – can only be assured if we faithfully follow the Universal Laws of Life, the Laws which form the framework of the Universe and that hold it together. These are the Laws by virtue of which all things are made and sustained. They are the Laws that were conceived by the Primary Creator before he started to create the worlds of spirit and form – before he issued the command: "Let there be Light." Without these Laws the Cosmos, the Stars and the Planets would simply not exist.

These Laws govern mathematically yet, with the spontaneity of mercy's flame, all manifestation throughout the Cosmos in the planes of Spirit and Matter. The Universal Laws are the signposts to the Truth of 'All that is'. They are our teachers and our guides and thus we ignore them at our peril.

"The greatest evil is not knowing God."
– Hermes Mercurius Trismegistus

The Universal Laws described here are the ones that I consider to be most relevant to the subject matter of this book, though in truth all of them impact upon the economy to a greater or lesser extent – seamlessly merging into each other like a giant spherical jigsaw puzzle. Indeed when shining the spotlight on these Laws it is difficult not to stray from one to another, as they all merge so perfectly well together.

And so as I dissect them you will likely spot instances where I cross the invisible boundaries between where one Law ends and another begins. This is done deliberately in order to show how these Laws work in the real world and also so that we might see the ingenuity and intent behind the design of All That Is – for truly it is a wonder to behold. I cannot say with any degree of certainty exactly how many Universal Laws there are or, indeed, whether or not a particular Law qualifies as 'Universal Law' as there is no definitive work of reference that comprehensively identifies these Laws.

Hermes & the Divine Pymander

However, based on the research I have done to fill the gaps in my own knowledge, I have come to the conclusion that there are seven core Universal Laws from which an indeterminate number of subsidiary Laws derive.

Probably the earliest surviving work of reference that confirms this is a set of seventeen short books collectively known as the 'The Divine Pymander' written by Hermes Mercurius Trismegistus in which he states that there are seven 'Great Principles' (Mentalism; Correspondence; Vibration; Polarity; Rhythm; Cause and Effect; and Gender) by which the Universe was created and is sustained. Hermes was one of the great sages of ancient Egypt who was hailed as 'The Master of Masters'. He is believed to have lived in Egypt long before the time of Moses and is regarded as the father of occult wisdom; the founder of astrology and the discoverer of alchemy. The best authorities believe that Hermes was a contemporary of the prophet Abraham (from the Old Testament of the Bible) and some of the Jewish traditions claim that Abraham was his student. After a reputed lifespan of three centuries the Egyptians deified Hermes, naming him Thoth, the 'Scribe of the Gods'. Tens of centuries later the Ancient Greeks also made him a God, though this time he was known as Hermes, the God of Wisdom. It was the Egyptians, however, who bestowed upon him the title 'Trismegistus', which means 'the thrice-great'; 'the great-great'; 'the greatest-great'. The name of Hermes Trismegistus was revered in all the ancient lands as he was regarded as the 'Fount of Wisdom'.

The modern-day term 'hermetically sealed' comes from the Hermetic practice of not 'casting pearls (of wisdom) before swine' whereby Hermes' teachings were only disseminated among those who were considered worthy of the prize. And thus, they remained secret to all but the most enlightened.

"The lips of wisdom are closed, except to the ears of Understanding."

— **The Kybalion**

The divine teachings that Hermes brought forth found their way into all the ancient lands and religions, though they cannot be identified with any particular country or faith, as the teachers of his writings warned that his secret doctrine should not be allowed to become crystallised into any particular creed. The wisdom of this caution is evident to all students of history.

The ancient occultism of India and Persia degenerated because those who had been teachers became priests and thus theology became mixed with philosophy creating a mass of religious superstition, cults, creeds and gods. The same happened in Ancient Greece and Rome. And again with the Hermetic teachings of the Gnostics and early Christians, which were lost at the time of the Roman Emperor Constantine. At the Counsel of Nicea in 325 AD Constantine saw to it that only those teachings that affirmed his power and control over his subjects made it into the authorised version of the Bible. Everything else was either destroyed, locked away or lost. This theft of Truth meant that the Roman Catholic Church was deprived of its very essence and spirit. And to this day the scriptures leave so many unanswered questions that what remains does not make complete sense. It is, therefore, not surprising that Christianity is haemorrhaging support as congregations continue to decline.

Thankfully Hermes, 'Divine Pymander', has survived and is free to download from the internet.

More recently the Ascended Masters have confirmed through their messengers that Hermes is an Ascended being who is known in heaven as the God Mercury.

THE KYBALION

Hermes 'Great Principles' were expounded upon in the book *The Kybalion* that was first published in 1908. It was authored by the 'Three Initiates' who, by referring to themselves in this way, obviously wished to remain anonymous. They stated that their intention was to create bridges that would link with the numerous teachings already in existence concerning God's Laws rather than to build a new 'Temple of Knowledge'. Since then other writers have added their own thoughts and interpretations of what the 'Truth' is as well as adapting what has already been written to appeal to the appetites and consciousness of contemporary audiences.

The Book of Enoch – that is believed to predate the Old Testament – is another rich source of enlightenment on the Universal Laws, as are the dictations given by the Ascended Masters through their messengers in embodiment. And, of course, the most notable of these are the scriptures of the eight true religions (Hinduism; Buddhism; Zoroastrianism; Taoism; Confucianism; Judaism; Christianity and Islam) that began to be recorded many thousands of years ago.

As mentioned previously, the 'official' scriptures have references to the Universal Laws as Hermes described them, though they do not state categorically that this or that particular teaching is based upon any specific Law. For example, Jesus' teaching about 'sowing and reaping' pertains to the Universal Law of Karma that is a subsidiary Law to the Great Principal of Cause and Effect, whereas Jesus' miracles were performed by the application of the science that is governed by the 'Great Principle of Vibration' – as we shall see later.

THE THEOSOPHICAL SOCIETY

As the Piscean Age has been drawing to a close the Ascended Masters have been very active in passing on their wisdom concerning the Universal Laws and this was most evident in the dispensation they gave to sponsor the Theosophical Society (TS) – formed by Helen Blavatsky in New York in 1875. The motto of the TS is:

"There is no religion higher than Truth."

Theosophists believe that "our every action, feeling and thought affects all other beings and that each of us are capable of and responsible for contributing to the benefit of the whole".

The Society's mission is "To encourage open-minded inquiry into world religions, philosophy, science, and the arts in order to understand the wisdom of the ages, respect the unity of all life, and help people explore spiritual self-transformation".

The following text is taken from the Society's American website:

"The Society is composed of students belonging to any religion or to none. Its members are united by their approval of the Society's Three Objects, by their wish to remove religious antagonisms and to draw together people of goodwill whatsoever their religious opinions, and by their desire to study religious truths and to share the results of their studies with others. Their bond of union is not the profession of a common belief, but a common search and aspiration for Truth."

In accordance with the Theosophical spirit, most Theosophists regard Truth as a prize to be striven for, not as a dogma to be imposed by authority. They hold that belief should be the result of individual understanding and intuition rather than mere acceptance of traditional ideas, and that it should rest on knowledge and experience, not on assertion. Truth should therefore be sought by study, reflection, meditation, service, purity of life, and devotion to high ideals.

At the same time, Theosophists respect the different beliefs. They see each religion as an expression of the Divine Wisdom, adapted to the needs of a particular time and place. They prefer the study of various religions to their condemnation, their practice to proselytising. Thus, earnest Theosophists extend tolerance to all, even to the intolerant, not as a privilege they bestow but as a duty they perform. They seek to remove ignorance, not punish it; peace is their watchword, and Truth their aim.

The three declared Objects of the Theosophical Society:

- To form a nucleus of the universal brotherhood of humanity, without distinction of race, creed, sex, caste or color.
- To encourage the study of comparative religion, philosophy and science.
- To investigate unexplained laws of nature and the powers latent in humanity.

Today the International TS has members in almost seventy countries around the world. The Society was influential in the founding of many later esoteric movements, a number of which were founded by former TS members. Some notable cases are Dr. Gerard Encausse (Papus), founder of the modern Martinist Order; William W. Westcott, co-founder of the Hermetic Order of the Golden Dawn; Max Heindel, founder of the Rosicrucian Fellowship; Alice Bailey, founder of the Arcane School; Rudolf Steiner, founder of the Anthroposophical Society; the Russian painter Nicholas Roerich and his wife Helena, founders of the Agni Yoga Society; Guy and Edna Ballard, founders of the 'I AM Movement'; among others.

The Ascended Masters most closely associated with the Theosophical Society are said to include: Djwal Khul; Kuthumi; Sanat

A GOLDEN AGE ECONOMY

Kumara; Lord Maitreya; Paul the Venetian; Serapis Bey; Master Hilarion; Jesus Christ and Saint Germain.

The Ascended Masters have sponsored many other organisations since then as they have been keen to bring forth higher teachings to help us to rise above the 'duality consciousness' that has dominated the Piscean Age of Jesus the Christ for the last two thousand years. Anyone who is interested in studying these teachings in greater depth than it is possible to give in this book will find many points of reference throughout this book.

In addition to Hermes' seven 'scientific' Principles there is another related category of Laws that we might call the 'Moral' Laws. Included in this group are the Ten Commandments that Moses received from Sanat Kumara – the Ancient of Days on Mount Sinai and the teachings that Jesus delivered during his Sermon on the Mount. And, more recently of course, there are the teachings that the Archangel Gabriel dictated to the Prophet Muhammad in the seventh century that are contained in the Koran and the writings associated with Sufism that could be described as the 'softer' version of Islam.

> "Enlightenment must come little by little – otherwise it would overwhelm."
>
> **– Idries Shah**
> (Sufi quotation)

These are the moral codes of behaviour that the Ascended Masters have brought forth through the ages in the hope that we might learn to have harmonious relationships with each and our planet. These 'Moral' Laws are connected to the 'scientific' Laws in the same way that everything that IS is connected to everything else.

> "I will write my laws in your hearts and minds, in your hearts and minds will I write them."
>
> **– Sanat Kumara**

If you examine the legal systems of the world you will see that all of them are, to some extent, based on these moral teachings, though at the same time it would also be true to say that a large number of laws on the statute books are not in alignment with the word of God having been put there by those with malevolent intent.

When it comes to power, to the economy and to the achievement of material success, what seemeth right unto man may not always be right unto God. As, when we see the grinding poverty and interminable misery that a large proportion of the people on this planet have to endure on a daily basis and compare it to the luxuriant lifestyles of the super rich, it is clear that whatever laws we have been following since Moses came down from Mount Sinai, they most certainly did not come from the heart and mind of God.

In the USA 5% of the population controls 63.5% of all wealth whereas the overwhelming majority, the bottom 80 percent, collectively hold just 12.8%. As the Economic Policy Institute has reported, the richest 10% of Americans received an unconscionable 100% of the average income growth in the years 2000 to 2007, the most recent extended period of economic expansion. And the Washington Post reported in 2011 that after adjusting for inflation, the average income of the top 0.1% of all Americans jumped by 385% between 1970 and 2008, while the average income for the bottom 90% of all Americans actually fell by 1%.

In the United Kingdom the richest 10% are 100 times better off than the poorest.

At the time of writing 14.3% of US citizens are receiving food stamps. Over one-third are surviving on government handouts and, according to the Federal Reserve, the average American family has lost 23% of their household wealth since 2007. Most shocking of the statistics, however, is that the true unemployment rate in the USA is nearly 23%, a figure which I suspect is similar in the UK when you read between the lines of the official figures.

However, the most damning statistic is that three billion people – about 45% of the population of the planet – live on an average of less than two dollars a day.

The fact that the majority of people on Earth have failed to manifest anything like an abundant life is proof enough that there is something very wrong with the way in which we organise our economic affairs – and yet it says in the Bible:

> "Fear not, little flock, for it is your Father's good pleasure to give you the kingdom."
>
> – **Luke 12:32**

And:

> "I am come so that they might have life, and that they might have it more abundantly."
>
> – **John 10:10**

Clearly we have not been acting as our Creator intended. We have not been heeding the wise words of the prophets, the great spiritual teachers and the Saints who have been sent here down the ages to show us how to bring forth the infinite supply of energy that is available to us naturally on Earth.

So what then are these Laws that we would be wise to follow if we are to tap in to the river of abundance that naturally flows in nature and yet is so lacking in the lives of humankind? What are these Laws that form the great rock upon which all the Temples of the True Faiths have been built? For the Ascended Masters tell us that if we were to study all the teachings they have ever given (in the pure form that they were originally given) for each of the true religions and compare them with each other we would find that there is a common thread of truth running through all of them, as in God's eyes the 'different' religions are not, in essence, different at all as they emanate from the one set of Laws that God used to create the Universe that I am about to describe.

> "There are no religions, there are only God's Laws."
>
> – **Kim Andrew Lincoln**

If you have studied any of the Universal Laws before you will know that they are collectively known by many different names, including: The Universal Laws; The Cosmic Laws; The Great Law; The Great Principles; The Spiritual Laws; The Natural Laws; and God's Laws – to name but a few. So to avoid confusion I have decided to use the two most common, i.e. The Universal Laws and God's Laws, unless I am specifically talking about Hermes' Great Principles.

Here, then, is my interpretation of the Universal Laws that if properly applied will enable us to establish a divine economy of unparalleled prosperity in this Golden Age of Aquarius that has just begun.

The Great Principle of Mentalism

"THE ALL IS MIND; The Universe is Mental."

– **The Kybalion**

This first of the seven 'Great Principles' is more commonly known as the Law of One or the Law of Divine Oneness and it states that we live in a world where everything is connected to everything else. And thus, everything we think, feel, say and do affects every other part of creation. This is the world of spirit, of thought and of mind where everything is spiritual because everything comes from God and God is Spirit. God is in all things and all things are in God.

> "Holy art thou, of whom all Nature is the Image. [Nature; the manifested or external Image of GOD (LIFE)]. For there is nothing which is not the Image of God. Yet thou sayest that God is invisible; but be advised, for who is more manifest than He? For therefore hath he made all things; that thou by all things mayest see him."
>
> – **Hermes Mercurius Trismegistus**
> (An excerpt from *The Divine Pymander*)

When you throw a stone into a pool the waves that form expand in a circular motion outwards touching everything in their path. The disturbance that this action creates is nature's way of telling us that it is impossible for anything or anyone to exist in isolation from any other part of creation, because everything that exists is imbued with the Creator's energy, and that energy is light – the basic building block of the universe – from which All That Is is made.

The Ascended Masters state that everything in existence has some

The Great Principle of MENTALISM

degree of consciousness and that this consciousness is an energy that started out as a thought in the Creator's mind that he wanted to create. The Creator then turned that thought into an action by applying the power of the spoken word to command that the process of creation begin.

This is explained in Genesis 1:3 where God said: "Let there be light" and there was light.

Scientists tell us that light is a form of energy and that all energy forms vibrate at different frequencies like the different radio stations that can be found when you turn the frequency dial on a radio. The densest matter vibrates at the lowest frequency and vice versa. Lead vibrates at a very low frequency, whereas the thoughts that come from the mind of God carry the highest frequencies. Indeed, when we pray from the heart with love and sincerity our thoughts travel straight to God. We establish a frequency link between the physical and spiritual realms and literally bring Heaven to Earth.

> "Heaven and Earth may be one world but there are many levels of consciousness."
>
> **– Kim Andrew Lincoln**

All our thoughts and deeds are recorded (with the assistance of the angels of record) by the Ascended Master known as the 'Keeper of the Scrolls' and then played back to us when we have to account for ourselves at the end of each incarnation. There are no secrets, as nothing that we think, say and do is hidden from God.

> "You cannot hide from the All-Seeing Eye of God."
>
> **– Kim Andrew Lincoln**

Thoughts are pure consciousness and because consciousness is an energy that vibrates at a frequency that corresponds with the purity of those thoughts, what we think affects everything. The mass consciousness, which is the sum total of thoughts of a similar vibrational pattern, is therefore an immensely powerful body of energy that can create, transform and even destroy worlds. There is no such thing as a 'natural' disaster as what goes on in our minds will eventually be out-pictured in nature.

> "Cataclysms like earthquakes are not the interplay of natural forces but the karmic penalties extracted by God through nature."
>
> **– Kim Andrew Lincoln**

You could say that what happens on this planet is determined by what we think about most of the time, so that when our thoughts are positive and pure we manifest in our lives the abundance that our Creator wants us to have. But when those thoughts are less than Christ perfection we create an entirely different experience.

It is said that we create for ourselves that which we focus our attention on. And that focus has an impact on the people and world around us because under the Law of Divine Oneness nothing can be separate from anything else because we are all one being.

Nothing is independent of anything else. Nothing stands alone because everything and everyone, every cell and every aspect of our beings is connected to every other. We are all part of the Universe and the Universe is part of us.

> "May you see yourself in every life who suffers. May you know that as long as life suffers, a part of you is suffering with that life, for God is one."
>
> **– Ascended Master Phylos the Tibetan**

Although we are all unique we can never be separate from the whole, from All That Is. Jesus stated this truth – that you cannot divide the Creator from his creation – when he said:

> "Verily I say unto you, Inasmuch as ye have done [it] unto one of the least of these my brethren, ye have done [it] unto me."
>
> **– Matthew 25:40**

It would also be true to say that what goes on in one country affects another as, for example, pollution of the water and the air cannot be contained or compartmentalised because we all drink the same water and breathe the same air.

The truth about the economy is that it is a state of mind and that the first thing we must do in order to transform a 'Dark Age' economy into a 'Golden Age' one is to hold the immaculate concept in our minds of the sort of economy that we would like to have and then imagine that we are already experiencing it. If enough people do this, then within a relatively short time, we shall, by the power of our thoughts, manifest that which we hold most dear. So that years from now when the student in the school economics class asks his teacher when the 'Golden Age' economy of the twenty-first century began they will say: "It started when most of us thought it had."

"A Golden Age is state of consciousness that begins when we think, speak and act as though it has already begun."
– **Kim Andrew Lincoln**

Hearts & Minds

"I will write my laws in your hearts and minds, in your hearts and minds will I write them," said the Lord.
– **Sanat Kumara**
(The Ancient of Days)

So if the universe is mental what exactly is the relationship between the heart and the mind? Well, the heart is the hub of life, physically and spiritually. The heart is the place where we commune with God. And, it is the centre from where radiates the love that nourishes the world. It is said that God is Love and that the greatest love of all is the love that the Creator has for his creation. So that where there is love there is the potential to create and where there is no love there is the potential to miscreate. Therefore, it could be said that love is the energy that comes before the thought to create.

A GOLDEN AGE ECONOMY

Love carries the highest vibrational frequency of any energy form. Love flows upwards from our hearts to our heads and then to God. The heart is below the head but in a sense it is above it because it is the source of God's love. Love radiates its warmth like the Sun. Nothing lives without love. It is the well-spring of life. And it is the Father of the noblest thought.

"That which is not born out of love will surely die."
– **Kim Andrew Lincoln**

If you have read any of the works of Shakespeare, Byron or Shelley you will know that these great poets could not have expressed thoughts of such truth, joy and beauty had they not come from the source of all love. Below is one of the best known examples of writing that comes from the heart:

> Shall I compare thee to a Summer's day?
> Thou art more lovely and more temperate:
> Rough winds do shake the darling buds of May,
> And Summer's lease hath all too short a date:
> Sometime too hot the eye of heaven shines,
> And oft' is his gold complexion dimm'd;
> And every fair from fair sometime declines,
> By chance or nature's changing course untrimm'd:
> But thy eternal Summer shall not fade
> Nor lose possession of that fair thou owest;
> Nor shall Death brag thou wanderest in his shade,
> When in eternal lines to time thou growest:
> So long as men can breathe, or eyes can see,
> So long lives this, and this gives life to thee.

– Sonnet 18 by William Shakespeare

We might say that our head is the chalice where we receive the creative thoughts of God and our Higher Self but whatever comes from God is

The Great Principle of MENTALISM

Love and God's love always comes from the heart first. For it is in our hearts that God implanted the fires of his flames of Power, Wisdom and Love. And it is these flames that when they burn brightly rise up and touch our minds so that we think positive thoughts that are in alignment with God's will.

> "If you are silent, be silent out of love; if you speak, speak out of love; if you correct, correct out of love; if you forgive, forgive out of love."
>
> **– St. Augustine**

When the energy of pure love flows from our hearts to our minds we make good decisions in both our personal and business lives.

The golden rule is that love is good for business because when we care for our customers, when we treat them as we would like to be treated ourselves they will keep coming back for more of whatever it is that we have to offer them.

> "You cannot take God out of the economy as God is in the economy and the economy is in God."
>
> **– Kim Andrew Lincoln**

THE LAW OF DIVINE LOVE

"Think not that I am come to send peace on earth: I came not to send peace, but a sword."

— **Matthew 10:34**

Divine love is not romantic love, neither is it unconditional love as many false gurus misguidedly claim:

"For God so loved the world that he gave his only begotten Son, that whosoever believeth in him should not perish, but have everlasting life."

— **John 3:16**

No, divine love is the love that parents have for their children. It is the love of the Father and Mother who desire for their children every advantage in life. These parents tell their children how things really are; they bring them up not by insulating them with illusory tales and falsehoods but by telling them the truth.

In the film *Jesus of Nazareth* Pontius Pilate asks Jesus the purpose of his mission and Jesus says that he has come to bring 'the truth' – the sword of truth that cleaves the real from the unreal.

When we tell the truth to those we love we are loving in the way that God and Jesus love us, which is the complete opposite of the way the forces of darkness and anti-Christ relate to us, which is the way of telling us only what we want to hear not what we need to hear in order to thrive, which is the truth.

Let us not forget the Serpent in the Garden of Eden who through the subtlety and sweetness of his lies tricked humankind (represented by Adam and Eve) into disobeying God's Laws that he knew would lead us unto hell and certain death.

The Law of Divine Love

The scriptures tell us that anything we create that is not constructed on the rock of Christ's truth – meaning in accordance with God's Laws – will not last because it has no reality. Where there is truth, there is wisdom and it was wisdom that Jesus came to impart – for wisdom means wise dominion which is just another way of saying 'knowing the truth'.

> "Love begets truth; truth begets wisdom; wisdom begets enlightenment; enlightenment begets mastery and mastery begets ascension."
>
> **– Kim Andrew Lincoln**

THE LAW OF HIERARCHY

"Order is heaven's first Law and that order manifests in the release of light from the Great Central Sun all the way down from the coordinates of hierarchy to our point in time and space."
– **Elizabeth Clare Prophet**
(from her book *Predict Your Future*)

When we think of the hierarchy within a large company we usually envision a pyramid with a Chief Executive Officer at the top and his subordinates below – in descending order of rank. In heaven, however, it is easier to imagine hierarchy as a circle with the Primary Creator in the centre where the greatest concentration of power is focused.

In our Universe the source of all power is the Great Central Sun. This is not a physical sun like the one in our solar system but a spiritual Sun, and it contains the highest concentration of God's energy in the Universe. It is from here that all things begin and end because it is where the ascended beings, Alpha and Omega represent and focus the Father/Mother God energies of the Great Central Sun.

As the male and female polarity of the Godhead, Alpha and Omega step down the life sustaining power from the Great Central Sun to the lower evolutions in the hierarchy. These beings operate at many levels or frequency bands and the closer they are in vibration to Alpha and Omega the greater the intensity of light they radiate. Unimaginable concentrations of energy pour out from these beings, such that if we were to stand in the presence of Alpha and Omega we would be instantly obliterated. This is why it says in the Old Testament: "No man can see God and live."

The significant point here is that God's energy is personified; meaning that the twelve aspects of *God consciousness that correspond to the numbers on the cosmic clock, spiral down from the spiritual

The Law of Hierarchy

realm to the matter world, via these powerful beings. They act like energy transformers so that the energy that originally came from Alpha and Omega is at a level that will not harm us.

Our purpose in being here is to out-picture, meaning to demonstrate by example, the twelve aspects of God consciousness that are also known as God flames, by bringing them into the physical realm of Earth. In other words, to be all that we truly are in God. We all carry within us a unique combination of these God flames so we could describe ourselves as individualised presences of God incarnate as well as the arms and legs of God walking on the Earth plane.

When we embody on Earth our mission is to switch on the light that we are given by the hierarchy, which is the individual aspects of God's being that we personify, and by our good works draw down more light into our beings so we and the people we interact with become enlightened. To 'shine our lights' means *to be* who we truly are. It is to 'set our fires' correctly so that the individual God flames we brought to Earth burn ever more brightly and consume the darkness.

The divine plan is that by this process God's Kingdom constantly expands as the darkness is filled with the light of all that we create. We are, after all, God's co- creators and we know intuitively that when our creations are constructed on the rock of Christ truth, meaning in accordance with God's Laws, they will stand both the tests of time and the Holy Spirit.

> "Blows the wind that castles break
> Back to sand now moving
> Back to the flow where no tower stands
> If it be not improving."
> **– Kim Andrew Lincoln**

(A verse from the poem *Blows the Wind* written in 2008 – NB: the 'Wind' is the Holy Spirit)

---

* The twelve aspects of God consciousness or God flames are: God-Power; God-Love; God-Mastery; God-Control; God-Obedience; God-Wisdom; God-Harmony; God-Gratitude; God-Justice; God-Reality; God-Vision and God-Victory.

All this explains why Jesus said that "Ye are Gods" for we are the Children of the Sun, the offspring of Alpha and Omega.

The Law of Transcendence

As our consciousness is much lower than God consciousness our reason for being is to transcend ourselves by constantly moving up the spiritual ladder until we attain full God consciousness. This is, however, a step-by-step process that will take time to achieve as we make progress via the numerous levels of hierarchy that bring us closer to God.

Our next step is to win our ascension and follow in the footsteps of Jesus and all the other great spiritual teachers who reside in the third kingdom of heaven. We, the Children of the Sun, are Sons and Daughters of God in training and it is the Ascended Masters that we are destined to become who help us do what they have done before.

"It is only by constantly transcending ourselves that we shall find our way home."

– **Kim Andrew Lincoln**

So who then are these enlightened beings from the spiritual realm that transfer and transform the awesome power of God's flames to those who walk upon the Earth plane?

Cosmic Beings

Well, surrounding Alpha and Omega is the first kingdom of the hierarchy which is the realm of the cosmic beings and the twelve solar hierarchies. Cosmic beings are aware of self as cosmos and are imbued with so much of the light of God that they can ensoul an entire cosmos. The Elohim who are the Creator Gods mentioned in the Old Testament, are numbered among their ranks and it was they who responded to the fiat from Alpha & Omega to create the world of form that includes our planet Earth.

The Law of Hierarchy

SOLAR HEIRARCHIES

We know the names of the solar hierarchies as the twelve signs of the zodiac. CAPRICORN sits on the twelve o'clock line of the cosmic clock and initiates Earth's evolutions in the Flame of God-Power. On the one o'clock line is AQUARIUS (God-Love) and on the two o'clock is PISCES (God–Mastery) and so on until we return to Capricorn. The other nine solar hierarchies are: ARIES (God-Control); TAURUS (God-Obedience); GEMINI (God-Wisdom); CANCER (God-Harmony); LEO (God-Gratitude); VIRGO (God-Justice); LIBRA (God-Reality); SCORPIO (God-Vision) and SAGITTARIUS (God-Victory).

The primary function of the solar hierarchies is to focus the twelve aspects of God consciousness that corresponds with each hierarchy to the lower evolutions so that if, for example, we were born under the star sign of Taurus the God quality that we would be intended to bring into the world in this life would be Obedience to God's Laws.

ELOHIM & ELEMENTALS

The Elohim are the most powerful aspect of the consciousness of God and include in their hierarchy the elemental builders of form. Elementals are the salamanders that control the fire element, the sylphs that control the air, the undines that control the water and the gnomes who control the Earth.

The first kingdom corresponds to the God-Flame of POWER.

SONS & DAUGHTERS OF GOD

The second kingdom in hierarchy is the kingdom of the Christed ones – the Sons and Daughters of God. These are the Ascended Masters who we are in a state of becoming. These Masters are our teachers and some of them are in embodiment now to guide us at this time of great change as we move from the age of Pisces, which Jesus lead, to the Aquarian age, which is the Golden Age of Saint Germain. Saint Germain embodied as Joseph the Father of Jesus as well as many other famous people including Merlin the magician and Francis Bacon who, the Ascended Masters have said, wrote the greatest works of English literature under the pen name of William Shakespeare.

This kingdom corresponds to the God-Flame of WISDOM.

ARCHANGELS & ANGELIC HOSTS

Finally, the third kingdom is comprised of the bands of angels who serve mankind under the command of the seven mighty archangels and their twin flames. Angels are beings who have not left the purity of God's consciousness, except in some cases where they volunteer to incarnate in human form in order to help mankind. Probably, the most famous example of where this has happened was Mary, Mother of Jesus, who is the twin flame of Archangel Raphael.

The relationship between angels and humankind is a very important one because angels assist us in our role as co-creators to create in the world of form. But they must do this in accordance with our divine plans and the Laws of God. Their duty is to serve, as it is through their service work that they ascend the spiritual ladder. The angels serve us at the level of our emotional or feeling bodies. They bring us hope, joy and laughter and sustain the concepts and ideas that we receive that are ours to hold in our kingdom, the second kingdom of hierarchy. The angels help us build desire because it is this emotional force that propels us to act and therefore to co-create in the world of form.

We all have a guardian angel that has been with us from the beginning and who will step in and help us if we ask. They must, however, always respect our free will. These beloved beings are full of love, joy and kindness and it is their greatest wish that we acknowledge them and seek their help. My first conscious encounter with my guardian angel was at the age of fourteen, when, due to my lack of care, I caused a can of petrol to explode in my hands, igniting the ground beneath me. As the flames rose up my body I realised that I would die

The Law of Hierarchy

without assistance, so I cried out to God to save me and immediately the fire went out. It was a miraculous escape, but it was not until decades later, when I discovered who my guardian angel was, that I realised that it was he, my beloved friend, who had saved me all those years ago. Since then I have lost count of the number of requests I have made to him, for every time I ask for his help it is given. It never ceases to amaze me what my angel is capable of doing for me, like pushing my car to a petrol station when it had run out of fuel and arranging for my keys to be found and returned to me after they had been lost on a busy sandy beach. If you don't know who your guardian angel is you can ask them their name and they will send it to you telepathically. I recommend that you get in touch!

This kingdom corresponds to the God-Flame of LOVE.

WE ARE IMPORTANT

The Ascended Masters tell us that we are part of the infinite and ever-expanding being that God IS, and thus we all have our place and our reason for being in God's great plan. We count because who we are and what we do is important. Our contribution has value because we are valuable. We are an essential part of the creative process because without God's co-creators planets would not become stars and the universe would not become more than it is now. Our mission is to fill the darkness with the light of God's being that we carry within us. It is a sacred duty that has the blessing and support of all the powers of heaven whose time and energy is focused on helping us to achieve this primary goal.

> "The only way to remove darkness from a room is to switch on your light."
>
> **– Kim Andrew Lincoln**

This is of immense importance to the economy, because when we know who we are and what our purpose here is, the revelation is a transformational experience. Our whole attitude and approach to life changes. We become motivated to fulfil our mission. Life has new meaning as we change direction from drifting sideways or sliding backwards to moving onwards and upwards. Productivity increases because we are happier and therefore more relaxed in our work. We are focused and our lives have meaning because we have a reason to get out of bed each morning. But more than this, we are empowered by the knowledge that we are an important wheel within the greater wheel of the universe. Knowing that we are Gods and that we have real power is a victory in itself because it takes power away from those who seek to control us, for no longer shall we be slaves.

"Power is awareness of truth."

– Kim Andrew Lincoln

This is but a a brief outline of hierarchy and I therefore strongly recommend that you read Elizabeth Clare Prophet's book *Predict Your Future* for it is an inspirational and highly informative work that goes into far more detail than is appropriate here.

THE LAW OF FREE WILL

Everything that is wrong with the way we conduct ourselves on planet Earth can be traced back to the war in heaven when the wisdom angels rebelled against the will of God. The scriptures tell this story, but essentially what happened was that God decreed that we, his co-creators, should have the right to exercise our free will and therefore the right to disobey his Laws. This is not to say that God is giving us an open invitation to swim in the sea of troubles that is the world of duality, because it is not necessary to do evil in order to know what evil is. As Children of the Sun – who are created in the image and likeness of God – we intuitively know that murder is wrong. And thus how to commit murder is not a lesson we need to learn. However, there are many among us (fallen angels) who are motivated to disagree, because the more they can persuade us to misqualify God's energy the more of our light they can steal. And this is the light they need to survive. So we must always be aware that the fallen angels are wishing and willing us to break God's commandments so they can prove that God was wrong to grant us free will.

> "Freedom is the freedom to make mistakes; it is not a God-given licence to miscreate."
>
> **– Kim Andrew Lincoln**

We have come to earth to acquire wisdom (wise dominion) which of all the God flames is the one that takes the longest to master. In his infinite wisdom God reasoned when he created us, which was after his angels, that we should have the choice 'to be or not to be'. God is love and because he loves us he wants us to be free to co-create with him. And love is all about setting things free.

A GOLDEN AGE ECONOMY

The two main human emotions are fear and love. When we feel fear we move further from God. When we feel love, God is working through us. One way or another all human actions are motivated by fear or love. Fear is the energy which contracts, closes down, draws in, runs, hides, hoards and harms. Love is the energy which expands, opens up, sends out, stays, reveals, heals and shares.

"Love is the seed and freedom is the flower it becomes."
– Kim Andrew Lincoln

Freedom brings with it the possibility that if we switch off our inner guiding light (our holy Christ selves) we may be turned to the left-handed path that takes us away from the Son and into the places where the dark forces abide. This is the counterfeit kingdom of relative good and evil and though we may know that killing is wrong there are many temptations in this garden of illusions to which we may succumb when our vibration falls. God, our guardian angels and all our guides in heaven always hold the immaculate concept that we will not stumble and fall on the path back home but if we do there is a backup plan which is designed to help us make a better choice so that we turn back onto the right road. This is the Law of Karma and its school of hard knocks where when we fall, we will experience the repercussions of our mistakes.

"In order to be MORE, God gave us the right to be LESS than we are now."
– Kim Andrew Lincoln

You can tell a child that if they touch something hot they will get burnt, but if the child steadfastly refuses to listen to your good advice then God's 'Plan B' is that they will have to experience what it is like to be burnt in the hope that they will not wish to continue with the experiment. Hopefully they will remember the pain, but also the good advice not to touch the hot item so that the lesson is learnt well without undue harm being done to the child.

The Law of Free Will

But what is the lesson here?

Well, it is that if we disobey our parents' guidance (God's Laws) there will be consequences that we may dislike, that are the direct effect of our disobedience. By granting us free will our divine parents gave us the freedom to master the lessons of life in a way that is appropriate to the level of our awareness. Their expectation is that whatever way we chose to learn, we will all reach the same conclusion – eventually. And that conclusion is that when we obey God's Laws our spiritual journey is swift, smooth and trouble-free.

Although some major events in our lives are astrologically predestined and others are 'exams' we have agreed to sit, we are free to mitigate the negative impact of such events, or even transcend them entirely. For by our good deeds and by demonstrating that we have learned past lessons we can minimise unpleasant experiences. And, as we put on the mantle of the Masters we are becoming, we detach ourselves from desire and become less affected by world events. We start to enjoy the warmth and joy that life has to offer, and all fear and negativity that once affected us passes us by. My point is that free will gives us the freedom to choose the experiences we want to have, which is the Love of God in action.

The Great Law also mandates that if we want heaven to intercede in events on Earth the request must come from a person in embodiment by means of a prayer, a decree or a judgement call. For even though the Ascended Host have all the answers they will never impose their remedies upon us. But what they will do is assist us when we make specific requests. They will suggest and present options for us to consider but they will never, ever, tell us what to do, as this would be a gross violation of our free will. But whatever choices we do make, the powers in heaven always hold the immaculate concept for the highest outcome – in accordance with our divine plans.

> "Ask, and it shall be given you; seek, and ye shall find; knock, and it shall be opened unto you."
> – Matthew 7:7

A GOLDEN AGE ECONOMY

Communism is the antithesis of freedom, and therefore the ultimate political and economic expression of everything that the Law of Free Will is not. It is a form of government rooted in the belief systems of the fallen angels and therefore the consciousness of anti-Christ and anti-Being. And, as we have seen with the collapse of the Soviet Union it is a tower of Babel that shall certainly fall.

> "This is the Age of Freedom and it is the destiny of this planet to become THE FREEDOM STAR."
>
> – **Kim Andrew Lincoln**

The Great Principle of CORRESPONDENCE

"The second great Hermetic Principle embodies the truth that there is a harmony, agreement, and correspondence between the several planes of Manifestation, Life and Being. This truth is a truth because all that is included in the Universe emanates from the same source, and the same laws, principles, and characteristics apply to each unit, or combination of units of activity, as each manifests its own phenomena upon its own plane."

– **The Kybalion**

In other words our outer world is a reflection of our inner world, in that what we focus our attention on and what we think about most will be reflected back to us in the conditions and circumstances that we experience in our lives.

What this Principle tells us is that each person is responsible for what happens to them as we are the architects of our own destinies. It explains why we are happy or sad, rich or poor; and that what is contained on the inside will become manifest on the outside. Inner beauty, which is harmony within, will manifest itself as physical beauty, which is harmony without – meaning harmony on the outside.

"For the peace flame to grow
Wipe war from your heart
When Peace is within
Outside it will start."

– **Kim Andrew Lincoln**
(A verse from the song 'Peacemakers' written in 2006)

A GOLDEN AGE ECONOMY

What I am saying here is that it is the content of our minds that matters because our thoughts are the first cause in the chain of being. Nothing happens unless we first have the thought that it should. No action can occur without the thought that gets the action going. We cannot act before we think of acting even though we may joke that we can. Therefore, if we want to improve any part of our lives we can only do so by changing the content of our minds. Positive thoughts beget positive physical outcomes; therefore we should choose our thoughts with care.

The Ascended Masters talk about holding the 'immaculate concept' for something that they would like to see manifest on Earth. What is meant by this is that for the highest possible outcome (the immaculate concept) to manifest we must first create an image in our mind's eye of whatever it is that we would like to happen and then hold that vision. This is the inner process we must initiate before the outer process, the result, can manifest. This is how we turn our dreams into a reality – by seeing within (our mind's eye) what we want to happen so that whatever that is can then become manifest without – in the physical world.

> "All successful people started out thinking that they were successful long before they ever became a success."
> – **Kim Andrew Lincoln**

Another way of explaining the Great Principle of Correspondence would be to say whatever we create on the inside will become manifest on the outside and that we cannot create anything on the outside until we have first created something on the inside. So we can see from this explanation how important our thoughts are and that we must be careful what we initiate in our minds, because this power, the awesome power of thought, is what the Lord God Almighty used to create the Universe. It is what makes things happen as I discovered for myself as a young man.

In the late 1970s I was a sales representative with Cussons UK, the famous soap manufacturer. The company had decided to test launch a new washing-up liquid called 'Morning Fresh' and so the management put together a team of their top sales representatives to sell the product

The Great Principle of CORRESPONDENCE

into retailers in the South Wales area, prior to the commencement of a TV advertising campaign. As this was the biggest and most important product launch in the company's history it was an ideal opportunity for me to make a name for myself. So I decided that I would persuade every shopkeeper I visited to order at least one case of Morning Fresh. I held the vision that all the buyers I met would agree to my proposals and burned that image of total success in my mind. A fortnight later, when the sales results were announced, I was informed that I had achieved the highest strike rate (97%) and that I had sold the most cases of Morning Fresh – none of which would have been possible had I not seen myself as winning first.

The most important message that the Great Principle of Correspondence conveys is that we are responsible for everything that happens to us, as our material and spiritual conditions are a direct reflection of the way we think, feel and act most of the time. We are the authors of our own success and/or misfortune because there is no such thing as good luck or bad luck.

LUCK = Labour Under Correct Knowledge.

When we operate in alignment with the Laws of God we are almost certain to be lucky because our right thinking will create a corresponding right result. And when we do not, the opposite will happen. This Law rules out any possibility of coincidence happening in our lives, as events do not occur randomly, but as a result of a first cause.

> "Under the Laws of God, coincidence, which is chaos by another name, cannot occur."
> **– Kim Andrew Lincoln**

The ramifications of this may be hard to accept as it is commonly believed that what is wrong in our lives is as a result of what other people have done or not done, or because fate has dealt us an unfavourable hand.

> "And why beholdest thou the mote that is in thy brother's eye, but considerest not the beam that is in thine own eye?"
> – Matthew 7:3

This is a false, though understandable view, given that while we are in embodiment it is almost impossible for us not to be driven, to some extent, by the illusions created by our egos. And this explains why we cannot always discern the difference between reality and illusion. For the ego is selfish and prideful. It has no heart and thinks that it is infallible. It reasons that all problems – all dissatisfaction with our lives – is caused by the mistakes and mis-creations of others, and thus it is others who must change because the ego is beyond fault.

> "The definition of insanity is doing the same thing over and over again and expecting different results."
> – Albert Einstein

The hard truth is that this entity we call the ego was created when we lost our connection with our spiritual parents, God the Father and God the Mother, as explained in the Old Testament in the allegorical story of the Garden of Eden. In this story all of us, represented by Adam and Eve, decided to experiment with the consciousness of duality, the fruit of knowledge of good and evil, and as a result, we became like sheep without a shepherd. Realising that we needed to replace the guidance we had lost when we turned away from our divine parents, we created the ego. The ego, however, is a false guru. It tells us what we want to hear and not what we need to know in order to grow spiritually. Moreover, the ego is like the arch-deceiver, the Serpent, a fallen angel skilled in telling the sweetest and most subtle lies. He tricked Adam and Eve into disobeying God's Laws so that they would follow the wrong path, the left-handed path of the consciousness of anti–Christ, which is also the way of the ego that leads to hell and death. The ego is like the wicked one – the devil and Satan – who misrepresents the truth by making us think that our misfortunes are the fault of others and that we can do what we want without consequences; that if it feels good it

The Great Principle of CORRESPONDENCE

must be right when in truth we are all subject to God's Laws and we pay a price when we break them.

The truth is that it is not others who determine our fate it is us, as we are in the driving seat and thus go where we please because we are in control of everything that we wish to experience. We are masters of those vehicles we call our minds and the fuel that moves us forward is the thoughts that only we can form. As we control our thinking we control everything else.

> "Harbouring a resentment
> Is sure to leave some resentment behind.
> How can this be good?
> It cannot.
> Therefore the wise
> Accept all responsibility."
>
> **- LAO TSU**
> (from Verse 79 of the TAO TE CHING)

Moreover, how we think, feel and act affects our planet, as we are energy and the planet is energy. And, all like energies, which are energies of a similar vibration, are attracted to each other. So when vast numbers of people send out the same negative energy, like the energy of fear, for example, this emotional energy collects together in a cloud and hangs in the astral plane, which is a dimension of spiritual consciousness where our emotions reside, located between the vibrational frequencies of Heaven and Earth.

When this dark cloud of emotional energy becomes too heavy it literally falls back to Earth like rain and is caught by the Elemental beings (the Salamanders, Sylphs, Undines and Faeries) that control the elements of fire, air, water and earth. They out-picture this energy with extreme physical conditions that correspond to the type of emotional energy we have released. It is above as it is below because the nature kingdom mirrors back to us what we have given out. So that when we see extreme weather conditions out-pictured, they are more than just a fluke of nature they are

A GOLDEN AGE ECONOMY

the by-product of the miscreations of mankind's hearts and minds.

When we send out feelings of anger and hate it develops into violent storms. And when it is fear, there is lack of rain that mirrors back our lack of identity with the reality of God. The opposite extreme, flooding from too much rain, is brought about by the consciousness of being ungrateful for the abundance that nature has brought forth.

Then there is abortion, the product of unwanted pregnancies which results in violence against all children of God. When a mother kills her offspring her heart is hardened to the sacredness of life. The return of this callousness of the mothers in the world is loss of property and loss of life attached to that property — when new life is seen as standing in the way of owning and possessing things. When mothers allow their unborn to be murdered, there is the consciousness of hatred of the Mother God. Whether that mother has hatred of the Mother God or not, she is tied to that hatred by allowing her unborn child to be murdered. Thereby, she is contributing to the mass weight of hatred against the Mother God and the resultant weight accumulates until it can no longer be held back from the physical, and abruptly out-pictures that hatred into our world. This hatred appears as violent upheavals in the earth, such as volcanoes, landslides or earthquakes, or it may appear as extreme weather conditions like hurricanes, tornadoes and other disasters in nature.

> "Sickly pale faces, sounds foreboding
> Tornadoes sweeping a violent warning
>
> What have we done to deserve such pain?
> Please forgive us Lord and calm this hurricane
>
> For six days and six nights
> The storm's been raging in mortal fight
>
> Devastation - injured people lie
> Panic- stricken thousands' more will die

The Great Principle of CORRESPONDENCE

> Please spare us Lord, on our knees we pray
> Crying for help on this judgement day."
>
> **– Kim Andrew Lincoln**
> (An extract from the song 'Storm' written in 1975).

So we can see that there is no such thing as a natural disaster. For indeed what we previously may have considered to be natural is in fact manifestly unnatural, for it is the effect of everything that is not of God but that has come from the thoughts and deeds of the Children of God who have not been acting in accordance with the Laws of God.

This explanation of the causes of 'natural disasters' has been adapted from a dictation given by beloved Pallas Athena, the Goddess of Truth, through the messenger, Lorraine Michaels, who runs the Ascended Master sponsored organisation, Theosophia Is The Way. You can read the full explanation on the website: www.theosophiaistheway.com

This then is the Great Principle of Correspondence that can be summed up:

"As above, so below, so below as above."

– The Kybalion

The Great Principle of VIBRATION

"He who knows the Law of Vibrations knows all."
– **Hermes Mercurius Trismegistus**

This Law states that everything in the universe vibrates and that different things vibrate at different frequencies. All things are constantly moving. And, if one thing slows down or stops it is transformed into something else.

Einstein discovered that all "matter is energy" and scientists have proven that we cannot destroy energy, only transform it.

Human beings are energy and although our skin appears solid it is actually trillions of rapidly moving molecules that vibrate at a specific vibrational rate. We vibrate at different frequencies. And how high or low that frequency is, is dependent upon how harmoniously or disharmoniously we have lived in past lives and our present life.

Just as the pebble we throw into the pool creates vibrations that appear as ripples that travel outward, the thoughts we send out are like ripples too, that extend into the Universe. And because these thoughts attract energies of a similar vibration we must be careful what we send out, because whatever that is, it will come back to us as circumstances that later manifest in our lives. If we want to manifest positive circumstances we must send out positive thoughts, because negative thinking will attract the same back. It is said that we become what we think about and the world that we have now is the result of the sum total of those thoughts.

An important point here is that higher frequencies transmute lower frequencies – meaning that negative thoughts can be transformed into positive ones simply by replacing them with positive thinking. In other words high frequency positive thoughts transform low frequency negative thoughts into high frequency positive ones.

Jesus has explained that when he walked the Earth two thousand

The Great Principle of VIBRATION

years ago the frequency at which his personal energy field (consciousness) vibrated was about fifty times higher than that of the average person. This explains why he was able to heal the sick and even raise the dead. It was the sheer power of his high frequency thoughts focused on the disease in his patients that restored them to health.

Even doctors today would acknowledge that the power of thought is such that we can think ourselves to health just as easily as we can think ourselves to death.

When Jesus turned water into wine he was applying his God Power and God Wisdom as a master alchemist to transform one substance into another by altering its vibration. The miracle of walking on the water was achieved by a similar process whereby Jesus temporarily increased his vibration so that his physical body became less dense and lighter, so that he literally floated upwards. The effect this created made it appear that Jesus was actually walking on the sea when in reality he was levitating above it. There are adepts in India who can perform similar feats of levitation today.

The Ascended Masters advise us that in fact matter is spirit and that the physical universe is merely an extension of the spiritual realm that has the potential to manifest God's kingdom on Earth. The scientific meaning of this statement is that the only difference between the physical world and the spiritual one is the rate at which they vibrate, so that if we wish to create heaven on Earth, all we have to do is to raise the vibration of our energy fields to the level of the ascended beings in Heaven, and we will be in Heaven.

That is why we are here: to raise our consciousnesses by serving others and so follow in the footsteps of Jesus and the other great spiritual teachers who demonstrated by their wonderful examples of raising others up how we can bring heaven to Earth, and thus how we can create *A Golden Age Economy*.

> "Verily, verily, I say unto you, He that believeth on me, the works that I do shall he do also; and greater [works] than these shall he do; because I go unto my Father."
>
> – John 14:12

And:

> "I have said, ye [are] gods; and all of you [are] children of the most high."
>
> – Psalm 82:6

The Secret of Eternal Youth

As with Jesus' miracles the secret of eternal youth and a longer life can be explained by the Great Principle of Vibration as, when we raise each other up, God gives us more light with which to co-create. And when we qualify that light by obeying his Laws our consciousness, and therefore our vibration, is raised too.

When our vibratory rate increases, our physical bodies look younger, healthier and more radiant because our inner beauty, meaning our beautiful thoughts, shine through and manifest as outer beauty – in accordance with the Great Principle of Correspondence.

We appear ethereal and our skin looks translucent as though it had been airbrushed of all its imperfections. And with a higher consciousness we tend to care more about the condition of our bodies as they are the temples of our souls that enable us to walk upon the Earth. Caring about our bodies means exercising regularly, eating a healthy, balanced diet and eating less food overall – simply because we need less calories to survive. This is because spiritual people carry more light within their energy fields and this light energy or prana is a substitute for food.

So what matters here is that we work on perfecting our spiritual beings first because then everything else will naturally fall into place as what happens on the inside will become manifest on the outside.

> "But seek ye first the kingdom of God, and his righteousness; and all these things shall be added unto you."
>
> – Matthew 6:33

The Law of Attraction

Jesus understood the Law of Attraction, which is related to the Great Principle of Vibration. It states that, as like attracts like, energies of a similar vibration will be attracted to each other, and so we must pay attention to the fact that if we send out low vibrational energy we will receive the same back. If, therefore, we transmit feelings of fear we will attract more fear into our lives. Whereas, if we smile into the mirror (of life), that same smile will be reflected back to us, because the Universe is a giant mirror that continually reflects back to us what we send out.

And thus, if we want to be prosperous we should first help others to be prosperous. So that when we do the universal mirror will recognise the vibration of prosperity that we are emitting and reflect it back to us.

"Whatever you choose for yourself – give to another first."
– **Jesus Christ**
(through the former Messenger, Kim Michaels)

Please note that we may get back more than we send out because under the Law when we 'multiply our talents' – by raising others up – we will be raised up too. We will be given more abundance to multiply, so that the more becomes even more and so on, and a virtuous spiral of ever increasing abundance is created. Jesus explained this in his parable of the 'talents' when he stated that the servant who had multiplied his talents the most was not only allowed to keep that which he had manifested but also the money of the servant who had buried his in the ground.

I believe that this is the source of the saying: "to those that have shall be given", but its meaning may also be that inaction is tantamount to negative action that may result in us losing even that which we have, but did not 'multiply'. And thus standing still and resting on our laurels is not a viable option in either personal lives or the world of commerce. For how many times have we heard stories of companies that have gone into liquidation and wondered what it was that caused them to go down? Well, sadly the truth is that whatever the causes were, incorrect action – meaning misqualified energy – would have been at the heart of it, because under Universal Law there is no such thing as bad luck, accidents or coincidence, or indeed, any other cause, that would appear to be beyond management's control.

When we witness the tragedy of a great company collapse or a country divided by conflict it is usually because 'something is rotten in the state of Denmark' – meaning that the upheaval is caused by the outpourings of disordered minds.

> "Even in chaos there is order, for in reality for every action there is a reaction."
>
> **– Kim Andrew Lincoln**

There is no escape from the Great Law. It is immutable. It is not random. It does not discriminate. It is no respecter of persons. It cannot be undermined, side- stepped or usurped. It is what it is. It is the Great Principle of Vibration

> "God does not play dice with the Universe."
>
> **– Albert Einstein**

The Law of Resistance

It is said that "what we resist persists" because that which we resist we draw unto ourselves like a magnet so that it perpetuates its influence upon our lives. Resistance is the face of fear that we must confront and conquer before a state of harmony can exist within us. If, for example, we have a strong resistance to a particular race of people, the only way that we can overcome it may be to incarnate as a member of that race in a future lifetime so that we can learn to detach ourselves from the negativity we perceive to be connected to them.

When we change our view about something it is usually because we come to see the situation for what it really is, meaning that we see it through the crystal clear vision of the 'Christ mind'. When this happens any disharmony that was attached to our old view usually disappears. To obtain wisdom or, as the Gautama Buddha put it, to become 'awake' is why we are here. Being wise and having wisdom is knowing the Truth of All That Is. And thus, changing our minds may be just another way of saying becoming aware of the truth. For when all resistance (fear) within our beings has gone we attain a state of bliss that is the Peace of the Buddha, which comes from being free from attachment to the things of this world.

"What we resist we become."

– Kim Andrew Lincoln

THE LAW OF FELLOWSHIP

"The power of love, wisdom and unity."
— **Kim Andrew Lincoln**

When two or more people of similar vibration are gathered together for one purpose, the energy they generate when focused on achieving that purpose will be far greater than the sum of their combined energies working alone.

The universal truth that underpins this Law is that if we want to change our world we will achieve far better results when we work together. The following verses from my song 'Look into the River' explore this truth in the context of what was happening in the world when I wrote it in 1979 and that is still happening today.

> Marching in your millions
> Down politician's row
> Rising now to halt the flood
> Of all the evil flow
> Crying at your daughters grave
> Won't bring her laughter back
> Stake the ground and save your sons
> From Serpent's* men in black
> Murder is a deadly sin
> No licence can allow
> The Watchers* you should be aware
> Are waving at you now
> All united in the Light
> Love streaming from our eyes
> With our voices winds will blow
> And all the tears will dry.

* Serpents and Watchers are fallen angels

THE LAW OF FORGIVENESS

When the apostle, Peter, asked Jesus how many times he should forgive those who sinned against him Jesus said that he should forgive them not seven times, but *seventy times seven.*

So why did Jesus say that we should forgive so many times?

Well, I think that the point Jesus was making is that when we forgive repeatedly we build a momentum of love and light that enables us to enter in to a higher state of consciousness. And this opens the door to communication with our higher selves (I AM presence) and our spiritual advisers in heaven. When we forgive we are given more light from God and thus we become lighter. When we forgive each other so much light is anchored in the Earth that a virtuous spiral is begun that burns the darkness away.

Until we forgive we are the prisoner of the person who offended us. When we forgive we release those fear-based energies of anger, resentment and hatred that are usually tied up with the sins that were committed against us and the sins we committed. Moreover, these energies can – if they are not released from our chakras – form into a ferocious beast that is almost impossible to tame. And we have all borne witness to this beast in the ongoing conflict between the Jews and the Arabs that began on another planet and was brought to Earth aeons ago by the lost souls that have incarnated here. And yet these protagonists do not forgive, for their enmity still threatens the peace on Earth today. So when Jesus implored us two thousand years ago to forgive he may have been mindful of the events that led to the mutual annihilation of the Laggard races on Maldek, which I shall explain in more detail under the Law of Relativity later on in this episode. Perhaps he was also warning us that what happened there could just as easily happen here if we do not keep forgiving those who do us harm.

"But if ye forgive not men their trespasses, neither will your Father forgive your trespasses."

– **Matthew 6:15**

When we forgive we do not condone a past imperfect action, but accept that it happened for a reason and that the sin will be balanced in the justice of God's plan.

"Dearly beloved, avenge not yourselves, but rather give place unto wrath: for it is written, Vengeance is mine; I will repay, saith the Lord."

– **Romans 12:19**

When we forgive we let go by drawing a line under the injury caused and keeping what is past in the past. Life is lived not in the past or the future but in the eternal now. History and the records of past misdeeds are certainly our teachers, but in order to ascend we must detach ourselves from the heavy burdens of past wrongs. Forgiveness is the key to achieving this so that when we forgive we free ourselves from the weights that have been holding us down.

Forgiveness
I AM forgiveness acting here,
Casting out all doubt and fear,
Setting men forever free
With wings of cosmic victory.
I AM calling in full power
For forgiveness every hour;
To all life in every place
I flood forth forgiving grace.

The above is a verse from the 'Head, Hand and Heart' decree that was written by the Ascended Host for our benefit. The full decree can be found on the Summit Lighthouse website and can be spoken daily as part of the forgiveness process that Jesus recommended two thousand years ago.

The Law of Forgiveness

When we forgive we may be unknowingly pardoning those whom we know and love because they are part of the circle of souls we have grown up with over many lifetimes, and through whom, the Laws of Karma have been dispensed by the mercy of God's flame. For it may be the case that in a past life our misguided actions caused the deaths of others. So that when that debt had to be repaid with our execution, it was our son from a past life who pulled the lever that took us from this world.

Consider that those whom we count among our friends on 'Facebook' or any other social media site may have been agents of God's justice at some point in our distant past. But we will probably never know who is who, and who did what because when we incarnate we have no conscious memory of lives past. Though we may have a feeling or even an inner knowing that we have known a friend in a previous life it is highly unlikely that we will be able to recall anything about the relationship.

These immortal words by Shakespeare tell part of the story:

> "All the world's a stage,
> And all the men and women merely players;
> They have their exits and their entrances,
> And one man in his time plays many parts."

– William Shakespeare
(An extract from his *As You Like it*)

So when we read between the lines of Shakespeare we can see that those who we thought were our enemies are in fact only playing their rightful roles in this play called life – a role which we all agreed they should play before we came into embodiment. For they the sinners, and we the sinned against, are all actors who rehearse scenes in different plays so that we might master particular lessons and then move on to a higher stage in life. So knowing this how could we possibly condemn those within our soul circle who act out their roles on the opposing side delivering their lines and their blows upon our persons? How indeed?

A Golden Age Economy

For the truth is that in this great play of life it is often our greatest foes who are our greatest friends both in the literal sense, and in the sense that they help us to win the 'Oscars' of life.

Forgiveness & the Economy

"Forgiveness is good for business."

– Kim Andrew Lincoln

It is cheaper to forgive than to fight through the courts for a victory that we can never win. Forgiveness saves time, stress and money. But more than this it makes us feel good and better able to face the challenges that we are presented with each day. How many good friends do we know whose lives have been turned upside down because of wrongs they will not forgive and lay to rest? Our most expensive mistakes are made when we refuse to forgive. Wars are fought when we fail to forgive. Sons and daughters die when parents cannot forgive. The following poem tells this age-old story:

Thou Shalt Not Kill

No glory in a million dead
Mankind not raised when brothers bled
How brave are they who took the hill?
Who was it said
Thou shalt not kill?

There is no light if none is shone
All wars engaged cannot be won
How many sons in conflicts spilled?
Said the All One
Thou shalt not kill

Two thousand years since Jesus came
Forgive thy foes he did proclaim

The Law of Forgiveness

Thy sword not raise thy arm be still
His words the same

Thou shalt not kill
Mahatma Ghandi beloved heart
Peaceful resistance did impart
An Empire beat by words and will
Said he to all
Thou shalt not kill

Now Saint Germain's new age we bring
His freedom song he bids us sing
And peace dispense that sweetest pill
So say we now?
Thou shalt not kill

Kim Andrew Lincoln

THE LAW OF REFLECTION

This Universal Law states that the positive and negative traits we respond to in others, we recognise in ourselves, meaning that that which we admire in others, we recognize as existing within ourselves, and that which we resist and react to strongly in others is certain to be found within ourselves, and that which we resist and react to in others is something that we are afraid exists within ourselves and finally that which we resist in ourselves, we will dislike in others.

> "Thou hypocrite, first cast out the beam out of thine own eye; and then shalt thou see clearly to cast out the mote out of thy brother's eye."
>
> **– Matthew 7:5**

THE GREAT PRINCIPLE OF POLARITY

"Everything is Dual; everything has poles; everything has its pair of opposites' like and unlike are the same; opposites are identical in nature, but different in degree; extremes meet; all truths are but half-truths; all paradoxes may be reconciled."
– **The Kybalion**

"Everything that is, is double."
– **Hermes Mercurius Trismegistus**
(from *The Divine Pymander*)

"I am the LORD (or LAW), and there is none else. I form the light, and create darkness: I make peace, and create evil: I the LORD do all these things."
– **Isaiah 45: 6, 7**

This Great Principle is the Law of mental vibrations that enables us to demonstrate our potential To BE all that we truly are in each embodiment. It permits us to express ourselves in a range of outcomes from the extremely negative to the highly positive. For the Law of Free Will allows us to take any road we choose and each choice that we make will initiate a series of causes and corresponding effects. We may balance or create karma. We may follow our divine plans precisely or not. But, whatever we decide, our spiritual parents and guides will hold the immaculate concept for us in their hearts and minds. They will see us finding the fastest and least troublesome route home, the path of least resistance, which is the one where we follow the Laws of God.

"It is only by constantly transcending ourselves that we shall find our way home."
– **Kim Andrew Lincoln**

A GOLDEN AGE ECONOMY

We all have positive and negative personal characteristics and all good traits are balanced by bad ones in the scales of personality. In astrology each of the twelve signs of the zodiac has its opposite. I am a Taurus and my opposite sign is Scorpio. It is said that opposites attract, which must be so as I have many dear friends born with the sun in Scorpio.

Before we come into embodiment it may be part of our divine plans to partner someone who has opposite personality traits to ourselves. The purpose here would be to draw out and reinforce that which is good and to moderate that which is not, so that both parties benefit from the interaction of their opposite's traits. This is the process of polarity integration where the aim is to find the 'Middle Way' of harmony and balance that leads to the sublime peace that Jesus exemplified during his life in Palestine. It is the way of Gautama Buddha, the King of Peace. It is the way of enlightenment that is the opposite of ignorance and darkness in all its many forms.

Evil means 'energy veil'. An energy veil is the illusion we created when we separated ourselves from the light of our Father/Mother God after we fell from grace in the Garden of Eden. It was then that we lost divine direction, which is the benefit of our divine parent's wisdom whose opposite is ignorance. So that evil means living in ignorance under the veil where there is an absence of light, i.e. under the cover of darkness.

> "Within the darkest of life's perceived trials and hardships lies the means as well as the ability to find and experience the light."
> – **Chuck Danes**

Every negative experience has its counterpart. And one way we can return to BEING (Be – in – God) who we really are, is through the experience of being who we are not. This is learning in the school of hard knocks, which means living in accordance with man's laws as opposed to God's Laws. It is allowing ourselves to be driven by the dictates of ego and thus immersing ourselves in the sea of illusions that is the world of unreality. It is not the preferred method of spiritual advancement, but as we all know it can be a very effective way of ensuring that a challenging lesson is learnt.

> "To BE or not To BE that is the question."
> **– William Shakespeare**
> (from his play, *Hamlet*)

The Great Principle of Polarity enables us to explore and experience life to the fullest extent through all its highs and lows. It is through us and the way that we choose to deal with the difficulties of daily life that God experiences Himself in the world of form, for as His children He is in us as we are in Him.

This inbuilt polarity of extremes that we find in every aspect of life – in emotions like love and hate and physical conditions like great wealth and poverty – can be a great teacher and a great leveller. By its existence and through its example it can humble the proud and give strength to the weak. For when we witness great acts of selflessness, charity and compassion we are humbled by the towering example of those who choose To BE the Christ, by shining their lights. For in that moment of realisation when we recognise that goodness in others, deep within us our heart strings are pulled and we are reminded that perhaps we could BE more than we are BEING right now. And that maybe it is time to take stock of our lives and the direction in which we are headed. We are alerted to the fact that maybe it is time to change course.

> "The acquisition of great wealth is often motivated by the experience of extreme poverty."
> **– Kim Andrew Lincoln**

The Great Principle of Polarity can teach us to see the good in all situations as the glass may be half empty but it is also half full. With this Law everything has opposites and those opposites are equal, as if it is six miles from north to south it must also be the same distance from south to north.

A GOLDEN AGE ECONOMY

When we accentuate the positive by looking for the good – even in the most difficult of situations – we send out the vibration of victory and the universe responds in kind by reflecting back to us the trappings of victory – in all its many guises.

A company is thriving. Its order book is full. It is making healthy profits and the employees are happy with their lot. All is rosy in the garden until one day disaster strikes. There is a mysterious fire and the entire factory is burned to the ground. So the business owners meet to assess the damage and decide what to do. There are two ways they can view the situation: either positively or negatively. On the plus side the factory is fully insured so the funds will be there to replace the building, machinery and stock, and to compensate the firm for the interruption. On balance the owners consider that the fire is a blessing in disguise as they were already considering a move to a bigger and better factory as the old one was expensive to maintain. Such a move would allow them to expand the business and reduce costs. All plusses which in the longer term will pay dividends. On the downside there is the problem of fulfilling existing orders and the possible loss of customers while the new factory is being made ready, but on balance the directors are not overly concerned by these temporary setbacks. All they can see is the potential to generate higher sales and profits in the future.

So, by refusing to be beaten by this unforeseen disaster, by choosing victory over defeat and by holding the immaculate concept for even greater success in the future the owners lay the mental foundation that will enable them to manifest all that they wish to achieve in the future; for under the Law you reap what you sow, you get back what you send out.

Needless to say this business goes from strength to strength and yet it could so easily have gone the other way had the owners taken a less than positive view of the loss of their factory by fire.

So from this example we can understand that it is how we perceive a situation that is crucial, because it is our mindset that determines events. Nothing happens that did not originate with the thought that it should. Everything starts out in the mind because the universe is mental in accordance with the first 'Great Principle'.

The Great Principle of POLARITY

"Matter is subject to Mind."
                                      – **Kim Andrew Lincoln**

At its most basic level the Great Principle of Polarity shows us the depths to which we can sink when we deny the divine within us and the great heights of spiritual attainment we can achieve when we chose To BE all that we are in God. By surrendering to our higher selves as opposed to allowing our lower (unreal) selves, i.e. our egos to rule our lives.

In the economy there are opposites and paradoxes too. For example, the ultimate expression of a capitalist economy, a fascist regime, is where one corporation owns and controls everything, whereas under the most extreme left-wing, communist model, it is the state that is omnipotent. Here we have two diametrically opposed political/economic systems that are in effect the same as so succinctly illustrated by the following quotation:

"Under capitalism, man exploits man. Under communism, it's just the opposite."
                                      – **John Kenneth Galbraith**

We could say that an enlightened economy is one that is characterised by the selflessness of its people whereas the opposite extreme would be one where the people are totally self-centred.

And the most enlightened free market system would be one where there are no investors who live off the sweat and toil of the employees but there are only owner-workers and managers who share the profits that they have generated by working together as a team for the greater benefit of all. There are two noteworthy retail businesses that have embodied this ideal: the John Lewis Partnership in the United Kingdom and the J C Penny Company of America. J C Penny, who founded the firm, operated his business in accordance with the 'Golden Rule', which was to treat his customers as he would want to be treated himself. And I am sure all those who love Jesus will recognise this is his second most important teaching – the first being: "The kingdom of God is within you". J C Penny is now an Ascended Master.

A GOLDEN AGE ECONOMY

One of the best examples of polarity is the extreme opposites of heaven and hell wherein lies the most profound paradox. This is that if we live long enough in darkness (ignorance) the misery of it will cause us to rebel against this captor as we rebelled against God in the Garden of Eden, when we fell for the lies of the Serpent. And in this awakening we will see that there is more to life than living in bondage to our desires and the suffering it brings, and that before we become so immersed in the 'sea of troubles' we have created that we drown, we will swim back to shore and take the right-handed path that leads us home.

The Great Principle of Rhythm

> "Everything flows, out and in; everything has its tides; all things rise and fall; the pendulum-swing manifests in everything; the measure of the swing to the right is the measure of the swing to the left; rhythm compensates."
>
> **– The Kybalion**

As we breathe in and out there is a period of the time that elapses between the in-breath and the out-breath. This is a cycle. This is rhythm and it beats like our hearts for an infinite time.

In the natural world the evidence of this Law of Cycles is plain to see. It is in the ebb and flow of the tides; the changing seasons of the year; the cycles of life, death and rebirth and in the rising and setting of our Sun. It is present even in the metre of the words that form the lines upon this page. Indeed rhythm is in all things and all cycles emanate from a single point of beginning, which was the first letter on the opening page of the Book of Life. And this, first and greatest, of all cycles began with the first breath that our Creator breathed after he had the thought that he was going to create. And what followed that in-breath was the out-breath and so the rhythm of life was established with this first cycle that was the birthing point from which all lesser cycles were born.

Rhythms of Life

It is rhythm that keeps everything in balance, for when the natural rhythms of Mother Earth are disturbed by the off-beats of an unenlightened world it can cause continents to collapse. Thus it is rhythm that maintains equilibrium and harmony in our world. Rhythm is the measured swing of the pendulum on the grandfather clock that moves equally from left to right from the centre starting point. For what goes out must come back and what goes up must come down.

Musicians will know that our hearts beat to the 2/4 time and that common time (4/4) forms the basis of most musical composition. The Ascended Masters tell us that there are seven basic rhythms of life and that each of the seven Chakras, which are the energy centres of our bodies, corresponds to a different one of these time signatures. The rhythms of life are 4/4, 3/4, 6/8, 2/4, 12/8, 5/4, 7/4 and 12/4. Misuse of rhythm is a black art perfected by the fallen angels that I will be discussing in more detail in Episode Two.

The Great Principle of Rhythm is in the biorhythms of our bodies and our mental and emotional states. It is in our mood swings, our good days and our bad. It is present in the rise and fall of fevers, in sickness and health, and in the cycles of abundance and the creation of great wealth. It teaches us that there is a right time to act, as success is so often dependent upon getting the timing right as Brutus so eloquently expounds in these famous lines from Shakespeare's play *Julius Caesar*:

> There is a tide in the affairs of men.
> Which, taken at the flood, leads on to fortune;
> Omitted, all the voyage of their life
> Is bound in shallows and in miseries.
> On such a full sea are we now afloat,
> And we must take the current when it serves,
> Or lose our ventures.

– William Shakespeare

An important lesson we can learn from this Law is how to rise above any negative energies that may be present in the downswing of the cycle that begins with the fall of the wave. For it is when the waves are crashing all around us that we need to keep the balance as it is only with a calm and collected mind that we can cope with stormy seas and steer our ships safely home.

The Great Principle of RHYTHM

"There is but One Life – One Life Underlying. This Life is manifesting through ME, and through every other shape, form and thing. I am resting on the bosom of the Great Ocean of Life, and rejoice as I feel the sway of its motion. Nothing can harm me – though changes may come and go, I am Safe. I am One with All Life, and its Power, Knowledge and Peace are behind, underneath and within me. O! One Life! Express thyself through me – carry me now on the crest of the wave, now deep down in the trough of the ocean – supported always by Thee – all is good to me, as I feel Thy life moving in and through me. I am Alive, through Thy life, and I open myself to Thy full manifestation and inflow."

– **Yogi Ramacharaka**

I was an athlete in my youth and was aware that my best times as a sprinter always coincided with the days when the biorhythms that governed my physical strength were strongest. Had I been able to run each race when these energies were at their peak I am sure that I would have won every competition. But life is not like that. We have to take the rough with the smooth, the good times with the bad, for whatever we do, we cannot escape the Great Principle of Rhythm – the cycles that are woven into the invisible fabric of spirit and form.

"All men reach and fall, reach and fall."

– (A line from the movie *Alexander* spoken by the Pharaoh Ptolemy Soter describing the extraordinary life of his dear friend Alexander the Great)

With the birth of every baby a new hand turns on the face of the cosmic clock as another cycle begins. For from the day we are first created we are confronted with the mountain of the Ascension that we must climb – our journey home to join our Father/Mother God in heaven. This exciting adventure is an expedition of discovery where our purpose is to obtain enlightenment, that state of sublime peace that comes from being non-attached to the things of this world.

Moreover, it is part of our mission of service to help our fellow brothers and sisters raise their consciousnesses, so that they too can be enlightened. Thus, by this process a causal link is established that serves to raise up all people and all life. This occurs when all dark places (under the energy veil of evil) are illuminated with light of our beings. And when this happens, when all ignorance has been transmuted by the threefold flame of our God POWER, God WISDOM and God LOVE, our victory is won. For only then can we ascend permanently to heaven and complete the cycle by returning home.

And once we have ascended, Mother Earth can follow us, as she too will have been so filled with the light of the Children of the Sun of her body, that she will be transformed into the Freedom Star that she was always destined to become. So here we have a description of the personal and planetary cycles that are being outplayed on every inhabited planet in this galaxy and universe. And from these examples we can visualise the step-by-step process whereby the immaculate concept is that we are constantly moving onwards and upwards in consciousness. It is the sequence of events that God set in motion when he decided to create this realm of frequencies that extend from his heart (at their highest point), to the world of matter where the densest of material resides. For we are light bodies and it is the amount and intensity of the light that our beings can hold that determines how close in vibrational frequency we are to our maker. Each step up the spiral staircase to heaven is not a movement of distance climbed, but a measure of consciousness raised. Every step is a lesson learned and another cycle gone by.

> "God is billions of souls that shine much brighter each moment of time."
>
> – Kim Andrew Lincoln

To learn more about how you can apply this Law of Cycles to your own life, I recommend the book *Predict Your Future* by Elizabeth Clare Prophet, which explains the science of the Cosmic Clock. The author was, prior to her recent ascension, a messenger for the Ascended Host and held the spiritual office of the Guru Ma. I strongly recommend all

Elizabeth Clare Prophet's books, videos and discourses, which you can access via the 'Summit Lighthouse' website.

The River of Life

We all know what happens when we go against the flow of the river of life, when we step off the track of the Great Law that was laid down to make our journey as smooth and comfortable as possible. For our Creator is a kind, compassionate and considerate God who, like any parent, wants the best for his children. So that when we 'kick against the pricks' it is the Laws of Rhythm and Karma that compensate and hopefully bring us back into balance. And what I mean by this, is that we will feel the pain of the thorns in our feet as we struggle to make progress through the thickets and bushes and all manner of obstacles that have been placed in our path to remind us that we have stepped off the highway to heaven, and that by this impossible route we will never find our way home. And so the lesson here is that with God's Law there is no compromise as it is what it is for a reason. There is no relative good and evil. There is only one way to go, and to live one's life, and that is in accordance with God's Laws. For when we are out of step and out of time it is inevitable that we will fall down.

"There are the things that are and the All that Is."
– **The Kybalion**

The Economy

Rhythm is inherent in our consciousness and because the universe is mental it is the contents of our minds that are out-pictured in the economy.

Consciousness drives the economy as much as it drives the price of shares. We may like to think that the financial markets are rational, but they are not. They are driven by the tide of emotional energies that emanate from our desires for the things of this world. Research and analysis may have their place, but it is mainly greed and fear that moves

A GOLDEN AGE ECONOMY

markets, as these low vibrational energies pull upon the collective consciousness like the strings on a helpless puppet. And so it is only when we rise above these energies that their grip upon us is released.

But herein is the paradox. For when we raise our awareness we see the markets with clearer vision and mind. We are alert to the reality of how unreal they are and that rather than feed them with more of our money we see the wisdom in letting them die from exposure to the truth – for reasons that will become clearer as you read on.

Corporate Karma

There is justice in God's plan as, when we misqualify his energy, God's Laws are there to compensate – to balance the scales.

Companies that provide poor service or produce sub-standard goods may profit in the short term of the cycles ascent, but when their customers realise what poor value they have received the cycle will begin to turn against them. Complaints and product returns will start rolling in. This will cause the companies' costs to rise and their profits to fall. And the profits that were made will be lost. Under the Law an individual, partnership or corporate entity will be allowed to transgress the Law for a time – in the hope that the firm turn itself around. But if it does not, the full force of the Law will descend, which may result in the business going to the wall – or worse.

As we know like attracts like, so it is likely that any karmic debt that has to be repaid will be appropriate to the crime. A company that deceives its customers may be deceived by its suppliers. And a manufacturer that sells inferior goods may find that its machinery keeps breaking down.

A business that breaks man-made laws may be fined or suffer some other sanction, but it will not make karma unless God's Laws are broken.

If a firm is prosecuted for a crime that does not contravene any of God's Laws then it may be that the punishment is to balance the books for something that was done previously that did contravene a divine Law. It is said that: 'God moves in mysterious ways', and this would be a good example.

The Great Principle of RHYTHM

Agents of the law of the land are most commonly the means by which God's justice is dispensed and therefore their work is a sacred duty. Indeed the forces of law and order operate under the protection of Archangel Michael, the Prince of Archangels, who, in response to our free will, calls and decrees, protects our consciousness, being and world.

Businesses that stand up to and peacefully challenge unjust laws will have their divine account credited. Companies that break both God's and man's laws but are treated too leniently will have the difference made up at a future time.

> Each person is weighed
> In the balance to say
> For what they've mis-sowed
> They will reap every day
>
> The Karmic Board Lords
> These decisions do make
> All tempered with mercy
> So the weight we can take.
>
> **– Kim Andrew Lincoln**
> (Two verses from the song 'Keeper of the Scrolls')

Those who fail to enforce the law of the land properly become party to the crimes they allow to go unpunished and so will make karma.

> "Dearly beloved, avenge not yourselves, but rather give place unto wrath: for it is written, Vengeance is mine; I will repay, saith the Lord."
>
> **– Romans 12:19**

The Law of Rhythm is no respecter of persons. For under the Great Law all are equal.

At the time of writing the British media is full of revelations about the miscreant behaviour of the nation's biggest selling Sunday

Newspaper, the *News of the World*, who, in a misguided attempt to secure exclusive news stories, had been hacking into the telephones of distressed citizens and celebrities. For sixty years this multinational media group, founded by Rupert Murdoch, had been on the ascendant and governments and politicians in the UK, America and Australia, where this group has its principal operations, have lived in fear of this organisation and the damage its papers can do (and have done) to their electoral chances. It is a fact that this corporation wielded far too much power for too long, so that now the knives are out for Mr. Murdoch and he will find himself on the receiving end of all that his businesses have been dishing out over the years and more. Indeed, I would be surprised if this corporation is still trading in anything like its present form three years from now.

"Nothing is hidden from the All-Seeing Eye of God."
– **Kim Andrew Lincoln**

I shall be talking more about the Laws of Karma that I have briefly addressed under this heading of Corporate Karma, as it is my view that the removal of Jesus' teachings on Reincarnation and Karma from the Bible have had a profoundly adverse effect on the economy and all other aspects of our lives here on Earth too.

THE GREAT PRINCIPLE OF CAUSE & EFFECT

"Every cause has its effect; every effect has its cause; everything happens according to Law; chance is but a name for Law not recognized; there are many planes of causation, but nothing escapes the Law."
– The Kybalion

"Be not deceived; God is not mocked: for whatsoever a man soweth, that shall he also reap."
– Galatians 6:7

This is the Law of Cause and Effect that is also known as the 'Causal' Law and the Law of 'Sowing and Reaping'. It is a key Universal Law being the sixth of the 'Seven Great Principles' documented by Hermes in his ancient role as 'Messenger of the Gods'. This Law states that nothing happens by chance or is outside of the Law because for every action (cause) there is a reaction (effect) that we 'reap what we sow'.

This is similar to Sir Isaac Newton's Third Law of Motion, which states that "for every action, there is an equal and opposite reaction".

The implications of this for the economy are immense because the physical conditions that we are experiencing now are the out-playing of causes that were set in motion in the past. And these deeds that were done cannot be undone unless they are transmuted by other actions that will mitigate their effects. For it is a little known fact that human beings have the power to invoke the spiritual fire of the Violet Flame to consume the cause, core, record and memory of all those things we wish we had not thought, said and done – both in this life and past lives – so that the returning karma – meaning the adverse effects of those negative energies – are either mitigated or cancelled out. When you invoke the Violet Flame, what you are doing is sending high vibrational energy to transmute lower vibrational energy so that the lower energy is in effect transformed into higher energy.

> "The economy may not be as we would want it to be, but it is nevertheless as it should be, under the Law."
> – **Kim Andrew Lincoln**

When Jesus advised us to "do unto others as we would have them do to us" he was making reference to the Causal Law and warning us to exercise control over our thoughts and actions so that we do not suffer the consequences of any negativity that we may transmit in our relationships with each other and the world at large. He was also giving us an invaluable guideline to follow, which is that we should recognise that if we wish to achieve positive results in our lives, we must make a conscious effort to be positive in our thinking, our speaking and our actions, as it will produce positive outcomes. We should control our emotional energy and adopt a disciplined approach to life. Rather than fail to plan we should plan to succeed.

THE LAW OF ACTION

In order to manifest things on Earth we must apply the Law of Action that is connected to the Great Principle of Cause and Effect. This means that we must engage in activities that support and reinforce that which we desire to achieve. We must decide what we want and then devise a plan of actions that will bring our plan to a successful conclusion.

If, for example, we wish to buy a new car, we should first decide on the make, model and the specification of the car we would like so that we can create a clear image of what it should look like in our mind's eye. We should then find a picture or photograph that replicates, and therefore reinforces that image, and hang it somewhere where it can be easily seen.

We should visit the dealer showroom, sit in the car and familiarise ourselves with all the controls. We should go for a test drive and saturate our senses with the feel, the smell and the sounds of the car.

We should now be able to accurately recreate an image of the car in our mind's eye. We should visualise that the car is parked on our driveway and imagine that we already own it. We should go on imaginary journeys in 'our' car with family and friends. We should think, speak and act in our daily lives as though the vehicle is already ours.

We should work out how we will pay for the car, so that if it is beyond our immediate means we can create (through our imagination) the circumstances that will enable us to meet the cost. Having said that, we must be realistic!

In short, we should turn the dream into a reality, firstly in our minds and then with physical actions so that by 'multiplying our talents' we maximise the opportunity to manifest the object of our desire.

If, however, our plans do not materialise we should not despair, but accept that either the timing is wrong or that we are not meant to have the car – for good 'spiritual' reasons.

Our actions may not guarantee success because what we want may not be in accordance with our divine plan. And, for this reason, we should understand that there may be times when our actions will not bear fruit because it would be harmful to our spiritual growth.

In this life I have learnt to recognise that when a brick wall appears in front of me it is a message from my spiritual advisors that either I must be patient or that my actions are inappropriate and that I am advised to seek an alternative course.

God gave us dominion over the Earth, so it follows that if we wish to create a Golden Age economy we must act in order to bring it about. If we do nothing, nothing will happen. If we leave it to others nothing will happen. We must initiate the action ourselves. And, we must believe that our actions will make a difference because they do – every single day – and in ways that we cannot possibly imagine.

Only by taking (right) action can we change this world into something that we really want.

The Laws of Inertia & Momentum

Allied to the Law of Action and therefore the Great Principle of Cause and Effect are the Laws of Inertia and Momentum.

The Law of Inertia states that: "An object at rest tends to stay at rest." The longer we procrastinate before beginning a task and the more time we spend not acting, the harder it is for us to get started. We must, therefore, initiate action in order to overcome the inertia of inaction.

"The journey of a thousand miles starts with a single step."
— **Ancient Chinese Proverb**

The Law of Momentum states that: "An object in motion tends to stay in motion." Once you get started, it is easier to keep going and make progress. After the decision to move forward has been made, the first step we make gets the momentum going.

The image of a steam train pulling out of the station helps us to understand the laws of inertia and momentum as we can see that it takes an enormous amount of energy to get the train to move from its stationary position. But, once the inertia has been overcome by the power that is released from the engine, the amount of energy needed to keep the train moving – and therefore to maintain its momentum – is not so great.

Life can be like this too, as it is easier and requires less effort to fall in with the momentum of the mass consciousness that is moving down the wrong road because long ago the Serpent in the Garden of Eden said that that was the right way to go. And, so sadly, this is what most people do; they go where the fallen angels lead them. They take the simple option, the one that is easier than thinking for ourselves what is the right way to go, which is of course the 'Middle Way' that Jesus demonstrated; the way of truth and honesty, of 'doing unto others how you would have them do unto you' and by speaking out against the evil and the lies of the devil. For it requires effort to think for ourselves, to stand out from the crowd, to question what the majority are doing and to forge ahead in a different direction because you feel in your heart that that is the right thing to do. But once you have made that decision, once you have applied your power and energy to moving forward on the right track, it is not so hard to keep going, as each right choice that you make makes it easier to make the next right choice and so on, so that the first wise decision eases the way for the next and you begin to build a momentum of doing right, of taking right action, which is living in alignment with the Universal Laws, which is just another way of saying obeying the God's Laws.

THE LAWS OF KARMA & REINCARNATION

"Consider that if you were God, the Primary Creator of All that is; would you allow even the smallest part of your being to infect the whole, or would you – out of love for all that you had created – do your utmost to save the All, by terminating that part of your being, which had already chosen the way that leads to death and was unrepentant for the wickedness it had done."

– **Kim Andrew Lincoln**

Allied to the Great Principle of Cause and Effect are the Laws of Karma & Reincarnation about which almost all evidence was removed from the Bible by the Roman Catholic (RC) Church in the sixth century. This was instigated on the orders of the Emperor Justinian who made any discussion of these Laws a serious crime. But, by calling such acts heresy, he affirmed the pre-existence of these Laws. Indeed, if you doubt the veracity of my last statement, consider why it would be necessary for the RC Church to outlaw something that did not exist.

Karma and Reincarnation were an accepted part of the Christian faith up until that time and Jesus gave many teachings on the subject that were subsequently removed from the Bible. These teachings were expanded upon by various treatises written by Origen of Alexandria (185 – 254 AD) who was probably the greatest and most influential Christian scholar whose doctrines on the pre-existence of souls, multiple ages and transmigration of souls and the eventual restoration of all souls to a state of perfection and unity with the Godhead were highly respected until they were completely disowned by the RC Church three centuries later following the Fifth Ecumenical Council (the Second Council of Constantinople).

However, there is still one remaining reference in the Gospel of John in

A GOLDEN AGE ECONOMY

the New Testament that Justinian's censors missed that refers to the pre-existence of souls and karma and that we have to pay for past misdeeds.

It is a short passage concerning a blind man that Jesus and his disciples came across in their travels. Jesus explains to his disciples that the blind man's affliction was not given to him because of crimes he or his parents had committed in past lives as the disciples had assumed, but that this man was the medium through which, by healing his blindness (which Jesus went on to do) Jesus could publicly demonstrate the awesome power of God working through him. And implicit in this is another message, which is that we should not assume that because someone has a physical impediment they are a sinner. This is because some people agree to carry the karma of the world on their shoulders for the greater good, as this particular blind man had clearly agreed to do. Here is the passage:

> "And as Jesus passed by, he saw a man which was blind from his birth.
> And his disciples asked him, saying, Master, who did sin, this man, or his parents, that he was born blind?
> Jesus answered, Neither hath this man sinned, nor his parents: but that the works of God should be made manifest in him."
> – (John 9: 1-3)

Now, I am not saying that this one passage is irrefutable proof that these Laws exist as those who are determined to prove the opposite would say that it proves nothing because the Bible is a work of fiction. What I am saying is that it is another piece of the puzzle that when combined with the others gives us cause to question the official version of events espoused by the Christian Churches, plus the fact that most of the rest of the world's religions (Buddhism; Hinduism; Sikhism; Jainism; Esoteric Christians; Kabbalist Jews etc) accept these Laws.

By censoring God's Laws Emperor Justinian committed the heinous crime of blasphemy and created negative karma for himself and the RC Church, whom, even to this day, refuses to recognise and reinstate these Laws into the scriptures.

> Open the archives, in Rome they do lay
> In Vatican City, the truth none will say
> Delay builds your karma; it's time to come clean
> Conspiracy over, act now and redeem.

- Kim Andrew Lincoln
(A verse from the song 'Den of Thieves' written in 2007)

This monumental theft of the Truth of Jesus' teachings by dark forces in the church's power elite has probably caused more problems on this planet than any other set of God's Laws that have been disregarded, and it has left several billion people in a state of utter confusion concerning the truth of All That Is.

> They say they love Jesus, these preachers of lies
> You stole from his truth and his message did hide
> Emperors and Bishops, the power elite
> The mission of Jesus, you trod under feet.

- Kim Andrew Lincoln
(A verse from the song 'Den of Thieves' written in 2007)

Indeed the story of how this key tenet of Christianity came to be covered up is as colourful as it has been calamitous for Christians. For Jesus has revealed through his former messenger, Kim Michaels, that the actual person behind the burying of these Laws was not the Emperor Justinian, but his wife, Theodora. She had been a famous prostitute and a sex performer (with animals) before she charmed her way, firstly into the Emperor's bed, and then into marriage.

However, with her new found status, she became embarrassed by the memory of her bestial acts in the Circus of Constantinople and determined to use the bishops, her husband and the full might of the law to expunge those unsavoury episodes in her past. She misguidedly reasoned that if a new law was passed that decreed that people could not be held to account for their past deeds then by some earthly magic her past sins would be eradicated and she would avoid being judged on them by the Lords of Karma when her embodiment ended.

> Two centuries later, another nail hit
> Empress Theodora, more crimes did commit
> The Law that is Karma, you 'reap what you sow…'
> Was not to her liking, so she struck the blow
> Her power, influence and deadly resolve
> Buried reincarnation, deep in the cold.
>
> **– Kim Andrew Lincoln**
> (A verse from the song 'Den of Thieves' written in 2007)

Her arrogance and pride was such that she thought that by changing man's law she could dodge the karmic consequences of her past actions. But clearly she misunderstood divine law because in reality we are judged in accordance with God's Laws NOT man's laws. In attempting to retrospectively wipe the slate clean Theodora did as so many in the power elite have done before and since, which is to usurp God's Laws when those laws do not suit their purposes. But as we know nothing is hidden from the 'All Seeing Eye of God' and 'God is not is not mocked' by such foolish acts.

And so it was that in the year 543 AD Emperor Justinian convoked the Fifth General Council of the RC Church and ordered the Pope to sign into doctrine whatever the Council decided, which the Cardinals (who were under Theodora's spell) had pre-agreed with the Emperor. However, as the Pope disagreed with this action he did not sign, so technically it never became law, although the Council acceded to the Emperor's wishes and produced fourteen new anathemas, the first of which, condemned reincarnation and the concept of the pre-existence of souls.

The irony is that in seeking to avoid paying the debts of her past Theodora's actions served only to increase them.

My Voyage of Discovery

I was raised a Christian in the Church of England and went to church and

Sunday school and even helped run the local Church Youth Club. And yet deep within me I always felt that there was something important missing from the Bible because it does not contain answers to key questions like:

Who are we?

and

Why we are we here?

And so in 2003, having spent a lifetime being interested in spiritual matters and believing in reincarnation, I decided to make a determined effort to find the answers to these two fundamental questions. Suffice it to say, the answers did begin to come, and are coming still, as I fill in more and more pieces of the jigsaw puzzle of my past lives on Earth and before.

In fact, I would say that the journey I embarked upon then was and is an essential part of my own healing process, as I had become so frustrated by all the things that I knew were wrong with the world, but felt powerless to change, that I had little peace of mind. I was stressed because I knew that I had solutions to many of the problems but no realistic way of putting them into practice. I now know that I was mistaken because every single person has immense reserves of power because we are God's children and have the flames of God POWER, God WISDOM and God LOVE burning within the secret chamber of our hearts. And thus, there are many things that we can do to change the world into something we want and all of them start with thinking the right thoughts.

The following two songs make reference to the two fundamental questions I referred to earlier. They also talk about the Laws of Karma and Reincarnation and the real power we have within us to change the world.

Tell Me WHO YOU ARE

Have you ever had the feeling
That there's something missing,

A GOLDEN AGE ECONOMY

There's more to life than your eyes can see?
When your mind roams far
Do you wonder like me?
Did I come from here?
Or a distant star?

And "ye are Gods", and "ye are Gods"
And Jesus said that "ye are Gods"
And "ye are Gods", and 'ye are Gods"
And Jesus said that "ye are Gods".

Have you ever had the notion
About our devotion
To a flat line world of duality?
Where there's little light
And you don't know why
But you wish you knew
How to make it right.

And "ye are Gods", and "ye are Gods"
And Jesus said that "ye are Gods"
And "ye are Gods", and "ye are Gods"
And Jesus said that "ye are Gods".

CHORUS:

Tell me what you see
When your eyes are open
Tell me what you hear
When your voice flows free
Tell me how it feels
When your heart is loving
Tell me who you are
Who you want to be

The Laws of Karma & Reincarnation

Have you ever had the feeling?
That you've lived before?
Been a King or Queen or Emperor?
Had déjà vu?
Gone white or blue?
Does the spirit world
Resonate with you?

Chorus

And "ye are Gods", and "ye are Gods"
And Jesus said that "ye are Gods"
And "ye are Gods", and "ye are Gods"
And Jesus said that "ye are Gods".

Chorus

Have you ever had the feeling
That you're something special?
That there's more to your reality?
With words so true
Do you think it might be,
When your heart does speak
That it's God in you?

© COPYRIGHT 2006 **KIM ANDREW LINCOLN**

THE KEEPER OF THE SCROLLS

Don't think you can hide
When your thinking is known
There is nowhere to run
When you're never alone.

Your life is a book

A GOLDEN AGE ECONOMY

What you think and you do
The light and the dark
The emotional you.

Don't fall for the lie
That this life is it all
Many lives you have had
Though you cannot recall.

In heaven's a soul
More than history old
Who records what we do
As our lives here unfold.

Like Jesus he looks
A loving Master too
From his great golden desk
He observes me and you.

His vision is awesome
Imperfections he sees
Though our mis-creations
He forgets instantly.

Your past's on the scrolls
And the record is clear
To balance your karma
Is the reason you're here.

Two parchments he holds
And each moment does add
Every choice we have made
In the lives we have had.

Each person is weighed

The Laws of Karma & Reincarnation

In the balance to say
For what they've mis-sowed
They will reap every day.

The Karmic Board Lords
These decisions do make
All tempered with mercy
So the weight we can take.

When life here is done
And Ascension we turn
All the entries of fear
In God's fire are burned.

Before we conclude
Of some help we do tell
For erasing karma
That does work very well.

Energy magic
Of the God St Germain
His gift to the people
Divine 'Violet Flame'.

If faithfully used
Can your journey make sweet
But rest ye assured
The Great Law you can't cheat

CHORUS:

He's the Keeper – He's the Keeper of the Scrolls
Know the Keeper – Know the Keeper of the Scrolls

© COPYRIGHT 2006 – 2010 **KIM ANDREW LINCOLN**

A GOLDEN AGE ECONOMY

Our Divine Plan

The great spiritual teachers (Ascended Masters) say that planet Earth is a schoolroom where – over many lifetimes – we learn the Universal Laws of Life through the experience of living in physical bodies in the material realm.

Before each embodiment we receive help in drawing up a life plan ('divine plan') that details everything we are intended to learn in our next incarnation on Earth. The overall plan is that after many lifetimes we will have mastered life's key lessons and balanced at least 51% of our karma, meaning that we will have repaid our debts to those we have wronged. And by the time this cycle of reincarnations ends, the immaculate concept is that our consciousness will have been raised to the 'Christ' level whereby we will qualify to ascend permanently to the spiritual realms of heaven as Moses, Jesus, Buddha, Krishna and countless others have done before. How long this process takes depends on how well we acquit ourselves while we are here on Earth, meaning the extent to which we either qualify or misqualify the energy (light) we are given. If we live our lives in accordance with the Universal Laws then our progress will be swift. But if we exercise our right under the Law of Free Will to transgress those laws then our learning experience will be via the school of hard knocks. So that if we continue to work below the level of our true potential by following the path that 'seemeth right unto man', then the lessons will keep coming back to us with ever-increasing force until we say 'enough is enough' and voluntarily make a better life choice.

It is said that 'what you resist, persists'. And when we resist our lives will inevitably be filled with struggle and strife.

And so it is with the economy.

When we work in harmony with the Universal Laws by pursuing economic policies that raise all life, the Universe will stand behind us and multiply what we do, so that everyone who 'multiplies their talents' will receive the abundance (material and otherwise) that the Creator wants us to have.

If, on the other hand, we decide to go against the Universal Laws, we can expect to reap what we sow – though the repercussions of what we sow may be a long time coming back to us. This is because the Creator will give us time to experiment by making wrong decisions in the hope that we will eventually learn from our mistakes and thus make better future choices – though our 'imperfect choices' may take many 'lifetimes' to correct.

Those souls who refuse to step onto the path of 'righteousness' and thus raise their consciousness will after an allotted time – and after every effort has been made by their 'guides' in heaven to turn them around – be erased by the Creator as individual spirit beings in what is known as the 'second death'.

These teachings also state that any structure we create whether it be physical, like a building, or intangible, like an economic policy, cannot survive unless it is created in accordance with the Universal Laws by which all things are made.

What we have been reaping in the financial world and economy is the cumulative effect of many imperfect decisions made in direct opposition to the Universal Laws that have perverted the intent and purpose for which money was created, which was and is as a medium of exchange and store of future value.

This downward spiral started when the Bank of England (BoE) was founded in 1694 and the 'something for nothing' culture of lending money for interest (usury) began in earnest and more specifically to finance a war with France.

Since then this 'tower of Babel' has be extended beyond the simple, but ingenious deceit of usury, to include the abolition of the gold standard in 1971 (where our paper money was exchangeable for gold) and the creation of a vast array of highly complex financial instruments that have further perverted, distorted and debased the financial system to the point where it is now in a state of progressive disintegration.

"If we live by the sword we will die by the sword and if we live by debt we will die by debt."

– **Kim Andrew Lincoln**

A GOLDEN AGE ECONOMY

Moving Onwards & Upwards

Inherent in God's divine plan for his creation is the opportunity for all life forms to progress up the spiritual ladder. And thus we learn that as human beings it is our purpose to ascend permanently to the spiritual realms of heaven and become Ascended Masters like Jesus. It is also in the divine plan for lower life forms – like those from the animal or elemental kingdoms – to step up in consciousness through their service work to humans and then to cross over and embody as humans themselves. At this point the newly promoted life stream will win their threefold flame (the kingdom of God within them), which then entitles them to be called 'Children of God' – a designated rank within the hierarchy. 'Son or Daughter of God' is the next rank up and is awarded to those who demonstrate a high degree of 'Christ' consciousness. We move up the ladder when we live by God's Laws and when we help to raise others up. But the converse is also true as when we act like fallen angels by trying to pull others down we will be pulled down too. This is because when we misqualify the energy (light) that God gave us to survive it causes our vibratory rate to fall and thus we become heavier and denser and therefore less enlightened. And if we continue to disobey God's Laws in different embodiments the Lords of Karma will see to it that more and more of the light that God gave us to sustain our lives is withdrawn. In other words our room for manoeuvre will be restricted so that we have less opportunity to cause harm to God's kingdom. But once we start backsliding we may eventually reach the point where our consciousness has become so low and our activities so inimical that we will be taken to the Court of the Sacred Fire for the final judgement. And if we still refuse to bend the knee to God the consequence will be that we are extinguished permanently as an individual life stream in the Lake of the Sacred Fire that is the 'second death'.

> "Those souls who are set upon a course of defiance and disobedience of God's Laws should know that both Lucifer and Satan have been judged and sent to their second deaths in the Lake of the Sacred Fire where all unrepentant life streams shall meet their end."
>
> – **Kim Andrew Lincoln**

The Law of Relativity

An easier-to-understand title for this Law that has its roots in the Great Principle of Cause and Effect would be the Law of Tests, as this Law states that we are continually tested for the purpose of strengthening our inner light and this in turn helps us to keep transcending ourselves and thus climb higher up the spiritual ladder on a journey back home. These initiations test our God Being at every level and in all its aspects. This enables us to truly understand who we are, and therefore To BE who we are while we are in embodiment.

> "To be, or not To be, that is the question."
> – **William Shakespeare**

The secret to successfully passing these tests is to welcome them with an open heart and to treat each one as an opportunity to move higher in consciousness. Whatever problems we are confronted with during these initiations, I have found that the best approach is to hold the immaculate concept that the difficulties we encounter will be resolved and to adopt a positive mental attitude, because if we think we can win our victory is already halfway won. If, however, we are so lost that we cannot see the wood for the trees we can ask our higher selves ('I AM' presence) and our guardian angels for help.

> "Ask, and it shall be given you; seek, and ye shall find; knock, and it shall be opened unto you."
> – **Matthew 7:7**

In my own life I have found that this always works and I am always amazed at the ingenuity of the powers of heaven in working those little miracles every day that we usually dismiss as coincidence but, in reality, are the helping hands of the beloved angels who serve us in so many ways.

This Law also teaches us to put our problems into proper perspective because no matter how bad things may appear to be for us there is always someone else who is in a worse position because everything is relative to everything else.

EARTH RESCUE MISSION

It is also possible for whole civilisations to backslide into oblivion and the Ascended Masters tell us that this happened to the lost continents of Lemuria and Atlantis many aeons ago.

In various dictations taken by their messengers the Ascended Masters have confirmed that the Old Testament story of Noah and the Great Flood is what happened to Atlantis in around 9,500 BC when disobedience of God's Laws reached such a level that the Ascended Host deemed it necessary that the entirety of the mis-creations of the fallen angels and Laggards be buried under the sea.

In the years that followed this cataclysm, the so-called 'ape man' that emerged from this episode was not an evolving species as the Darwinians would have us believe, but mankind in degenerate apparel. The base physical form that we wore was a reflection of the extremely low level of consciousness that we had sunk to prior to the Great Flood. The Great Principle of Correspondence tells us that what is within is without and so it came to pass that, as we had been behaving like animals, we began to look like them.

This was probably the darkest time in the history of our planet for there was not one soul in embodiment who had enough light within them with which to build a momentum for turning the situation around. Earth was on the verge of being written off as a spiritual school room for evolving souls when beloved Sanat Kumara, aka the Ancient of Days, stepped in and offered to mount a rescue mission. His plan was to embody on Earth and anchor his light and thus begin the long process of teaching those who subsequently incarnated, the Universal Laws of Life.

The Law of Relativity

This takes us to the tale of the 144,000 spiritual warriors who volunteered to assist Sanat Kumara, which, of course, is the story of the prophets, the saints and the great spiritual teachers like Gautama Buddha, Lord Maitreya and Jesus who came here from all parts of this Universe to help raise the light and thus push back the great tide of darkness that had overwhelmed our planet and nearly destroyed it.

> "And I looked, and lo, a Lamb stood on the mount Sion, and with him an hundred forty and four thousand, having his Father's name written in their foreheads."
>
> – **Revelation 7:4; 14:1-5**

THE LOST PLANET OF MALDEK

Another interesting piece in the jigsaw of Earth's pre-history is the story of the two 'Laggard' races, so called because of their continual warring and inability to come to terms with each other that culminated in the total obliteration of their home planet, Maldek – once part of our solar system. I say 'once' because it no longer exists as a single planet but more as a collection of tiny pieces of planet, which we know today as the 'Asteroid Belt'.

The Ascended Masters also confirm that the hatred between these races was such that they tried to destroy each other with nuclear weapons, but went too far and wiped out their planet too. The karmic debt this created was so great that two-thirds of those who died went to the second death while the remaining third were given another chance to reconcile their differences. They have been incarnating on Earth ever since and we know them today as the Jewish and Arab races.

THE TRUE MEANING OF 'SAVING US FROM OUR SINS'

Many Christians believe that one of Jesus' main reasons for coming to Earth was to 'save us from our sins' – meaning to absolve us from all future sin – a belief that probably has its roots in the following Bible quotation:

> "And she shall bring forth a son, and thou shalt call his name JESUS: for he shall save his people from their sins."
> – **Matthew 1:21**

But is this interpretation correct? For it would be contrary to both Karmic Law and the Law of Free Will, as we are all personally responsible for what we do, and thus if we were permitted to sin without limit and without sanction we would not learn from our mistakes, our spiritual development would stop and our reason for being would be nullified.

Therefore, I suggest that the true meaning of these words is that through his suffering Jesus held back the repayment of karmic debt that had accumulated in the past, both as an act of mercy and for practical reasons, but did not mitigate it for all time.

Indeed, the Ascended Masters tell us that the Lords of Karma exercise their discretion in deciding how much karmic debt we should repay in each lifetime and that some individuals agree to take on an element of group karma in order to alleviate the burden on humanity. The debt they take on can manifest itself in different ways of which disabilities for which there is no apparent cure, or that do not respond to treatment: deafness, poor eyesight and limb deformities are common examples.

Jesus' suffering held back the descent of karma because people needed time to inwardly digest his teachings – many of which countermanded what had been previously taught, because dark forces had infiltrated the Judaic religious hierarchy and perverted the Mosaic Code. And so it was that just as Gautama Buddha had incarnated on Earth in order to correct the lies that had been inserted into Hinduism, Jesus' came to do the same for Judaism.

By explaining how without sinning we can have the abundant life that our Father wishes us to have Jesus 'saves us from our sins' in the sense that he gives us the means by which we can choose not to keep

The Law of Relativity

sinning and this I believe is the true meaning of the quotation in Matthew 1:21. But whether we heed Jesus' advice is a free will choice that each one of us has to make. Believing in Jesus is not sufficient in itself to cancel out negative karma. We must stop making it, or do enough good deeds to pay off the debt. Christians are no more special than anyone else. There is no easier path for believers in Jesus where you can sin and still ascend, as we are all equal under the Law.

Some other aspects of Karmic Law that have been revealed by the Ascended Masters are that Karma does not begin to descend until the age of twelve and that those who die young (before thirty) usually do so because they have a large amount of debt to clear.

If we set in motion karmic conditions they will return to us much like the action of a boomerang. The more karma we have the more time it takes for the return of that karma. The less karma we have the quicker we will receive back that which we sent out—for good or ill.

When we come into embodiment we are given an allotment of light to sustain our physical bodies that is increased with our good deeds and reduced with our bad. If we do not replenish light lost we will eventually die, and for those who continually misqualify their light with their miscreations, death will come at an early age, for the good do not, generally speaking, die young.

The Laws of Karma and Reincarnation are plausible and logical and provide an explanation for the seemingly inexplicable. For instance, what possible purpose is served by a baby dying before it has had an opportunity to experience life? Well, under Karmic Law the reason might be to account for past sins, but what is the Catholic explanation? Well, they don't have one, because it is heresy under church law to even discuss such matters.

The Law of Reincarnation explains the phenomenon of déjà vu, which is when you visit a place and immediately become aware that you have been there before but have not. The reality is that you have been there, but in a past life.

And then we have the many incidences of love at first sight. How can you instantly fall in love with someone you have never met before? Well, this is a case of past life lovers who are most likely soul mates and possibly twin flames – though this is rare – who are likely to have had numerous relationships going back many thousands, if not millions, of years. I know many people today who I have known before this life and am constantly meeting more.

Why Karma & Reincarnation are Important to the Economy

Knowing and *believing* that we are accountable and will have to pay for the harm that we do is a powerful constraint that is likely to stop large numbers of people from misqualifying God's energy. If crime is reduced significantly as a result of this truth being disseminated we will all benefit financially because dealing with the effects of crime wastes huge amounts of our money. We are talking: insurance costs; policing costs; court costs; probation costs; prison costs; hospital costs; social costs; lost production costs; inflation costs; speculation costs; interest costs etc.

The cost of all crime, which includes those crimes that are not reported, and those crimes which some people do not even consider to be crimes, but in reality are truly gargantuan crimes, is on such a scale that if these costs did not have to be borne by you and I then our governments would probably be able to eliminate most taxes. I will look at this some more in Episodes Two and Three.

The Laws of Abundance & Supply

These Laws are also related to the Great Principle of Cause and Effect and apply to blessings we receive when we multiply our talents, help others or render service to the planet. They are also known by other names such as the Law of Compensation or Receiving or Increase and/or Success.

We have all heard the saying that it is better to give than to receive but what does this really mean in relation to God's Laws and the economy?

Well, my understanding is that when we give we invoke the boomerang of abundance, which is just another way of saying that we set ourselves up to receive more blessings from God. In short when we give we receive. It is a reciprocal arrangement.

When we give we send out the energy of giving and this energy carries with it the vibration of love so that when we are charitable, caring and compassionate the universe will act in like manner and reflect back to us those same energies.

Our highest thoughts go straight to God and God will multiply that which is in alignment with his Laws because we are being more of what God Is – as his co-creators. The ultimate compliment we can pay to God is to be like him – to do as he does. God returns our good deeds by increasing the amount of light we have to work with. And that light manifests as abundance that can take on many forms. It may be more money, it may be more friends or it may be more children. But whatever it is it will mirror what we originally gave and it will be multiplied to a degree that is proportionate to the vibrational frequency of the original gift.

A GOLDEN AGE ECONOMY

"He does not live in vain who employs his wealth, his thought, and his speech to advance the good of others."

– **Hindu proverb**

Abundance

Jesus said through his former messenger, Kim Michaels, that: "Whatever you want for yourself you should give to another first."

This is the key to receiving greater abundance whether it be individually in our business lives or for the economy as a whole. The following examples illustrate what this means in practice.

Before a financial adviser can make a lot of money they must first ensure that their clients make a lot of money, because then they will boast to their friends how well they have done and how smart they have been by taking their advisers advice. What will happen next is that the adviser will receive so many referrals that they will be unable to cope with the amount of business that will come their way.

If we feel that we are lacking in friends, the best way to win more is to be a good friend to as many people as possible, so that when someone pours out their heart to us and tells us all their troubles, we should give them our time and our understanding. Be compassionate, be a good listener and be a wise counsellor. In short, be a good friend. If we follow this simple rule they will not only return the favour, but they will also introduce us to their friends, so that we can repeat the exercise.

"They who give have all things; they who withhold have nothing."

– **Hindu Proverb**

Probably the best book I ever read on this subject other than the scriptures is the classic by Dale Carnegie called *How to Win Friends and Influence People*.

And when it comes to selling products and/or services businesses will do well to remember that:

The Laws of Abundance & Supply

"People buy people first and anything else second."
– **Kim Andrew Lincoln**

A candidate for political office who wants to get elected needs people to vote for them, so what do they do? Well, the answer is simply that the politician must support the needs of people they intend to represent – they must pile on the service *before* they can expect any support in terms of people's votes.

"Help thy brother's boat across, and Lo! Thine own has reached the shore."
– **Hindu Proverb**

For abundance to flow towards you, you must first believe that it will, and better still that the abundance is already flowing, right now, to where you are. See yourself as winning and the universal mirror will reflect back to you that victory, so that you receive that which you focus your attention on, that which you are already seeing in your mind's eye. If you don't believe me go to a mirror right now, smile into it and tell me what you see. Is it not the expression on your smiling face being reflected back to you?

"Where your attention goes the energy flows."
– **Kim Andrew Lincoln**

The secret to abundance is service – service to life. In order to be in the flow of abundance – the river of life – we must first render service. Service that raises all people and all life, meaning that what we 'sow' is beneficial to individuals, to society and the planet as a whole.

When our service is selfless, when we serve others because we believe in our hearts that it is the right thing to do you we are serving ourselves, because when we raise up others we shall be raised up too, for Jesus said: "As ye sow so shall ye reap."

Abundance is like a fire.

A GOLDEN AGE ECONOMY

We do not say to a fire "give me heat" (abundance) without first putting in the essential preparatory and service work. What we do is gather kindling and wood and arrange it in such a fashion that the fire will burn vigorously when lit. This is the rendering of service part, or the sowing prior to the reaping. We do this knowing that once the fire has started (because we have set it correctly) it will get hotter and hotter as we keep piling on wood. But note that there is always a time lag after applying more wood before the heat reaches a new peak in intensity. And once this ascending spiral of abundance is established through service it becomes a powerful force that builds into a momentum that generates so much prosperity that is difficult to imagine for those who have not experienced it.

Had it not been for the damming of the river of abundance by the power elite – over the last two centuries alone – we would all be enjoying a standard of living that is somewhere between ten and a hundred times higher than we have now – but that is a conservative estimate, for a pyre of prosperity much greater than this is possible when we multiply our talents to the full.

It is, however, a rule that in order to reap abundance we must first be ready to receive it, meaning that we are in the right state of mind, which is a state of harmony where we are free from fear and doubt and having any sense of lack or want for the things of this world. We must also have faith in the fact that it is God who is the provider of all the good things that we need and that he will deliver them to us at the appropriate time. It also means that in order to attract abundance we must first send out the right signals to the universe because as we know from the Law of Attraction like attracts like, and so if we want abundance we must act and feel as if we are already abundant, because the universe will then recognise the frequency of those signals and respond in kind. In other words, we must raise our thoughts and feelings to the vibration of that which we wish to receive, which will be the vibration of love as all things that we receive from God are always given in love. So we could say that to those who have (harmony) shall be given more (abundance).

SUPPLY

> I AM free from fear and doubt,
> Casting want and misery out,
> Knowing now all good supply
> Ever comes from realms on high.
> I AM the hand of God's own fortune
> Flooding forth the treasures of light,
> Now receiving full abundance
> To supply each need of life.

The above verse comes from the 'Head, Hand and Heart' decree that was written by an Ascended Master for our benefit. When recited daily this decree will help us to manifest everything we need to make our stay on Earth as bountiful as possible, for it says in the Bible:

> "Fear not, little flock; for it is your Father's good pleasure to give you the kingdom."
>
> **– Luke 12:32**

WHAT 'ABUNDANCE' REALLY MEANS?

The first part of the word abundance i.e. 'abun', means 'Our Father – the two opening words of the Lord's Prayer. The words 'a-bun' are Aramaic, which was the language spoken in Jesus' time. In a dance, it is by tradition that the man leads and the woman follows. The symbolism here is of the feminine (Omega) aspect of our beings – that corresponds to our physical bodies – being directed by the masculine (Alpha) aspect – that corresponds to our spiritual side or 'I AM Presence' that is God in us. In other words if we allow ourselves to be guided by divine direction we can enjoy the dance of living in the physical world because our Father will bestow upon us all the abundance that is his good pleasure to give. And this can be further refined to mean that if we follow God's Laws we will be able to create a Golden Age economy on Earth.

A GOLDEN AGE ECONOMY

> "Desirelessness is the alchemy for precipitation."
> — **The God of Gold**

When we are utterly free of the desire to possess money we find ourselves in the position where more abundance will flow towards us than we have ever known. There are, however, some people on Earth to whom, for spiritual reasons connected to their mission on Earth, this law does not apply. But for the vast majority it is desirelessness that is the key to precipitating money and abundance.

> "When we become unattached to possessions and money we become independently wealthy."
> — **Kim Andrew Lincoln**

INCREASING PERSONAL ABUNDANCE

When we receive an increase in abundance we should multiply it wisely but also give over an appropriate amount to God (charity) in gratitude for what we have received. And, provided that we use the extra funds efficiently, the increase will be repeated and repeated and repeated. But, as quickly as we become self-indulgent and profligate in our spending, the dispensation will be withdrawn.

Money may be the root of all evil but it is not in itself evil. Money is a form of energy that facilitates commerce and the expansion of the abundant life that God wants us to have. It is not a requirement that we should be robed in sackcloth and live like paupers, but what we must avoid is excess. It is the frugal consciousness, the flowing consciousness, the giving and receiving consciousness that must be pursued.

The Law of Disintegration

The Tower of Babel is an enduring symbol that reminds us that any structure that is not built in accordance with God's Laws will not hold fast to the buffeting of the winds of the Holy Spirit; for that which is not of God, which is not imbued with the twelve aspects of God consciousness, shall not stand the tests of time and space. The scriptures tell us that the Holy Spirit is everywhere and that it is constantly probing the structures we build for weakness. So that if we start building outside of the parameters that God has set – i.e. in the soft and shifting sands of unreality – those structures will have to be rebuilt; for firstly they will start to shake and then they will begin to disintegrate, and eventually they will fall down.

We are seeing evidence of this now in the economy and in other aspects of society that I will be examining in Episode Two of this book But suffice it to say, that when we create we operate in accordance with God's Laws, so we can be confident that whatever form our creations take they will endure. But, if there is any element of mis-creation in our enterprise, it will be exposed and found wanting, for nothing is hidden from the All Seeing Eye of God. And, as we know, the Law of Karma states that we cannot escape the effect of any causes that we have set in motion; for all our debts to life must be repaid.

> Blows the wind that humbles all
> That strips selfish ego
> Break down the illusions we create
> Awaken us to knowing.
>
> **- Kim Andrew Lincoln**
> (A verse from the poem 'Blows the Wind' written in 2008)

It is becoming increasingly clear to those who have eyes to see and ears to hear that the fallen angels have built a counterfeit kingdom on Earth. But we should not be alarmed, nor despair in this knowledge, for fear is the fuel that feeds what dark forces do. Indeed, we can sleep soundly in our beds knowing that those who love and obey the Law shall have the Law as their protection, but those who disobey the Law and refuse to bend the knee to God; they shall not pass!

For this is the time of the Armageddon described in Revelation. It is the time when the perpetrators of evil and wickedness are witnessing the destruction of everything they thought was real but, in truth, is iniquity and illusion. And this is also a time of great celebration. For, as the ways of darkness pass into oblivion the seeds of a new age are being sown as the New Jerusalem rises from the earth and the Golden Age of Love, Enlightenment and Freedom begins.

NB: The scientific equivalent of this Law of Disintegration is the Second Law of Thermodynamics which states that all imperfect forms will eventually be returned to their base state, which is another way of saying that all *imperfect* forms will, in time, be ground into dust.

The Law of Gratitude

"Gratitude is not only the greatest of virtues, but the parent of all the others."

– Cicero

When we are grateful for the sun that shines and the rain that falls and for all the other wonderful gifts that are our Father/Mother God's pleasure to give, we are infused with feelings of joy and happiness that travel out into the universe. But, as we know, the universe acts like a mirror, so that what we send out will be reflected back to us, but in greater measure.

Gratitude is an affirmation of thankfulness that when expressed sincerely, with love and affection from the heart, is positive in every respect. When we thank others for their service, for their consideration, for their kindness, or for whatever they have done to warrant our thanks, it makes them feel good about themselves and it also makes them feel good about us. Too many people in this world feel worthless, so when we thank them, our gratitude makes them feel worthy again, that they count and that they are valued.

When we keep showing gratitude we are giving of ourselves and thus we initiate a virtuous spiral of positive outcomes that raises our spirits and the light on Earth.

"When we are grateful we give to others and when we give we receive back more in return."

– **Kim Andrew Lincoln**

When we develop an attitude of gratitude we prepare the way for abundance to flow into our lives. We send out the message that we are ready to receive more because we are grateful for what we have already received.

The Great Principle of Gender

> "Gender is in everything; everything has its Masculine and Feminine Principles; Gender manifests on all planes."
> — **The Kybalion**

My first academic encounter with the Great Principle of Gender was at the tender age of eleven when I started to learn the French language at school. I had the privilege of being taught by an inspirational teacher called Sydney Winters, who had trained at the Sorbonne University in Paris and consequently could speak French like a Frenchman. He told the most outrageous jokes in class and it was this, plus his exacting standards as a teacher, which earned him the love and respect of his pupils. It was a very sad day for me when, having won the school prize for French three years later, I learned that Sydney was to become Head of Languages at another school. I learnt nothing new from his replacement and subsequently my interest in the subject went rapidly into decline. So Sydney, this is my tribute to you and also to all the other truly great teachers that excel at the art of drawing out the best in those they serve.

As any past or present student of French will know, the world and everything in it, is divided into those things which have 'le' in front of them and those that have 'la'.

'Le' denotes that the article is masculine and 'la' that it is feminine. And one of the hardest things in learning French is remembering which gender prefixes apply in each case, which brings me to the Great Principle of Gender.

This seventh Hermetic Principle embodies the truth that gender manifests in everything and that the masculine and feminine principles are embedded and active in all phenomena and levels of life. But in the Hermetic sense gender and sex are not the same. The word gender is derived from the Latin root meaning: 'to beget; to procreate; to generate; to create; to produce'. So gender has a much broader meaning than sex. The latter is defined as: "the property or quality by which organisms are classified as female or male on the basis of their reproductive organs and functions". So it follows that sex is no more than a manifestation of gender on the physical plane of life.

Indeed, gender manifests on all three planes of existence: the Physical, the Mental and the Spiritual. It manifests at its most elemental level on the physical plane in the differences in bodily design between men and women and the act of sex for the purpose of procreation.

But whilst importance may be attached to having sexual relations beyond that which is necessary to bring reincarnating souls back into embodiment, it is nevertheless, our ultimate goal to liberate ourselves from the wheel of life, death and rebirth through the extinction of all desire.

On the mental plane that operates at a higher vibrational frequency than the physical we can observe some more subtle examples of gender. For instance, the masculine principle of mind corresponds to the objective, conscious, voluntary and active mind, whereas the feminine principle corresponds to the subjective, sub-conscious, involuntary and passive mind.

The highest frequency plane is the spiritual one. Spirit is defined as the masculine polarity of the Godhead and the coordinate of Matter. It is God as Father, who of necessity includes within the polarity of himself God as Mother and hence is known as the Father/Mother God.

It is the plane of the 'I AM Presence' which comes from the 'I AM THAT I AM' (Exodus 3:13-15). When Moses ascended Mount Sinai to meet God (Sanat Kumara) for the first time, he asked him what he should call him and God replied: "I AM THAT I AM."

The 'I AM Presence' is the individualised presence of God focused for each individual soul. It is the God-identity of the individual. It is where the Ascended Masters dwell in the kingdom of God and, as such, is a place of perfection.

The following song is about the 'I AM Presence' that Jesus referred to as "... the Father in me which doeth the work" – (John14:10) and "the Kingdom of God (that) is within (us) you" – (Luke17: 20-21).

'I AM' INSIDE OF YOU

I AM inside of YOU
As always I have been
And yet you search the stars for me
And think you are apart from me
I AM inside of YOU.

I AM inside of YOU
For you and I are ONE
Seek me within and I will flow
With answers that you long to know
I AM inside of YOU.

I AM inside of You
As ever I shall be
My love sustains you through your heart
You are the light that I did spark
I AM inside of YOU.

I AM inside of You
I wait your bidding call
Open your heart and mind and hear
Your inner voice is mine my dear
I AM inside of YOU.

I AM inside of YOU
This Truth will set you free
Follow the path my Sons did show
And born in you the Christ will grow
I AM inside of YOU.

I AM inside of YOU
My Mansions are not clay
No golden calf is made of me

The Great Principle of GENDER

Within your heart I AM this day
I AM inside of YOU.

I AM inside of YOU
You are the door to me
This simple truth I offer you
My Kingdom waits for you to free
I AM inside of YOU.

I AM inside of YOU
No limit has my love
I gave you all for you To BE
Below all that you are Above
I AM inside of YOU.

Chorus

I AM, I AM,
I AM, Inside of YOU

© COPYRIGHT 2006 **KIM ANDREW LINCOLN**

Matter is the feminine (negative) polarity of the Godhead, whereas Spirit is the masculine (positive) polarity. Matter acts as a chalice for the kingdom of God and is the abiding place of evolving souls. Matter is distinguished from matter (lowercase m) – the substance of the earth, which blocks rather than radiates divine light and the Spirit of God.

The word 'Matter' derives from the Latin 'Mater', which means Mother. Mothers nurture their young and so it is the purpose of everything that occupies the Matter world to become More than it is now by moving onwards and upwards in consciousness. This applies to individuals as much as it does to businesses as enlightened people will create enlightened companies and they will generate an enlightened economy where all people can thrive.

When I talk about the feminine 'negative' polarity I am not

insinuating that the fairer sex and the Omega aspect of God is inferior to the Alpha. On the contrary, what I am saying is that this 'negative' is, in fact, a positive, in the sense that the two components of gender are essential parts of a divine whole, meaning that one cannot function without the other. A good example of this is electricity where without the negative polarity electric power would simply not flow.

We could say that the Father (Alpha) aspect of the Godhead directs the process of creation that God has envisioned and the Mother (Omega) aspect is the means by which that divine plan is achieved. And what is that plan? Well, it is simply to fill the darkness with the light of our Beings. It is to raise Earth to Heaven, which, of course, is what we are here to do.

Another way of delineating the male and female aspects of the Godhead would be to label the Alpha aspect the expanding part and the Omega aspect the contracting part, so that what you have are two apparently opposing yet complimentary forces working together in such a way that life can keep growing in the balanced and controlled manner that Jesus called the 'Middle Way'.

If you visualise the creative process (meaning life itself) as an explosion, the energy that is pushed outward, by the force of the explosion, is the thought and the command to create that is the positive, expanding, masculine Alpha power. But what holds that power in check and stops it from becoming destructive and degenerative – as the explosive energy dissipates – is the negative, contracting, feminine, Omega force.

The Elohim are the Creator Gods who represent the Omega aspect. They are the builders of form and their job is to step down the high frequency energies that emanate from the God head into lower vibrating frequencies that cause pure light to solidify into matter. And this matter is the solids, liquids and gases that are the constituent parts of planet Earth.

At the human level the Alpha is the essence of our original creation by God. And the Omega is the More that we become as we go out into the physical realm.

> "I have said, Ye are gods; and all of you are children of the most High."
>
> – (Psalm 82:6)

We fit into God's plan as his co-creators by virtue of the fact that we are his children. We were created as spirit out of God's being, but we were given bodies so that we could walk on the Earth and continue the job of creation that the Elohim began but did not complete.

In the Book of Genesis we are told that God spent six days creating the world and that he rested on the seventh day. So what does this mean? Was God, who is the source of all energy, so tired after creating the universe that he needed to rest? Or is it more likely that it was his intention to delegate the job of completing his work to his children? Is the deeper meaning of God's command to take dominion over the Earth and all its creatures and go forth and multiply, that we should infill the dark places on the Earth with God's light, which is the light of heaven that, as his children, we hold in our hearts?

This light is the threefold flame of the Christ that is the spark of life anchored in the secret chamber of the heart in the Children of God. It is the sacred trinity of God Power, God Wisdom and God Love that is the manifestation of the sacred fire of God. It is the essence of all that God Is and it defies description.

> "The only way to know God is to become the fullness of all that God Is."
>
> – **Kim Andrew Lincoln**

The threefold flame, which the Fleur de Lys emblem* represents, is

---

* The Fleur de Lys emblem was used on the coat of arms of King Clovis, the first of the Louis Kings of France, who united the people of France under the teachings of Jesus Christ. King Clovis is said to be an incarnation of Ascended Master Lanello who was Mark Lyle Prophet, the founder of the Summit Lighthouse, before he ascended in 1973. His other past lives have reputedly included Noah and Mark, the evangelist, author of the Gospel of St Mark in the New Testament of the Bible, Source: Ascension Research Center.

contained within the secret chamber of our hearts, which is a spiritual chamber located behind the heart chakra. It is surrounded by great light and protection and is the connecting point of the cord of light that descends from our 'I AM Presence' that is the source of divine energy that sustains the beating of our physical hearts. It gives life, and purpose to life. It is what connects us to our Creator and his creation. It is the place where we commune with our Holy Christ selves and where we fan the fires of our own threefold flame.

> "It is not the food in our bellies or the blood in our veins that sustains our beings; it is the light of God, which is the love that our Creator has for all of his creation."
> **– Kim Andrew Lincoln**

When Jesus declared that: "the kingdom of God is within you" (Luke 17:20-21) he was talking about the 'I AM presence' that all God's children have. He also referred to the 'I AM presence' as "… the Father that dwelleth in me..." Here is the full quotation:

> "Believest thou not that I am in the Father, and the Father in me? The words that I speak unto you I speak not of myself: but the Father that dwelleth in me, he doeth the works."
> **– John 14:10**

The significance of these words cannot be overstated as when you combine them with the previous quotation (Luke 17:20-21) you have the bones of what is arguably Jesus' most important revelation. And yet, for fifteen hundred years, it has suited the Christian churches to disregard these teachings – for reasons that I will reveal in episode two of this book. Suffice it to say that had Christians known the true extent of their divinity I believe that our world would be much more enlightened than it is now.

TWIN FLAMES

At the human level arguably the most significant manifestation of gender is the twin flame relationship, which is the soul's masculine or feminine counterpart conceived out of the same white-fire body, the fiery ovoid of the I AM Presence. What this means is that the whole of our Being is comprised of two complimentary parts, made up of that half which is predominantly male (Alpha) and the opposite half which is predominantly female (Omega).

In the Christian faith probably the most famous twin flames are Jesus Christ and Mary Magdalene – both of whom are Ascended Masters. This explains why it was that Jesus appeared to Mary Magdalene first after his ascension and not to his other disciples, for it was Mary whom he loved the most as she was (and is) his other half.

> The disciples were men, except Magdalene
> The twin flame of Jesus, no text will proclaim
> She was most beloved and thirteen did make
> Her light shone the brightest, this truth no-one spake.
>
> **– Kim Andrew Lincoln**
> (A verse from the song 'Den of Thieves' written in 2007)

The Universal Laws teach us that life is all about balance and thus the Ascended Masters have explained that the psychology of a perfect male has within it 60% masculine (yin) characteristics and 40% feminine (yang) characteristics. For the perfect female the ratios are 60% feminine and 40% masculine.

Nevertheless, some people come into embodiment with ratios different to these because they have carried with them an imbalance in their psychology that arose in past lives. The cause will have most likely been some traumatic experience or series of experiences that involved improper or unnatural relationships, the manifestations of which are divinely planned to be healed or part-healed in this life. No-one can ascend until they have balanced their masculine and feminine aspects.

For a more detailed explanation of twin flames I recommend the book *Soul Mates and Twin Flames* by Elizabeth Claire Prophet which you will find on the 'Summit Lighthouse' website. There is also a great deal of information about twin flames and how they are created on the website 'Theosophia is the Way' run by Lorraine Michaels who now holds the spiritual office that Elizabeth Claire Prophet formerly held. Elizabeth Clare Prophet was a messenger for the Ascended Host and is now an Ascended Lady Master herself.

Gender and the Economy

Gender is crucial to the economy because it is the progenitor of balance and thus an essential component for a 'Golden Age' economy to manifest is a balanced mix of Alpha and Omega energies.

When the economy is balanced there is enough forward movement to prevent stagnation and decline, but insufficient thrust to cause overheating. The expanding male energy is kept in check by the contracting female energy and this allows growth to be achieved in a sustainable way.

In the 1980s I ran a marketing services agency and exhibition organising company with my wife and business partner, Elizabeth, and remember well the comments that our accountant used to make about the personalities of the two directors. He said that I was the high flyer and that Elizabeth was the one who kept my feet firmly on the ground. Although we joked about this he was actually being complimentary by implying that between us we embodied the perfect balance of Alpha and Omega qualities that make for a good partnership. For had Elizabeth been a high flyer too the business would have blown itself out in a very short time and conversely had I been like my wife it would not have expanded as quickly as it did.

A successful economy is a macrocosm of the immaculate concept for the human family, having within it a perfect blend of Alpha and Omega energies. We all know that a family with a father and no mother is not ideal any more than one with a mother and no father.

Recruitment firms understand the necessity for gender balance within the workplace as, without it, the right people would end up in the wrong jobs. For example, those who excel in sales and marketing are usually blessed with predominantly Alpha male personalities while those who prefer administrative roles tend to exhibit a preponderance of Omega qualities.

Alpha occupations would include designers, architects and composers while those in the omega mould would be accountants, musicians and nurses.

Each sex has its own particular skills set because the male and female brains are not the same.

Nothing times nothing equals nothing. And so without the interaction of the two key components for the creation and expansion of the universe – the Alpha and the Omega aspects of God – there would be no world and there would be no economy. This then concludes my summary of the last of the seven Great Hermetic Principles.

Usury (Riba)

Quotes from the Bible

"He that putteth not out his money to usury, nor taketh reward against the innocent, he that doeth these things shall never be moved."
Psalm 15:5

"If thou lend money to any of my people that is poor by thee, thou shall not be to him as a usurer, neither shalt thou lay upon him usury."
Exodus 22:25

"Take thou no usury of him or increase: but fear thy God; that thy brother may live with thee. Thou shalt not give him thy money upon usury nor lend him the victuals for increase."
Leviticus 25:36 – 37

"He that by usury and unjust gain increaseth his substance, He shall gather it for him that will pity the poor."
Proverbs 28:8

"In thee have they taken gifts to shed blood; thou hast taken usury and increase, and thou has greedily gained of thy neighbour's by extortion, and hast forgotten me sayeth the Lord God."
Ezekiel 22:12

Usury (Riba)

Quotes from the Qur'an (Koran)

"Those who devour usury will not stand except as stands one whom the Evil One by his touch hath driven to madness. That is because they say: Trade is like usury but Allah hath permitted trade and forbidden usury. Those who after receiving direction from their Lord desist shall be pardoned for the past; their case is for Allah [to judge]; but those who repeat [the offence] are companions of the fire: they will abide therein forever."
– Qur'an 2:275

"O ye who believe! Fear Allah and give up what remains of your demand for usury if ye are indeed believers."
– Qur'an 2:278

"O ye who believe! Devour not usury doubled and multiplied; but fear Allah; that ye may prosper."
– Qur'an 3:130

"For the iniquity of the Jews we made unlawful for them certain [foods] good and wholesome which had been lawful for them; in that they hindered many from Allah's way. That they took usury though they were forbidden; and that they devoured men's substance wrongfully; we have prepared for those among them who reject faith a grievous punishment."
– Qur'an 4:160 – 161

Other Quotes

"Usury is unnatural."

"Money exists not by nature but by law."

"The most hated sort of wealth getting and with the greatest reason is usury, which makes a gain out of money itself and not from the natural object of it. For money was intended to be used in exchange but not to increase at interest And this term interest (tokos), which means the birth of money from money, is applied to the breeding of money because the offspring resembles the parent. Wherefore of all modes of getting wealth, this is the most unnatural."

Aristotle 384 BC – 322 BC
(Greek Philosopher; student of Plato and teacher of Alexander the Great)

Of all the definitions of usury Aristotle's (above) is in my view the best explained. Usury is regarded as a misqualification of energy by the great spiritual teachers because they say that it is a perversion of the intent and design for which money is created, which is as a medium of exchange and store of future value. They warn us that when we rely upon interest from savings to provide ourselves with an income or we lend money for profit we are not multiplying our talents in the way that God intended because we are using money not as a means to an end but as an end in itself, whereby money is being used to make money out of money.

The Ascended Master, Saint Germain, has stated in recent years through one of his previous messengers, Kim Michaels, that we qualify God's energy when we are rewarded according to our willingness to multiply our talents:

1. Through our ingenuity of bringing forth new ideas, new inventions, better ways of doing the same old tasks.
2. Through our willingness to take risks by taking an initiative by doing something that no one has done before and therefore we cannot know what the outcome will be.
3. By our willingness to put forth the labour that is needed in order to get the economy to run.

Saint Germain's comments clarify what it means to multiply our talents as they suggest that any activity that involves making money from

Usury (Riba)

money would have karmic consequences.

Just consider for a moment what would happen if we all decided that instead of working for a living we would become money lenders resting on our laurels and waiting for the interest to come rolling in as money lenders do. Well, the world would be chaos as nothing would get done; no goods would be manufactured; no food would be produced and there would be no shops or markets where we could go and buy the necessities of life. In a very short time life on earth would come to a grinding halt and money, which had become the sole focus of our attention, would no longer be needed because there would be no goods and services to exchange. The reality is that when money becomes an end in itself life loses all meaning and purpose. The wicked serpents have two names, which are debt and interest, and they are the root cause of all the world's financial problems today. When we do not multiply our talents, when we chose to do what seemeth right unto man, but not unto God, there will be consequences, for the Great Principle of Cause & Effect is no respecter of persons, and the Lords of Karma, the dispensers of justice will ensure that all (karmic) debts are repaid.

The well-known writer on the iniquities of our financial system, Ellen Brown, has reported that according to Mangrit Kennedy, a German financial researcher, interest now takes up 40% of the cost of everything we buy!

The Importance of Gold

"The Gold Standard is a Good Standard because it is the God Standard."

– Kim Andrew Lincoln

The simple truth is that without gold there can be no economic recovery and no Golden Age economy.

A Golden Age is one based upon the gold standard. And that standard is the God standard of the Christ consciousness that Jesus demonstrated two thousand years ago. It is the standard we have come to Earth to manifest. So we can see that there is a spiritual aspect to gold as well as a practical one. The Gold standard is the standard of 'The Golden Rule', which is to do unto others as we would have them do unto us.

Gold is important alchemically because it is precipitated sunlight and as such balances the flows of energy that affect our minds, our emotions and thus our physical bodies. Gold is divine and is necessary for the stability of our consciousness and the stability of our economy.

If we do not wear gold on our bodies the balance of the elements is not held and we will experience greater mental and emotional disturbance. It is vital, therefore that we maintain permanent physical contact with gold in its pure form by handling it as currency and wearing it as jewellery.

Gold is the lodestone of Alpha and Omega because it reminds us, at the soul level, of where we came from, which is the great throne room decorated in white and gold in the Great Central Sun. For it is from here that all Children of the Sun leave the realms of spirit to incarnate on Earth.

The God of Gold and the God Tabor tell us that the Elementals have

The Importance of GOLD

been trained by the Elohim to precipitate gold and thus they cause it to grow in veins that expand in the earth. The Elementals out-picture human consciousness in the physical conditions we see like the weather, so that when we are good they grow more gold. The amount of gold in circulation represents our outer attainment and gold that remains undiscovered represents that portion of our Christ minds that remain to be brought forth. There is an infinite supply of gold available to us for use as currency and adornment and the amount we can harvest from the earth is directly proportionate to the amount of light we draw down to Earth.

Gold contains great light that is so intense that it will change our forcefield and consciousness. So that if there is any residue within us at subconscious levels of greed and selfishness, possessiveness and attachment, then the presence of gold will amplify these tendencies and we will make karma for the misuse of that gold. This is one reason why so many people on Earth have so little abundance. It is because abundance produces in them greed, debauchery and immorality and this misuse of the light causes them to create more and more karma. Thus, the Lords of Karma have determined that those who have misqualified the energy of abundance should repay their karma by living with less abundance. Consequently, what has been divinely ordained should not be interfered with by totalitarian regimes based on socialism and communism that would seek to undo what heaven has done.

We know that the love of money is the root of all evil and so it is vital that we become non-attached to the coin of the realm. We must see gold for what it really is, which is a medium of exchange and an alchemical formula. For gold, when it is in flow as energy passing hand to hand in transactions of commerce, regulates the conduct of that commerce intrinsically within itself.

This is explained by the God of Gold below:

"... The cosmic law of supply and demand actually works itself out in the economies of the nations through the free flow of gold itself. Gold, in fact, is a talisman of the Great Central Sun. And therefore, when you give and receive gold, you cannot misqualify that gold with greed, because gold resists the vibration of greed, whereas you take the paper money and the copper and nickel coins, and you find that even silver itself is able to retain a vibration of greed. But not gold, beloved ones. It repels it instantaneously, and therefore retains that purity of the Goddess of Purity, focused by her, that comes from Alpha and Omega. And therefore there is an upwards spiral in the consciousness, and gold becomes an instrument of the soul liberation of a planet and a people. Beloved ones, it is this message that must be spread abroad."

– From a dictation given by the God of Gold with the God Tabor, through the messenger for the Great White Brotherhood, Elizabeth Clare Prophet, in 1977.

THE LAST WORD FROM JESUS
(– for now)

"All who put down God's Laws as primitive and for the unenlightened are walking the path to perdition.

Follow them not or you will be walking the same path to perdition as they. And there is an end to that Path — the Final Judgment in the Court of the Sacred Fire. Yes, walk ye in the Light of the Way and know the true Jesus that I AM."

– JESUS CHRIST, 4TH SEPT 2011,
(through his messenger, Lorraine Michaels, from the 'Ask Jesus the Truth' website)

EPISODE TWO

Disobedience of The LAW

"All who sin apart from the law will also perish apart from the law, and all who sin under the law will be judged by the law. For it is not those who hear the law who are righteous in God's sight, but it is those who obey the law who will be declared righteous. (Indeed, when Gentiles, who do not have the law, do by nature things required by the law, they are a law for themselves, even though they do not have the law, since they show that the requirements of the law are written on their hearts, their consciences also bearing witness, and their thoughts now accusing, now even defending them.) This will take place on the day when God will judge men's secrets through Jesus Christ, as my gospel declares."

– Romans 2:12-16

CONTENTS

Introduction	137
The Power Elite	142
The Duality Consciousness	151
The Power Elite's Plan	154
The Tentacles of the Power Elite	174
Greed Is NOT Good	177
The Biggest Crime of All Time	189
Speculation & Investment Risk	209
Perversion of the Gold Standard	221
Perversion of the Health Care System	223
Global Warming & Free Energy	231
Globalisation & International Trade	235
The Perversion of Music	238
The Perversion of Religion	244
Some Thoughts on Atheism	248
War Is	250
Some thoughts on Politics, Politicians, People Power & the Economy	252
The Perversion of the European Dream	256
The Deception of Inflation	259
Deflation can be Good	262
Quantitative (Stealing) Easing	264
The Bankers' Manifesto	268
Some More of My Thoughts on Money & Monetary Policy	270
To Borrow, or Not to Borrow, that IS the Question	274
The Un-Free Market	280
Regulation Gone Wrong	283
Taxation – the Good, the Bad & the Ugly	286
Big Brother & Bureaucracy	292
More of My Thoughts on the Fractional Reserve Banking System	295
Funny Money	296

A GOLDEN AGE ECONOMY

The Possessions Have Gone	298
Ye Shall Know Them by the Words of Those Who Know Them Best	301
Ye Shall Know Them by Their Own Words	306
The Key Points of the Illuminati Code	308
Wake Up	313

INTRODUCTION

"This book is really about how un-free we are and how we can free ourselves from the clutches of those who have enslaved us with their counterfeit economy and dualistic thinking."
— **Kim Andrew Lincoln**

THE STORY OF NOW

The story of our times is a tale of two economies – the real and the unreal. For now is the time when all that has been hidden is being exposed. It is the time of the curtains falling on the power elite as the spotlight of public scrutiny shines into every dark corner of their illusory and shadowy world. It is now that the full extent of their lies and deceptions relating to our economic system are being revealed. For the power elite it is the time of their judgement for the harm they have done. And for the rest of us it is now that we must confront the reality that for too long we have been living in a dream world, and that we must now wake up and acknowledge that any economic system that tries to serve the few at the expense of the many cannot endure, because it is in opposition to the Universal Laws of Life. And it is now that we must take responsibility for what we have allowed to happen on our watch – that which we have created, through the filter of our mistaken belief systems, we must uncreate. It is now that we must accept that what we have lost, and any losses to come are the hard lessons in the school of life that are the consequences of not separating the wheat from the chaff.

But not all is doom and gloom, for while it is a time of endings, it is also a time of beginnings, a time for laying new foundations that, provided they are set in the bedrock of Christ reality in accordance with the Universal Laws, will enable us to create unparalleled abundance as we manifest this new Aquarian Age of Peace, Freedom, Enlightenment and Universal Love. Our planet is stepping up a gear we must either move with it, or be left behind.

> "You can be a spectator in the Grandstand of life or you can run the race and win."
>
> – Kim Andrew Lincoln

2012 & THE MAYAN CALENDER

Most people accept the existence of cosmic cycles that, during the period when one ends and another begins, bring about significant changes in the level of consciousness of a planet and its people. The length of these cycles can vary enormously and the longer they are, the greater the changes that will occur during the transition period. When one cycle ends and another begins we experience 'growing pains' because in order to transcend ourselves by expanding our awareness we must periodically 'shed the skin' of our old selves before we can step up the ladder of consciousness. But if we resist this process we will be subject to more 'struggle and strife' via the school of hard knocks.

> "Transcendence is the essence of life."
>
> – Kim Andrew Lincoln

One of the stories of the ancient Mayan people of Mexico is that they were seasoned space travellers who came here many thousands of years ago bringing with them detailed knowledge of these cosmic cycles. It is claimed that they developed an accurate calendar that recorded when these cosmic cycles occurred. But intriguingly, their calendar stopped on 21-12-2012, which some have taken to mean is the date when all physical life on Earth comes to an end. This is one interpretation, but is it correct? Well, not according to the Ascended Masters, for they have said that the Mayan calendar relates more to the fallen angel timetable for world domination that it does to anything else.

Introduction

THE AGE OF AQUARIUS

Nevertheless we are coming to the end of a major 25,800-year cosmic cycle and another smaller cycle of 2,150 years has just begun. This is the Aquarian Age, also known as the 'The Golden Age of Saint Germain' because it is Saint Germain, who, in addition to holding the office of the God of Freedom, is also the hierarch of this age, as Jesus was the hierarch of the Piscean Age that is now ending.

ARMAGEDDON

The transitional period we are in now is the 'Armageddon' described in Revelations, which is why there is so much upheaval. We are witnessing the judgement of the old unenlightened ways as the winds of the Holy Spirit bring down the towers of Babel that form the counterfeit economy. And, with this clearing out, we are being given the opportunity to replace the old ways of running the economy with new and better ways of working that are in alignment with the Universal Laws relating to abundance and wealth creation. If we raise our game, the power elite, who are the architects of the old ways, will find that as we take our power back – by taking responsibility for ourselves, their power, which was the power we gave them, will wane and everything they have been fighting to introduce will come to nothing.

NEW WORLD ORDER

The other possibility is the one portrayed in Revelation that paints a picture with very striking imagery of what living in a New World Order world would be like, which according to my research, is everything that an Age of Freedom is not. Indeed it is more akin to the world envisioned by George Orwell in his chilling novel *1984*. I am convinced that as a work of prophecy Revelation was intended to serve as a warning of what may happen if we do not wake up and transcend the consciousness of the old ways that we now know do not work.

A GOLDEN AGE ECONOMY

"The purpose of prophecy is to motivate a change in events, not to foretell them."

– Kim Andrew Lincoln

I believe that this will be an uncomfortable time for those who resist the changes that need to happen, because resistance creates the sort of turmoil that we have been experiencing in the economy and natural world for a long time now. When we look closely at the economic system that operates in the West and most other parts of the world – as I will be doing in the following chapters – you will see why we are not receiving the prosperity that our Creator intended we should have.

An Economy Designed to Fail

The power elite have designed the system so that they get all the choice cuts of meat, while the rest of us are left with the scraps. The perverted structures that the power elite have put in place were designed specifically to increase their wealth and privilege at the expense of everyone else, while ensuring that the gulf between rich and poor grows ever wider. This economic model is based on the lower consciousness of the age that is now ending. It is a model that is collapsing before our eyes – despite some outer appearances to the contrary – and in spite of the best efforts of the power elite to keep their unreal creation on the life support machine of taxpayers' cash. The power elite in government say that the pain of the austerity measures is being shared out, but that it is not so, as the burden is being heaped upon the backs of the poor and middle classes. In my view the unreal parts of our economy, which includes most of what the City of London and Wall Street do, will not survive. This is good news because a Golden Age economy cannot manifest until they fall.

The consciousness of 'Greed is Good' as epitomised so well in the films *Wall Street* and *Wall Street – Money Never Sleeps* is gasping its last breaths because all that is socially and economically useless, should not and shall not survive. In this Aquarian Age none of the 'old skin' structures can be allowed to stand and so the 'Armageddon' described

Introduction

in Revelation is in effect the 'reaping' of the power elite for their perversion of our economy and every other aspect of our lives here on Earth.

As we know, what we resist persists, and so, by not yielding to the inevitable, the governments of the world – who are either members of the power elite or who serve their interests – have been reckless with our economies, thereby ensuring that the next collapse will be much worse than in 2008. They have failed to learn the lesson that an economy run for the benefit of one group at the expense of another is not sustainable, and will therefore be subject to the Laws of Disintegration.

> "The Holy Spirit is a mighty wind that breaks down all structures not built on the rock of Christ Truth."
> **– Kim Andrew Lincoln**

THE POWER ELITE

"Ye shall know them by their fruits."
– Matthew 7:16

"And there was war in heaven: Michael and his angels fought against the dragon; and the dragon fought and his angels, and prevailed not; neither was their place found any more in heaven. And the great dragon was cast out, that old serpent, called the Devil, and Satan, which deceiveth the whole world: he was cast out into the earth, and his angels were cast out with him. And I heard a loud voice saying in heaven, Now is come salvation, and strength, and the kingdom of our God, and the power of his Christ: for the accuser of our brethren is cast down, which accused them before our God day and night."
– Revelation 12:7-10

The power elite are those who exercise control or influence over the economy and policies of governments on this planet and that embrace the consciousness of the fallen angels. They see themselves as being separate from God and consequently have no issues with breaking God's Laws. Their consciousness is based on duality. The ranks of the power elite are drawn from many races and planets in the Cosmos, as Earth is a giant melting pot with such a diversity of cultures and creeds that it would take many books to describe them all. Earth is four and a half billion years old and the history of intelligent life here is much more than our history books have recorded and what even the Ascended Host has revealed. Suffice it to say that those beings in embodiment now have come here with many levels of consciousness. They range from those who are fallen angels, the laggard races from Maldek and various uninvited invaders from other systems of worlds, to the children of the sun and those who are 'empty vessels' known as 'mechanised man'. The power elite are fallen ones, meaning that they have fallen in consciousness to a level, such that they have no respect or care for the rights and aspirations of others. The centre of their universe is self, wealth and power. These fallen ones are either fallen angels embodied as human beings or those who follow these forces of anti-Christ. They believe that they are superior to everyone else, that they have a divine right to rule and that the right to self-determination applies only to them because they are the wise ones whose role is to instruct and control the people.

> "I believe that the divine right of Kings is a deceptive precept dreamt up by the power elite in order to establish, assert and maintain their control over the people in perpetuity."
> **– Kim Andrew Lincoln**

The power elite look upon the people of Earth as their slaves, as sheep, who should be herded into pens and told what to do. Eons ago they decided that by a combination of force of arms and deception, they would take unto themselves the riches of this world by stealing the labour and the property of the people. Metaphorically speaking, they applied brakes to the wheels of fortune, so that the natural cycles of abundance in nature would be slowed down. They dammed up the rivers and stopped that which is essential to life from flowing. They blocked out the Son, Jesus Christ, who had come so that all people might have life and that they might have it more abundantly. And they perverted the teachings of the other prophets that God had sent too. They redirected the rainfall into reservoirs and stored up crops in their barns and warehouses, and horded all manner of foodstuffs and goods, so that there was not enough for the people. They created a consciousness of lack, whereby the majority were persuaded to accept less so that the power elite could have more. Yet in truth it is possible – in an enlightened economy – for all to have more. What God had freely given for the benefit of all, the power elite took for themselves and their kind; for they have not love, not faith, not hope, not charity.

The power elite and those who slavishly follow their philosophy have perverted everything that is good, everything that is pure, everything that is of God – from the money we need to exchange goods and services to our democratic system and even the music we listen to in order to enrich our lives and raise our spirits.

> "Communism is the ultimate expression of the mindset of the anti-Christ."
>
> **– Kim Andrew Lincoln**

The Ascended Masters inform us that Karl Marx, the founder of communism, was a fallen angel, as are many of the 'rock stars' in the music industry today. Revelation 9:1-6 foretold the rise of the drug culture that accompanied the introduction of rock music brought forth by Elvis and The Beatles. And it is no coincidence that sometime before these performers came to prominence the fallen angels were released from the bottomless pit having spent eleven thousand years in captivity.

> "The Beatles were among the fallen angels released from the bottomless pit."
>
> **– Lorraine Michaels**
> (From her book *The Unseen Power in I AM*)

Probably more than half of the world's political leaders are members of the power elite – who include fallen angels. They dominate the world of banking and finance, science, religion, commerce, the media and entertainment industry, the food industry, the pharmaceutical industry, the oil industry, education; the military, the secret services, the higher echelons of the civil service and all the principle international organisations like the United Nations, the World Bank, the International Monetary Fund, the Bank of International Settlements and many charitable foundations that serve as front organisations for the dark aims and nefarious activities of the power elite. They are also behind criminal organisations like the Mafia.

The Power Elite

We shall know them by their fruits for they represent everything that freedom and love are not. The tentacles of the power elite's anti-Christ agenda reach into every aspect of life on Earth such that a full description of their activities would fill the pages of many books. In order, therefore, to prevent this book from becoming too lengthy and overtly negative, I have focused my attention on those areas of the economy where this 'beast' has caused most harm. For be under no illusion: these souls are Satanists. They worship Satan and Lucifer, and have taken on the consciousness of the anti-Christ, which is everything that is not of God and that opposes God. For they have brought their pride and thus their rebellion against God's Will and God's Laws to Earth.

The 'power elite' aim to own and control as much of the world's wealth as possible. They will happily bleed the people dry in order to enrich themselves. In their eyes the poorer others are the more superior and richer they feel. They are like a band of vicious 'robber barons' intent on stealing our incomes our assets and our freedom. The level of contempt these Illuminists have for the Children of the Sun is demonstrated by their description of us as 'useless eaters'. When you look around and wonder why the world is in such a mess, where nothing seems to work, where there is poverty, spiritual decay, greed, tyranny, exploitation and war, you will understand that this is not God's doing. It is the work of the fallen angels who determined that they would prove God wrong by destroying his creation – the Mother and the manchild. For theirs is the consciousness of anti-Christ and anti-Being that is behind the persecution of women and the blaming of women for all the ills of the world. It is these followers of Lucifer, called the Illuminati, who are the 'accusers of the brethren' and who condemn others for witchcraft, when in truth they are the practitioners of the greatest wickedness and evil. It is also these fallen ones who preach that women should walk behind men because they are lesser beings when the truth is that men and women are equal.

The power elite and Illuminati are one and the same. They embody the consciousness of the fallen angels, for in the main they are fallen angels, and this consciousness is born of separation from God, of selfishness of anti-love and of anti-Christ. It is the consciousness of pride with all its many garments. It is the "… way that seemeth right unto a man, but the end thereof are the ways of death" – Proverbs 16:25.

> "The power elite's aim is to own everything and thus control everyone."
>
> – **Kim Andrew Lincoln**

The reality is that everything on this planet has been set up to keep us from knowing the truth about who we really are and why we are here. But, as these fallen ones are now discovering, seven billion voices cannot be silenced and seven billion people moving forward into the light is a force with which they cannot contend.

The greatest battle that has ever been fought and that is still being fought on Earth is the battle for free will – for the right to choose how we live our lives. The dualistic argument that people can only be safe if their freedoms are taken away is a Luciferian concept that originated with the rebellion of the wisdom angels who waged war in heaven over this issue and who wage war still, here on Earth. But it is a war, nevertheless, that they shall not win, for they shall not pass!

MECHANISED MAN

In his book *The Soulless One*, Mark Lyle Prophet, an anointed messenger for the Ascended Host until his ascension in 1973, tells the story of an alien race called the Anunnaki who colonised Earth aeons ago and used their skills as geneticists to create a slave race of 'human' automatons. These mechanised beings looked exactly like we do today as their genetic makeup was based on human DNA, but the codes were altered to make them compliant.

> They were disconnected to low vibrate
> In negative mode ninety five per cent
> Denied their pleasure of spice and fruit

> So that what remained was of bitter root.
>
> **– Kim Andrew Lincoln**
> (A verse from an untitled song written in 2004)

They did not carry the threefold flame because they were not created entirely in the image and likeness of God, but, because they had the christic seed that the Children of the Sun have, God gave them his light so that they could walk upon Earth. God also made it possible for them to progress up the spiritual ladder by multiplying their talents and to receive the threefold flame, once they had attained a certain higher level of consciousness. By granting mechanised man life, it was God's will that they should transcend themselves and become more than their Anunnaki creators had intended. Indeed, it was God's desire that they should break the bonds of their enslavement. And so it is that by God's grace and mercy's flame all those in embodiment on Earth today have the opportunity to become co-creators with God and thus to bring heaven to Earth. Mechanised man is still incarnating here and probably makes up the bulk of the world's population today.

Half-Man & Half-Beast & the Sinking of Atlantis

During the experimental phase of the Anunnaki genetic manipulation programme the creatures of Greek mythology were created. These included the Minotaur (man with the head of a bull); the Satyr (half-man, half-goat) and the Centaur (part man, part horse). In God's eyes, however, these creatures were mis-creations because they were brought forth by breeding between humans and beasts. So, to put an end to this abominable work, and other iniquitous activities, the elementals caused Atlantis to be buried under the sea in the great flood. What makes this history so interesting is that Mark Lyle Prophet who wrote about it – from accounts given to him by the Ascended Host – was a key character in these events because he had previously embodied as Noah, who built the Ark that saved the animals nearly twelve thousand years ago.

A GOLDEN AGE ECONOMY

THE ANUNNAKI

What is important to know about the Anunnaki is that their consciousness is at a similar level to that of Lucifer and his fallen angels. The Anunnaki represent the 'dark side' as depicted by the Darth Vader character in the *Star Wars* movies. And by all accounts they probably make up a substantial number of the power elite embodied on Earth today.

In Episode One I talked briefly about the twelve aspects of God's being (God consciousness) that is wholly positive; but these God qualities have their opposites that are perversions of the perfection of all that God IS. Everything that is good can be perverted by everything that is 'bad' – if we do not hold to the light. So we could say that the consciousness embodied by the Anunnaki and the fallen angels is the opposition to our being all that we can be, as we perform our plays in the 'Grand Theatre' of Earth.

THE HUMAN PERVERSIONS OF GOD CONSCIOUSNESS

GOD QUALITY	PERVERSION OF THAT QUALITY
God-Power	Criticism, condemnation and judgment and all black magic
God-Love	Hatred and mild dislike and all witchcraft
God-Mastery	Doubt, fear, human questioning and records of death
God-Control	Conceit, deceit, arrogance and ego
God-Obedience	Disobedience, stubbornness & defiance of the Law
God-Wisdom	Envy, jealousy and ignorance of the Law
God-Harmony	Indecision, self-pity and self-justification

God-Gratitude	Ingratitude, thoughtlessness and spiritual blindness
God-Justice	Injustice, frustration and anxiety
God-Reality	Dishonesty, intrigue and treachery
God-Vision	Selfishness, self-love and idolatry
God-Victory	Resentment, revenge and retaliation

When the Anunnaki designed mechanised man they 'switched off' nearly all of their potential for spiritual growth but left just enough for these beings to function properly and receive God's light. As a consequence of this tampering, mechanised beings are characterised by their lack of sensitivity, self-centredness and "I'm alright Jack" attitude to life. However, they make excellent actors and mimics and can just as easily be led down the left-handed path that leads to death as the right-handed one that leads to eternal life. My point is that mechanised man is easily influenced, which is important for the salvation of this planet as I shall explain later.

The Anunnaki first invaded Earth about half a million years ago and have been coming and going ever since – though not in the last two decades. They are essentially a warrior race with a history of conquest in our solar system and elsewhere in the Milky Way. Their creation story is that they have a right to go where they please and take what they want without any care or concern for the people and planets they subjugate and/or destroy. They are cold-blooded beings and operate a rigid class system. They love pomp, ceremony and pageant and are expert in mind control. In his book *The Twelfth Planet*, Zecheria Stichin talks about the Anunnaki and the enormous influence their presence has had on our culture and the way we conduct our affairs. He also points to the scientific evidence that proves that we are not alone and how the ancient civilisations that grew up in Babylon (Iraq) and Egypt could not have achieved what they did without technology and learning that was far beyond what the indigenous peoples had attained.

The Anunnaki have been incarnating in human bodies here for a long time now as have many other races from planets across the cosmos. On Earth most of us strive to live in peace and harmony. We have no memory of who we are or where we are from. But what many people are now realising is that there are dark forces at work on Earth who are intent on stopping the divine plan for this planet from manifesting, and that the source of this evil is the consciousness embodied by the fallen angels. Apart from the fallen angels in embodiment this consciousness is also common to the Anunnaki and elements within the laggard races and others who have also incarnated here in human bodies. What is taking place now is a battle for supremacy between these forces of darkness and the warriors of light who have come here with Sanat Kumara and who carry the sword of truth in their right hands. They are the 144,000 mentioned in the Bible.

So what is the relevance of all this deep history to the economy and restoring it to perfect health? Well, in order to solve any problem we need to first establish the nature and cause of the problem – meaning that we need to know what is really behind it. Dealing with the symptoms of sickness may bring some relief but it will not cure the disease. What we must do is find the root cause. And to do that we have to position ourselves so that we can see the big picture, for then the remedy is so much easier to see. I will be returning to this subject in Episode Three, by which time I trust that all will be much clearer.

THE DUALITY CONSCIOUSNESS

The duality consciousness is the mindset of the power elite. It is the thinking that the ends justify the means and that it is perfectly acceptable to break God's Laws if it serves the so-called 'greater good'. It is the belief that you can remove evil by doing evil and that you can guarantee the freedom of a country's citizens by passing laws that take their freedoms away. In America the Patriot Act and the National Defense Authorization Act (NDAA) are good examples of this mentality as, under the 'Prolonged Detention Order', citizens can be detained by the military indefinitely without trial, having committed no crime. They only have to be suspected of doing something that the government does not like to have all their rights under the Constitution and the Bill of Rights taken away. The NDAA even permits citizens to be tortured and murdered by the government, without due process of law.

The duality consciousness is the absurd notion that it is justifiable for one country to invade another to change the regime, without first asking the people if that's what they want, and then to use 'shock and awe' firepower that kills hundreds of thousands of that country's citizens and then to boast to the wider world that you have done so for their benefit and not the profit of your own corporate sponsors.

God never commanded
We kill in his name
No peacemaker sanctions
A bombing campaign.

Peacemakers of Gaia
Don't bend to the line

A GOLDEN AGE ECONOMY

> That war can bring peace
> When war is a crime.
>
> **– Kim Andrew Lincoln**
> (Two verses from the song/poem
> 'Peacemakers' written in 2006)

Dualistic thinking is not the sole preserve of the power elite. But, when it is applied as government policy, a great deal of harm is invariably done, and usually to those who are least able to defend themselves. Many western governments, for example, have an undeclared policy of tolerance for high levels of unemployment because they see it as an effective way of keeping wages down. Moreover, when unemployment is high, workers tend to be more compliant and flexible in their dealings with their employer because they are in constant fear of losing their jobs. This changes the balance of power in favour of employers and enables them to hold wages and working conditions down. This suits the power elite because it increases their power over the people and enables them to make more money.

> "Duality is an illusion – there is no such thing as relative good and evil. All that is good comes from the heart of God and all that is not comes from somewhere else."
>
> **– Kim Andrew Lincoln**

What is not of God has no reality, no permanence – therefore it cannot endure. Governments are always trying to justify the unjustifiable because their economic policies do not work. The duality consciousness, therefore, walks hand in hand with failure because it is a mis-creation that originates from the mind of anti-Christ. It is the thinking that states at a sub-conscious level that in order to prove God wrong the power elite are entitled to use all means at their disposal to destroy God's co-creators and God's kingdom. It is the mindset that allows the use of dualistic arguments to trick the people into

The Duality Consciousness

misqualifying God's energy with the intention that they we will then destroy themselves and the planet and thus prove the power elite right and God wrong.

"The duality consciousness is the ego and the anti-Christ in disguise."

– Kim Andrew Lincoln

The Power Elite's Plan

"Woe to the inhibiters of the Earth and of the sea for the devil is come down unto you, having great wrath because he knoweth that he hath but a short time."

– **Revelation 12:12**

Background

The origins of the power elite's plan for world domination can be traced back to the angel rebellion of 500,000 years ago. The rebellion leader was Lucifer, whose name means 'light bearer'. He held the office of archangel and was therefore the most enlightened of all the wisdom angels. But Lucifer disagreed with God's plan to give human beings free will. He believed that humans would misuse this freedom and harm themselves and the rest of God's creation. He was jealous of the high rank that God had given his co-creators because up until that point only archangels had free will, which they had won through exceptional service to God. All other angels had to follow the archangel's instructions. Lucifer perceived humankind's elevated status as an effective demotion for him because his wisdom was greater than mankind's. So Lucifer refused to serve God's co-creators and ordered those angels who reported to him to do the same. He refused to do what John the Baptist had done for Jesus which was to decrease so that Jesus could increase. In his pride he failed to understand that the teacher must give way to the student so that the All can be raised.

"The greatest amongst us are the servants of all."

– **Kim Andrew Lincoln**

The Power Elite's Plan

So what followed was a war between the forces of light lead by archangel Michael – who stands for the power and will of God – and the forces of 'darkness' lead by Lucifer and the 'Satan' angels who had joined him in his rebellion against God's will. Lucifer was defeated and consequently he and a third of the angels fell (in consciousness) to Earth from where they resolved to destroy the mother and the manchild, meaning the Children of the Sun and the Sons and Daughters of God.

> "And his tail drew the third part of the stars of heaven, and did cast them to the earth: and the dragon stood before the woman, which was ready to be delivered, for to devour her child as soon as it was born."
>
> **– Revelation 12:4**

So this was the first fall, but the Book of Enoch tells the story of another band of angels called the 'Watchers' who fell to Earth much later, but this time it was because they lusted after the 'daughters of men'. When these Watchers mated with human women they produced an offspring of giants called Nephilim. These beings were ravenous and consumed all the people's food. The Nephilim were monsters in size and iniquity. Goliath, who lost his duel with King David, was one of these creatures. The Nephilim's time on Earth, however, was relatively short as they were all wiped out in the earthquakes and the great flood that sank Atlantis.

The Watchers were masters of war and every form of wickedness imaginable. They passed on their knowledge of these ways to the children of the sun with the intention that they (we) would give up our light through sin. This was most important to the Watchers because when they fell to Earth they stopped receiving God's life sustaining light and so became reliant upon stealing it from the Children of the Sun. But they could only do this when the Children of the Sun shed their light through mis-creation. And so we can see that through this process humankind and the fallen angels became tied and bound to each other by karma, and both groups have continued to re-embody, side by side, to the present day.

Moreover, into this cauldron of rebellion and conflict came other groups including the Laggards, the Anunnaki and Mechanised Man. It was the Laggards who discovered nuclear power, how to create life in test tubes and how to use ultra-sonic waves, laser beams and astral rays as healing tools and weapons. Aeronautics, space travel and the manipulation of DNA are also technologies that originally came from Maldek with the third of their population that were allowed to embody here. And we should not forget that it was the satanic science of nuclear power that was the cause of that planet's destruction. The Laggard races are also materialists who believe that the acquisition of wealth is not a means to an end but an end in itself. And this is the same consciousness of greed for power and money that has consumed the bankers, and that is displayed by so many who work in the City of London and Wall Street today.

What I have described above and in other chapters of this book is but a very small part of what is known today about the history of the fallen angels and the origins of evil. For a more detailed understanding of this subject I recommend the books *Fallen Angels Among Us* and *Fallen Angels and the Origins of Evil* by Elizabeth Clare Prophet, available from the Summit Lighthouse, plus **all** the books written by Lorraine Michaels, which can be purchased from her website: www.theosophiaistheway.com, Lorraine's websites and books contain the most up-to-date teachings released by the Ascended Masters.

From what the Ascended Masters have revealed from the Hall of Records in heaven we can begin to understand what lies behind the present discord and disharmony on earth today. But there is much more to know.

STRATEGIES

Everything that fallen angels have done and are doing now is focused on proving God wrong for giving humankind free will. So their objective is to get us to fail on every level so that the divine plan for each person and the planet as a whole does not manifest. To achieve this they have tried to imprison us in a false world, a counterfeit kingdom that has been constructed on foundations of sand so that its structures have no strength, no substance and thus no permanence. It is an illusory mis-created world riven with deception and half truth. Jesus and all the other spiritual teachers came here to bring us the truth because the fallen angels have spent aeons feeding us everything but the truth. Their basic plan has been to divide us in order to conquer us so that they can then control us. And once they can control us they will have won because then we will no longer be able to exercise our free will.

Removing our freedom and thus preventing this new Golden Age of Freedom from manifesting is their most cherished aim.

The fallen angels' time is short. For they have been judged and when they take their leave of the Earth by physical death they will go to the second death and thus be permanently extinguished as individual life streams. Both Lucifer and Satan (who were separate beings) have already gone that way and are no more.

THE MARK OF THE (MONEY) BEAST

What we have seen in the last fifty years or so has been a substantial increase in the efforts of the power elite to bring the people of this planet under their control. What we know, from accounts given by ex-members of the Illuminati, is that the power elite have a strategic plan, which is basically to own everything and control everyone. And the reality is that they stand a chance of achieving these aims if we allow them to establish their New World Order and one world money system prophesied in Revelation:

> "And he caused all [beast] both small and great, rich and poor, free and bond to receive a mark in their right hand, or in their foreheads: And that no man might buy or sell save he that had the mark or the name of the beast, or the number of his name (666)."
>
> – **Revelation 13:16-18**

A GOLDEN AGE ECONOMY

> It's the Number of the Beast
> Rising now it richly feasts
> It's the number triple six
> In your flesh a money trick
> Do not cheer if you have bled
> Blessed not are those who wed
> Graven license for to sell
> Buy the goods of living hell
> Do not take this poisoned cup
> Know again – and so rise up
> Truth is love and Fear is hell
> Awaken now and break the spell.
>
> **– Kim Andrew Lincoln**
> (An extract from the song 'Number of the Brand'
> written in 2005)

This money system is based on the existing technology used in debit and credit cards and thus could just as easily be inserted under the skin as it is contained within a plastic card. And when linked to an international super-computer in Brussels the myriad forms of data that could be stored in these microchips would enable the power elite to track everyone and know everything about our business and private lives as well as our physical movements and trading transactions. Indeed, with such a system in place the authorities could make it very difficult for us to operate effectively – let alone buy and sell. This is what the illuminati-sponsored boffins have been working towards for many years and you will note that periodically it becomes possible to do more and more with these devices such that notes and coins have almost been dispensed with so that the money and banking system that we currently use is comprised almost entirely of electronic money where all transactions are just credit and debit entries on computer screens. In the UK, banks are trying very hard to do away with notes and coins in circulation and it will be a happy day for them when cheques and cash have been completely eliminated. For if they can achieve this then they will be free to set their money beast lose on an unsuspecting world. If we drink of this poisoned cup we will be under their total control and it will be very difficult to break away. So I say now that we must resist by all legal and peaceful means the introduction of this scheme. And we can do this by using cash and cheques more and cards less. This will frustrate their plans because cash transactions are not traceable and the fractional reserve banking system that I will be explaining shortly is more difficult to manipulate when people use cash as opposed to electronic money.

Of all the nefarious schemes that the power elite have introduced and are planning for the future this is the most evil in terms of the impact it will have on our personal liberties. And thus no matter how generous the incentives are to persuade us to implant the mark of the beast in our foreheads or right hand we must resist them at every turn so that this chilling prophecy that Jesus dictated to John of Patmos is not fulfilled.

If you still find this hard to believe, what follows is a transcript of an excerpt from a documentary made by the late film-maker Aaron Russo, who used to be friends with Nicholas Rockefeller, until he found out what he and his friends are planning for us all. I cannot prove beyond reasonable doubt that this interview is absolutely genuine or that the Nicholas Rockefeller who gave the interview is a real member of the famously rich Rockefeller family, so you will have to make up your own mind. Here is the interview:

Nicholas Rockefeller:

"By having this war on terror, you can never win it so you can always keep taking people's liberties away. The media can convince everybody it's [the war on terror] real. Say it over and over and over again and that's when people believe this."

Aaron Russo:

"What are you doing this for? This is not a good thing people."

A GOLDEN AGE ECONOMY

NICHOLAS ROCKEFELLER:

"What do you care about people for? Take care of yourself and your own family."

AARON RUSSO:

"What are the ultimate goals here?"

NICHOLAS ROCKEFELLER:

"The goal is to get everybody in this world chipped with an RFID chip with all their money and information on it. And if people want to protest what we do or violate what we want, we just turn off the chip."

NB: The Rockefeller family is probably the second richest on the planet. Only they know what they are truly worth, but some estimates I have seen put their fortune in the region of $30 trillion, which is about one tenth of what the House of Rothschild is said to be worth. The original Rockefeller riches came from oil (Standard Oil) but since then they have diversified their interests into all the biggest and most profitable industries.

FALLEN ANGELS IN THE CHURCH

Many books have been written about the conspiracies of the Illuminati (Luciferians) and the legions of secret societies and other organisations that are part of their wicked world wide web. Movies have been made and many websites have been published that profess to know their secrets from inside information. Now this is all well and good and has been genuinely helpful in exposing what is going on behind the scenes, though we need to exercise our discernment; as truth and misinformation are often interwoven to confuse us more. But when you think about it, the essential elements of this global conspiracy have been known about for aeons, for they have been written into every history book and into the scriptures of all the world's true religions.

In the Christian faith the fallen angels were the 'accusers of the brethren'. They embodied as the Scribes and Pharisees who questioned Jesus and pressurised the Romans into crucifying him – though the Romans had no quarrel with Jesus. The Illuminati of old are the wolves in sheep's clothing whom about Jesus warned us. And so we can see that, from the beginning, the power elite infiltrated the hierarchy of the church and perverted the original teachings so that the Children of the Sun would stay in ignorance of the truth and their divinity. These dark forces trampled on Christianity by censoring so much of what Jesus had taught that what remained did not make sense. And Islam has gone a similar way for it has become synonymous with warring and terrorism and with Buddhism falsehoods were implanted so that it has become an 'anything goes' philosophy where wrongdoing is not condemned.

By sowing the seeds of apostasy amongst young and old the power elite have sought to sever our connection to God and thereby prevent us from achieving enlightenment. And their success is measured by the number of people who are so confused that they do not know what to believe. The duality consciousness of the fallen angels has spread through the world like a virus for they have redefined morality and made a mockery of the truth.

Divine Right to Power

In the field of politics the intervention of the fallen angels is evident in the royal bloodlines and the precept of the divine right of Kings. Long ago these fallen ones tricked the people into thinking that God had appointed the monarch to rule as his proxy on Earth. Once this idea had taken root, royal families came to be regarded more as deities than human beings. In ancient Egypt the Pharaohs were treated more like Gods than men. However, by the middle of the seventeenth century cracks had started to appear in the idea that Kings and Queens were beyond reproach. In England, King Charles I played the hand of his divine descent as a defence for his tyranny, but lost the game and his head, as his nemesis, Oliver Cromwell, saw through the whole charade. And so democracy (of a sort) was reborn. However, this hard-won victory for the light was short-lived because, as the taste for democracy grew, the fallen angels found ever more subtle ways to retain their grip on the levers of power.

> "A monarch who devotes themselves tirelessly and selflessly to the task of representing the nation will earn the love and respect of the people and will, in this way, be elevated in accordance with the greatness of their works. In the United Kingdom the person who best demonstrated these qualities was Princess Diana. She was, we thought, destined, though clearly never intended, to become Queen, and at the time of her passing was probably the most loved – and certainly the most famous – person in the world. Her legacy lives on through her sons."
> – Kim Andrew Lincoln

BANKERS CONTROL GOVERNMENTS

> "Whoever controls the money system controls the nation."
> – Kim Andrew Lincoln

It was the world's richest and most powerful banking dynasty, the House of Rothschild that actively encouraged the party political system. They knew that the blame for the damage the fraudulent money and banking system would do to Europe's economies would fall on the politicians whom the people thought managed the economy. Indeed, it was this particular banking house that funded both sides in the Napoleonic wars and whose fortune was thus founded on death and destruction.

By 1850 the Rothschild family had reputedly amassed a fortune of £250 billion. What that figure is today is difficult to calculate but if you adjust it for inflation it we would certainly come to many $trillions. I have seen estimates that say they are now worth $300 trillion but this figure is at best a guess – though certainly possible.

The Power Elite's Plan

> "The party political system was established to divert attention away from the real cause of our economic problems, which is the fractional reserve banking system and the bankers created party politics so that politicians would be blamed for the economic mess that banks keep making."
>
> – **Kim Andrew Lincoln**

Once the House of Rothschild had indebted the governments of Europe into its control it turned its attention to the United States of America who had just won their independence from the British Crown. The Rothschilds fought long and hard to gain control of America's money system though they were vociferously opposed by Presidents Thomas Jefferson, Andrew Jackson, Abraham Lincoln and J. F. Kennedy.

NB: In the Addendum at the end of this episode I have made available an extract from President Andrew Jackson's farewell speech in which he talks about his battles with the bankers and the importance of keeping taxes low. It is beautifully written prose and well worth the read.

It is alleged in some quarters that Abraham Lincoln was shot not because of his position on slavery but because of his opposition to the Rothschilds' plan. But never thwarted by temporary setbacks, the Rothschilds eventually got their way and in 1913 the Federal Reserve Act was passed and this former colony of Great Britain began the long slide into the mire of economic slavery based on debt.

> "The people that run America are the people that pay for the President, which in the main are the private banks that own the Federal Reserve."
>
> – **Kim Andrew Lincoln**

The Federal Reserve name was chosen deliberately to suggest that it is government owned. The Fed acts like a central bank in that it is the lender of last resort but, unlike the Bank of England (BoE), it is not state-owned.

A GOLDEN AGE ECONOMY

"The powers of financial capitalism had another far-reaching aim, nothing less than to create a world system of financial control in private hands able to dominate the political system of each country and the economy of the world as a whole. This system was to be controlled in a feudalist fashion by the central banks of the world acting in concert by secret agreements arrived at in frequent private meetings and conferences. The apex of the system was to be the Bank for International Settlements in Basle, Switzerland, a private bank owned and controlled by the world's central banks which were themselves private corporations."

– Carroll Quigley, 1966

CORPORATOCRACY

The illuminati control of the world's wealth and resources is not confined to the banking sector, but to every sector. The thirteen core bloodline illuminati families are more powerful than we ever thought, for the global corporations they own and control exert so much influence over world affairs and daily life on this planet that the system of government in the West would be better described as a corporatocracy than a democracy.

But trying to determine who owns what is extremely difficult because in order to evade taxes the really rich stay that way by not disclosing all that they own and earn. The sum total of their wealth is not capable of being audited because in the main it is held in assets that are not easily traced like gold and other precious metals. These would have been extracted from mines owned by the elite and then secretly stored in private vaults beyond the taxman's reach. In addition they hide and disperse their wealth through trusts and charities they control as well as making extensive use of tax havens.

The power of the illuminati comes from its obsession with secrecy as their dealings are done in the shadow economy. If an illuminati family buys a business they will do it in such a way that its connection to the family or any member of the family is concealed. For if the true extent of the power that these people wield was widely known there would be a hue and cry so loud that our elected rulers would be forced to rein them in. Exposure of the illuminati's activities, secrets and modus operandi is the last thing they want, which is one of the reasons why I am writing this book.

In the film *Devil's Advocate* there is a scene where the devil, played by Al Pacino, is teaching his lawyer son how to win cases in court. He says:

> "Don't get too cocky my boy. Don't ever let 'em see you coming – that's the gaff. You gotta keep yourself small, innocuous. Look at me, underestimated from day one. You'd never think I was master of the universe."

Here are some things we do know:

Among the largest companies in the world are: Bank of America, JP Morgan Chase, Citigroup, Wells Fargo, Goldman Sachs and Morgan Stanley – all bankers and investment bankers. And of all the shareholders who own the above there are four firms – all of whom are fund management groups – who own significant stakes in all these banks. They are: State Street Corporation; Vanguard Group; Black Rock; and Fidelity. According to their websites these four firms have funds under management of about $7.5 trillion, which is approximately three times the Gross National Product of the United Kingdom.

> "For more than a century, ideological extremists at either end of the political spectrum have seized upon well-publicized incidents to attack the Rockefeller family for the inordinate influence they claim we wield over American political and economic institutions. Some even believe we are part of a secret cabal working against the best interests of the United States, characterizing my family and me as 'internationalists' and of conspiring with others around the world to build a more integrated global political and economic structure – one world,

if you will. *If that's the charge, I stand guilty, and I am proud of it."* [my emphasis]

– David Rockefeller

The truth is that big business tells our elected representatives what to do. Most, but not all, of our politicians are in some way under the influence of these companies so that corporate wish lists are at the top of the agenda when government policy is made. Lobbying of politicians by big business is conducted on a massive scale, as is the amount of money that is lavished on ensuring that companies always win at the expense of the people. The corporate power elite are always grateful for services rendered so that when accommodating politicians leave office they usually find it easy to secure well paid employment with those firms they have helped. And this sends out a message that it pays politicians to cooperate with business, and so the cycle of self interest and corruption continues to spin, and the grip the illuminati and their proxies have on the levers of power is assured. The power elite are very protective of those who serve their interests but woe betide anyone who leaves the fold and moves into the light.

Mind Control Through Education

The illuminati go to great lengths to control the minds of the young as they are a rich source of light that can be harvested, but also because they are the future and they need to bring on the new breed in the ways of wickedness. And so to this end they have constructed an extensive network of educational establishments to cater for the needs of the children of the power elite and others who they consider can be turned to their way of thinking. The English public school system and the Oxbridge universities are the most obvious bastions of the power elite in the UK, and America has its equivalents, like Yale and Princeton. Scholarships are awarded to the brightest and many of these are funded directly by illuminati organisations. The 'Rhodes Scholars' is one notable example. Illuminati influence over young minds extends into many other areas including the music and entertainment industry, which I will cover in more detail later on.

Opinion Formers

One way the illuminati attempt to get people to come over to their way of thinking is through the establishment of research institutes and academic bodies that promote ideas and policies that are supportive of their agenda. There are many thousands of these organisations operating throughout the world and some of the most influential ones are described in the next chapter.

An Interest in Arms

Americans were given the right to bear arms under their constitution to protect them from tyrannical governments. It is no surprise, therefore, that there has been an ongoing campaign (most likely funded by illuminati money) to remove this right, because you cannot completely control the population if they have the means to fight back. And it is this desire for control that drives the fallen angels to expend untold sums of money on homeland security and offensive weapons development when a tiny fraction of what is actually spent would be sufficient to cover legimate defence needs. In England the fallen angels in authority are obsessed with surveillance as there are more than five million security cameras pointed at the people. We are told they are meant to protect us from crime and terrorism but in truth they serve as the State's spying tool. In the UK in 2010 there were three million officially sanctioned spying events carried out under the anti-terror laws.

Another reason why some countries maintain an excessive military presence is to support the commercial interests of the corporations that control the government. As one of the biggest businesses is the oil business, we can understand why the US government has been, and remains so, keen to invade countries that have large reserves of oil. But it's not just oil, as there are other spoils

A GOLDEN AGE ECONOMY

of war to be won. Once an invaded country's infrastructure has been destroyed the big conglomerates move in and make even more money from the rebuilding work that needs to be done. The British power elite were past masters at this. Britain only became Great Britain when the power elite used its military muscle to further commerce in foreign lands. Following the suppression of India by the East India Company in the eighteenth century a great expansion of the British Empire took place when the House of Rothschild bankrolled Cecil Rhodes' expeditions to conquer Africa. His strategy was to create a pretext for war and then to invade the target country using overwhelming force to subjugate the indigenous people. What followed was the 'theft' of those countries' natural resources and then the establishment of trading opportunities for businesses back home. The Greeks did it and then the Romans and the Mongols after them. It is a classic Anunnaki strategy and it continues today with the USA.

Control of the Media

All parts of the mass media, if not owned, are controlled by the power elite. The media never rock the boat. Dramatic events that are cries for freedom by the people are played down so that the status quo is maintained. The national media present the same 'safe' stories and push similar political lines. Every time the economy is discussed these broadcasters dance around the subject but never explain what is really going on. For example, you will never hear the phrase 'fractional reserve banking' used or get an explanation from the so-called experts of how it works, and yet it is the root cause of all our economic ills.

One of the few places you will find honest and in-depth news coverage is via the internet. But discernment is needed here too, because whenever the power elite's duplicity is exposed they try to kill the story. But if they cannot they will move to discredit or even remove the source for they care not who they hurt and kill.

A Divided Society

"Behind all conflicts are elements of some belief that is based on a lie."
   – Ascended Master Padma Sambhava

Meat and drink to the illuminati is the low vibrational energy of fear and so it is a key part of their plan to divide society into as many opposing factions as possible for the purpose of creating tension between the sides. The truth is that we are ALL ONE so the fallen angels have tried to create the illusion that we are different and separate from each other. If you can divide people by race, social class, sexual preference, political views, religion and whatever else you can create the potential for conflict and preferably war which is their ultimate aim. Of course these points of difference are not real, but through propaganda and misinformation we are made to believe that they are, so that we will fear that which we are not familiar with and do not fully understand. Fear breeds hatred and hatred breeds conflict. This was the strategy the Nazis employed to get their soldiers to kill Jews. They fed them the lie that Jews were inferior to Germans and even lower in the evolutionary chain than animals and therefore they could be eliminated without a second thought. In Northern Ireland the conflict was focused along religious lines and in the French and Russian revolutions it was economic inequality and envy that were the seeds of division and war.

So why do the power elite want to create division?

Well, firstly it is to distract us. For if we can be persuaded to fight among ourselves then we will be too busy to notice how we are being robbed and enslaved by bankers and other corporate thieves. Secondly, when we are preoccupied in fear-based activity we create karma which stunts our spiritual growth and that makes us easier to control. While we remain unenlightened we are unlikely to rise up against our oppressors. Thirdly, when we create karma we shed our spiritual light, which the fallen ones need to survive. Fourthly, conflict – especially terrorism – enables the power elite to justify the confiscation of our freedoms and civil liberties in order to 'keep us safe'. Note how draconian anti-freedom laws were introduced after 9/11 and ask yourself whether you truly believe that the demolition of the twin towers was carried out by terrorists acting alone. Fifthly, war and terror are good business for the corporations owned and controlled by the power elite.

> War is a banquet
> On which demons feed
> All courses our light is
> Our fears what they need.
>
> **- Kim Andrew Lincoln**
> (A verse from the song 'War is...' written in 2007)

A Sick Society

The Ascended Masters say that this planet was designed by the Elohim to support ten billion people in embodiment. The fallen angels, however, have a much lower figure in mind, which, according to some sources I have seen, is closer to half a billion. But whatever the target number is, the feeling I get from my research is that it is clearly a lot less than the seven billion souls currently here.

> "Depopulation should be the highest priority of U.S. foreign policy towards the Third World."
>
> **- Henry Kissinger**

So why would the fallen angels want to depopulate Earth? And by what method have they chosen to carry out this evil plan?

As to method, their main weapon is silent and unseen. It is difficult to identify and isolate as a specific cause of death. It kills slowly by stealth and it is the primary cause of cancer on Earth. It is poisons developed and manufactured by businesses owned and/or controlled by the power elite. These toxins are deliberately administered into the air (e.g. chemtrails*) and water (e.g. fluoride). They are the harmful

---

* For more information about 'Chemtrails' Google it and follow your nose.

ingredients that go into the everyday products we use in the home and in industrial processes. They are in the pollution that is poured out by factories into our rivers and that is incinerated into the air. They are the by-products (radiation) of accidents that occur in the production of nuclear power (e.g. Chernobyl – USSR; Three Mile Island – USA; and Fukushima – Japan). They are the oil from spills and the dispersants that pollute our seas. They are the heavy metals (mercury) that are found in most vaccines and the fillings that fill our teeth. These metals destroy our bodies and minds. They are in the preservatives and other toxins found in fast food and processed food. They are the deadly saturated fats (i.e. transfats) and sugar-filled foods that have no nutrition in them and that are largely responsible for the epidemic of obesity. They are monosodium glutamate (MSG), also called yeast extract. They are the sugar alternatives like aspartame that attack the central nervous system. They are the 'Frankenstein' foods that are made from genetically modified organisms produced by companies such as Monsanto.

These mis-creations have the potential to cause untold damage to our health and the world ecosystem. They are in the food irradiation process that damages the nutritional value of much of what we eat. We are lulled into thinking that we are eating a healthy and balanced diet that will maintain our physical health, when in fact we are being deprived of nutrition. They are in the narcotics that were never part of the divine plan for this planet for they were created not by God but by man under the influence of the Watchers, who sought to control us by dragging us down into degradation and death in order to take our light. The Ascended Masters tell us that plant-based drugs like marijuana and opium were genetically created plants that originated from the great advancement of Luciferian science on Atlantis and Lemuria that occurred before written records were kept on Earth. And they are in the prescription drugs that do not so much cure the condition but manage it so that big pharmaceutical companies' (Big Pharma) profits are maximised. They are the side effects that these pharmaceutical solutions cause. They are the treatments that are so toxic (e.g. chemotherapy) that the clinicians who handle them put themselves at great risk of developing the cancers these drugs are supposed to cure.

In 1986 Big Pharma was given immunity from prosecution by the United States government for any harm to people that their vaccines cause. This is an alarming development because if the power elite are intent upon population reduction then what better way to achieve it than through a programme of mass vaccinations. It would be easy, for example, to hide an undetectable killer cocktail in a flu vaccine and then to blame the subsequent deaths on flu.

> "Man-made poisons have reduced human fertility rates."
> **– Kim Andrew Lincoln**

Starting another World War (nuclear) and causing mass starvation are additional ways in which the power elite may be planning to slash the population and their reasons for doing so can be explained as follows. Firstly, it is their avowed aim to kill the mother and the manchild in order to prove God wrong. Secondly, when they create a climate of fear and suffering it causes our light to be released which they need to live. Thirdly, with a smaller population there are more resources and therefore more luxuries for the elite to enjoy while the people that remain are forced into menial work and service to the elite.

Wheat Amongst the Chaff

> "I know thy works, that thou art neither cold nor hot: I would thou wert cold or hot. So then because thou art lukewarm, and neither cold nor hot, I will spue thee out of my mouth."
> **– Revelation 3:15-16**

Even though the forces of darkness occupy most of the key positions of power and influence in society today we should not despair because the hierarchy of light have also placed their agents in high places. And when enough of us have awakened and we start to reclaim our power from the elite these spiritual warriors will be thus empowered to help

The Power Elite's Plan

end our enslavement as Moses did for the Israelites in Egypt over three thousand years ago.

Since I began writing this book I have become aware of the identity of some of these light workers, though, for obvious reasons, I will not unmask them here. Suffice it to say that despite the opposition there is a way out of all this darkness as you will find by the time you have finished reading this book.

The source of most of the material under this heading of 'A Sick Society' has come from the website: www.naturalnews.com. And, for this reason, I strongly recommend it to anyone who is interested in finding out more about living a healthy lifestyle. Here you will find invaluable information on healthy eating and alternative treatments to disease that use the natural remedies available to us from nature's storehouse, as opposed to the chemical-based compounds concocted by Big Pharma. The webmaster, Mike Adams, also exposes the quackery behind the vaccines business that has so much to answer for because of its use of heavy metals and other dangerous substances.

I should also like to point out that my recommendations of this website and other websites or books mentioned in this book are made purely on merit alone.

THE TENTACLES OF THE POWER ELITE

BANK OF INTERNATIONAL SETTLEMENTS (BIS)

The black heart of the power elite's international fractional reserve banking system is the BIS which controls the central banks of most Western and developing nations. The BIS acts as a financial agent for international agreements, collects financial information on the global economy and serves as lender of last resort to prevent global financial collapse. It is owned by the Federal Reserve, Bank of England, Bank of Italy, Bank of Canada, the Swiss National Bank, Nederlandsche Bank, Bundesbank and Bank of France. It is without doubt the most powerful bank in the world.

The BIS was originally set up in 1930, ostensibly to receive the reparation payments from Germany that were agreed at the Treaty of Versailles. However, it is more likely that the main reason for its establishment was to increase the hold that the illuminati controlled banking families had over the world financial system and thus advance their one-world government agenda. Some sources claim that the BIS helped to fund Germany's expansion after Hitler became Chancellor in 1933, while others say that his intention was to completely cut the Zionist banking cartel out of the loop. My own view is that the reparations imposed upon the German people were made deliberately harsh so as to cause an economic collapse that would enable Hitler to seize power and start another war. It is noteworthy that within four years of becoming Chancellor, Hitler had built the strongest economy in Europe. He instigated a massive programme of public works that was paid for with credit notes issued by the government. This infuriated the private banks as this form of 'money' was created debt-free and thus not subject to interest. However, the banks did later benefit from Hitler's leadership as once he had invaded Poland, and the UK had declared war on Germany, the allies needed to borrow vast sums of money to fight the war, money which the Rothschild's and other banks were happy to lend. The House of Rothschild is still believed to be the principal power behind the throne of the BIS.

THE EURO

The Euro had always intended to be a stepping stone towards a single world currency, which is why there is such a determination on the part of the core European states to make it work.

THE COUNCIL ON FOREIGN RELATION (CFR)

The CFR is the North American offshoot of the British Royal Institute of International Affairs whose membership comprises solely of illuminati from Canada and the USA. This semi-secret organisation was established in 1971. The CFR exercises considerable control over the major western powers and its primary objective is the creation of a one-world government and currency. At the heart of this organisation is the Rockefeller family who reputedly fund its operations from the profits of their massive corporate interests in oil, banking, insurance, pharmaceuticals, chemicals, transport and machinery, food, airlines, computing and technology.

THE TRILATERAL COMMISSION (TC)

The TC is another Rockefeller creation and semi-secret society that was founded in 1973 by high-ranking members of the power elite, David Rockefeller and Zbigniew Brzezinski. It came into being because existing organisations such as the United Nations were too slow in establishing a single world government. This organisation is subdivided into three blocks of nations comprising the USA, Japan and Western Europe. Its members are invariably freemasons. The Trilateral Commission controls, through the CFR members, the whole US

A GOLDEN AGE ECONOMY

economy, politics, military, oil, energy and media lobbies. The members are chairmen of different companies, bankers, real estate agents, economists, scientists, lawyers, publishers, politicians, union leaders, presidents of foundations and newspaper columnists.

THE BILDERBERGERS

One of the power elite's most powerful secret societies is the Bilderberger group formed by Prince Bernhard of the Netherlands, a former SS officer, and the Polish socialist Joseph Retinger, a founder of the European movement. The organisation's name comes from the Hotel Bilderberg in Holland where they had their first meeting in 1954. The core membership comprises of thirty nine people who make up the steering committee. Their meetings are held annually in secret in different locations and the membership of a hundred and twenty is drawn from the financial elite of Western Europe, the US and Canada. Also invited are political leaders from different countries whose expenses are paid by the group. What is discussed at these meetings is rarely reported (unless there is a leak) as many of the world's media barons are Bilderbergers themselves. As with all other illuminati organisations their goal is to achieve a one-world government by the year 2012 and to set up a global army through the United Nations. The reason the Bilderbergers invite politicians to their meetings is to try to persuade them to betray their own countries by selling out their sovereign states to the European Union and the American Union (USA, Canada and Mexico), contrary to the constitutions of the countries they represent. It is reminiscent of the treachery of King Charles I who recruited foreign troops to fight against his own people in the English Civil War.

Other organisations that were set up under the influence of the illuminati include the United Nations, the International Monetary Fund (IMF), World Bank, the Skull & Bones and the Round Table to name but a few. If you want to know more about the illuminati just type that word into Google and follow your nose, applying the usual discernment as not everything published on the internet is factually correct.

Greed is NOT Good

"Our perverted financial system was born out of the same dark desire of greed for power and money that is now destroying it."
– **Kim Andrew Lincoln**

In this chapter I give a brief overview of what is wrong with our financial system, and comment on some of the key events of the last decade in the world of investments, money and banking. In succeeding chapters I will look in more depth at the component parts of our economy so that by the end of Episode Two you will be in no doubt of the need for change. How a Golden Age economy came to be is the subject of episode three.

Stockmarkets Are Controlled and Manipulated

When I started giving investment advice in 1992, I thought that the stock market was a place where everyone had a reasonable chance of building a store of wealth to draw on when needed. It was not until March 2000 when the dot.com bubble burst, and the value of 'technology funds' fell by 80%, that I finally realised that an international 'power elite' were controlling and manipulating investment markets and the economy to the point of killing the goose that lays the golden egg.

I was even more horrified when I discovered that about $33 trillion had been legally stolen from private investors and pension funds during the dot.com scam – money which the victims will never recover!

A GOLDEN AGE ECONOMY

"I suddenly realised I had joined the wrong mob."
– **Lucky Luciano**
(comparing Wall Street to the Mafia)

BANK GREED BACKFIRES

Following 9/11 global investment markets plummeted and the FTSE 100 index of leading UK companies fell over 50% to 3300. Fear of a global recession made the central banks slash interest rates and by 2003, when they hit 1% in the US and 3.5% here, the banks had sown the seeds for the next bubble – property – which burst in 2007/8.

What people do not realise is that the rise in property prices is a systematic way by big banks and mortgage companies to steal the value of people's labour, as when the price of a house doubles, the amount of interest that the buyer has to pay goes up exponentially. Thus, the purchaser needs to spend an inordinate amount of income in order to pay back the mortgage, giving inordinate profits to banks and mortgage companies. These lenders have a selfish interest in allowing property prices to go up indefinitely and they will not stop until borrowers can no longer pay the interest and the system collapses under its own weight – which is happening now.

Since the inception of the present money and banking system, called 'fractional reserve' lending – over three centuries ago – the private banks have been lending money to governments, businesses and individuals. The banks have devised all manner of schemes through which they can lend ever more money to the point where we and our American and European cousins are 'all borrowed up' and sinking under the weight of debt.

I remember when in December 2003, after spending over a year thinking about the potentially devastating effects that so-called 'natural' disasters and atrocities like 9/11 could have on my client's investments, I wrote down what I thought might happen if Al Qaeda struck again – as they had promised to do – and what advice I would give to safeguard my clients' wealth. What came out of this was my 'Safety First Strategy' for cash savings, investments and pensions and some other areas of financial planning like mortgages and 'protection' insurance.

What I did not realise then was that a follow-up attack would not be needed to destroy the financial system as – with the benefit of hindsight – we can see that 9/11 was in fact the catalyst for the property boom that led to the sub-prime crisis which caused the 'credit crunch', and the catastrophic economic problems we are facing today.

As a result of their unbridled greed after 9/11, the banks and mortgage companies effectively fired an Exocet missile into the foundations of the financial system weakening them further. And yet despite this costly warning shot, virtually nothing has been done to prevent it from happening again, as the unregulated derivatives market expands and the financial 'tower of Babel' becomes ever more unstable.

'Derivatives' Could Bring the 'Tower' Down

Essentially derivatives are complex financial instruments that derive their value from another asset like shares, commodities, bonds and loans. Derivatives were devised by banks and financial institutions to turbo-charge investment returns in the same way that if you pour petrol on a fire you get bigger flames and more heat.

Derivatives are a relatively recent development that have undermined the world's financial system and made it highly unstable. Trading is conducted – not in things of real value like goods and services – but in money itself. This is a world of illusions where the emotions of fear and greed run rampant and can therefore be highly damaging to real businesses and the real economy on which we all depend, to provide for our daily needs.

> "Derivatives are yet another weapon in the armoury of the power elite designed to relieve the people of their legitimately earned wealth."
>
> – **Kim Andrew Lincoln**

A GOLDEN AGE ECONOMY

The derivatives business can best be described as a giant casino where the amount of money gambled is about twenty times the value of the world's annual production of goods and services.

The multi-billionaire investor Warren Buffett called derivatives 'time bombs' and 'Financial Weapons of Mass Destruction'. And George Soros, the infamous speculator, who made a fortune by forcing the Bank of England to devalue the pound, said of the derivative, credit default swaps: "It is Damocles sword waiting to fall."

> "The power elite regard the people as their servants and an endless revenue source."
>
> – Kim Andrew Lincoln

In 2002 the Bush administration passed the Commodity Futures Modernization Act, which completely deregulated the derivatives market and unleashed a ravenous marauding beast.

> "In a casino they gamble for money, in Wall Street they play for the world."
>
> – Kim Andrew Lincoln

Credit default swaps are one type of derivative that can be explained using the following analogy:

Imagine that not one, but many investors could take out an insurance policy on the same multi-million pound office building that they did not own and collect the insurance value if it burned down. Now this is fine if there are few office fires; but what the insurers are beginning to realise is that these buildings were constructed in such a way that they will easily ignite. No checks are made to ensure that the insurers have sufficient reserves to pay all the likely claims and, unlike ordinary insurance companies, which in the case of a mass disaster payout can turn to re-insurance companies, no such re-insurance exists for credit default swaps. And, as the insured office buildings are all effectively located in the same area, a fire in one can quickly spread to the others and the sum of potential claims could bring the global financial system down.

Insurers suffered massive losses from credit default swaps in 2008. American International Group, the world's largest insurer at the time, had to be bailed out by the US government, and it is alleged – though not admitted – that the collapse of the fifth largest US bank, Bear Sterns, was caused by losses from credit default insurers. And, had it not been for the swift intervention of the Federal Reserve Bank, who lent JP Morgan Chase the cash to buy out Bear Stearns, the financial firestorm I have described might well have already happened.

Derivatives trading is speculation taken to the extreme. All derivatives do is provide an opportunity for financial institutions like banks to make vast profits (or losses) by taking huge risks – invariably with others people's money. It is a something-for-nothing business!

"In a 'Golden Age' economy financial centres like the City of London and Wall Street would not exist as their activities are designed not for the creation of wealth but for its transfer from the people to the power elite."

– Kim Andrew Lincoln

THE WORLD'S MONEY & BANKING SYSTEM IS A GIANT PONZI SCHEME

A Ponzi scheme is essentially a pyramid selling scheme in which a continuous stream of new investors must be recruited at the bottom of the pyramid to support the investors at the top. With our money and banking system, however, it is new debtors (borrowers) that are needed to support the creditors (lenders) at the top. This giant Ponzi scheme that operates in most civilised countries is built on fractional reserve lending, which allows banks to create money (credit) as debt with nothing more than accounting entries on a computer screen. Banks are allowed to lend something in the region of thirty times more than their 'reserves', which means that they are in effect counterfeiting the money they lend.

"All bank loans, meaning all money, is created out of thin air, on computer screens, solely on the strength of the borrower's income, lifestyle and assets. The truth is that banks have very little real money to lend; what they do have is willing borrowers, for in reality it is the borrower that creates the money for the loan but the banks that benefit."

"Banks don't lend you something of theirs they lend you something that is already yours."
                                            – Kim Andrew Lincoln

In this way the banks create about 97% of the money supply. The problem, however, is that the banks only create the principal, and not the interest that is also needed to pay back their loans. This means that the bank must find an ever-increasing number of new borrowers to create enough money to cover the interest on the old loans that make up the money supply.

"Banking's biggest secret is that all the money we have ever borrowed was ours to begin with."
                                            – Kim Andrew Lincoln

The scramble for new borrowers has gone on for so long now that the West has become irrevocably indebted to the bankers' private money cartel. This Ponzi scheme has finally reached its mathematical limits! When the bank's supply of creditworthy borrowers dried up, they turned to uncreditworthy ones who in many cases had no income, no job and no assets. So to avoid losses from default, they moved these toxic mortgages off their balance sheets by repackaging them as mortgage securities and selling them to investors. To persuade investors to buy them, these securities were insured with derivatives called credit default swaps. But the housing bubble itself was another Ponzi scheme and eventually there were no more borrowers to be sucked in at the bottom who could afford the ever-inflating home prices. When the uncreditworthy borrowers defaulted on their mortgages, investors stopped buying mortgage-backed securities and the banks were left holding these babies and nursing a bundle of losses. What most people do not realise is that the economic crisis is not in the real economy, which is fundamentally sound – or would be with proper money and banking system to enable it to run smoothly. No, the problem lies with the fractional reserve banking system itself, which is fundamentally flawed, and has now reached the point where it can no longer sustain itself.

> "Sane people would think that the operation of the fractional reserve banking system was a work of fiction – a carefully crafted novel about financial crime. But when you tell them that it isn't, they are so shocked, so dumbfounded, that they simply don't believe you. This book aims to persuade them otherwise."
> **– Kim Andrew Lincoln**

THE COMMODITIES BUBBLE

When the property bubble burst, the market manipulators moved all the money they had made from it into commodities. Their plan was to pump up prices in oil, precious metals and basic foodstuffs and so encourage other investors to join them in the hope of making a quick killing. Of course, the players always remain in control and will continue to manipulate commodity prices both up and down until they have sucked in as many investors as possible, at which point they will sell out at the top of the market, leaving everyone else to wonder how they managed to lose so much money when prices suddenly collapse.

THE BOND BUBBLE

The Rothschild banking family made their original fortune 'speculating' on the price of government bonds during the Napoleonic wars. To ensure that they always profited from their trading they set up a network of carrier pigeons who flew between the capitals of Europe delivering written news of the winners and losers of each battle. Armed with this 'inside information' they were able to manipulate the bond market to their maximum advantage. In the space of a few years they became the wealthiest and most powerful family on the planet.

It is my belief that there will be a massive bubble in UK government bonds (gilts) and that their rise will coincide with a crash in the money and banking system. My prediction is that as the price of non-guaranteed investment assets like shares, commercial property and corporate bonds fall, pension funds and private investors will be forced to seek the safety and guaranteed returns that gilts provide. There will literally be nowhere else for them to invest their cash, so a tsunami of money could hit the gilts market forcing prices up.

How the Fractional Reserve Banking Came into Being

> "Essentially what banks do is counterfeit money. But to do this they must first create demand for borrowing and what creates the greatest demand for borrowing is war."
>
> **– Kim Andrew Lincoln**

Fractional reserve banking came into being in the UK when the English King, William of Orange, wanted money to build ships to fight the French but could not raise the money he needed from taxes alone because the people would not stand for it. So he entered into an unholy alliance with the emerging bankers of Europe who had started out as the goldsmiths who stored the excess money that people had legitimately earned. They stored the gold in their vaults and realised that they could make money out of lending that gold and charging interest. And since it was very rare that all of the people would demand all of their gold at the same time, they started lending out the money that people had deposited in their vaults, even though it was not theirs to lend. And thus, the kings of Europe were open to the suggestions of the bankers, who suggested that instead of having money that was based on gold or silver – thus the money had an inherent, indigenous value – you created a new type of money, called fiat money that was money by decree, where the king issued a law that this newly created money was now the legal tender, the legally approved form of money in society, and all people had to accept it as payment for goods and services. Whereby, the bankers could create this money and lend it to the king, who could then use it to buy the goods and services needed to finance his war.

> "I believe that Abraham Lincoln was shot – not for his stance on slavery – but for his introduction of debt-free money in the form of the 'greenback', which had it become established, would have wiped out most of the bankers' profits."
> **– Kim Andrew Lincoln**

And so you see now the beginning of a money system, where there is no longer a direct correspondence between the amount of money and the amount of goods and services. There is now a disconnect between the money and something of real value, which means you can now create excess money – money that is not the result of someone multiplying their talents, but is literally created out of nothing by the bankers lending money, charging interest for it, but actually lending more money than they have reserves for in their vaults. Thus, the emergence of the system called fractional reserve banking, which is what the banking system in most of the civilised world is based on today.

> "Nobody knows for sure who was behind the assassination of JFK, but what we do know is that within a few months of his death America was at war with North Vietnam."

> "It is a fact that almost every ill on this planet can be traced back to the bankers and their fractional reserve banking system."
> **– Kim Andrew Lincoln**

INFLATION IS A HIDDEN FORM OF TAXATION

This new money system allowed governments to effectively tax people without them realising it using a 'hidden tax' called inflation. It works like this. In a perfectly 'balanced' economy the amount of money in circulation would always be equal to the value of all the goods and services produced by that economy. Under these conditions the value of the money – or its purchasing power – will remain constant with the money serving only as a means of exchange and as a store of future value.

Provided that there is a direct connection between the amount of money and the things of real value i.e. the goods and services produced, then the economy can grow and people can be confident that if they work harder and/or smarter they can earn more money and the value of their money will not change.

What fractional reserve banking does is pervert this pure money system. This happens because the private banks that create this surplus money disconnect the amount of money in circulation from the value of goods and services being produced. They create too much money that is now chasing too few goods and services. The result is that once all this excess money has worked its way through the system the price of goods and services will rise by the amount of excess money in circulation. So, if you double the amount of money in circulation the price of goods and services may eventually double too. But the government bought what they needed at prices prevailing before the surplus money was brought into circulation, so they get the benefit of the excess money because they bought the goods and services at old prices. The rest of us, though, pay the new price. And so you can see that the difference between the old price and the new price is not only the amount of the price rise (i.e. the level of inflation) it is also the amount of the hidden tax that we have all had to pay that was created by the government, so that they could finance their war. Now governments use this deception to finance anything they want – not just wars.

Fractional reserve banking creates two imbalanced conditions. Firstly, it disconnects the money supply from the things of real value and in so doing steals the value of peoples labour by creating the 'hidden tax' of inflation. And secondly, it imposes an additional tax burden on the people because the interest on government debt is funded from taxation. Both these things make us poorer because they result in a transfer of wealth to the power elite who control and benefit from the money system they created out of their dark desire of greed for power and money. A. M. Rothschild, the most powerful banker on the planet, said that if you allowed him to control a nation's money, he did not care who made the nation's laws, for he knew that the nation could be controlled through the money system.

> "The greatest earthly power is the power to create money and the greatest evil done on earth is the perversion of money, perpetrated by the private banking monopoly."
> **– Kim Andrew Lincoln**

Were it not for new inventions and more efficient ways of working which increase productivity, then the effect of inflation over the last two centuries would have completely destroyed the value of our labour. If you also look closely at the activities of the banks you cannot fail to see that they are primarily engaged in one activity – although it is often disguised – and that is creating mountains of debt on which they receive interest. But now we have reached the point where this imbalanced system is teetering on the verge of collapse.

> "We never elected bankers to run our economy, yet they do so through their control of the money and banking system."
> **– Kim Andrew Lincoln**

FROM INFLATION TO DEFLATION

The 'Credit Crunch' of 2008 was the warning sign that the fractional reserve banking system – that creates excess money and is therefore inflationary – was beginning to collapse under its own weight. The sub-prime lending crisis of that year had bankrupted some of the biggest banks and severely weakened those that survived, forcing them to rein in their lending. And this, in turn, led to a fall in spending by individuals

A GOLDEN AGE ECONOMY

and companies as credit facilities were reduced or withdrawn. And, even though inflation increased – caused in part by commodities speculators – the economic clouds that started to form were deflationary as the amount of money in circulation continued to fall.

As a counter-measure, governments pumped the equivalent of trillions of pounds of taxpayers' money into the banking sector and reduced interest rates to historically low levels. These measures, however, had little positive effect, so the central banks started to print money ('quantitative easing'), in order to redress the shortage of money. Again, the success of this policy has been muted as most of the extra money has been used by the banks for speculative purposes and not for investment in the real economy where it is most desperately needed. Indeed, only about 8% of bank lending is made to fund industry and production.

One effect (intended or not) that quantitative easing is having, and that governments are downplaying, is that as most of this printed money is finding its way into stock markets, it is causing share prices to rise and thus creating the illusion of a general economic recovery – albeit that this 'recovery' is confined to the financial markets. What this means in the cold light of day is that when the next crash occurs, the magnitude of the fall in stock prices will be all the greater as the bubble bursts.

When taken together these policies are no more than a series of adrenaline shots administered to the patient in the vain hope that it will stop them from dying when what the patient really needs is a new heart.

If governments continue to try and resolve the terminal condition of excess debt by borrowing more, there can be only one outcome, and that is the total collapse of the monetary and banking system.

> "If alien beings had wanted to subjugate and impoverish the people of this planet by stealing all their wealth – without the people realising what was happening – they would use the fractional reserve banking system to do it, and the truth is, that that is exactly what has happened."
>
> **– Kim Andrew Lincoln**

THE BIGGEST CRIME OF ALL TIME

AN EXPOSÉ OF 'FRACTIONAL RESERVE' BANKING THAT IS THE ROOT CAUSE OF ALL OUR ECONOMIC ILLS

The biggest secret in the world today has nothing to do with aliens, the unexplained aspects of Princess Diana's death or who was really behind 9/11. The biggest secret is, in truth, not a secret at all, because the information is already in the public domain, but is not spoken about directly, because if it were to become widely known, the grip on power of the financial elite, who control the world through the money and banking system, would be lost and their massive fortunes put at risk.

The purpose of this chapter, therefore, is to bring this information, with a full understanding of how it affects us, into the glare of public scrutiny and debate, so that we have the ammunition to end the tyranny. This is the biggest and most important story of our times. It is the revelation of how the 'fractional reserve' banking system (FRBS) undermines the economy and enslaves the people. In this chapter I explain in very simple terms how the bankers have not only been stealing our money, but how they have also been preventing us from receiving the abundance to which we are entitled by divine law. This scheme for transferring our wealth to the banks is a work of pure genius. It is the greatest Ponzi scheme ever devised and has resulted in its perpetrators amassing fortunes measured in tens, if not hundreds of trillions of pounds. In fact it is so ingenious that we are not even aware that we are being robbed.

This chapter is, in many respects, the most important in this book because once you have read and inwardly digested its contents you will hold the key to understanding how the system works, or more precisely, how it does not work. I reveal how this deception operates so that you can see it for what it really is – a tower of Babel that must fall, if we are to create a Golden Age economy.

Deception One

There Is Lack of Money

The first deception is that there is no alternative policy to the one that most governments in the west started to pursue in 2010, which was to bring in austerity measures that involve massive cuts in government spending and increases in taxes.

The simple truth is that if we abandoned the fractional reserve banking system and replaced it with a 'sound money' system this unfolding economic tragedy could be avoided. If you think about it logically, why is it that that our crumbling schools cannot be rebuilt or our pot-holed roads repaired? It is not for want of the labour, materials or equipment, as we have all of these in abundance. No, the problem we are told is the lack of money. But are the politicians right? Is there really a shortage of cash or is there something they are not telling us? Well, under the fractional reserve banking system that operates in most countries the primary source of the money that we need to cover our daily living expenses and transact business is the private banking network. However, since the 'Credit Crunch' of 2008, the banks have been saying that they have less money to lend because people are defaulting on their loans. But what they are not revealing is that people are defaulting on their loans not because they are feckless, or irresponsible, or incompetent business people, but because the banks who charge interest on these loans are not creating the money to cover the interest payments. Now I am going to repeat that because it is absolutely essential that this point is understood in order to fully appreciate how this aspect of the fractional reserve banking system operates:

THE BANKS DO NOT CREATE THE MONEY TO COVER

The Biggest Crime of All Time

THE INTEREST PAYMENTS THAT THEY CHARGE ON THEIR LOANS.

They create the money to cover the capital, which is the amount that is credited to your bank account when your loan is approved, but they do not create the money to cover the interest, which you have to pay back in addition to the capital. So if you borrow £5,000 on which the total interest is £2,000 the bank only creates £5,000. But you will need to find £7,000 to pay back the loan in full. If this point is still not clear in your mind, I suggest you take a look at a loan or mortgage agreement and see how much the lender requires you to pay them back and then compare that figure with the amount that you were advanced when the loan was agreed. The difference between the two figures is the amount of interest that you will have to pay back, but which the bank did not create and put into circulation so that you could pay it back!

So you can see that this shortage of money must cause problems in the economy, because the banks have – by not creating the money to cover the interest – made it impossible for *all* people to pay back their loans.

DECEPTION TWO

BANKS WANT YOUR MONEY

So why have the banks made it impossible for all people to pay back their loans? Well, it is to create a situation whereby those who are forced to default on their loans forfeit their property (i.e. their real assets like land, homes, shares, etc.) to the banks because that is what the banks really want – tangible assets as opposed to more bank notes, which have no intrinsic value and lose value over time through the effects of inflation. After all, the banks created this 'funny money' themselves out of thin air by making accounting entries on their computer screens every time they make a loan. The reality is that bank notes are worthless pieces of paper that the banks ultimately don't want. The reason banks prefer real assets to bank notes is that the 'fractional reserve' banking system constantly devalues the purchasing power of the money created by banks through the device of inflation – which I will explain later on – whereas real assets will usually hold or even increase in value as prices are made to rise.

How the Banks Create Money

About 97% of the money in circulation today is electronic money, created as debt, in the form of loans, overdrafts and credit cards. The remaining 3% is in notes and coins issued by the state.

In order to create money (as debt) all a bank needs to do is find someone who is willing to borrow money, which, unsurprisingly, is not difficult.

It works like this.

When a bank makes a loan, the amount of the loan is entered on the banks accounts simultaneously as an asset (credit) on one side of their balance sheet and as a liability (debit) on the other. So on the balance sheet the £1,000 loan is regarded as an ASSET of £1,000 – because the loan agreement is a legally binding document that entitles the bank to receive the loan capital back, over a specified time period, plus an additional amount in interest. Now even if the loan is not secured on a particular asset that you own like your house or car the bank still has the legal right to take your property to the value of the outstanding debt in the event that you default – a legal right that is rigorously enforced.

On the other side of the balance sheet the loan is treated as a LIABILITY of £1,000 because there is a risk to the bank that you will not repay all or part of the loan.

The bank's profits come from charging interest on the loans, which, when paid back by the borrower, creates profits that increase the bank's cash (capital) assets. But once the loan is repaid in full the asset and liabilities it generated fall off the bank's balance sheet. So in order to increase their assets and profits banks must keep making new loans. There is another crucially important reason why the bank must keep lending and that is to stop the entire money and banking system from collapsing as started to happen in 2008 – as I shall now explain.

The Biggest Crime of All Time

DECEPTION THREE

THE FRBS IS SUSTAINABLE AND CANNOT COLLAPSE

I mentioned earlier that the banks do not create the money to cover the interest on their customers' loans which in turn makes it impossible for everyone to repay what they owe.

So how can this situation be resolved?

How are you – and everyone else who borrows money – going to find the money to pay the interest if that money was not created in the first place? Well, a rational person would reason that it is impossible to repay that which was not created. And they would be right! However, on a limited time basis only, it has been possible for this flawed money system to operate, because the banks have ensured that by lending more and more money to an ever-increasing customer base (including those with no means to repay) they have created enough 'CAPITAL MONEY' in the system, which people could compete for in order to make their interest payments. 'CAPITAL MONEY' refers to the initial loan amount before the interest element is added. This is the amount of money that the bank actually creates when they credit a loan amount to your current/cheque account.

But we have now reached the point in the UK, and in most other advanced Western nations, where individuals, companies and the state have borrowed as much as they can reasonably afford to repay in capital and interest. You could say that we are 'all borrowed up' as the banks have exhausted the potential pool of borrowers, who up until now have kept the system afloat. This giant Ponzi scheme has reached the point of no return and has over a period of over three hundred years (in the case of the United Kingdom) has started to collapse. This is because the banks are not making enough new loans to keep the supply of 'Capital Money' at a sufficient level whereby it will also cover the interest payments that the banks require (in accordance with the terms of their loan agreements), but do not create.

What started to happen in the west with the onset of the 'Credit

Crunch' in 2008 was that the spiral of ever-increasing lending went into reverse and became negative lending, whereby overdrafts were called in, credit card facilities reduced or withdrawn and loans to all but the most credit-worthy customers denied. And, as the available pool of 'Capital Money' diminishes those people with existing loans will find it even harder to pay their interest, so that an ever-increasing number will default and have their assets seized by the banks. Without a redesign of the monetary and banking system this problem cannot be resolved!.

So, to summarise, we have established how the FRBS creates 'Capital Money' (and not 'Interest Money') and that through a flexible but aggressive approach to lending the private banks have, after being bailed out by the taxpayer, been able to keep this giant Ponzi scheme temporarily afloat.

We also know that the true intent and purpose behind the FRBS is for the banks to acquire an increasing share of the people's real (non-cash) assets when they default on their loan repayments. And that it is impossible to pay back the 'Interest Money' on those loans as the banks never created it in the first place.

DECEPTION FOUR

THERE IS NO COMPETITION FOR THE RESTRICTED SUPPLY OF MONEY

Before I move on to explain how the FRBS steals even more of your money through the 'Profit Multiplier', inflation, deflation and the creation of asset bubbles, I wish to explain the problems that arise from the 'competition for money'.

Competition for money occurs as there is not enough of it to go round because the banks did not create 'Interest Money'. So you can see that usury (i.e. charging interest on loans) is the root cause of the problems associated with the FRBS, because if there was no interest to pay it would be possible – through a system of centralised control – to devise a way for ensuring that there would always be enough money in the system for people to exchange the value of the goods and services produced in the economy.

Another negative aspect of the FRBS is that it creates disharmony between people.

We are forced to compete for this essential resource of money because the banks deliberately restrict its supply. We compete for this money by working as employees or by running businesses so that we can 'win' the money from others in order to pay the loan interest. But this money – that only some of us are able to win – can only come from the pool of 'Capital Money'. So, in fact, if only some people are successful at winning the money they need to cover their interest payments, the rest must inevitably fail. Faced with the prospect of failure to secure a big enough share of that Capital Money to repay the 'Interest Money' due could mean the loss of one's home – or through conflicts about money, one's marriage too, so that families fall apart. It is a sad fact, therefore, that some desperate people will resort to crime in order to fund their loan repayments. So this system sets people against each other by creating an environment of conflict where we are forced to fight each other for the money we all need to pay back the 'Interest Money' that was never created and put into circulation in the first place.

This system is divisive in the extreme!

So, the FRBS works against the interests of the majority who wish to create a society based upon peace and harmony between people. It has a cost to all of us and that cost is met through the taxes that most citizens have consented to pay in order to deal with the social and other costs associated with disharmony in society.

DECEPTION FIVE

THE PROFITS THAT BANKS MAKE FROM LENDING MONEY IS THE DIFFERENCE BETWEEN WHAT THEY CHARGE BORROWERS IN INTEREST AND WHAT THEY PAY IN INTEREST TO DEPOSITORS

We now come to the part of the FRBS scam that allows banks to

A GOLDEN AGE ECONOMY

multiply their profits by lending much *more* than they receive in deposits. Now this plays havoc with the money supply because more (and sometimes less) 'Capital Money' is created than is needed to buy the goods and services produced. When too much 'Capital Money' is created inflation results and when there is not enough, deflation follows.

In the UK, fractional reserve banking started in the early seventeenth century when goldsmiths issued promissory notes (IOUs) for the gold and silver coins that people had deposited with them for safe keeping. After a time these promissory notes came to be treated as real money because people knew that if they took them to the goldsmith he would promise to pay the bearer the amount on the promissory note in gold. So in this way promissory notes became bank notes or paper money – though unlike today's money, this old money was backed by gold and/or silver. However, the goldsmiths soon realised that as everyone did not demand the return of all their coins at any one time they could lend this gold and silver out – even though it was not theirs to lend – and charge interest on it. And they made these loans simply by issuing more banknotes than they had gold and silver in reserve in their vaults. The ratio of notes they issued in relation to the amount of gold they held in reserve is where the term 'fractional reserve banking' originated. So if the goldsmith issued ten times more banknotes than he had gold in his vaults the fractional reserve was one in ten or ten per cent. Of course, this practice was fraudulent, but was later made legal by King William of Orange who granted the concession to the Bank of England on condition that it lent him the money he needed to finance his war with France. The Bank of England (BoE) was set up as a private company in 1694 and has continued to provide finance for the government by buying bonds (aka gilts) on which it receives interest and that interest is paid by taxpayers. The BoE was nationalised in 1947.

However, since the abolition of the gold standard during the course of the twentieth century our money is no longer backed by gold, but is instead fiat money, which is money issued by the decree of the issuer. And this money is effectively worth what the financial markets say it is worth. So in essence what we have now is a system where one bank note supports the value of another banknote and yet both banknotes have no inherent value. Another development has been the advent of the electronic age and the virtual elimination by the banks of notes and coins from circulation. Today 97% of money is electronic money, and this money is nothing more than numbers entered onto a computer screen.

So this very simplified summary brings us to the present version of fractional reserve banking which works like this:

You would think that if banks charge 10% interest on loans and pay 3% interest to depositors their profit would be 7%, but it's not, it's 87%. This is because for every £100 deposited, the bank only keeps £10 in reserve. The remaining £90 is lent out. The borrower takes their £90 loan and deposits it in a bank. The bank holds back 10% (£9) and lends the balance of £81. This process is repeated until the original £100 deposit has multiplied into £900 worth of loans generating £90 of interest. The bank paid out £3 interest on the original £100 deposit so their profit is £87 (87%).

NB: When banks lend money the usual procedure is that once the loan has been authorised the borrower's current/cheque account is credited. As the loan is invariably spent on goods and/or services the cash will not normally stay in the borrower's account long enough for it to accrue interest. This is why, in the above example, the bank pays out so little in interest but makes such huge profits from depositors. The 'profit multiplier' is the 'fractional reserve' element of the FRBS and lies at the heart of all the world's financial problems. It is the cause of the vast inequalities in wealth between the mega-rich and poor and is responsible for keeping most people in bondage to the banks.

*The fractional reserve lending ratio of one in ten used in this example is for illustrative purposes only. In practice the ratios most banks use are much higher. In fact in the UK and the USA there is presently no regulatory limit, which means that the profits banks make from charging interest are substantially higher than those quoted in my example. In reality, however, banks do not need saver's money at all to make loans. All they need is willing borrowers as most money today (97%) is electronic money created out of thin air on computer screens.

A GOLDEN AGE ECONOMY

The FRBS was born with blood on its hands and continues to this day to grow fat on the profits of death. When you look closely into the ownership of armaments manufacturers and businesses that supply the means to wage war you will see that the banks benefit either directly or indirectly from these companies operating profitably. The FRBS destabilises the economy and makes it impossible to control. Historically usury was illegal and with good reason. Only when it is made so again can we create a sound money system and thus the conditions that will allow a genuine and sustainable economic recovery to begin.

> "If you allow me to control the nation's money, I do not care who makes the nations laws because I know that I can control the nation through the money system."
>
> – **A. M. Rothschild**,
> (Founder of the House of Rothschild)

The House of Rothschild were the prime movers in the expansion of the FRBS from its beginnings in Europe and its spread to America and the rest of the world.

> "I believe that banking institutions are more dangerous to our liberties than standing armies. If the American people ever allow private banks to control the issue of their currency, first by inflation, then by deflation, the banks and corporations that will grow up around the banks will deprive the people of all property until their children wake up homeless on the continent their fathers conquered."
>
> – **Thomas Jefferson**
> (Founding Father and 3rd American President)

> "Capital must protect itself in every possible manner by combination and legislation. Debts must be collected; bonds and mortgages must be foreclosed as rapidly as possible. When, through a process of law, the common people lose their homes they will become more docile and more easily governed through

the influence of the strong arm of government, applied by a central power of wealth under control of leading financiers. This truth is well known among our principal men now engaged in forming an imperialism of Capital to govern the world. By dividing the voters through the political party system, we can get them to expend their energies in fighting over questions of no importance. Thus by discreet action we can secure for ourselves what has been so well planned and so successfully accomplished."

– USA Bankers' Magazine, **August 25 1924**

"It is well that the people of the nation do not understand our banking and monetary system for if they did, I believe there would be a revolution before tomorrow morning."

– Henry Ford
(Founder of the Ford Motor Company)

Deception Six

The Govt's 2% Annual Inflation Target Is Beneficial to the Economy and the People

The FRBS deliberately creates more money than is needed to exchange the value of goods and services produced in the economy. This results in inflation. And, as we all know inflation steals the value of our savings and the money in our pockets because as prices rise we are able to buy less.

The most astounding fact is that had we had a sound money system for the last two hundred years, our living standards today would be between **ten** and a **hundred** times higher – and that is a conservative estimate!

Inflation Steals the Value of Our Labour

To put those numbers into perspective, a person on earnings of £25,000 now would, at the lower end of my projection, enjoy the standard of

A GOLDEN AGE ECONOMY

living of someone on £250,000 today and at the higher end a staggering £2,500,000 p.a. Please take a few moments to relate the implications of those projections to your own situation, because when you do, you will understand why I have entitled this chapter 'The Biggest Crime of All Time'

With a sound money system there would be plenty of jobs, stable prices and we would be looking forward to a future of massive and sustainable levels of economic growth in a society where poverty had been eliminated and where all people who wanted to work would share in the country's prosperity.

Inflation is a crime because it steals our wealth, yet it goes unreported, because we do not realise that we are being robbed. Had it not been for our ingenuity in bringing forth new technology, which has kept costs down – inflation would have completely devalued our labour. To understand how new technology raises living standards, compare the cost of today's computer with a similar model bought twelve months ago and it's about half the price. Technology puts money in our pocket because it reduces the cost of making goods like computers and we benefit by having more to spend on other things. Technology may enable one person to do the work that needed a hundred people two centuries ago. Yet we have not reaped the full economic benefit of this technology because it has been largely offset by the effects of inflation.

INFLATION IS PUBLIC ENEMY NUMBER ONE

And, even though the UK government knows how to prevent it – by balancing the amount of money in circulation with the value of the goods and services produced – they insist on maintaining inflation, by having an annual inflation target of 2%. Yet in spite of this target they consistently exceed it, as the 'official' level of inflation (Retail Prices Index) has been nearer 4% over the last twenty-five years. The truth is that governments love inflation because it devalues their debts and stretches their budgets. But they are living in a fool's paradise because with a sound money system – that is operating at maximum efficiency

The Biggest Crime of All Time

– it would be possible to provide for everyone's needs with extremely low levels of taxation.

The downside of inflation for the people with cash savings is that our money is being constantly devalued because we always earn a lot less in interest from money placed on deposit than the true rate of inflation. The present money system was designed specifically to create inflation which is, in effect, a hidden tax that governments use to extract more money from us than we realise. Governments have been using this trickery ever since to hide the real cost of their overspending.

A sound money system, however, would eliminate inflation (and deflation) and enable us to benefit from the massive increases in living standards that new technological advances normally bring, but which have been denied us by the wealth sapping effects that inflation has had on our incomes since the founding of the Bank of England. Another important point to note is that the creators of inflation (banks and governments) benefit from it because with their advance knowledge of the likely consequences of their actions, they can buy the goods and services they need at the old, lower prices, which are the prices that applied before the excess money in the economy caused the price of goods and services to rise. For example, if the banks created double the amount of money that was needed to buy the goods and services produced in the economy, it is certain that prices would eventually double. So those who can buy what they will need now will save, while those who wait will pay more. So if the banks and the government know that their actions are going to cause inflation down the line they can plan their purchases accordingly and thus avoid paying the higher prices that we will all have to pay.

A 'sound money system', however, would ensure ever-rising living standards because the value of money would be constant while innovation and more efficient ways of working would force the price of goods and services down. The gap between the rich and poor would be reduced and poverty eliminated.

A GOLDEN AGE ECONOMY

DECEPTION SEVEN

DEFLATION (AND INFLATION) ARE PART OF THE 'ECONOMIC CYCLE', WHICH WE MUST ACCEPT AS THE PRICE OF DOING BUSINESS IN THE MODERN WORLD

Whereas inflation is caused by an excess of money in circulation, meaning that there is more money than there are goods and services to buy, deflation is the exact opposite. Inflation is an upward spiral of rising prices whereas deflation is a downward spiral of falling prices. Like inflation, deflation is a by-product of the systemically flawed FRBS.

What has started to happen is that because the banks are creating less money, the money supply is shrinking so that there will be less money in circulation than there are goods and services. Eventually this imbalance will force the price of goods and services down. When people see that prices are falling, they will delay spending in anticipation that prices will fall further. This delay will force manufacturers and service providers to drop their prices even more – in order to stimulate demand – and thus a negative deflationary spiral is created. What we have been experiencing with the economy since the 'Credit Crunch' began in 2008 is the beginnings of a massive deflationary spiral that has been caused by the shortcomings of the FRBS and which central banks around the world have been trying to correct by 'Quantitative Easing', which means, in effect, that they are printing more money.

The core problem, as I have said, is that we are all 'borrowed up', so the banks have less and less people to whom they can lend. Their money creation scheme is grinding to a halt, with the result that the amount of 'Capital Money' in circulation is insufficient to cover the 'Interest Money' demands from the banks. This means that there will be an ever-increasing number of people defaulting on their loans. The banks will be forced to keep increasing their provisions for non-performing loans, and the value of any assets they are able to seize will keep falling, as when there is a shortage of money, the price of goods falls and thus the value of cash money rises. What is happening now is that the FRBS is grinding to a

The Biggest Crime of All Time

halt. It is like a train that is slowing down because it is running out of track and like all Ponzi schemes it will run out of time too.

In previous times deflationary spirals have usually followed periods of overheating (inflation) in the economy caused by the banks creating too much 'Capital Money'. To remedy this situation the Bank of England raised interest rates to make borrowing more expensive, so that fewer people took out loans. When this policy worked the amount of surplus money was reduced and inflation fell. The banks can only create money if they have customers willing and able to borrow. And we taxpayers know to our cost that desperate banks will lend to anyone in a bid to keep the system afloat. Banks believe that they are too big to fail and that governments will bail them out rather than let the system fall. Using interest rates to control the money supply is a blunt financial instrument that unless wielded with extreme care and foresight results in either an under or overshoot of inflation or deflation depending on whether or not the accelerator or brake is being applied. It is this constant applying and releasing of the brakes that gives rise to the economic cycles of boom (inflation) and bust (deflation) which have been a constant feature of western economies since the inception of the FRBS. In truth these cycles are unnatural because they are caused by the perversion of money that lies at the black heart of the FRBS. With a sound money system they would simply not occur.

If you hold the view (which our political leaders and bankers do) that inflation is acceptable, then you could say that this 'Monetary Policy' has generally worked over the last thirty years. But that was then. Now, we are in the 'End of Times' era because the FRBS is all 'borrowed up'.

The best example of how devastating deflation can be was the period that followed the Wall Street Crash in 1929. Known as the 'Great Depression' this era was characterised by soup kitchens; mass layoffs of workers, as factories closed for lack of demand for their goods and the mass movement of people in search of work. Unemployment hit 25% in the UK and America. Ordinary people experienced great hardship during this time while the banks busied themselves seizing people's homes and businesses for non-payment of loans. Loans of

A GOLDEN AGE ECONOMY

money – remember – created out of nothing and for which the banks received real assets in return. The 'Great Depression' continued until World War II broke out – an event that was engineered so that the banks could make yet another fortune financing the massively expensive programme of production for destruction.

DECEPTION EIGHT

ASSET BUBBLES ARE A NATURAL RESULT OF THE ECONOMIC CYCLE

When the property bubble burst the market manipulators moved all the money they had made from it into commodities. They pumped up prices in oil, precious metals and basic foodstuffs and so encouraged other investors to join them in the hope that they would make a quick killing. Of course, the players remained in control and continued to manipulate commodity prices up and down until they had sucked in as many investors as possible, at which point they sold out at the top of the market, leaving everyone else to wonder how they managed to lose so much money when prices eventually collapsed.

These are just a few examples of some of the very real scams that the bankers have been able to engineer because of the control over the economy and investment markets that the FRBS gives them.

Since the FRBS began, banks have been lending money to governments, businesses and individuals. They have devised all manner of schemes through which they can lend ever more money to the point where we have become all borrowed up and are sinking under the weight of debt.

DECEPTION NINE

THAT PRIVATE BANKS ARE NOT SUBSIDISED BY THE TAX PAYER

The truth is that most banks on Earth are subsidised by the taxpayers

The Biggest Crime of All Time

of the countries in which they operate. This occurs because governments underwrite the cash balances in their citizens' bank accounts – up to a preset limit. This means that if a bank goes bust the government undertakes to make good the losses up to the limit of their country's protection scheme. In the United Kingdom that limit is the equivalent of 100,000 euros (£85,000), which equates to an annual subsidy to the banking sector of up to £130 billion. In 2010 it was estimated that the banks would have lost £70 billion had it not been for the generous financial support of the UK taxpayer. The amount of tax money pledged every year to support the banks is the same as what is spent on Education and Defence. What makes this worse, is that by not having to set aside this money from their own resources, the banks are free to gamble with it in the 'casinos' of the City of London and Wall Street, through what they call their 'investment banking' arms. Here vast profits can be made but also lost that could send the financial system into meltdown, as would have happened in 2008 had the banks not had a massive injection of taxpayer cash.

"We pay the banks to rob us."

"The banks' funny money scam started to collapse with the onset of the Credit Crunch in 2008. Since then the financial system has been kept alive on the respirator of taxpayer bailouts and back door money printing called 'quantitative easing'.
– **Kim Andrew Lincoln**

The second subsidy that banks benefit from is the right to print money – a colossal concession as 97% of money is created by banks out of nothing – and without them paying a penny for the privilege. Indeed, if such a concession were auctioned today, I suggest that the banks would have to pay licence fees to HM Treasury amounting to many tens of billions of pounds per year.

The power to create money used to belong to the British people, but over the years the banks have ingeniously transferred this responsibility to themselves. The government took this power back in 1844, but since then the banks have figured out a way round the rules as electronic money was not covered by the legislation.

> "The single richest banking dynasty – via its vast and secretive network of international, interrelated businesses, organisations, trusts and foundations, probably controls between a third and a half of the wealth on this planet."
>
> – Kim Andrew Lincoln

A Summary of How Fractional Reserve Banking Destroys Society

It steals our wealth through the creation of excess money, which causes inflation and means we can buy fewer goods and services than we could before the inflation occurred.

It forces people to compete for the shortage of money resulting from the banks not creating the money to cover the interest on loans. This guarantees that because there is not enough money to go round a large number of people and businesses will fail causing unemployment, homelessness, suicides, divorce, family break-ups and crimes of hardship.

It guarantees the systematic transfer of wealth in the form of real assets, like property, to the banks from debtors who default on their loans because the system makes it impossible for all borrowers to repay their loans. This is because only enough money was created by the banks to pay the loan capital – not the interest.

It facilitates the creation of asset price inflation, which enables banks to boost profits from higher lending as people have to take out bigger loans when the price of assets like houses are artificially increased.

It enables banks (through manipulation of the money supply) to make capital gains on repossessed property acquired for nothing, in a recession they created, and later sold at an inflated price in the boom, which again, they created.

It enables banks via the 'profit multiplier' facility to marshal the vast sums of money they hold on behalf of depositors for the purpose

The Biggest Crime of All Time

of manipulating investment markets and thus make huge capital gains.

It creates huge inequality in the distribution of wealth whereby the thirteen richest illuminati families are said in some quarters to own and/or control about 80% of the world's wealth.

It creates disharmony in society as people are forced to compete for money by fair means and foul.

It prevents under-developed nations from rising out of poverty because the burden of interest payments uses up their foreign currency reserves that would be better spent on investing in their development needs.

It ensures that the private banks have effective control of the country, its people and its resources because they control the creation and distribution of the official medium of exchange, i.e. the money that we all need to live.

It forces up the price of commodities like basic foodstuffs so that the poor and those on fixed incomes are made to go hungry. This occurs when the central banks conduct quantitive easing (money printing) which encourages speculation in the financial markets in commodities like basic foodstuffs.

It forces ordinary people to pay taxes that they would not have had to pay had our money been created free of debt. Most taxation is levied upon the people in order to fund the failure that the FRBS creates in the economy.

It forces taxpayers to subsidise banks because of the guarantees that the government gives to savers in the event that the banks become insolvent.

It is a Ponzi scheme and as such will eventually collapse which will cause massive financial dislocation to most people on Earth.

> "To preserve our independence, we must not let our rulers load us with perpetual debt. We must take our choice between economy and liberty, or profusion and servitude. If we run into such debts, we must be taxed in our meat and drink, in our necessities and in our comforts, in our labors and in our

A GOLDEN AGE ECONOMY

amusements. If we can prevent the government from wasting the labor of the people under the pretence of caring for them, they will be happy."

– Thomas Jefferson

SPECULATION & INVESTMENT RISK

"In a casino they gamble for money; in Wall Street they play for the world."

– **Kim Andrew Lincoln**

In the UK the financial regulator, the Financial Services Authority (FSA), was set up to protect the investing public from sharp practice, dangerous products and unsuitable advice in the financial services industry. It regulates banks and building societies; insurance companies; the investment fund management industry; the stock market and financial intermediaries who provide advice and other services to the investing public.

As regulated individuals financial advisers have to be qualified by examination and competent through experience to make investment recommendations that hopefully will prove profitable to their clients over time. Financial Advisers are, if they are to maintain their authorisation to work in the industry, obliged to operate in accordance with certain rules and regulations proscribed by the FSA. The pronouncements of the FSA are law for those regulated by them – even though the FSA is not directly accountable to Parliament for the rules and judgments it makes. And for regulated firms that fall foul of their rules there is no appeal.

Now you would think that an organisation that wields so much power would be able to keep financial firms free of scandal and wrongdoing, but not so; as since the establishment of the FSA the media has been full of stories about the failure and collapse of financial institutions and the loss of investor's money caused in part by poor supervision by the FSA of the biggest firms and its failure to foresee trouble brewing in the wider economy. The cost of regulatory failure to the taxpayer has been hundreds of billions of pounds in bailout money paid to keep the weaker banks in business and the losses so far incurred by the state in taking either full control or a substantial stake in some of our biggest banks.

So why has regulation failed so miserably? Why has it had so little effect in curbing the worst excesses of the banking and investment industry? Why are bank customers and investors still being disadvantaged when the vast majority of regulated firms are operating in accordance with the rules? Well frankly it is because these businesses are working as they were always intended to work and that is to liberate the unwary and the unwise from their wealth. The truth is that the City of London and the other financial centres serve little useful purpose. Most of what they do is, in one way or another, designed to relieve the masses of their money. The entire edifice is built on a sea of illusions that promises everything, but delivers nothing that helps to elevate humankind.

> "If gambling is an illness then the City of London is a very sick place."
>
> – **Kim Andrew Lincoln**

However, having said that, I have some sympathy with the FSA as it is impossible to successfully regulate a financial system that is so systemically flawed and which permits so many of God's Laws to be flouted.

Just imagine how hard it would be for a building regulator to enforce rules pertaining to building construction if they had to enforce a rule that states that the side walls of all buildings must be constructed so that they lean at a certain angle. Such a rule would run contrary to the laws of gravity that state that maximum strength is achieved if walls are built vertically. Now I am not saying that it is physically impossible to construct buildings with angular walls but I do maintain that if the building industry was forced to comply with such rules there would be very serious safety issues and construction costs would soar. Indeed I would venture to suggest that all structures built in accordance with such rules would eventually fall down.

But this is how our financial system has been constructed!

My experience as an Independent Financial Adviser (IFA) during the time that the FSA has been in existence is that the amount of regulation has grown in line with the increasing number of failures in our financial system. In fact the amount of time that IFAs have to spend complying with the rules is so great that clients with small and medium sized investment portfolios are no longer profitable to manage. So in trying to protect investors with a mountain of regulation the unintended consequences are that all but the wealthiest of clients are denied access to the gold standard of investment advice. And if the burden of regulation continues to increase as it has, I can see a time soon when the vast majority of IFA practices will shut up shop because the costs and risks of doing business will be too great.

> "The truth is that you cannot stop investors from losing money because the investment business is imperfect and a million rules and regulations cannot make it perfect."
>
> – Kim Andrew Lincoln

SPECULATION IS THEFT

When you speculate, when you invest money in the financial markets, you are breaking God's commandment, which says: "Thou shalt not steal". Speculation is theft because when you win on the markets it is always at someone else's expense and when you lose someone else gains.

Here's how:

Investor 'B' buys a share from Investor 'A' for £1 and holds that share for 12 months. Investor 'B' then sells that share for £1.20 to investor 'C'. Following a collapse in the stock market investor 'C' panics and fearing great loss sells their share for 0.90 – though it subsequently falls to 0.35.

So who has gained and who has lost?

Well, Investor 'B' made a capital gain of 0.20 by holding his share for a year. Investor 'C' on the other hand sold out at a loss of 0.30 and the investor he sold to also lost because that person held on to the share and it eventually bottomed out at 0.35 and has yet to recover. So they have made an unrealised or 'paper loss' of 0.55.

> "The truth about speculation is that for every winner there is a loser and for every loser there is a winner."
>
> – Kim Andrew Lincoln

When brokers speculate in soft commodities like wheat, rice and cocoa they invariably force up the overall price of food and thus deprive the poor of enough to eat. In March 2011 Kraft, one of the world's largest food manufacturers, estimated that about half of the increase in the price of the foodstuffs it buys could be attributed to speculators who buy and sell commodities but never take delivery.

Since the onset of the Great Recession of 2008 the price of food has rocketed whereas the price of many other goods has fallen. In poor countries as much as 60-80% of people's incomes is spent on food, compared to 10-20% in industrial countries. This explains why food price inflation has such a disproportionately adverse effect on the poor. What makes this situation worse is that the poor are not fully compensated for food price inflation through increases in wages and the indexation of their social security benefits because these increases are usually determined by the changes in the Consumer Price Index, which gives food a lower weighting, as it is designed to reflect price rises for those on average as opposed to low incomes. Over time the cumulative effect of these underpayments has increased poverty to such an extent that we are now seeing food riots in some countries and in the UK young children have been reported stealing food from shops because their parents cannot afford to feed them properly.

Another distasteful development has been that ordinary investors are starting to regard food as a potential investment due to rising demand and falling supply so it is possible that the element of food inflation caused by speculation may well increase if governments do not step in and end this immoral activity.

Another area of the commodities business where speculators have enjoyed rich pickings at the expense of ordinary people is oil.

In serving no-one but themselves professional speculators misqualify energy and create karma because in trying to make money out of money they do not 'multiply their talents' but make their living off the backs of those toil daily to produce the food and the products and services that we all need to conduct life on Earth.

Be under no illusion: the so-called 'investment' banking business is totally ruthless. It takes no prisoners. There is only one rule and that is to make as much money as possible. Tell me how this can be doing unto others what you would have them do unto you? This is definitely not 'doing God's work'.

> "Most investment decisions made by investment bankers are motivated by the deadline by which their next performance bonus is calculated."
>
> – Kim Andrew Lincoln

The power elite use complex financial instruments like derivatives to make inordinate profits for themselves. These instruments are designed to relieve the people of as much of their legitimately earned wealth as possible and are based on the 'something for nothing' culture which is rooted in the power elite's false belief that the people are their servants and an endless revenue source. Essentially their creations are giant honey traps where they use their cunning and guile to tempt the unwary into participating in their elaborate, gambling schemes. The activities of the power elite in financial markets have undermined the financial foundations of society because they are predatory and destructive. The City of London and Wall Street are home to the best examples of the type of businesses that these money changers have created. Before the economic crash the most powerful and predatory of them were known as 'Masters of the Universe'. The truth, however, is that they are masters of deception and the towers of 'Babel' they have built will eventually collapse under their own weight.

A GOLDEN AGE ECONOMY

Assessing Investment Risk

As I write this (January 2011) the FSA is saying publicly that they are not happy with the way financial advisers assess and document their clients' threshold to investment risk and that this may result in unsuitable advice being given. I agree – but for different reasons. Moreover, I suggest that there is no satisfactory method of meeting the regulator's requirements in this respect, as I will now explain. My first point is based on the proposition made by the Ascended Master Jesus Christ, who several years ago stated through his former messenger, Kim Michaels that:

> "There is no argument you can construct by using words that cannot be counteracted by using words."

Jesus is making an extremely profound point here. In effect he is saying that the exclusive use of the written word is inadequate to convey the fullness of meaning, so that in relation to investment risk, words by themselves cannot sufficiently define it, assess it, document it, describe it, quantify it and rationalise it. Indeed there are no words in the English language precise enough to define comprehensively and conclusively all that investment risk is with its multitude of permutations and possibilities. And, as we know that words are open to misinterpretation, the difficulty is compounded when the same word or phrase can mean different things to different people at different times, and in different circumstances. This is especially true when it comes to defining what risk is and an individual investor's threshold to it. My own experience is that one's attitude to risk is a variable feast in that it changes according to personal circumstances and the multitude of external factors that one is confronted with at the time. And there are the intangible factors such as intuition or gut feeling which are hard, if not impossible, to express in words alone. Walking down the street would not normally be regarded as a high risk activity unless of course it is raining hailstones the size of cricket balls and doing so would put your life at risk. Similarly, investing in the stock market during a raging bull market is not as risky as doing so when there is clear evidence of a bear market and your investment horizon is short. One person's risky investment is another person's no risk investment because different people perceive risk differently. It is not sufficient to say that a person is a 'cautious investor' a medium risk or even 'high risk investor' because risk is subjective and relative to other factors that are themselves constantly changing.

A good example of this is the fractional reserve banking system. Here we have a massive privately owned Ponzi scheme that is inherently unstable, difficult to control and destined to fail. Essentially bankers determine what is going to happen in the economy through their control of the quantity of money (credit) in circulation, and this in turn has a huge impact on stock markets. When there is an excess of money prices are bid up and the resultant inflation will have a detrimental effect on the value of fixed interest securities like gilts, whereas when the banks printing presses stop rolling and credit becomes scarce, the prospect of deflation causes conventional gilt prices to rise. The banks engineer these boom and bust cycles to maximise their profits and in so doing the price of shares, commodities, currencies and property are also affected.

So what can an individual investor do to account for the effect that the manipulation of the economy through the money and banking system is going to have on the future value of their investments let alone take account of any direct intervention in the markets by the major players?

"Risk is all about perception but in the main it is completely misunderstood."

– Kim Andrew Lincoln

You could say that what many people would regard to be a no risk investment – i.e. a bank deposit account – is in fact, during these testing times, a high risk investment where there is the potential for significant capital loss. This is because there is not enough capacity within the various national compensation schemes to pay out all claims in the event of severe economic downturn or collapse.

It is also a fact that once money has been deposited in a bank, the bank is both legally and contractually free to do with that money what it wants, which may include reinvesting it in the most risky of ventures that could bring the bank down – as has happened many times in recent years.

As the law currently stands depositing sums of money in a bank in excess of the statutory compensation limits, is, in my view, a high risk strategy because that money will most likely be gambled on 'casino banking' type investments called derivatives that are so dangerous that they have the potential to decimate the world's financial system in an instant. The amounts gambled by banks on derivatives is something in the order of $700 trillion which is a frightening sum when you consider that the value of all goods and services produced on this planet in a year is a mere $70 trillion. By the same token in the current economic environment (2011) I would regard long-dated conventional gilts to be a low risk investment in a scenario where base rates are either falling or a constant and where there is the prospect of long term deflation.

How many self-proclaimed cautious investors bought into the dot.com bubble scam and lost because they thought they could make a quick killing and not lose money because everyone else was doing it. Well, I was one, and it was as a result of losing a large part of my pension fund in 2000 that my whole approach and understanding of the true nature of investment risk changed. It was also at this time that I realised that there is no such thing as free markets, as they are manipulated by powerful players from the world of investment banking, the fund management industry, hedge funds, sovereign wealth funds and central banks. And therefore, it is so often the case that massive fluctuations in the financial markets are not natural, are not 'Acts of God', are not the result of free and unfettered interplay between investor equals, but are in fact the nefarious activities of the market manipulators mentioned above, whose sole objective is to relieve small investors and pensioners of their hard won wealth through the legal but immoral workings of our 'un-free' markets.

Speculation & Investment Risk

Better to Regulate Investment Products

In the United Kingdom it is not the investment products that are regulated but the financial advice that goes with them. So if we do not use an authorised financial adviser but instead purchase our investments and pensions on an 'execution only' basis we are virtually on our own if things go wrong. For only if it can be demonstrated that the advice we received was unsuitable (which is a matter of opinion) can we seek redress for any losses suffered. The exception is where product providers go bust, but compensation is limited, so large investments with one provider will receive little protection. With this system, investment product providers benefit because if their products are found wanting, which is often the case, it is usually the adviser who recommended them that gets the blame and will have to compensate the investor. This, in my view, is unfair because product providers do not always fully disclose how risky their products are. For it is often the case that risk is played down in order to attract more funds, as investors are always looking for the holy grail of low risk combined with high returns. Increasingly investment products use derivatives to mitigate risk but paradoxically derivatives are so risky themselves that even those who design them do not really know the true extent of the risks that investors take. The collapse of Lehman Brothers in 2008 was brought about by massive losses from trading derivatives.

The best financial advisers are those who anticipate events and invest their clients' money accordingly. It is not sufficient to go with the crowd because the crowd is irrational and driven more by fear than facts. But advisers who do have their clients' best interests at heart and do not go with crowd in terms of their investment recommendations run great risks because if they get it wrong the Ombudsmen who adjudicate on clients' complaints will usually make judgements based on conventional wisdom that in recent years has not been wise at all. Furthermore my own experience of Ombudsmen is that they do not have sufficient understanding of investment markets and products to make judgements that would stand up in a court of law. And this is important because financial advisers have no right of appeal.

A better system for investors and advisers would be if the products were regulated so that there would be less doubt as to what investors are buying into. But in order for this to work properly the regulator would have to come clean about how potentially harmful these products are and that people would be advised to avoid them as the financial system is inherently unstable. The FSA would be forced to admit that what it regulates is not fit for the purpose, which I suspect it would not be prepared to do.

The crucial point here is that the monetary and banking system and the speculation business are the primary means by which the power elite control the economy and steal our wealth so they are unlikely to do anything that will expose the inner workings of their systemically flawed and corrupt system.

A Summary of the Risks Investors Face

As I have said, it is impossible to measure risk accurately as there are too many variables to consider – all of which are in a continuous state of flux. These variables include:

Internal Risks

Changing client circumstances – unforeseen changes in a person's financial circumstances may have negative implications for any investment portfolio, if it has to be rearranged in order to cater for the new situation.

Client perception/understanding of investment risk – this is impossible to measure accurately and will always be subjective.

Client investment experience – investors who have only ever done well from investing will tend to have a higher threshold to investment risk than those who have had their fingers burnt.

Client honesty – people do not always tell their advisers the truth and sometimes do not disclose all relevant information. This could cause problems at a later date.

Client intelligence – clients with low intelligence may find the whole business of investing too difficult to understand and thus they may be steered in directions they would not have otherwise have gone had they fully understood the ramifications of what their adviser had recommended.

EXTERNAL RISKS

Product risk – product providers do not always declare the real risk of the products they market to investors.

Currency risk – fluctuating currencies can increase/decrease the real value of investment returns

Inflation risk – inflation destroys the real value of investment returns.

Political risk – economic policies change and this affects markets. Taxes change.

Environmental risk – extreme weather and significant 'natural' disasters will affect investment markets.

Terrorist risk/False Flag operations/Black operations – the markets plummeted after 9/11.

War risk – hostilities usually have negative impact on investment markets.

Adviser risk – financial advisers have varying skills but qualifications are not a substitute for wisdom and/or common sense. Small firms can be more flexible and fleet of foot than larger ones.

Regulatory risk – the way that regulatory bodies expect those they regulate to operate can sometimes be harmful to client interests – especially in times of great financial turmoil when the need for speed is hampered by the burden of compliance. Excessive regulation adds cost, which must be met by investors.

Any assessment of investment risk that takes place as part of the advice process will be a guide at best, and valid only on the day it is done. And any form of words that are used to quantify an investor's threshold to risk is open to misinterpretation. The hard facts are that any sane person who (knowing all the risks involved) contracts with a financial institution that does not give an absolute guarantee that their capital will be returned, in full, at any time, under any circumstances and without loss of purchasing power by inflation, is laying themselves open to a potential capital loss. But having said that it would also be true to say that nothing is safe because the power elite have undermined the foundations of the investment universe with weapons of mass destruction (derivatives) that may yet bring the entire edifice down.

When we speculate in the financial markets we misqualify energy. We may be as wise as a serpent, but when we speculate in the markets, we can never be as harmless as a dove. Speculation is theft by another name.

> "Jesus said: do unto others as you would have them do unto you but his fine words fell on deaf ears in the City."
>
> – Kim Andrew Lincoln

IF THERE WAS NO INFLATION THERE WOULD BE NO NEED FOR SPECULATION

The primary purpose of investing money in the markets is to maintain the value of one's capital against the effects of inflation. Thus, if there was no inflation, there would be no need to invest. This is demonstrated in the following example:

If inflation is 4%, the interest on your investment is 5% and the tax rate is 20%, you would be no worse off than if your investment earned no interest and prices stood still. Moreover, if there was no inflation; no interest; no speculation and our currency was backed by gold, I suggest that not only would our financial system be unassailable but we would have laid the foundations for a Golden Age economy to manifest.

> "The unholy trinity are: **fractional reserve banking, usury** and **speculation.**"
>
> – Kim Andrew Lincoln

Perversion of the Gold Standard

> "In the absence of the gold standard, there is no way to protect savings from confiscation through inflation. There is no safe store of value."
>
> – **Alan Greenspan**
> (Former Chairman of the Federal Reserve)

What has happened on Earth is that the fallen ones and elements from the Laggard races who have incarnated here and who have no Christ consciousness have sought to amass the world's supply of gold, taking it out of circulation, placing it in their vaults and offering us a paper substitute. And yet, even though it is the Christ consciousness of the sons and daughters of God that is responsible for this gold in circulation, it is the fallen ones who have it in their possession, and thus in accordance with cosmic Law, control events upon Earth.

When we accept paper money as a substitute for gold we cut ourselves off from the very necessary cosmic Christ energies that are conveyed to us through the medium of gold by Alpha and Omega. The absence of pure gold in the form of coins used for currency is one of the key reasons why there is such a serious condition in the psychology of men, women and children on Earth today.

The importance of owning pure gold cannot be overstated. For nothing that we could possibly own is more precious, more valuable and more beneficial to our physical and spiritual well being than a piece of pure gold that we wear upon our person.

Gold is the principal weapon that the fallen ones and their cohorts are using to destroy our civilisation. Note that governments around the world have sold off their gold reserves and that currencies of the world are in the main no longer backed by gold. President Richard Nixon took

A GOLDEN AGE ECONOMY

America off the gold standard in 1971 when gold was thirty-five dollars an ounce. Now it is over seventeen hundred dollars an ounce and the value of a dollar has been destroyed through the effects of inflation. The manipulation of the price of gold by the power elite in the banks and finance houses has put our money in their pockets. They have gold and all the power that goes with its ownership and we have worthless pieces of paper that buy less and less each year. In England wherever we go on the high street there is someone who wants to buy your gold, though it is usually for only about forty per cent of the market value.

"They who control the gold control the world."
– **Kim Andrew Lincoln**

What has been perpetrated on Earth is a giant fraud through the printing of money without backing. And, this excess money, of which there is much more in face value than there are goods and services to buy, will surely cause the collapse of the economies of the world, and we in the West and elsewhere will be trapped in this global conspiracy. In the main the power elite are fallen wisdom angels in embodiment who understand the ancient knowledge and know what power the possessors of gold hold – and they have known this all along – and therefore it has always been their plan to separate us from our gold, to keep us down by disempowering us both spiritually and economically.

The economies of the United Kingdom, America and the West have been built upon sand and are now sinking under the weight of their own misqualified energy. So from an individual perspective it is important therefore that we do not compound the problem by adding more floors to the towers of Babel. What we must do is rebuild our personal economies on the rock of the Christ consciousness in the hope that others will follow our example and the process of rebuilding can begin.

Perversion of the Health Care System

> "The vast majority of drugs – more than 90% – only work in 30-50% of the people."
>
> – **Dr Allen Roses,**
> (President of Genetics, GlaxoSmithKline)

The origins of disease can be traced back to the Garden of Eden when Adam and Eve left divine direction and followed the suggestion of the Serpent to partake of the fruit of relative good and evil – the duality consciousness. As a result humankind took all future direction from the ego and thus fell into a state of disharmony and discord, which is what the fallen angels (Serpents) wanted. This is the true meaning of **dis-ease.**

> "The remedy for all conditions lies in the content of our minds."
>
> – **Kim Andrew Lincoln**

In his 'Great Principle of Mentalism', Hermes states that the universe is mental and that all conditions originate in the mind. And so it is with disease, for when we separated ourselves from our divine connection we created a number of false Gods to fill the gaps in our fractured psychology. And one of these false Gods was the pharmaceutical industry, which is as much a tower of Babel as our counterfeit economy based on debt, usury and speculation. Big Pharma represents a lesson we must learn, which is that the secret to perfect health lies within not without. It is the wisdom of knowing that we must look for healing within the God self that resides within our hearts. And when we do, we will be empowered and the fortunes of Big Pharma shall begin to decline.

A GOLDEN AGE ECONOMY

> "Jesus did not write prescriptions but he cured the incurable and raised the dead."
>
> – Kim Andrew Lincoln

The Governor of the Bank of England said in 2010 that of all the ways of running our economy "we have chosen the worse one". Well, that could also be said of our healthcare system as we tackle the outer, physical manifestations of disease, meaning the symptoms, with surgery and drugs rather than dealing with the root cause of the condition, which is in the mind. Modern medicine is more about managing diseases than it is about curing them, as management is more profitable than cure. Drugs are the first call when they should be the last. Greater emphasis is needed on the prevention of disease and this should be taught in medical schools. But if a physical remedy is sought we should first look in nature's storehouse as it contains the cures for most ailments.

Presently, Big Pharma is run almost entirely by dark forces. It is the most profitable industry in the world and a key player in the illuminati's plans for depopulation. Dark forces within governments work hand in hand with Big Pharma to remove and make illegal all competing cures so that there is only one solution i.e. costly pharmaceuticals. But these kill more people than illegal drugs like cocaine. In the USA the Food & Drug Administration (FDA) protects Big Pharma's profits by making it almost impossible for manufacturers of natural remedies to operate and thus competition and consumer choice is reduced. Another trick of the Big Pharma solution to sickness is that these chemical compounds have so many side effects that you need more drugs to deal with the side effects and the side effects of the side effects. This creates an ascending spiral of demand for drugs while patients' bodies become exhausted and stressed from saturation by these harmful substances. Instead of recovering, patients get increasingly sick as the drugs and the disease take their toll on their health and their finances.

> "It is more profitable for a pharmaceutical company to manage a condition with expensive drugs than it is to cure it."
>
> – Kim Andrew Lincoln

Animal Testing

> "You cannot profess to protect one part of life by harming another."
>
> **– Kim Andrew Lincoln**

Another abhorrent practice associated with this industry is animal testing. We are told that testing is necessary to ensure that new drugs are safe for humans to use, but how can this be when many of these products are so dangerous to our health. Of course, the duality consciousness will justify any action no matter how cruel in the name of the so called 'greater good'. Big Pharma says that the ends justify the means, but this can never be because we are all one being and thus harm done to one part of life is harm done to all.

> "A small evil does not serve the greater good."
>
> **– Kim Andrew Lincoln**

What we send out comes back to us so those people involved in this business will create serious karma and will thus find themselves on the receiving end of the pain and suffering they have inflicted on helpless animals at some future point in time.

> "If the believed solution to any problem or condition involves harming any part of life it is the wrong solution."
>
> **– Kim Andrew Lincoln**

A Sick Society Does Not Work

As disease is a manifestation of separation from God it is wholly negative. And in economic terms it has a cost to individuals and society that can be measured by the proportion of our taxes and personal spending that is taken up by it. And even though privately run and state healthcare services employ many people and generate substantial GDP, it is wasted energy because most disease is preventable.

A GOLDEN AGE ECONOMY

In the USA healthcare spending is nearly 20% of GDP and, for every dollar spent on healthcare in America, ten cents is spent on pharmaceuticals. As a financial adviser I know only too well what the true cost of sickness is, as my advice to clients has been to insure against it. But this is dead money, for how much better would it be if that money could be spent on something that raised people up.

HEALTHCARE PRIORITIES

"Psychology not pharmacology is the answer to most disease."

– **Kim Andrew Lincoln**

Doctors are supposed to make patients better not drug companies richer, therefore it would seem to me to be appropriate for the medical profession to consider the possibility that there may be more than one way to cure disease and that perhaps they should start by studying Hermes' seven Great Principles and the teachings of Christian Science brought forth by Mary Eddy Baker. In 1879 this lady established the Church of Christ Science based on the teachings and healings of Jesus Christ. She was the only woman in history to found a major religion and ascended in 1940. In the Ascended Master octaves of heaven she is known as Theosophia, Goddess of Wisdom. Mary Baker Eddy embodied as Mary, the sister of Lazarus whom Jesus raised from the dead. The basic tenet of Christian Science is that all *dis-ease* has its root in the mental body, which means that chemical solutions are unlikely to be 100% effective as Dr Allen Roses of GlaxoSmithKline has so bravely stated. Christian Science has the answers to many of the questions that doctors have been asking through the ages but which the commercial side of medicine has been happy to dismiss for the reasons of the bottom line and other aspects of the fallen angel agenda that are exposed in this book. The Christian Science website is: www.christianscience.com

Perversion of the Health Care System

POISONING BY VACCINATION

What is certain about the vaccine business is that the controversy that surrounds it is as big as the annual sales it generates. In 2010 worldwide revenues were about $25 billion with approximately half of that coming from the USA. From small beginnings vaccines have become one of the most lucrative segments of the pharmaceutical industry.

In his website www.naturalnews.com the health campaigner Mike Adams claims that the criticism and controversy surrounding vaccines is centred on eight key areas:

Vaccines are not proven to be safe or effective.

Vaccines contain dangerous substances – including mercury, aluminium, formaldehyde (declared a carcinogen by the US National Institute of Health) and cancer-causing viruses.

Vaccines cause serious health problems. These are some of the diseases that have documented associations with vaccines: allergies and eczema, arthritis, asthma, autism, acid reflux requiring an infant to take proton pump inhibitors which have many side effects, cancer, diabetes (infant and childhood), kidney disease, miscarriages, long list of neurological and autoimmune diseases, Sudden Infant Death Syndrome (SIDS), and many, many more.

Vaccines can have serious side effects including: arthritis, bleeding disorders, blood clots, heart attacks, sepsis, ear infections, fainting (with reports of broken bones), kidney failure requiring dialysis, seizures/epilepsy, severe allergic reactions, such as hives and anaphylaxis and sudden death. The National Vaccine Injury Compensation Program (NVICP) has awarded more than $1.2 billion in damages to children and adults injured by vaccines.

Vaccines are the perfect medium for the dissemination of poisons designed to control and/or reduce the population.

Vaccine manufacturers and doctors in the US are immune from prosecution and being sued when people are harmed by vaccines. Both are protected under the 1986 National Child Vaccine Injury Act.

Vaccines create a huge market for other drugs to deal with the negative impact that vaccines have on human health.

A Golden Age Economy

Vaccine legislation in the US state of California now allows twelve-year-old children the ability to consent to being injected with HPV vaccines (e.g. Gardasil) without their parents' knowledge. Although HPV vaccines are designed to prevent cervical cancer they are linked to the maiming and even killing of countless children. Moreover, their effectiveness has been questioned in many quarters.

My own view is that following the research into these treatments I will never allow myself to be vaccinated again. As to the thoughts of the Ascended Masters on this subject I will let you draw your own conclusions from this extract from the 'Decree for the Youth' that was published on the Theosophia Is the Way website on 20th February 2011. This website is sponsored by the Ascended Host.

Vaccine Decree

"... Blessed Holy angels, deliver all youth from all dark forces and black magicians! Mighty Astrea, encircle the youth of the world with your mighty circle and sword of blue flame! Encircle the sinister attack on youth and their future through population control, vaccination and the poisoning of their minds and bodies!
I demand and command the binding and the judgment of the entire production and distribution of vaccinations that are filled with toxins and poisons, and all who promote them and attempt to make these vaccinations for children mandatory..."

The Great Cancer Deception

"Cancer is big business and it keeps getting bigger."
– Kim Andrew Lincoln

The market for conventional cancer treatments is about twice the size of the vaccine market and is one of the largest and fastest growing in the pharmaceutical industry. 1 in 2 men and 1 in 3 women are now expected to be diagnosed with some form cancer in their lifetimes. It is my belief, based on comments made by the Ascended Masters relating to the primary cause of cancer, that the rise in its incidence is directly related to the increase in the use of environmental poisons and the adulteration of our food with toxic chemical compounds. Thus cancer is a disease that has largely been created by the power elite, meaning that it is a part of the fallen angel agenda to depopulate our planet and therefore I do not expect the pharmaceutical industry to come up with a cure for cancer anytime too soon as it is far more profitable for them to manage the condition than eliminate it.

> "There is already a cure for cancer, it's just that most people have not yet realised it."
>
> – Kim Andrew Lincoln

What I do see happening, however, is a big increase in alternative forms of cancer treatment that, unlike chemotherapy, radiotherapy and surgery, are not harmful and have no side effects, such as the antineoplastons treatments that have been pioneered by Dr Burzynski at the Burzynski Research Institute in Houston Texas. This treatment has caused brain tumours to vanish in children and has been successful with many other cancers afflicting both young and old. Antineoplastons are unique protein chains made from amino acids. But there are many other types of treatment out there including the use of herbs, supplements, dietary protocols and heat treatments that have proved to be effective but which the medical mainstream in the UK and USA have dismissed because of the hold that the pharmaceutical industry has over doctors and politicians alike.

Looking for a cure for cancer is certainly one side of the coin, but the other is prevention, which means stopping the use of poisons altogether. But the light is strong and it is penetrating through the energy veil (evil) and therefore I have no doubt that this global conspiracy will be dealt with as the cracks are already appearing in the establishment's wall of lies as the truth comes out.

I wish to thank the 'Health Ranger', Mike Adams of

A GOLDEN AGE ECONOMY

naturalnews.com whose sterling work in exposing criminal activity in this area has opened my own eyes and caused me to re-evaluate my whole approach to food and healthcare. I recommend www.naturalnews.com as a good starting point for anyone who wishes to learn more about the points raised in this chapter.

GLOBAL WARMING & FREE ENERGY

The Ascended Masters tell us that Earth was designed to support ten billion souls and yet there are vast tracts of land in the northern hemisphere incapable of supporting human life because it is too cold. This poses the question of whether it is part of the divine plan for this planet to warm up so that those areas that are not presently suitable for human habitation become so.

I believe that the argument of whether or not carbon fuels are responsible for global warming is the wrong argument, and that what we should be debating now is how we can best conserve our planet and how we can most effectively channel our energies and resources into the search for free, sustainable and harmless energy sources. I am convinced that if we make a determined effort to stop polluting the ecosystem with unclean and dangerous fuels that upset Earth's balance and deplete its resources, then our sincerity will be recognised and our calls for help will be heard, and the Ascended Host will release (through the right people in embodiment) the technology that we need for the cheap and clean energy that will power the new Golden Age economy.

Coal, oil, gas and nuclear power are the energy sources of the Dark Age we are leaving behind, as the Golden Age of Aquarius takes its first steps into our consciousness. And whilst I accept that there is great resistance to change from the power elite who are still reaping huge profits from these demon fuels (of which oil is preeminent) there is urgent need for change for the sake of our health, our wealth and our planet.

Oil is used as an economic weapon. Our dependence upon oil has been the cause and excuse for too many wars. Oil is a commodity and source of inordinate profits for speculators and oil companies. Oil is used as an economic tool to transfer wealth from the oil-consuming nations to the oil-producing nations and the multinational oil corporations. According to *Fortune* magazine in 2011, five of the top ten largest corporations in the world are oil companies. They are Royal Dutch Shell; Exxon Mobil; BP; Sinopec Group; and China National Petroleum. If we were able to stop using oil we would remove a major hold that the illuminati has over our lives and our economy.

I believe that the truth behind the global warming lobby is that it is a smokescreen for raising taxes. The power elite have no genuine interest in saving the planet – in fact, quite the opposite – but what they do want is to make us think that they care, and that they are green as this distracts us while they carry on polluting. Let's face it, levying tax on the burning of carbon-based fuels is a clever idea if you can make people believe (through false science) that incinerating carbon is the cause of global warming. If governments had a genuine desire to reduce carbon emissions they would have made it possible for clean energy sources to be developed in ways that only governments can, but they have not, and so solutions that were invented over a century ago were strangled at birth so that carbon kings like the Rockefellers (Exxon Mobil) could grow rich and powerful at our expense.

Alternative Energy Forms

One of many of the power elite's secrets in this area has been their suppression of the development of alternative sources (e.g. radiant energy) that are cheap and pollution-free. In the UK today about 20% of people are living in fuel poverty, which means that they are forced to spend more than 10% of their incomes to heat and light their homes. Consequently there is a pressing need for clean and cheap fuel yet governments have done little to encourage its development. Their answer has been to wed us to wind and solar power, which are even more expensive and, in the case of wind, much less reliable than existing carbon based fuels. With nuclear power the situation is even worse. Despite clear evidence of the dangers of nuclear power from the Fukushima disaster, the UK government is still recklessly planning to allow an expansion of generating capacity, even though it is the most expensive and potentially lethal of options and the Germans are decommissioning their nuclear plants.

The consequence of this unenlightened energy policy is that domestic energy consumers are being held to ransom by the energy suppliers who are effectively running a cartel. And this injustice is compounded by the regulator who allows them to keep raising their prices, and by successive governments who have failed to protect the interests of the people they are supposed to represent.

As we know everything in the universe is made of energy and thus it should be possible to devise a method of inexpensively harnessing some of this energy in a way that is not harmful to people or the environment.

RADIANT ENERGY

Nikola Tesla was the 'Einstein' of electricity whose brilliance made him so many enemies that after his death the power elite tried to erase him from history. Yet his genius gave us the Tesla Coil found in every TV set and his pioneering work in wireless communication was such that when Marconi made the first transatlantic transmission he was using seventeen of Tesla's patents. Radar, microwave ovens, fluorescent lights and electric motors were invented by Tesla. And when he introduced Alternative Current (AC) it shook the establishment to its core because his AC-powered machines were much more efficient than DC ones. So to discredit him DC power advocates claimed that AC was hazardous to human health. Moreover they tried to perpetuate this lie, by using AC generators to discharge death sentences in New York State. And though they were unable to kill AC technology their efforts did put an end to Tesla's radiant energy research. A century ago Tesla discovered how to harness the sun's energy by converting the ambient temperature of the air into mechanical energy. He documented the entire method and resolved many of the practical issues but the power elite prevented him from completing the work. His 'self-acting' engine is a fuelless power plant capable of producing energy anywhere and at any time. And now a hundred years later others have finally achieved what Tesla was not allowed to finish.

A GOLDEN AGE ECONOMY

Other types of engines that have been developed include those that use hydrogen and magnetic energy as their power source, but none come close to the one that powered the last Golden Age and that, if we play our cards right, could just as easily power the next.

Crystalline Energy

The source of power to which I refer is not entirely unfamiliar as it has been used in modern times, though in modest ways, and this is the energy that comes from crystals. This energy source is currently in watches and (crystal) radio sets but tens of thousands of years ago it was the primary power source in the highly advanced civilisation of Atlantis. What is little known about crystal energy, however, is that apart from being natural, free and harmless, it has other attributes that are beneficial to our spiritual, mental and physical wellbeing. I will be returning to this subject in Episode Three.

Globalisation & International Trade

I believe that trading between peoples and nations is an essential part of the collective divine plan, because it is through international trade that we learn about ourselves and people from different cultures and this helps us to become more enlightened. In the last forty years, however, a new type of economic exchange between nations has evolved that is wholly motivated by greed and threatens social cohesion – particularly in the mature economies of the West. I am talking about globalisation and the practice of multi-national corporations proactively seeking to produce their goods and services in the lowest cost location. This causes jobs lost in higher wage countries to be transferred to those places with the lowest wages, poorest working conditions and least worker rights. For Industrial conglomerates, it is increasingly the case that production is being shipped out to areas where there is scant regard for environmental protection and worker safety. As a tour of the ex-steel-making towns of Ohio (USA) and the industrial wastelands of the West Midlands (UK) will prove, these policies destroy communities and place huge burdens on the taxpayer, who is left to foot the bill for the unemployment, crime and social deprivation costs that result.

"The price of cheap Chinese shoes is the West's lengthening dole queues."

"When low prices are achieved by paying low wages, workers are exploited by employers and consumers."
— **Kim Andrew Lincoln**

In an enlightened free enterprise system it would be unthinkable to allow one group to benefit at the expense of another because under the

A GOLDEN AGE ECONOMY

Great Principle of Cause and Effect, "As ye sow so shall ye reap", which in practice means that the exploiters can expect to experience what it is like to be exploited.

> "The oppressors will become the oppressed."
> – **Kim Andrew Lincoln**

As consumers we become party to this oppression when we buy the goods and services of companies who are known to exploit workers, either at home or abroad, or that operate in a manner that is detrimental to the planet or any part of life. We can avoid creating karma by making every effort not to do business with such companies. When one country exports goods to another country at prices that are lower than the importing country can produce them – because the exporter is paying its workers lower wages than the importer – the importer would be right to impose an import duty to close the price gap in order to protect both the jobs of the workers in their own country and the wages and conditions of the workers in the exporting country. And, by the same token, when one country deliberately manipulates the price of its currency to give itself an unfair trading advantage, other countries would be within their rights to protect their own producers by imposing a 'balancing levy' on the guilty parties' imports.

If all countries adopted a code of ethics to enforce fair trading in the manner described above, then the economic dislocation and consequent social problems that trade imbalances cause could be avoided.

> "Free trade does not mean the freedom to exploit others."

> "There is no virtue and benefit in trade that is not conducted in accordance with the laws of fairness and natural justice."
> – **Kim Andrew Lincoln**

When there is consideration in commerce, when we treat others as we would like to be treated, we open the doors to the storehouse of abundance that our Creator wants us to have. This means that not only shall we receive more material riches, but also that we can spend less time working and have more time to do the things that truly make us happy.

Competition between companies is to be encouraged as this is the primary motivator for the innovation and invention that ultimately leads to increases in our standard of living and eliminates want and poverty in the world. Businesses that ignore the need to transcend themselves through a continuing process of improvement will be left behind and eventually disappear.

The imposition (by international agreement) of tariffs on traders and nations that do not conduct themselves in accordance with God's Laws is a measure of last resort that should be intended to correct errant behaviour when all other means of persuasion have been exhausted. It is not a weapon that can be deployed to support industries that are inefficient, because their owners have failed to innovate or to 'subsidise' States with dark agendas.

If there is any attempt to inhibit trade by unjust means, trade wars will result and we will all be poorer.

Consumerism

> "Consumerism is enslavement to the things of this world. It can only perpetuate suffering as all desire is suffering when you are attached to your desires."
> **– Kim Andrew Lincoln**

As the Aquarian Age begins to blossom, I believe that we will transcend our desire for a wholly consumer-based society to a more spiritual one, and thus enable abundance in all its forms to fully manifest. An enlightened society is one where we spend more of our time doing the things that make our hearts sing, and less time providing for our basic needs.

> "An enlightened society is one where our days are filled with joy."
> **– Kim Andrew Lincoln**

The Perversion of Music

"Every discordant condition on this planet could be dissolved and consumed by the right kind of music."
- **Beloved GODDESS of MUSIC**
(through the Messenger Edna Ballard 16/1/1944 Chicago, Illinois, USA)

In October 2007 I attended a spiritual workshop in England, organised by two messengers of the Ascended Masters, one of whom was Lorraine Michaels, whose writings and websites I have referenced many times in this book. During this four-day conference Lorraine gave a lecture on the misuse of rhythm in music by the fallen angels. These were the angels released from the bottomless pit by the Lords of Karma in the middle of the twentieth century, many of whom later embodied on Earth and became musicians during the explosion of pop music culture of the swinging sixties that started in London and America's West Coast. As a musician and songwriter myself, who was part of the progressive rock music scene in North London in the seventies and early eighties I found the truth of what Lorraine revealed during her lecture to be very distressing. Quite frankly I did not want to believe her, though I knew at an inner level that she was right and ever since that time my whole approach to music has completely changed – for the better. In 2010 I decided to write a song to explain to others what I have learnt on this subject, which you can read for yourself in the Ballad of Voodoo Rock below. And, for anyone who wishes to learn more about the science of music I strongly recommend David Thame's seminal work, *The Secret Power of Music*.

In economic terms pop and rock music and the youth culture that goes with them are big business. But what is so important about music is that it is inordinately more powerful than the money it generates…

THE BALLAD OF VOODOO ROCK

This tale begins in heaven
Before the angel wars
When elevated some became
Above God's love and laws.

Mighty angel Lucifer
Rebellion did lead
He thought he was too great to serve
God's co-creator's needs.

The Serpent, pride, had risen
One third thought they knew best
That God was right to grant free will
These angels vowed to test

So raged a war in heaven
For service and free will
Though always was the outcome known
So strong was Michael's will.

With Lucifer defeated
His regiments cast down
The battle moved to planet Earth
Where continents would drown

Destruction of the manchild
By sound these angels schemed
For science has so proved today
The harm some sounds can be.

A GOLDEN AGE ECONOMY

Their plan went into action
Two Continents laid waste
Lemuria and Atlantis
Wrong rhythm did erase.

These crimes called for their binding
Archangels did the deed
Into the bottomless pit they cast
This Illuminati seed.

One thousand times eleven
In years from then to here
The given time for man to learn
How not to live in fear.

Great masters have been teaching
Through scripture to this day
And God sent beautiful music
What's good for us to play.

Sacred music was released
The music of the Spheres
The Classical great composers
God wanted us to hear.

They showed us proper rhythm
Pure light and harmony
In words and sound, perfection
So balanced we could be.

They hoped we would not follow
The songs of those returned
Dismissing their destructive sounds
That we could now discern.

The Perversion of Music

The Lords of Karma ordered
So from the pit they came
As Revelation prophesied
The sun went dark again.

Embodying like humans
To Earth the Fallen came
Locusts with the scorpion's sting
To 'rock' the light again.

The fifties saw their songs re-sung
The King was in the lead
Then the boys from Liverpool rose
On smoke and acid dreams.

Soon 'metal' bands found favour
The hordes of heavy rock
Perversions, drugs and alcohol
Their armoury of stock.

Songs of anti-love the norm
Distort the Mother light
Add to the sum of all our fears
With words of death and spite.

Satan adored with song decrees
Those two-horn-fisted signs
An invitation to be served up
To forces serpentine.

The sound that rocks the cradle
That makes the babies cry
These sounds of such disharmony
God's light misqualify.

A GOLDEN AGE ECONOMY

The sound that rocks the rhythm
The syncopated beat
Can make souls lose their reason
For being – and their peace.

This devils tool of rhythm
Based on the voodoo beat
The source of jazz, rock, rap and pop
That's played on every street.

Though voodoo rock may feel good
It fools you like a cheat
For pleasure gained your light is drained
Small fix for big defeat.

When rhythm is distorted
By 'rocking' of the beat
The pleasure comes from light built up
That's suddenly released.

This takes place in our chakras
Those seven discs of light
That round our spinal column spin
Without which there's no life.

'Rock' concerts serve a banquet
Where demons go to feed
These vampires of the spirit
To live our light do need.

The 'Fallen' knew this science
How it could win the day
They sold us drugs and rock 'n' roll
To steal our souls away.

The Perversion of Music

Their Earth war won – not certain
Their judgement – it will come
The question is what choice we make
We 'Children of the Sun'.

Fear ye not who've heard or read
This truth we do reveal
For we have taken of this fruit
As once it did appeal.

Take this ballad to your heart
Consider carefully
And trust that God in you will play
The Final Victory.

Chorus

So how do they 'ROCK' the rhythm?
By stressing the weaker beat
Not the first one of the measure
But with the lesser they defeat
In a waltz the time is three – four
With the accent on ONE, two, three
Now turn it around and you're 'rocking'
As the last beat is stressed heavily.

© COPYRIGHT 2010 **KIM ANDREW LINCOLN**

The Perversion of Religion

Rather than write a long dissertation on the perversion of Christianity and other faiths by the fallen angels in church hierarchies I have encapsulated my thoughts in a song that extends to less than six hundred words.

DEN OF THIEVES

They say they love Jesus, these preachers of lies
You stole from his truth and his message did hide.

Emperors and Bishops, the power elite
The mission of Jesus, you trod under feet.

These words an indictment, your record of shame
So all who love Jesus, will know of your game.

Their falsehoods enslave us, our minds they control
It's time to abandon, the blinds of their fold.

Called is their judgment, for blasphemy done
Our Mothers' decreed it, and so it will come.

Her statues blood crying, are saying to all
Break out of this prison, climb over the walls.

For, the Kingdom of God, seek not in their church
As it lies deep within, your heart you must search.

The Perversion of Religion

Right from the beginning, was made the offence
So much was omitted, the message lost sense.

The intent was unholy, it seemed right to man
The motive was power, control of the land.

They made Jesus a God, thus set him apart
So we would not follow, in time with his heart.

Consider the 'Council', of three twenty-five
In Nicea the truth, was buried alive.

No, Jesus was human, with lives here before
A spiritual teacher, who lifted God's Law.

He came to enlighten, to raise us all up
To all of God's children he offered his cup.

He set an example, good works he did do
With compassion he healed and judgment passed too.

He said God is the doer, who lives in us all
To walk with your Father, step up, do not fall.

Two centuries later, another nail hit
Empress Theodora, more crimes did commit.

The Laws about Karma, you 'reap what you sow…'
Were not to her liking, so she struck the blow.

Her power, influence and deadly resolve
Buried reincarnation, deep in the cold.

Many gospels were 'lost' by thieves of the day
But some of those hidden, have found light today.

A GOLDEN AGE ECONOMY

The truth is emerging, the records of shame
Ego illusions, the duality game.

The 'Born Again' movement, that Luther did start
Another distortion, that keeps us apart.

Superior notions and spiritual pride
The reason for conflict, that binds and divides.

And so is the story, with other faiths too
From the East to the West, more lies the world through.

Look unto to Mecca, the truth did not hold
Jihad in the gospel – demons in the fold.

The children of Moses, were chosen they thought
More equal than others, the line that they bought.

But none are more special all equal are we
For God does not favour, we earn victory.

Belittled were women, this case we do make
The bishops were fearful, their power at stake.

The disciples were men, except Magdalene
The twin flame of Jesus, no text doth proclaim.

She was most beloved and thirteen did make
Her light shone the brightest, this truth no-one spake.

Open the archives, in Rome they do lay
In Vatican City, the truth none will say.

Delay builds your karma; it's time to come clean
Conspiracy over, act now and redeem.

The Perversion of Religion

The sands are a-shifting, our structures do shake
All houses divided and so they will break

Restore our Lords teachings and end all your games
Kneel or be summoned to the Court of the Flame.

Chorus

Blind leaders of the blind
Into the ditch ye shall fall.
When you follow the ego
You find nothing at all.

© COPYRIGHT 2007 **KIM ANDREW LINCOLN**

Some Thoughts on Atheism

When people say: "if there was a God, he would not let his people suffer so", I say that God gave us free will and the guidance of his laws, which we could choose to obey or not. What we have been seeing on Earth is the results of those choices.

—

Even the fallen angels – the forces of anti-Christ – believe in God. For they knew that when they rebelled against God's Will and fell to Earth as a consequence they would no longer receive the life-sustaining flow of God's light into their beings, but would have to take that light from God's children – his light bearers on Earth – by tempting them into sin, so that their light would be forced from their chakras, so that the fallen ones could drink it in like vampires feeding on the light of man. They knew that God had given them a limited time to either continue their rebellion by destroying mankind or to repay their karmic debt with good deeds. And they knew that they would be called for judgement to the Court of the Sacred Fire on the God Star Sirius and that the unrepentant would surely die in the second death that awaits both angels and human beings who continually refuse to bend the knee to the Lord God Almighty beloved Alpha and Omega.

—

It is not the food in our bellies or the blood in our veins that sustains our beings; it is the light of God, which is the love that our Creator has for of all his creation.

Some Thoughts on Atheism

—

Duality is an illusion – there is no such thing as relative good and evil. All that is good comes from the heart of God and all that is not comes from somewhere else.

—

What is not of God has no reality, and therefore it cannot endure.

—

Some people call themselves atheists because they are angry with God for what they mistakenly think he has done or not done, while others are so confused by the staggering amount of misinformation and chaos in this world that they don't know what to believe.

—

Some people think that things will never be right on this planet because people are inherently bad. I believe that human beings are inherently good because we were created in the image and likeness of God – who is wholly good. What was not good was the rebellion of some of God's angels who for eons have sought to destroy us and our beautiful planet, Earth.

—

Don't blame God for the ills of this world; look instead to the fallen angels: Lucifer and the wisdom angels who followed him, Satan and his seed, the Watchers and the Serpents who fell from heaven to wreak havoc on Earth. But look also to that other deceiver, the ego, for truly it is the serpent within.

WAR IS

War is what happens
When we lose our way
War is the ego
Prolonging its stay.

War is the darkness
We came to dispel
War is a nightmare
An Earthly-made hell.

All war is Civil
For Brothers are we
Sisters and parents
Have no enemy.

War is the ego
The lower self's voice
The liar we let in
When given the choice.

War is for business
Despicable team
Destruction, production
The devil's own scheme.

War is no answer
When none can be found
Bankers finance it

War Is

Their interest compounds.

War is a banquet
On which demons feed
All courses our light is
Our fears what they need

War is for power
Control of the land
People and planet
That Lucifer planned.

Chorus

War is for Profit
War is for greed
War is the spawn
Of the anti-Christ seed

© COPYRIGHT 2007 **KIM ANDREW LINCOLN**

Some Thoughts on Politics, Politicians, People Power & the Economy

"Politics is about the illusion of difference."
– **Kim Andrew Lincoln**

The root cause of all our economic problems, the cancer that is eating away at the tree of our economic life, is the money and banking system based on debt. Everything else that is wrong with the economy is a symptom of this diabolical disease. The truth is that the British State has had a love affair with bankers ever since they got into bed together in 1694. This was the year that the Bank of England was founded and the systemically flawed practice by banks of lending out more money than they had in deposits (fractional reserve lending), was given the royal seal of approval. Politicians give the impression that they are angry with bankers for destroying our economy and stealing our wealth but under the surface the bond of love is as strong as ever. Politicians have the power (through the will of the people) to end the vice-like grip that the private banks have over our economic life, but even now, when the evidence is so strong of the harm that fractional reserve banking does, our political leaders still bow down and kiss the hand that feeds them. Never was a divorce so much in the public interest as it is today.

"We are slaves to a debt-dependent system."
– **Kim Andrew Lincoln**

If politics is the art of the possible then all incumbent and prospective politicians should know that they will find it impossible to solve their country's problems until 'fractional reserve' banking is replaced with

Some Thoughts on Politics, Politicians, People Power & the Economy

a sound monetary system that is backed by gold.

All politicians say they want change – if only they meant 'change for the better'. Politics is a business. We pay politicians to meddle in our affairs and then at the end of the year they submit a bill for the mess they have made. But the trouble is that the mess and the bill keep getting bigger. What amazes me most is that when politicians are spending their own money they are usually quite wise, but when it's other people's money probity and prudence go flying out of the window.

Politics is irrelevant while the private banks control the creation and distribution of money. The essence of our political and economic system is that politicians distract us with policies of no importance, while the bankers steal our wealth. When governments start to put the interests of the people above their own, real prosperity will follow. Until that time the mature economies of the world will continue to falter and fall.

> "What differentiates the policies of the two main political parties is that we shall achieve financial oblivion faster with one than the other."
>
> **– Kim Andrew Lincoln**

Information is power, which is why politicians spend so much of their time and our money trying to keep it from us. However, the internet was invented to provide the people with a passport to free, uncensored information. The powers in heaven made this possible; so we must not permit the power elite to undo the good work that they have done. The truth is that fear is a tool that governments use to control people and stop them from finding out the truth. FEAR = False Evidence Appearing Real.

> "Politicians raise the flag of freedom at election time and take it down in office."
>
> **– Kim Andrew Lincoln**

A GOLDEN AGE ECONOMY

PEOPLE POWER

"The Ship of State floats on the Sea of the People. If the State makes the People angry the ship will be tossed about and may sink."

– Kim Andrew Lincoln

The strength of a pyramid lies not with its capstone but the blocks of stone beneath. Remove the capstone and the pyramid remains; take away the supporting stones and the capstone will come crashing down. Politicians take note, your power comes from the people and that which is given, which is not so easily earned, can so easily be taken away.

If the top ten per cent of the most spiritually enlightened people on Earth today were to demand that their countries be governed in accordance with the God's Laws, as opposed to man's laws, the middle eighty per cent of people would support them, and, within a very short time, there would be a Golden Age on Earth.

"The wealth of the western world has been built on the bones of a billion slaves."

– Kim Andrew Lincoln

Consider the real reason why US citizens were given the right to bear arms in the Constitution? Was it to protect white men and women from marauding Indians or was it to prevent the power elite within the institutions of State from overreaching themselves and replacing the tyranny of rule by a British King with the tyranny of a Big Brother state as so chillingly portrayed by George Orwell in his seminal work of prophecy, *1984*?

"The most important function of government is to protect the individual liberties of its citizens most governments, however, do the exact opposite."

Some Thoughts on Politics, Politicians, People Power & the Economy

"The power to control events rests with the people. Politicians keep forgetting this. We must remind them at the next election."
– Kim Andrew Lincoln

We were created in the image and likeness of God; therefore, we are the children of God. We have the POWER of the threefold flame of God Power, God Wisdom and God Love burning within our hearts. We have the POWER to change the world. We have the POWER to create Heaven on Earth. We have the POWER to cast out the dark ones and their darkness, the evil doers and their deeds. We have the POWER to end ALL tyranny and oppression. Now is the time to use that POWER for good.

The Perversion of the European Dream

"With any new legislation the devil is always in the detail. In the EU, however, the devil is everywhere."

– Kim Andrew Lincoln

The idea for a United States of Europe came from the Ascended Master, Saint Germain, who had used his considerable skills and influence to ensure that the United States of America was set up in accordance with its divine plan. Indeed, it was America's destiny to become the example that new and emerging nations might follow so that they would be best placed to benefit from the significant advances that the Aquarian Age will bring. In addition to sponsoring the United States of America, Saint Germain is the hierarch of the Aquarian Age, as Jesus Christ was the hierarch of the Piscean Age that has just passed. The Age of Aquarius will span the next two thousand one hundred and fifty years. It is also called the Golden Age of Freedom – as Saint Germain holds the spiritual office of the God of Freedom. This incoming age of freedom, peace, enlightenment and universal love can also be referred to as the Golden Age of Saint Germain.

In order to do for Europe what he had done for America, Saint Germain sought the cooperation of Napoleon who, at the time, was the predominant military and political power on mainland Europe. Napoleon, however, had an altogether different agenda and was not prepared to accommodate Saint Germain's plan for achieving an enduring peace. So followed two hundred years of the power elite playing out their petty rivalries and ego games, egged on by the banking houses who went on to make vast fortunes financing the carnage from the countless wars that ensued. This was a period of unprecedented tyranny, butchery and genocide, which concluded at

The Perversion of the European Dream

about the same time the EEC was formed. This is not to say that with the establishment of the EEC human kind had found an antidote to war – far from it – as the terrible events in Bosnia subsequently proved; no, my assertion is that the power elite's agenda switched from warmongering for profit, to doing the groundwork that they believed would be necessary to achieve their ultimate objective. Whereas Saint Germain had envisioned a United States of Europe as a brotherhood of nations coming together for the common good and for the advancement of commerce, the power elite saw it as springboard on which to move closer to their goal of world domination with a single currency and one-world government at the heart. The horrors played out in the world wars were the justification for the creation of the League of Nations and its successor the United Nations, and later the European Economic Community (EEC). Having deliberately started these wars the power elite then presented their solution for a permanent peace through the offices of the UN and EEC – though their real intention was that these bodies should be the primary mechanism for advancing the Illumunati's totalitarian regime. Communism did not spontaneously erupt in Russia, China, North Vietnam and Cambodia; it was carefully planned and financed by the power elite so that they could get in some practice before the main event. Now they are phasing in their New World Order in the West under the cloak of the phoney war on terror that began under George W. Bush's Presidency. In the EEC the individual sovereignty of the member states is being eroded by more majority voting and the increasing power given to unelected Commissioners, who are puppets of the bankers and multinational corporations.

> "European Commissioners thought that democracy was such an enlightened institution that they voted against it."
>
> **– Kim Andrew Lincoln**

The direction is clear. We are being duped into allowing the creation of a global fascist tyranny where corporations tell us what to do because they own and control everything. Of course, all of this can be stopped

A GOLDEN AGE ECONOMY

and I am sure that it will be, as there is a powerful momentum for change building across the globe as people link hands via the social networks that have been enabled by the internet.

The Deception of Inflation

"In the absence of the gold standard, there is no way to protect savings from confiscation through inflation. There is no safe store of value."

– Alan Greenspan

"Inflation is the one form of taxation that can be imposed without legislation."

– Milton Friedman

"The best way to destroy the capitalist system is to debauch the currency. By a continuing process of inflation, governments can confiscate, secretly and unobserved, an important part of the wealth of their citizens."

– John Maynard Keynes

Money exists for two purposes: to act as a medium of exchange and a store of future value. Any government, therefore, that seeks to deliberately devalue the purchasing power of their currency by means of a positive target for inflation is committing an act of grand theft against its citizens as well as perverting the intent and purpose for which money was created. By having an official inflation target (2% p.a. in the UK) the government is giving us advance warning that they intend to rob us, knowing that there is little we can do defend ourselves from the crime.

"There should only be one target for inflation – no inflation."

– Kim Andrew Lincoln

A GOLDEN AGE ECONOMY

Not only is this cruel but it creates an atmosphere of fear amongst the most vulnerable members of our society who spend their days worrying about whether they will be able to afford to pay their bills. Inflation is unfair because it causes people on fixed incomes to lose (the elderly and poor) and people with assets (the rich) to gain. The harsh reality is that it is usually those who can afford it least that suffer the highest rates of personal inflation.

> "Those who think that inflation is a good idea should be charged with treason."
>
> **– Kim Andrew Lincoln**

Inflation is theft because it steals the value of our labour, and thus any monetary and banking system and/or policy that is operated in conjunction with a system that deliberately creates inflation (e.g. quantitative easing) breaks God's Commandment which says: Thou shalt not steal.

The blame for inflation lies squarely with government as they allow the cause of inflation i.e. the fractional reserve banking system to continue to erode our wealth. Governments want us to believe that they control inflation by moving interest rates up or down (monetary policy), but the truth is different. Private Banks control inflation because not only do they create money, but with the founding of the Bank of England in 1694 they were granted the right to create excess money (via 'fractional reserve' lending), which is what causes inflation. And this system that operates in the UK is also used in most other countries too.

Let me be clear: the *sole* cause of inflation is an excess of money in circulation, meaning more money than there are goods and services available to buy. If inflation arises by mistake, it is forgivable, but if it happens by design it is treachery. Inflation and cancer affect humans in the same way, they die slowly and painfully.

Consumer Price Index (CPI)

Another way that we are deceived with inflation is in the way in which the inflation rate is calculated. The CPI assumes that we all buy the same basket of goods each month, which of course we do not. In reality what happens is that poorer people spend a higher proportion of their incomes on basics like food and fuel, which are the items that historically have risen the most, whereas those on above average incomes spend more of their earnings on expensive consumer goods like computers and TVs that over the years have tended to fall in price because of innovation and economies of scale. This is borne out by research conducted by Age UK who found that 'Silver RPI' has averaged 4.6% p.a. since Jan 2008 – nearly 50% more than the 3.1% average for RPI* over the same period. What this proves is that the one consistent fact about the official inflation figures is that nobody believes them because they only apply to Mr and Mrs Average who do not exist in the real world.

> "The inflation rate is like the unemployment rate in that the true rate for both is probably twice the official rate."
> – Kim Andrew Lincoln

A more accurate system would be to compile the index on the basis of different income bands, which would help the poorest who are disadvantaged most under the present method or better still do away with inflation altogether which could be achieved with 'sound money'.

> "The difference between CPI and RPI is that the latter is nearer the truth than the former."
> – Kim Andrew Lincoln

> "When pay and benefit levels are linked to CPI, as opposed to RPI, people are effectively getting a pay cut, not a pay rise."
> – Kim Andrew Lincoln

---

* The Retail Prices Index (RPI) includes mortgage costs which CPI does not and so is more representative of people's overall expenditure. In the UK the government changed to using to CPI as its preferred measure of inflation in order to save money on state pensions and social security payments as CPI always gives a lower figure than RPI.

Deflation Can Be Good

One definition of deflation in today's economic environment would be where increasing debt and falling prices reinforce each other in a damaging downward spiral. But it is not the only definition.

There are two types of deflation; the good and the bad.

Good Deflation

Good deflation is where the prices of products and services are constantly falling because innovation and new inventions enable them to be made and marketed more cheaply. Consumers benefit because their money goes further and manufacturers and service providers are happy because these lower prices increases the size of their potential market. And with the increase in output, economies of scale are possible and this in turn brings production costs even lower so that sales and profits go up. This positive deflation is also likely to lead to an increase in employment opportunities and thus an ascending spiral of abundance is created.

Bad Deflation

Bad deflation is where prices fall because there are more goods and services available for sale than there is money in circulation to buy them. This happens under the present 'fractional reserve' banking system when the private banks who create about 97% of money as debt decide – for their own purposes – to reduce the amount of purchasing power in the economy by reining in credit facilities in the form of loans, credit cards and overdrafts. And, as we all know to our cost, the shrinking of the money supply occurred on a massive scale with the so called 'Credit Crunch' that started in 2008. But this event was and is something far more

Deflation Can Be Good

worrying because it happened as a result of our systemically flawed money system that is now collapsing under the weight of our individual and collective indebtedness. What has happened is that the burden of our loan repayments has become too great to bear, to the point where we cannot borrow any more. Without able and willing borrowers the banks cannot create enough new money, so the supply of money contracts and there is less and less money to buy what is produced. In this scenario the only thing that producers can do to balance what is made with the ever-decreasing amount of money in people's pockets, is reduce prices. But as prices are being constantly adjusted to redress this imbalance people wise up to what is going on and delay their purchases on the expectation that prices will fall further. And, the more they delay the more prices come down. But obviously there will be a point beyond which prices cannot fall, without firms selling at a loss, so when this point is reached they go out of business and the workforce shrinks. Now there is even less money in circulation as the economy has entered into a negative downward spiral where unemployment keeps rising and the whole economy is turned into dust. This negative deflation is what politicians and economists fear most because once the downward spiral starts it is very difficult to reverse – as was the case with the Great Depression of 1929, which ended only when the economies of the world were turned over to war production in 1939, and there was a massive increase in money creation through government borrowing to finance the cost.

Bad deflation is what happens when the financial system is based upon the 'fractional reserve' banking model that is used in most countries today. What drives government policy in the UK is fear of bad deflation. Ministers are so desperate to avoid it that they have instructed the Bank of England to inflate the economy by at least 2% p.a. by changing interest rates and/or quantitative easing. But by adhering to this policy what the government is doing is throwing out the baby (good deflation) with the bathwater (bad deflation) so that the benefits from those parts of the economy that are working well are not being passed on to the people in higher living standards.

This travesty would not occur if it was the state that controlled the money supply and not the private banks.

QUANTITATIVE (STEALING) EASING

"QE is a last-ditch attempt by the central banks in the UK and US to extinguish the flames while Rome burns, but all it will do is cause more of the city to be consumed."

– Kim Andrew Lincoln

"In March 2009, the Monetary Policy Committee announced that, in addition to setting Bank Rate at 0.5%, it would start to inject money directly into the economy in order to meet the inflation target. The instrument of monetary policy shifted towards the quantity of money provided rather than its price (Bank Rate). But the objective of policy is unchanged: to meet the inflation target of 2% on the CPI measure of consumer prices. Influencing the quantity of money directly is essentially a different means of reaching the same end.

Significant reductions in Bank Rate have provided a large stimulus to the economy but as Bank Rate approaches zero, further reductions are likely to be less effective in terms of the impact on market interest rates, demand and inflation. And interest rates cannot be less than zero. The MPC therefore needs to provide further stimulus to support demand in the wider economy. If spending on goods and services is too low, inflation will fall below its target.

The MPC boosts the supply of money by purchasing assets like Government and corporate bonds – a policy often known as 'Quantitative Easing'. Instead of lowering Bank Rate to increase the amount of money in the economy, the Bank supplies extra money directly. This does not involve printing more banknotes. Instead the Bank pays for these assets by creating money electronically and crediting the accounts of the companies it bought the assets from. This extra money supports more spending in the economy to bring future inflation back to the target."

– Bank of England (BoE) 2011

The above text was taken from the BoE website, www.bankofengland.co.uk and is both a justification for and short explanation of QE. It all sounds very impressive but the truth is that this measure of monetary policy is yet another subtle tool of economic destruction that operates like the law of diminishing returns whereby the more you do it, the more you are forced to do it, until there comes a point when you have done it all that you can and can therefore do it no more.

"QE is the equivalent of feeding your belly with the contents of your own body."

– Kim Andrew Lincoln

QE has been used by the Federal Reserve and Bank of England (but not the European Central Bank as they disagree with it) because they have run out of policy options for propping up the fractional reserve banking model. In their heart of hearts they know that this systemically flawed system is collapsing but will not admit it for fear of what the public might do.

"QE is proof positive that monetary policy does not work."

– Kim Andrew Lincoln

It would be more accurate to describe QE as 'quantitative stealing' because it loots our incomes and savings. The problems associated with QE are:

It creates inflation.
When a central bank like the BoE buys government bonds (e.g. gilts)

the sellers of those bonds (banks and other financial institutions like insurance companies) invariably use the sale proceeds to speculate with in the markets. And knowing that the central bank has announced a pre-agreed programme of bond purchases they may well buy more of the same gilts that they have sold because the central bank's purchase programme is designed to force bonds prices up and thus government borrowing costs down. In this scenario financial institutions can make virtually risk free profits. The problem is that the money created out of nothing by the central bank does not find its way into the real economy where it is desperately needed, but instead is used in a merry go round of socially useless speculation. When this funny money is gambled on commodities like oil and wheat it forces up the cost of food and fuel, which hurts everyone – and the poorest most.

> "Quantitative Easing does nothing but make speculators rich and inflation rise."
>
> – Kim Andrew Lincoln

It encourages rampant speculation.
As explained in the chapter 'Speculation & Investment Risk', speculation is theft, which is contrary to God's Commandment. It is also making money out of money, which is not multiplying the talents but a misuse of the purpose for which money was created. And thus both these activities will create karma.

> "Quantitative Easing is a funny name for the printing of funny money and speculating with it on funny things. Unfortunately no-one is laughing."
>
> – Kim Andrew Lincoln

It devalues the currency.
The financial markets are not mocked when governments debase the currency by printing money that is not connected to anything of real value but instead is used for useless speculation. Since the beginning of 2008 the British pound has lost 20% of its value, which has happened

Quantitative (Stealing) Easing

because the pound has depreciated in value against the currencies of most of our major trading partners as a result of QE.

It reduces pensioners' incomes.
Another disastrous effect of QE is the reduction it is causing in pension incomes for those who have built up a pension fund and are now converting that pot of money into an income for life with an annuity purchase. Falling gilt yields – a result primarily of QE – are destroying annuity rates and many retirees are now locking themselves in at record low levels. Presently a £100,000 pension fund will buy a 65-year-old man a single life level annuity – which does not increase with inflation but pays out for at least five years if you die before then – of £5,932. However in July 2008 the same fund would have bought an income of a third more and if you go back to the halcyon days of 1990 it would have produced an income of £15,000. If interest rates rise the situation may improve (though I think it unlikely) but that is no comfort for those who need the security of a guaranteed income now.

> "QE is a despicable act of desperation designed to give the impression that the people in charge know what they are doing."
> **– Kim Andrew Lincoln**

It creates a false sense of security.
It is true that when vast sums of funny money are force fed into the financial markets the price of securities will tend to increase in the short term and this gives the holders of those securities a nice warm feeling. But the reality is that this benefit is an illusion because all the negative impacts that this policy brings with it serve only to accelerate the economic decline that the central bank was trying avoid in the first place.

> "Many critics would wonder whether QE policies actually heal, as opposed to cover up, symptoms of an unhealthy economy."
> **– Bill Gross**
> (Manager of PIMCO, the world's biggest bond fund)

The Bankers' Manifesto

Congressman Charles A. Lindbergh, Sr. revealed the Bankers' Manifesto of 1892 to the U.S. Congress somewhere between 1907 and 1917. The source was an article written by Louis Even and published in *United States Bankers Magazine* 1892. Here it is:

> "We (the bankers) must proceed with caution and guard every move made, for the lower order of people are already showing signs of restless commotion. Prudence will therefore show a policy of apparently yielding to the popular will until our plans are so far consummated that we can declare our designs without fear of any organized resistance.
>
> Organizations in the United States should be carefully watched by our trusted men, and we must take immediate steps to control these organizations in our interest or disrupt them.
>
> At the coming Omaha convention to be held July 4, 1892, our men must attend and direct its movement or else there will be set on foot such antagonism to our designs as may require force to overcome. This at the present time would be premature. We are not yet ready for such a crisis. Capital must protect itself in every possible manner through combination (conspiracy) and legislation.
>
> The courts must be called to our aid, debts must be collected, bonds and mortgages foreclosed as rapidly as possible.
>
> When, through the process of law, the common people have lost their homes, they will be more tractable and easily governed through the influence of the strong arm of the government applied to a central power of imperial wealth under the control of the leading financiers.

People without homes will not quarrel with their leaders. History repeats itself in regular cycles. This truth is well known among our principal men who are engaged in forming an imperialism of the world. While they are doing this, the people must be kept in a state of political antagonism.

The question of tariff reform must be urged through the organization known as the Democratic Party, and the question of protection with the reciprocity must be forced to view through the Republican Party.

By thus dividing voters, we can get them to expend their energies in fighting over questions of no importance to us, except as teachers to the common herd. Thus, by discrete actions, we can secure all that has been so generously planned and successfully accomplished."

Some More of My Thoughts on Money & Monetary Policy

Money

The intent and purpose of money is as a medium of exchange and short term store of future value. To use it for any other purpose is to misqualify energy and thus contravene God's Laws as explained by Jesus in his parable of the talents.

Money is a means to an end that should never be allowed to become an end in itself.

Money is simply a form of energy. If we choose to qualify that energy we shall be raised up and receive more. But if we become as money changers and pervert the intent and purpose for which money was created by using it as an end in itself, the light will be drawn from our bodies and we shall lose all that we thought we had gained – and more.

There was a time when our money was worth as much in itself as the value of the goods for which it was being exchanged.

Money that has no intrinsic value is not *real* money.

Eight hundred years ago Robin Hood took back from the rich what they had taken in taxes from the poor. Today the rich (banks) steal from us all by means of a fraudulent ponzi scheme called 'fractional reserve lending'. What banks do is create electronic money (out of thin air) as an interest-bearing debt, using the borrower's assets as security for the loan. They then seek to 'acquire' those assets by forcing borrowers to default on their loans. This is engineered by only creating enough money for borrowers to repay the loan capital – not the loan interest. This system has survived because over time banks have managed to create sufficient new money into circulation to cover the interest payments. Ultimately, however, this scheme is doomed to fail and will collapse under its own weight – as is now happening.

Fiat money is not something the Italians invented; it is money issued by decree of the state who specifies the form of money that shall be used by the people for the purpose of exchanging goods and services. Fiat money is either paper money or electronic money and therefore has no inherent value. It is worth what the state says it is worth.

It Is Borrowers, Not Banks, that Create Money

Under the fractional reserve banking system money is created as debt by being borrowed into existence. Without willing borrowers there would be virtually no money.

Lenders don't create money, borrowers do.

Banks create money on the good credit of borrowers.

The biggest misconception about banks is that they are full of money. They are not. Most people have this mental image that when they are granted a loan, the bank manager goes to a giant safe in the bank's vaults and returns with bundles of bank notes. The reality, however, is that the banks only have a small amount of cash from deposits – about three per cent of the total they lend. But what they do have is lots of willing borrowers who have assets (like property) that the banks can use as security to create money – out of nothing. This is electronic money that is literally typed into existence on a computer screen when a loan is agreed. What the banks are in effect doing is lending you your own money because without you and your assets, the banks cannot legally create money.

Monetary Policy

Monetary policy is an intellectual conceit because it is not possible to control the economy with interest rates alone when large numbers of people are up to their necks in debt and cannot afford to borrow any more. Zero interest rates will not persuade them to spend, and excessive money printing only creates asset bubbles and inflation and devalues the currency. In these circumstances there are no monetary levers left to pull that do not create more problems than they solve.

For the time being the only thing that is keeping the global economy afloat is the printing presses of the world's central banks. They will become like the Emperor with no clothes because the shrinking value of their paper can only cover them for so long.

Monetary policy is a triumph of theory over reality. Japan's two decades of deflation have proved that it doesn't work.

You cannot resolve a problem of too much debt by borrowing more.

In a nation where money is created as debt, reducing the national deficit is the imperfect solution for the imperfect economy.

You cannot build an economic recovery by changing the numbers on bank computer screens.

We are living on borrowed time on which the banks are charging interest.

Monetary Reform

It's not massive cuts in public spending that's needed its fundamental reform of the monetary and banking system.

Some More of My Thoughts on Money & Monetary Policy

It's not rocket science. If we want sustainable prosperity, money must be created debt free. All governments have to do is ignore the threats of the bankers and pass the right laws.

You do not need a first class honours degree in economics to know that if all money is created as debt there will come a time when the nation will be unable to repay the accumulated interest.

Without sound money there will be no economic recovery.

A Sound Money System

Set up a sound money system and the economy will continually expand, do nothing and it will contract and die.

The establishment of a sound money system will necessitate a return to the gold standard, which is a good standard because it is the God standard

When you have sound money there is no limit to the number of jobs that can be created if you have work to be done, the people to do it the and materials and equipment they will need.

Sound money = no debt, no interest, no inflation, no bad deflation, sustainable economic growth and low taxes – simples.

They who hold the gold control the world.

TO BORROW, OR NOT TO BORROW, THAT IS THE QUESTION

"Neither a borrower nor a lender be, For loan oft loses both itself and friend, And borrowing dulls the edge of husbandry."
– **William Shakespeare**
(*Hamlet* Act 1, scene 3, 75-77)

The wisdom of Shakespeare is the truth of Saint Germain, the Ascended Master who is the God of Freedom. In dictations via their messengers on Earth the Ascended Masters have revealed that Saint Germain was Francis Bacon in a previous embodiment, the author of *Hamlet*, and all the plays and poetry penned under the name of William Shakespeare.

Contemplating the calamitous mess the world economy is in, it is not difficult to agree with the sentiments expressed in *Hamlet*, as recent teachings given to students of the Ascended Masters by Saint Germain have categorically stated that the root cause of the world's economic problems is the fractional reserve banking system that creates debt that is impossible to repay. And this debt arises by borrowing money that is itself created as debt via the fractional reserve banking system that I have described in earlier chapters. Thus, it is easy to answer the question that the title of this chapter poses, which is that we should try to avoid borrowing money. But it is simply not sufficient to say this without first giving a comprehensive explanation as to why this should be so.

So what are the spiritual reasons that underpin this truth?

Well, in my research for this book I came across an article that used the above quote from *Hamlet* as its title. It is one of ten articles in a series called 'Kernels of Wisdom' that were published in *Theosophy* magazine in 1952. The Theosophical Society is the publisher of this magazine, and,

To Borrow, or Not to Borrow, That is the Question

as you may recall, it was the first Ascended Master sponsored organisation that I described in Episode One. When you read the article below, you will no doubt feel the vibration of truth that emanates from the words as it progressively convinces you that for you to borrow money is not what our Creator intended.

Kernels of Wisdom

"Neither a borrower nor a lender be; / For loan oft loseth both itself and friend. / And borrowing dulls the edge of husbandry."
– **Shakespeare**

THE economy of Nature is the orderly expression or manifestation of three great powers, – creation, preservation and destruction, or regeneration. The economy of nations and civilizations rests upon a similar trinity, particularized as production, distribution, and consumption. In the prudent administration of a family, or of the life of a single individual, the triune scheme is seen in work, frugality, and sharing. Whenever any one of these sides of the triangle is neglected or misused, balance is upset. This does not mean that all three aspects of a power must be equally operative at one and the same time, for there are cycles of creation just as there are cycles of destruction. There are times when it is appropriate for man to work and produce, and there are periods for resting and distributing. But in the perfectly balanced organism, all three powers of the Godhead must be present functionally, if not in actuality. Brahma, Vishnu, and Shiva are necessary parts of every plan.

Much of the economic framework of our civilization is based upon the practice of lending and borrowing. This is true not only of big business, of industry, and of commerce in general, but also of family and private life in the easy-payment plan of installments. But is this condition a healthy one toward which we may point with pride and satisfaction? Is it the result of co-operative work with Nature, or is it an abuse of some phase of

A GOLDEN AGE ECONOMY

natural economy? Might it not be that the man who finds himself bankrupt, and dependent upon others for support, is one who has either failed to work or has neglected, at some point in his cycle, the principle of preservation or thrift? And perchance the man who lends, at interest, knows not the creed of Shiva, the Sacrificer, Regenerator, Sharer.

It is easy to justify acts of lending and borrowing, to assure one's self that in so doing he is either helping a 'needy soul', or is being helped himself. But is this necessarily true? One may well question whether money always renders real help. The Karma of the individual to whom the loan is made is to be considered. Is his burden thereby lessened? Is he assisted in this way if he has a tendency to sloth, a neglect of frugality, a disregard of the principle of husbandry? Well and good to feel the desire to help, lest the spirit of brotherhood and charity perish from the face of the earth, but equally important is a knowledge of what help really is. It might be that in lending money to a friend, we are actually interfering, quite unconsciously to ourselves, with the Divine Law in its work of effecting an adjustment in the person's life – an adjustment moreover which can be achieved in no other way than through suffering, poverty and want. The Law of Karma does not punish. In bringing trial or difficulty into the life of an individual, it acts as justice, free of evil design, or of any purpose of inflicting injury. Karma is the impersonal law of man's own soul, working always for good – however painful the experience may seem to be.

"Loan oft loseth both itself and friend." Yet, how many individuals, knowing this to be true, have the courage of the Soul's own law, to decline a loan to an irresponsible friend? Lest we give the appearance of unbrotherliness, we weaken and yield, forgetting that the truest form of brotherhood and helpfulness is oftentimes shown in frank dealing, in the spiritual position of the man who has the courage to say "No". Yet such is the nature of modern friendship that it can seldom stand the

To Borrow, or Not to Borrow, That is the Question

test of frank dealing, and is often measured by the extent to which it is possible to make a 'touch', as the saying goes.

"He who goes a-borrowing goes a-sorrowing." Not only does borrowing bring added care for the property of other people — it destroys self-reliance in the man himself. In the light of good judgment, lack of funds may well serve as an indication to the individual that something is wrong in the course he pursues, that the step he plans is either false or premature, or that he is going in debt, not for need but to satisfy a personal desire. Perhaps wisdom would say that unless all the principal factors in a contemplated move are present, one would better wait, and create in himself a feeling of satisfaction with things as they are — at least until such time that the ways open up for natural change. Borrowing, moreover, never solves problems, but only puts off the day of reckoning. The man who borrows gambles with the future. For who knows what tomorrow will bring? Where is the person who can say with certainty that when the time for paying back a loan comes, he will be in better circumstance than he is at the present moment? The impulse to borrow indicates an unwillingness on the part of men to face their present situations squarely. Afraid to take inventory of ourselves, we poultice our ailments with a loan, upon the uncertain prospects of tomorrow. Oh for the courage to give up extravagant desires and to live within the limit of one's means!

The growth and success of money-lending agencies have grown out of the realization on the part of individuals that borrowing and lending among friends is a dangerous practice, that in the final analysis it does not pay. Inspired not by the motive of helping others, but of realizing an interest on the dollar, loan agencies take advantage of the human frailty of unthriftiness, of the uncontrolled desire for things. Hence usury – the pounds of flesh exacted in payment by the Shylocks of modern times. And banks and agencies have found by experience that people who begin the practice of borrowing are likely to remain regular customers. The habit once commenced has a tendency to repeat, so that some remain debtors for the balance of their lives.

Under high and wise social conditions there would never be need for lending and borrowing, or for the humiliating experience of going into debt. Nor would there be any feeling of possession. Consider the social structure of some of the South American aborigines, and of the Red Indians of the United States. Members of their communities never held the possessive attitude toward anything that they had. Everything was the property of the tribe. If one family or individual happened to be in need, someone else who had more than enough supplied it – not as a loan, with interest compounded, but as a sharing, the rightful due of a fellow man. One reason perhaps why we, as a people, find ourselves in debt is because we seek to possess, because we have been brought up with a false conception of independence, of ownership, of separateness. For to the extent that any person thinks he is separate and can own something for himself, just to that extent does he cut himself off from the Whole – bringing in time a condition of need. Possessiveness always brings indebtedness. As Mr. Judge (one of the founder members of the American Theosophical Society who was its Vice President in the 1890's) says:

"Remember this, that you own not one thing in this world. Your wife is but a gift, your children are but loaned to you. All else you possess is given to you only while you use it wisely. Your body is not yours, for Nature claims it as her property."

To reflect a moment upon the bounty of Mother Nature, upon the fact that without her gifts man could not remain on earth, is to sense the beneficence of gratitude and indebtedness for the untold blessings one receives through the bond of human brotherhood — to the farmer for growing food, to the miner for digging coal, to the electrician for having mastered his craft, for the thousand-and-one benefits we daily accept at the hands of others without giving the matter a thought. Can it be that nothing is due in return? Is it possible that Nature's Law will permit a man to continue his path of selfish borrowing without recompense or retribution?

The only legitimate borrowing and lending, in the highest sense of the term, are the loans we receive from nature and the gifts that are offered in return. The universal principle of reciprocity, the natural wheel of give and take, which is inherent in all life, provideth sustenance to every living creature that exists upon the face of the earth. But, according to The Bhagavad-Gita: "He who doth not keep this wheel already set in motion revolving liveth in vain, O Son of Bharata." Brahma, Vishnu and Shiva, on the highest spiritual plane of being, keep the wheel in motion through Creation, Preservation and Destruction, or Regeneration, thus sustaining the economy of Nature as a whole. Man's is the task to do the same thing in his own sphere – through work, frugality, and sacrifice.

– To Borrow, or Not to Borrow, that Is the Question
(published in *Theosophy* magazine, 1952)

"Look, I'm very much in favor of tax cuts, but not with borrowed money. And the problem that we've gotten into in recent years is spending programs with borrowed money, tax cuts with borrowed money, and at the end of the day that proves disastrous. And my view is I don't think we can play subtle policy here."

– Alan Greenspan

"Credit is a system whereby a person who cannot pay gets another person who cannot pay to guarantee that he can pay."

– Charles Dickens

THE UN-FREE MARKET

"Underlying most arguments against the free market is a lack of belief in freedom itself."

– **Milton Friedman**

It is not surprising – in a world where everything has been turned on its head – that markets are not free. The idea of freedom is not a concept that sits well with fallen angels, given that they fell because they did not agree with God's decision to give his children free will. Even in the West where democracy was born, the power elite's idea of a free market is one where rich and powerful corporations are allowed to bleed the people dry with their monopolies and restrictive practices. And when you consider that there are about 35,000 lobbyists in Washington DC it is not surprising that the big corporations always get their way because the reality today is that corporations call the shots – not Presidents. Look closely and you will see that Wall Street runs the White House.

Heaven bestowed upon America the mantle the 'Land of the Free', for under the sponsorship of Saint Germain, the God of Freedom, it is America's destiny to be the example that other nations might follow. To America people have flocked from the four corners of the world in search of freedom and liberty in all things, but especially in commerce and enterprise, for is it not in America that the customer is king? But sadly there are those who seek to snuff out America's freedom flame. They have employed much trickery in the law and in regulations to take away these hard won freedoms so that the so called 'little' people, the 99%, have no choice but to trade with these illuminati controlled corporations who have either taken over or wiped out all competition with the help of their puppets in Washington DC. .

In the United Kingdom it is the same as just four companies

The Un-free Market

dominate the grocery trade with 68% of the market. And one of these four, Tesco, controls nearly 30% of all grocery sales. Not content to confine its sphere of operations to out-of-town superstores, Tesco has embarked on a programme of buying up all the small independent grocery stores in the UK's towns and villages, so that in some conurbations the only place you can buy groceries is from a selection of different sized stores all badged with the Tesco brand. America has its retail mammoths too. Wal-Mart is now the world's biggest corporation according to the Fortune Global 500 for 2011. And like Tesco, Wal-Mart has decimated the local 'mom and pop' stores in communities where they have opened. Once these little shops close they rarely reopen, because when retailers like Wal-mart have gained a footing they are almost impossible to dislodge. The resources of these massive multiples are so great that they can afford to engage in predatory pricing (where goods are sold below cost) in order to drive away any competitor brave enough to challenge them.

As a citizen of the UK I thought I lived in a democracy, but within my lifetime it has become a corporatocracy. But all is not lost, because although giant corporations may be rich and powerful in the mass marketplace, it's the consumer that really holds the cards. The marketplace may not be as free as we would like, but it is democratic in the sense that as consumers we have the choice to vote or not with our cash and our credit cards. We are not always compelled to do business with big corporations. But where there is no choice we can pressurise them into changing unacceptable behaviour and practices. And if that does not work we can make a determined effort to stop doing business with them, or if that is not practical, we can let our elected representatives know what we think of these firms so that pressure is brought to bear for change. Monopolies must be broken up and markets made free!

"We do not have a free market, we have a free-for-all."
– **Kim Andrew Lincoln**

I suggest that if we do not like what a particular commercial organisation is doing we should write to the Chief Executive Officer (CEO) and tell them that we will not buy any more of their product/s until they change what it is that we do not like. We should tell the company that we have suggested to our friends that they do the same. I promise you that if a CEO received a hundred such letters something would be done because it would become a commercial imperative.

My personal protest against News International for hacking people's phones was to stop buying the *Sunday Times* newspaper. So Rupert Murdoch and the other shareholders of this mega media corporation have lost over a £100 per annum in sales from me alone. If a hundred thousand people did as I have done they would be down ten million pounds, which I think they might notice.

As consumers we have immense power, but only, if and when, we choose to use it. Bankers may well control the world today but tomorrow that could change, if we changed our minds about whom we do business.

> "The only way that has ever been discovered to have a lot of people cooperate together voluntarily is through the free market. And that's why it's so essential to preserving individual freedom."
>
> **– Milton Friedman**

Regulation Gone Wrong

An uncharitable view of regulation would be to say that its purpose is not to protect the poor from the rich, the simple from the clever or the weak from the strong, but it is to conceal the snares of the devil under a mountain of paper so that the people will not see the traps.

One way the power elite undermine democracy is by removing people's freedoms by the back door using quangos that write rules and regulations contravening laws made by the elected representatives of the people. A common trick is to make rules retrospective or prejudicial to parties in competition with businesses run by the power elite. Ostensibly the purpose of regulation is to protect the sheep from the wolves, but as it is the wolves (the power elite) that set up the regulatory system, it is not surprising that the regulators have a tendency to act as though they are agents of this beast called the private corporate monopoly.

> "With regulators there is always a risk that the poacher turned gamekeeper will become the poacher again but with the added benefit of the gamekeeper's experience."
> **– Kim Andrew Lincoln**

Regulation is usually weakest where it needs to be strongest because the power elite decide who and what should be regulated and by how much. Therefore, if a commercial activity that they control is highly profitable they will try to ensure that its regulation is either non-existent or scaled down, so as not to spoil the party. The best example of this is the $700 trillion derivatives business. This is the most economically toxic activity known to man and yet it is virtually unregulated. On the other hand, if a trade is being conducted that is in competition with the power elite or that is in conflict with their New World Order plans they will use the regulatory system to clamp down on it so that the trade cannot operate profitably for the burden of regulation that has been imposed. This is presently the case with the industry that I work in, which is being regulated to death because Independent Financial Advice is the gold standard and therefore much better than the so-called advice services provided by the high street banks. Moreover because independent advice is largely in competition with the banks and because it helps clients to minimise their tax bills it is at odds with the power elite's aim of maximising both bank profits and tax revenues.

The regulated will always seek advantage and favour with the regulator. And they will seek to infiltrate the regulator and turn him into a wolf so that the regulator becomes the agent of that beast. When we attempt to regulate that which is not in alignment with God's Laws we afford the original transgression a perceived legitimacy and make what was wrong worse. You cannot make theft right by regulating it.

> "When we rubber-stamp wrongdoing we compound the crime."
> – Kim Andrew Lincoln

Next to defence and law enforcement the regulation of economic life is the state's most important duty because we live in a Dark Age world that is governed by the duality consciousness and the law of the jungle. It is a sad fact that most regulation is not fit for purpose, but then it was never intended that it should be. Never was this more the case than in the financial world where my own experience of regulation is greatest.

Financial Regulation

> "A regulator that was doing its job properly would shut down the entire financial system on the grounds that it is systemically flawed and therefore wholly inimical to the interests of the people it is supposed to serve."
> – Kim Andrew Lincoln

Regulation Gone Wrong

When wrongdoing is exposed in some dark corner of the financial world the political response is often to call in the regulators. This always seems to calm everybody down because the consensus of opinion is that once an activity comes under government control it somehow becomes safe and respectable. But sadly that is the perfect smokescreen that enables the scam to continue, though perhaps in a less offensive form.

If one is realistic, trying to regulate the business of speculation will never work well because the motivation of the biggest speculators who control the markets is to consume the millions of small investors who, in their innocence, think that investing in the markets is a good way to increase their wealth. Regulators know this but deliberately and conveniently turn a blind eye so that the unwary continue to be eaten by the sharks.

> "The world's financial regulators are either agents of the beast (the private banking cartel), pawns of the governments who gave them life, or an unhealthy combination of the two."
> **– Kim Andrew Lincoln**

The greater the number of financial crises we have the fatter the financial rulebooks become; but no matter how many more rules they make the truth is that speculation – where you seek to gain something for nothing, by not multiplying your talents – is a misuse of God's energy and those who misqualify that energy will be subject to the Law of Karma.

> "The greatest sin of the City regulator is their refusal to publicly acknowledge that the fractional reserve banking system is a massive fraud that is systemically flawed and utterly corrupt. The only effective way to regulate speculation, usury and fractional reserve banking is to abolish them."
> **– Kim Andrew Lincoln**

The truth is that had our money system not been perverted by the bankers and other members of the power elite there would be little need for financial regulation now.

Taxation – the Good, the Bad & the Ugly

"A thief takes without asking, the taxman affords you the courtesy of telling you first."

– **Kim Andrew Lincoln**

When Jesus said: "Render unto Caesar the things which are Caesar's, and unto God the things that are God's" (Matthew 22:21) did he literally mean that we should pay whatever the taxman demands, or is it more likely that his words were intended for Roman ears. Jesus knew that the Romans would take what he said literally because it suited them to do so, as it has suited all governments since. But when we look at Jesus' statement in the context of his other teachings we can extract a different meaning entirely; something like: we should only pay what is reasonable, what is fair, what we can realistically and comfortably afford – but more importantly, only what we consent to.

We have to remember that when Palestine was under Roman rule it was impossible for a consensual relationship to exist between the Governor and the governed. The Romans were foreign invaders who reigned through oppression, fear and cruelty. There was no debate about what was an appropriate amount of tax, you either paid them what they wanted or suffered the consequences. Had Jesus encouraged the Jews to challenge Roman tax demands he would have been setting them up for a great deal of suffering, which I am sure he would have wished to avoid. I believe that Jesus was addressing a Roman audience with his tax statement and that the form of words he chose was designed to keep the peace, because Jesus is the Prince of Peace, as Gautama Buddha is the King of Peace. When taken together with his other teachings, I think that Jesus was really saying that if we do not consent, meaning that if there is no agreement by the majority, that what is asked for in tax should be paid then in accordance with natural justice and the Law of

Free Will, there is no moral or legal obligation to pay. Of course, I am talking about a democracy here, so different rules would apply in a situation where people are unable to exercise their free will.

> "Taxation that does not have the wholehearted support and consent of the people is not taxation at all. It is theft. It is extortion. It is tyranny."
> – Kim Andrew Lincoln

When the state breaks God's Laws the people have a moral obligation to stand up for what is right, but to do it peacefully, in accordance with God's Laws. This was the approach that Gandhi took with the British Raj and it was the right approach. The Indians did not consent to British rule and therefore they were within their rights (under divine Law) to withhold the payment of all taxes demanded by the British if they had chosen to do so. In a democracy, however, if we withhold taxes we would misqualify energy as the right procedure would be to effect change by lobbying, legimate protest and the ballot box.

In the USA today filing a federal income tax return is, in fact, voluntary, because there is no statute or regulation that requires the vast majority of US citizens to file and pay income taxes – or to have taxes withheld from the money they earn. Neither the IRS nor the Congress can cite an authorising law or regulation. Juries have been acquitting defendants in failure-to-file income tax return cases due to lack of demonstrable evidence that there is any law or regulation that requires it.

Should there be a mass awakening to this truth and the people en mass decide to enforce their legal right not to pay income tax the federal government would run out of money very quickly. So this is one legal strategy that US citizens could employ to force the government to abolish fractional reserve banking and thus take power from the few and return it to the many.

> "Taxation is the stuff of politics. Politicians spend their time debating it but all that happens is that taxes keep going up."
> – Kim Andrew Lincoln

A GOLDEN AGE ECONOMY

The power elite use the device of high taxation as a control mechanism. People who have given over a large part of their income in taxes to fund wasteful government schemes are forced to focus their attention on earning a living and thus have little time to spend on spiritual pursuits that will raise their consciousness and lead them to question the way their country is being run.

> "No matter how much tax a government takes they will always want more."
>
> – **Kim Andrew Lincoln**

We have high taxes because we have fractional reserve banking. Abolish the latter and within a relatively short time the former could be massively reduced. Taxes are levied to pay banks interest on the money they create out of nothing as a debt that the people are liable to pay, but if our money was debt free we would not need to levy income tax to pay this interest.

Once a government has run out of ideas they resort to raising taxes and therefore a minister that promises to raise taxes is not a wise man.

> "To suggest that taxes should be raised in a recession is like asking a man who has just lost two pints of blood in an accident to become a blood donor."
>
> – **Kim Andrew Lincoln**

The best measure of worth of any elected body with tax-raising powers is the extent to which they do not exercise those powers. As with so many things in life you will find that when it comes to taxes less is always more. Nothing kills enterprise like taxes and so it is a fact that the most enterprising economies have the lowest taxes.

> "Taxes are increased by the wicked, the unenlightened and the incompetent."
>
> – **Kim Andrew Lincoln**

Taxation – the Good, the Bad & the Ugly

In the UK in the 1980s, Margaret Thatcher's government proved that the best way to increase tax revenue was to reduce the tax rate. At that time the top rate of income tax was 83% but by the time the then Chancellor, Nigel Lawson, had reduced it in stages to 40% the actual tax take had risen substantially as higher earners were encouraged to return to the UK and complex tax avoidance schemes were abandoned.

"Whatever you tax, you get less of."
— **Alan Greenspan**
(Ex-Chairman of the US Federal Reserve)

High taxes discourage work and if the unemployed are better off on benefits, those in work are being paid too little and taxed too much.

"We have a system that increasingly taxes work and subsidizes non-work."
— **Milton Friedman**

The handbook of UK tax legislation has more than doubled in length since 1997 to a door stopping 11,520 pages. The purpose behind complexity in the tax system is obscurification – meaning an intention on the part of government to hide the true level of taxation under an incomprehensible web of taxes and tariffs, rules and regulations. Tax systems that are difficult to understand require an army of state bureaucrats to administer and legions of advisers in the private sector to steer taxpayers through the maze of red tax tape.

"Taxation is above the line, inflation is below the belt."
— **Kim Andrew Lincoln**

Furthermore tax advice is expensive and is therefore only the preserve of the rich. All this activity is unproductive. It does nothing to create wealth but merely redistributes it in a regressive manner from poor people to the power elite. Simple, transparent taxes are an anathema to governments because it is too easy for ordinary people to work out for themselves how much tax they are really paying. And thus simple taxes are invariably honest taxes.

As with usury and speculation, taxation can also be a mechanism for the transfer of wealth from the people to the power elite. Two good examples of this would be the multi-trillion dollar bank bailouts that preceded the collapse of Lehman Bros and the lax tax rules that allow multi-national corporations to control the amount of tax they pay by moving profits and losses between their various operating businesses throughout the globe and by locating their Head Offices in the most tax-friendly jurisdiction.

"One third of the top 700 UK companies pay no corporation tax."
– Kim Andrew Lincoln

This legalised evasion of taxes by big business means that ordinary people have to make up the shortfall of taxes lost to these schemes and in this way private citizens subsidise the corporate sector.

"It is the policy of the power elite to impoverish the middle classes so that just two groups remain: the super-rich and their slaves the poor."
– Kim Andrew Lincoln

ODE TO TAX

The rich shall pay some
The super-rich less
Billionaires will do better
For they shall pay none
The poor will suffer
For they shall be bled
As a penny is too much
For those in the red
So the class that gets clobbered
By the fall of the axe

Is the one in the middle
That pays most of the tax

- Kim Andrew Lincoln

A Good Tax

If there was such a thing as a good tax, it would be a sales tax levied on purchases of non-essential items where the tax rate is either fixed on all items subject to the tax, or alternatively, where the rate of tax increases in line with the degree of luxury of the product or service. A luxury yacht, for example, might attract the highest rate, whereas essential items like bread would not be taxed at all. The thinking behind such a tax is that the richest people pay the most tax when they spend on luxuries. This would be a foolproof way of ensuring that the wealthiest people shouldered the bigger share of the tax burden. It would also mean that goods and services that are 'essential to life' would carry no tax and thus aid those on the lowest incomes. This sales tax would replace all forms of income and capital taxes, which are unfair and destructive to wealth creation and would be the only means through which government is funded. Obviously, if the graded tax rate option were chosen, the level of tax that should be applied to different goods and services is a subjective matter that would occupy the time of the slimmed-down tax authorities, who would have little else to do. This tax would be appropriate for any country as it could be adapted to meet the particular circumstances and revenue needs of each nation. Rich people sometimes flaunt their wealth because it makes them feel superior. They are, therefore, unlikely to object to a 'luxuries tax' that makes their purchases more expensive as it will serve to reinforce their feelings of wealth and superiority, as well as raise revenue equitably.

"When taxes are simple, fair and transparent they are cheap to collect and less likely to be evaded."

- Kim Andrew Lincoln

BIG BROTHER & BUREAUCRACY

"Bureaucracy, never content, seeks always to expand."
– **Kim Andrew Lincoln**

The size and reach of government is limited only by the imagination of the power elite, and thus governments will always expand while they have taxes to expend. In Dark Age economies countries spend too much of the people's money trying to prop up (and thus disguise) those unworkable policies that contravene God's Laws. And a bureaucracy that keeps growing in size is proof of that failure. In 1881, Great Britain was the richest nation on earth with 50,000 Civil Servants. By 2011, however, when the country had fallen to seventh place in the league table of nations, the number of central government staff had climbed to over half a million – though they managed much less. Clearly something is wrong here as these numbers tell us that failure breeds failure and the cost of that failure is measured by the increasing taxes we are forced to pay. And as we know, high taxes drag the economy down.

"Inefficiency and bureaucracy are like conjoined twins: the size of one is directly related to the other".
– **Kim Andrew Lincoln**

You would think that the power elite would want government to operate efficiently, but you would be wrong, for these dark forces have come to bring the nations and their peoples to their knees. They have come to kill the mother and the manchild and to cripple the financial system so that they will have the excuse to introduce their one-world scheme complete with the mark of the beast.

Big Brother & Bureaucracy

In the UK we have a reality TV show called *Big Brother* where a group of people live together in a large house and in every room there are cameras monitoring their every move. This may be TV, but it is reality too, for this is what our governments do. They watch us, they track us, they record what we write and what we say, for every day and in every way we are spied on. And governments and their agencies employ a huge army of people to do it – all paid for out of our taxes. The power elite are obsessed with controlling the minions. Interference is their middle name and they will not rest until we have all been tagged, sedated and herded into cages like sheep.

Big governments have big budgets and so vast sums are spent on technology that is deployed to control the people. And this technology is developed by the very corporations that have the political elite in their pockets. And a failing economy must be propped up, so public money is poured into bailing out the banks that lost their depositors' money in the casinos of the City and Wall Street. Grants must be given to companies to take on unemployed workers who are then dispensed with when the subsidies run out. In the chapter "The Biggest Crime of All Time" I described the main ways in which the fractional reserve banking destroys the economy, and it is this failure that the power elite use to justify the expansion of the state. The more workers that are taken on the greater the states control over the people. For if your livelihood is dependent upon the state you are more likely to do your employer's bidding. This is the client state.

"Bureaucracy is like a hungry baby – it wants to be fed."
– Kim Andrew Lincoln

There is a limit to how far any government can go in expanding its base of operations because once the state's share of the national income exceeds 50% there will not be enough money coming in from the private sector to meet the costs of government. Failure is an expensive business, as the Romans discovered when the barbarian hoards went into mass revolt, and the Empire could no longer afford to defend its borders. The oppressors became the oppressed, as the cost of failure, which was the cost of running a tyranny, was too high. The USSR went bust for similar reasons and if the West does not correct itself it will eventually go the same way – in accordance with the Law of Disintegration. This Law is also known as the second law of thermodynamics and it states that all imperfect forms will eventually be returned to their base state, which means that they will collapse.

The challenge for any democracy is to hold the march of the state and its bureaucracy in check. The two questions that must be asked at least once a year by ministers are: how can we do more with less, and how can we reduce the overhead costs of government so that the people can pay less in taxes?

MORE OF MY THOUGHTS ON THE FRACTIONAL RESERVE BANKING SYSTEM

Since King William of Orange gave the bankers the keys to his kingdom, meaning the power to create money, it is not surprising that they have made the most of the opportunity.

The FRBS was designed specifically to transfer the wealth of citizens and nations to the private banking network. It has succeeded.

The banking halls are full of fallen angels; for how better to control the world than through a money and banking system that feeds off the peoples labour and keeps them enslaved through usury and debt.

China, India and the rest of Asia are on an economic roll right now as all Ponzi schemes rise before they fall. But when that old serpent called debt has coiled itself around the people so they cannot breathe, the day of reckoning will come and the towers of fractional reserve banking in the East will fall.

Only the greatest alchemists can create something out of nothing, but that's what banks do every day.

A bank is a legally constituted licence to print money.

The best place to learn how to counterfeit money is in a bank.

The difference between a privately owned bank and a money counterfeiter is that the latter has no licence, does not charge interest, and gives you the money at a discount.

Funny Money

We are controlled through the money system
By greedy banks who dominate
But they have built a tower of Babel
That one day will disintegrate.

Stop corruption of the money system
End this theft of our wealth by stealth
Abundance is our right in God's Kingdom
In money, happiness and health.

Perverted money – something for nothing
Reaping reward from other's sweat
Stealing the value of people's labour
With too much money, too much debt.

It started out with the wars in Europe
How to pay for the crippling cost
A clever banker set up the system
Ensuring that the people lost.

We're money slaves without understanding
Of how the system robs us blind
With penal taxation by inflation
And interest – that's another crime.

Money detached from things of real value
This system siphons wealth away
And we support it by working smarter
We need to find another way.

Funny Money

What we want is a sound money system
Currency that is backed by gold
We say no to created inflation
We want money whose value holds.

Radical change needs Golden Age thinking
And laws that will these bankers shock
Wake up now see a system that's failing
The money machine runs amok.

Chorus

We can put a stop to this funny money
We can bring an end to this anti-Christ tool
We can see what's right with crystal clear vision
We can see a world with real money rules
We don't want no more…
We don't want no more…
We don't want no more of your funny money
We don't want no more of your funny money
We have had enough of your funny money
We can see a world with real money rules
We don't want no more of your funny money
We don't want no more of your funny money
We have had enough of your funny money
We can see a world where real money rules.

© COPYRIGHT 2008 **KIM ANDREW LINCOLN**

THE POSSESSIONS HAVE GONE

Don't need any credit
I have inner means
My balance keeps growing
A God given scheme.

Don't need any bankers
And their crazy scams
Derivatives, debt piles
Their world is a sham.

Don't need to be greedy
Take more than I need
As all heavy treasure
Will sink in the sea.

Don't need your projections
They're illusory
But the truth it is certain
Just seek it and see.

Don't lust after power
Ego's currency
With all its begetting
A dark history.

The Possessions Have Gone

Don't need any pensions
Right doing provides
My barn is now empty
I've nothing to hide.

I see what you're selling
All drugs by degree
And all of them dated
With no guarantees.

You seem to be clever
The way that you walk
But I will not weaken
To your dirty talk.

The bible of devils
Divide, bind and rule
The lie and the liar
Who thinks we are fools.

It's in Revelations
The devil's own brand
No buying or selling
Without a chipped hand.

No longer an owner
My possession has gone
He has nothing in me
That he can make wrong.

I've lost my attachments
And let the light through
The flame of freedom
Has consumed my blues.

A GOLDEN AGE ECONOMY

CHORUS

So I'm kicking off my shoes
I'm not singing the blues
All's right with me now
That's my good news!
The things of this world
Will only give you pain
So be infinite peace
And come alive again.

© COPYRIGHT 2003 **KIM ANDREW LINCOLN**

YE SHALL KNOW THEM BY THE WORDS OF THOSE WHO KNOW THEM BEST

ON THE MONETARY & BANKING SYSTEM (FRBS):

"Of all the ways of organising banking, the worst one is the one we have today."

"The words 'banking and crises' are natural bedfellows."

"For a society to base its financial system on alchemy is a poor advertisement for its rationality."

"And it is hard to see why institutions (meaning banks) whose failure cannot be contemplated should be in the private sector in the first place."

"Ever since the Industrial Revolution we have not cracked the problem of how to ensure a more stable banking system."

"Change is, I believe, inevitable. The question is only whether we can think our way through to a better outcome before the next generation is damaged by a future and bigger crisis. This crisis has already left a legacy of debt to the next generation. We must not leave them the legacy of a fragile banking system too."
– **Mervyn King,**
Governor of the Bank of England
(New York City, 25-10-2010)

"The issue which has swept down the centuries and which will

A GOLDEN AGE ECONOMY

have to be fought sooner or later is 'the People versus the Banks.'
- **Lord Acton**
(Lord Chief Justice of England, 1875)

"I am a most unhappy man. I have unwittingly ruined my country. A great industrial nation is now controlled by its system of credit. We are no longer a government by free opinion, no longer a government by conviction and the vote of the majority, but a government by the opinion and duress of a small group of dominant men."
- **Woodrow Wilson**
(The US President who signed the Federal Reserve into existence in 1913)

"Everything predicted by the enemies of banks, in the beginning, is now coming to pass. We are to be ruined now by the deluge of bank paper. It is cruel that such revolutions in private fortunes should be at the mercy of avaricious adventurers, who, instead of employing their capital, if any they have, in manufactures, commerce and other useful pursuits, make it an instrument to burden all the interchanges of property with their swindling profits, profits which are the price of no useful industry of theirs."

"I believe that banking institutions are more dangerous to our liberties than standing armies. If the American people ever allow private banks to control the issue of their currency, first by inflation, then by deflation, the banks and corporations that will grow up around [the banks] will deprive the people of all property until their children wake up homeless on the continent their fathers conquered. The issuing power should be taken from the banks and restored to the people, to whom it properly belongs."
- **Thomas Jefferson**

"Gentlemen, I have had men watching you for a long time and I am convinced that you have used the funds of the bank to speculate in the breadstuffs of the country. When you won, you divided the profits amongst you, and when you lost, you charged it to the bank. You tell me that if I take the deposits from the bank and annul its charter, I shall ruin ten thousand families. That may be true, gentlemen, but that is your sin! Should I let you go on, you will ruin fifty thousand families, and that would be my sin! You are a den of vipers and thieves. I intend to rout you out and, by the Eternal God, I will rout you out ... if people only understood the rank injustice of the money and banking system, there would be a revolution by morning."

– **Andrew Jackson**
(4th US President – in a speech given in 1828 addressing central bankers)

"When a bank lends it creates money out of nothing."

– **R. G. Hawtrey**
(One-time Assistant Under-Secretary to the US Treasury)

On the Power Elite

"The powers of financial capitalism had a far-reaching plan, nothing less than to create a world system of financial control in private hands able to dominate the political system of each country and the economy of the world as a whole... Their secret is that they have annexed from governments, monarchies and republics the power to create the world's money..."

– **Prof. Carroll Quigley**
(Renowned late Georgetown macro-historian (mentioned by former President Clinton in his first nomination acceptance speech), author of *Tragedy and Hope*. "He [Carroll Quigley] was one of the last great macro-historians who traced the development of civilization... with an awesome capability." – Dr. Peter F. Krogh, Dean of the School of Foreign Service, Georgetown)

"The real truth of the matter is, as you and I know, that a financial element in the large centres has owned the government ever since the days of Andrew Jackson."

– Franklin D Roosevelt
(US President 1933 – 1945)

"If you want a vision of the future, imagine a boot stamping on a human face – forever."

– George Orwell
(Author of the prophetic novel *1984*)

"People simply disappeared, always during the night. Your name was removed from the registers, every record of everything you had ever done was wiped out, your one-time existence was denied and then forgotten. You were abolished, annihilated: vaporised was the usual word."

– George Orwell
(An extract from his book *1984*)

"We hang petty thieves and appoint the great ones to public office."

– Aesop
(Famous Greek fable writer from the 6th Century BC)

"The purpose of this financial crisis is to take down the U.S. dollar as the stable datum of planetary finance and, in the midst of the resulting confusion, put in its place a Global Monetary Authority (GMA – run directly by international bankers freed of any government control) – a planetary financial control organization."

– Bruce Wiseman

"The rich, by unfair combinations, contribute frequently to prolong a season of distress among the poor."

– Thomas Malthus

"Many people want the government to protect the consumer. A much more urgent problem is to protect the consumer from the government."

– Milton Friedman

Ye Shall Know Them by the Words of Those Who Know Them Best

"Capitalism is the astounding belief that the wickedest of men will do the wickedest of things for the greatest good of everyone."
— **John Maynard Keynes**
(World-famous British economist)

On the Economy

"The economy now is a fiction. The first five-year stretch of transition from August 1987 to August 1992 was the beginning of the destruction of the material world. We have progressed ten years deeper into the transition phase by now, and many of the so-called sources of financial stability are in fact hollow. The banks are weak. This is a delicate moment for them. They could crash globally, if we don't pay attention. Now, people are paying attention."
— **Carlos Barrios**
(Mayan elder, ceremonial priest and spiritual guide of the Eagle Clan).

"By a continuing process of inflation, governments can confiscate, secretly and unobserved, an important part of the wealth of their citizens ... in a manner which not one man in a million can diagnose."
— **John Maynard Keynes**

On Speculation

"The mother of all evil is speculation – leverage, debt. The bottom line is borrowing to the hilt, and I hate to tell you this, but it's a bankrupt business model; it won't work, it's systemic, malignant and it's global and like cancer it's a disease and we've got to fight back."
— **Gordon Gekko**
(Extract from a speech by the character Gordon Gekko, played by the actor Michael Douglas from the 2010 film *Wall Street – Money Never Sleeps*, directed by Oliver Stone)

YE SHALL KNOW THEM BY THEIR OWN WORDS

ON THE MONETARY AND BANKING SYSTEM (FRBS)

"Banking was conceived in iniquity and was born in sin. The bankers own the earth. Take it away from them, but leave them the power to create money, and with the flick of the pen they will create enough deposits to buy it back again. However, take it away from them, and all the great fortunes like mine will disappear and they ought to disappear, for this would be a happier and better world to live in. But, if you wish to remain the slaves of bankers and pay the cost of your own slavery, let them continue to create money."

– **Sir Josiah Stamp**
(Director of the Bank of England – appointed 1928. He was reputed to be the 2nd wealthiest man in England at that time. The Bank of England was privately owned until it's nationalisation in 1947)

"I am afraid that ordinary citizens will not like to be told that the banks can, and do, create and destroy money. And they who control the credit of the nation direct the policy of governments, and hold in the hollow of their hands the destiny of the people."

– **Reginald McKenna**
(Chairman of the Midland Bank (now part of HSBC) when addressing a meeting of Shareholders on 25th January 1924)

"Such was the case, and I could have financed the country for a further like sum had the war continued." [Asked if that amount was available for productive purposes in this time of peace, he answered, "Yes".]

– Sir Denison Miller
(During an interview in 1921, when he was asked if he, through the Commonwealth Bank, had financed Australia during the First World War for $700 million)

In 1891 a confidential circular was sent to American bankers and their agents, containing the following statements:

"We authorise our loan agents in the western States to loan our funds on real estate, to fall due on September 1st 1894, and at no time thereafter. On September 1st, 1894, we will not renew our loans under any consideration. On September 1st we will demand our money – we will foreclose and become mortgagees in possession. We can take two-thirds of the farms west of the Mississippi and thousands of them east of the great Mississippi as well, at our own price. We may as well own three quarters of the farms of the west and the money of the country. Then the farmers will become tenants, as in England."

– The above quotation was reprinted in the *Idaho Leader*, USA, 26 August 1924
(It has been read into Hansard twice: by John Evans MP, in 1926, and by M. D. Cowan MP, in the Session of 1930-1931)

THE KEY POINTS OF THE ILLUMINATI CODE

In the following pages is described the illuminati strategy to subjugate the people of Earth and to bring this planet under their total ownership and control. It explains how these fallen angels plan to remove most of the population and enslave those they permit to remain. It is one of the most chilling documents you are ever likely to read and confirms everything I have alerted you to in this book. I did not discover these 'Key Points' until I had almost completed the second episode of this book, and my attempts to discover the author have, unsurprisingly, been unsuccessful. Therefore, I cannot say for sure that this is an actual illuminati document – although it is similar to one that was accidentally lost by the illuminati and published by the forces of light over two hundred years ago. My intuition, however, tells me that it is authentic, because the words are imbued with the low vibrational energy of spiritual pride, superiority, contempt, malice and menace. You decide.

THE KEY POINTS OF THE ILLUMINATI CODE

- An illusion it will be, so large, so vast it will escape their perception.
- Those who will see it will be thought of as insane.
- We will create separate fronts to prevent them from seeing the connection between us.
- We will behave as if we are not connected to keep the illusion alive. Our goal will be accomplished one drop at a time so as to never bring suspicion upon ourselves. This will also prevent them from seeing the changes as they occur.
- We will always stand above the relative field of their experience for we know the secrets of the absolute.
- We will work together always and will remain bound by blood and secrecy. Death will come to he who speaks.

The Key Points of the Illuminati Code

- We will keep their lifespan short and their minds weak while pretending to do the opposite.
- We will use our knowledge of science and technology in subtle ways so they will never see what is happening.
- We will use soft metals, ageing accelerators and sedatives in food and water, also in the air.
- They will be blanketed by poisons everywhere they turn.
- The soft metals will cause them to lose their minds. We will promise to find a cure from our many fronts, yet we will feed them more poison.
- The poisons will be absorbed through their skin and mouths; they will destroy their minds and reproductive systems.
- From all this, their children will be born dead, and we will conceal this information.
- The poisons will be hidden in everything that surrounds them, in what they drink, eat, breathe and wear.
- We must be ingenious in dispensing the poisons for they can see far.
- We will teach them that the poisons are good, with fun images and musical tones.
- Those they look up to will help. We will enlist them to push our poisons.
- They will see our products being used in film and will grow accustomed to them and will never know their true effect.
- When they give birth we will inject poisons into the blood of their children and convince them it is for their help.
- We will start early on, when their minds are young, we will target their children with what children love most, sweet things.
- When their teeth decay we will fill them with metals that will kill their mind and steal their future.
- When their ability to learn has been affected, we will create medicine that will make them sicker and cause other diseases for which we will create yet more medicine.
- We will render them docile and weak before us by our power.
- They will grow depressed, slow and obese, and when they come to us for help, we will give them more poison.

A GOLDEN AGE ECONOMY

- We will focus their attention towards money and material goods so they may never connect with their inner self. We will distract them with fornication, external pleasures and games so they may never be one with the oneness of it all.
- Their minds will belong to us and they will do as we say. If they refuse we shall find ways to implement mind-altering technology into their lives. We will use fear as our weapon.
- We will establish their governments and establish opposites within. We will own both sides.
- We will always hide our objective but carry out our plan.
- They will perform the labour for us and we shall prosper from their toil.
- Our families will never mix with theirs. Our blood must be pure always, for it is the way.
- We will make them kill each other when it suits us.
- We will keep them separated from the oneness by dogma and religion.
- We will control all aspects of their lives and tell them what to think and how.
- We will guide them kindly and gently letting them think they are guiding themselves.
- We will foment animosity between them through our factions.
- When a light shall shine among them, we shall extinguish it by ridicule, or death, whichever suits us best.
- We will make them rip each other's hearts apart and KILL THEIR OWN CHILDREN.
- We will accomplish this by using hate as our ally, anger as our friend.
- The hate will blind them totally, and never shall they see that from their conflicts we emerge as their rulers. They will be busy killing each other.
- They will bathe in their own blood and kill their neighbours for as long as we see fit.
- We will benefit greatly from this, for they will not see us, for they cannot see us.

The Key Points of the Illuminati Code

- We will continue to prosper from their wars and their deaths.
- We shall repeat this over and over until our ultimate goal is accomplished.
- We will continue to make them live in fear and anger though images and sounds.
- We will use all the tools we have to accomplish this.
- The tools will be provided by their labour.
- We will make them hate themselves and their neighbours.
- We will always hide the Divine Truth from them, that we are all one. This they must never know!
- They must never know that colour is an illusion; they must always think they are not equal.
- Drop by drop, drop by drop we will advance our goal.
- We will take over their land, resources and wealth to exercise total control over them.
- We will deceive them into accepting laws that will steal the little freedom they will have.
- We will establish a money system that will imprison them forever, keeping them and their children in debt.
- When they shall band together, we shall accuse them of crimes and present a different story to the world for we shall own all the media.
- We will use our media to control the flow of information and their sentiment in our favour.
- When they shall rise up against us we will crush them like insects, for they are less than that.
- We will recruit some of their own to carry out our plans, we will promise them eternal life, but eternal life they will never have for they are not of us. The recruits will be called 'initiates' and will be indoctrinated to believe false rites of passage to higher realms. Members of these groups will think they are one with us never knowing the truth. They must never learn this truth for they will turn against us. For their work they will be rewarded with earthly things and great titles, but never will they become immortal and join us, never will they receive the light and travel the stars. They will never reach the higher realms, for the killing of their own kind

will prevent passage to the realm of enlightenment. This they will never know. The truth will be hidden in their face, so close they will not be able to focus on it until it's too late. Oh yes, so grand the illusion of freedom will be, that they will never know they are our slaves.

- When all is in place, the reality we will have created for them will own them. This reality will be their prison. They will live in self-delusion.
- When our goal is accomplished a new era of domination will begin. Their minds will be bound by their beliefs, the beliefs we have established from time immemorial.

But if they ever find out they are our equal, we shall perish then. THIS THEY MUST NEVER KNOW. If they ever find out that together they can vanquish us, they will take action. They must never, ever find out what we have done, for if they do, we shall have no place to run, for it will be easy to see who we are once the veil has fallen. Our actions will have revealed who we are and they will hunt us down and no person shall give us shelter. This is the secret covenant by which we shall live the rest of our present and future lives, for this reality will transcend many generations and life spans. This covenant is sealed by blood, our blood. We, the ones who from heaven to earth came.

This covenant must NEVER, EVER be known to exist. It must NEVER, EVER be written or spoken of for if it is, the consciousness it will spawn will release the fury of the PRIME CREATOR upon us and we shall be cast to the depths from whence we came and remain there until the end time of infinity itself.

WAKE UP

Part One

Wake up – we've been sleeping
Oh we are so cold
The ice we have been reaping
Has slowly taken hold.

Wake up – draw the curtains
Sunshine melts away
The fears that have us captives made
Release them all today.

Wake up – let the light in
Find the inner key
Unlock the god-flames waiting
So long for us to free.

Wake up – the illusion
That we are apart
For nothing is that was not of
Our Father from his heart.

Wake up – Sons and Daughters
Warriors of Earth
The mission bells are calling
We cast before our birth.

Wake up – to deception

A GOLDEN AGE ECONOMY

Divide, bind and rule
Ego and the anti-Christ
So long have had us fooled.

Part Two

Wake up – your inner search
Wake up – the man-made church
Wake up – doctrinal rules
Wake up – the ego's tools
Wake up – they box you in
Wake up – see God within
Wake up – break out the fold
Wake up – don't be controlled

Wake up – the female side
Wake up – what men deny
Wake up – balance is might
Wake up – to equal rights
Wake up – to Mother light
Wake up – religions see
Wake up – your women free
Wake up – and balanced be

Wake up – we are All One
Wake up – the One in All
Wake up – and heed the call
Wake up – let out your love
Wake up – and rise above
Wake up – the Christ in you
Wake up – I AM in you
Wake up – all that is true

Wake up – you're not alone

Wake Up

Wake up – Ascended Host
Wake up – your brothers close
Wake up – they're here with love
Wake up – for "Ye are Gods"
Wake up – for God is we
Wake up – for we are God
Wake up – to what we're not

Wake up – from fear and strife
Wake up – there's more to life
Wake up – from riches more
Wake up – two thirds are poor
Wake up – the have nots raise
Wake up – as Jesus saved
Wake up – see life as one
Wake up – birth Christ the Son

Wake up – spirit of truth
Wake up – illusion great
Wake up – divided state
Wake up – God did not make
Wake up – we caused our fall
Wake up – the sexes all
Wake up – not just women
Wake up – the false Eden

Wake up – reap what you sow
Wake up – our ego's hold
Wake up – let God unfold
Wake up – give up the ghost
Wake up – God's not remote
Wake up – hail one in all
Wake up – God is in all
Wake up – to God is all

A GOLDEN AGE ECONOMY

Wake up – and spread the news
Wake up – God is in you
Wake up – there's more to life
Wake up – there's spirit life
Wake up – God – Father
Wake up – God – Mother
Wake up – your brother
Wake up – each other

Wake up – duality
Wake up – polarity
Wake up – the two extremes
Wake up – outside them be
Wake up – there is no scale
Wake up – the Holy Grail
Wake up – Christ self this day
Wake up – the Middle Way

Wake up – pull eye beams out
Wake up – help neighbours too
Wake up – so all can see
Wake up – reality
Wake up – first love yourself
Wake up – then others too
Wake up – forgive what's past
Wake up – the Christ in you

Wake up – to scarcity
Wake up – illusion be
Wake up – there is no lack
Wake up – bounty is fact
Wake up – the false world view
Wake up – begin anew
Wake up – and help the poor
Wake up – all life adore

Wake Up

Wake up – to this bad dream
Wake up – ungodly schemes
Wake up – our burdened Earth
Wake up – karma returned
Wake up – as forests burn
Wake up – as seas invade
Wake up – as levees break
Wake up – we did this make

Wake up – to Bush and all
Wake up – twin tower fall
Wake up – his terror fight
Wake up – less civil rights
Wake up – security
Wake up – they test to see
Wake up – how loud we shout
Wake up – to freedom's rout

Wake up – to bankers' greed
Wake up – the house price boom
Wake up – a banking scam
Wake up – bank profits feed
Wake up – to interest paid
Wake up – your wages raid
Wake up – this beast is loose
Wake up – it kills the goose

Wake up – corporations
Wake up – domination
Wake up – exploitation
Wake up – slave nations
Wake up – cheap Chinese shoes
Wake up – to worker blues
Wake up – support their rights
Wake up – abundant life

A GOLDEN AGE ECONOMY

Wake up – to End of Days
Wake up – Grand Cycle ends
Wake up – new blowing wind
Wake up – Aquarius
Wake up – to Saint Germain
Wake up – his Golden Age
Wake up – we will succeed
Wake up – END POVERTY

© COPYRIGHT 2005 **KIM ANDREW LINCOLN**

ADDENDUM

CONTENTS

An excerpt of President Andrew Jackson's Farewell Speech   323

An Excerpt of President Andrew Jackson's Farewell Speech

What follows is about half of President Jackson's farewell speech in which he addresses taxes and control of the money supply. This is brilliant, not only in terms of the content, but also in the way it is written. There is a web link at the end of the extract, so please feel free to pass it on.

"There is, perhaps, no one of the powers conferred on the federal government so liable to abuse as the taxing power. The most productive and convenient sources of revenue were necessarily given to it, that it might be able to perform the important duties imposed upon it; and the taxes which it lays upon commerce being concealed from the real payer in the price of the article, they do not so readily attract the attention of the people as smaller sums demanded from them directly by the tax gatherer. But the tax imposed on goods enhances by so much the price of the commodity to the consumer; and, as many of these duties are imposed on articles of necessity which are daily used by the great body of the people, the money raised by these imposts is drawn from their pockets.

Congress has no right, under the Constitution, to take money from the people unless it is required to execute some one of the specific powers entrusted to the government; and if they raise more than is necessary for such purposes, it is an abuse of the power of taxation and unjust and oppressive. It may, indeed, happen that the revenue will sometimes exceed the amount anticipated when the taxes were laid. When, however, this is ascertained, it is easy to reduce them; and, in such a case, it is unquestionably the duty of the government to reduce them, for no circumstances can justify it in assuming a power not given to it by the Constitution nor in taking away the money of the people when it is not needed for the legitimate wants of the government.

Plain as these principles appear to be, you will yet find that there is a constant effort to induce the general government to go beyond the limits of its taxing power and to impose unnecessary burdens upon the people. Many powerful interests are continually at work to procure heavy duties on commerce and to swell the revenue beyond the real necessities of the public service; and the country has already felt the injurious effects of their combined influence. They succeeded in obtaining a tariff of duties bearing most oppressively on the agricultural and laboring classes of society and producing a revenue that could not be usefully employed within the range of the powers conferred upon Congress; and, in order to fasten upon the people this unjust and unequal system of taxation, extravagant schemes of internal improvement were got up in various quarters to squander the money and to purchase support. Thus, one unconstitutional measure was intended to be upheld by another, and the abuse of the power of taxation was to be maintained by usurping the power of expending the money in internal improvements.

You cannot have forgotten the severe and doubtful struggle through which we passed when the Executive Department of the government, by its veto, endeavored to arrest this prodigal scheme of injustice and to bring back the legislation of Congress to the boundaries prescribed by the Constitution. The good sense and practical judgment of the people, when the subject was brought before them, sustained the course of the executive; and this plan of unconstitutional expenditure for the purpose of corrupt influence is, I trust, finally overthrown.

The result of this decision has been felt in the rapid extinguishment of the public debt and the large accumulation of a surplus in the treasury, notwithstanding the tariff was reduced and is now very far below the amount originally contemplated by its advocates. But, rely upon it, the design to collect an extravagant revenue and to burden you with taxes beyond the economical wants of the government is not yet abandoned. The various interests which have combined together to impose a heavy tariff

An Excerpt of President Andrew Jackson's Farewell Speech

and to produce an overflowing treasury are too strong and have too much at stake to surrender the contest. The corporations and wealthy individuals who are engaged in large manufacturing establishments desire a high tariff to increase their gains. Designing politicians will support it to conciliate their favor and to obtain the means of profuse expenditure for the purpose of purchasing influence in other quarters; and since the people have decided that the federal government cannot be permitted to employ its income in internal improvements, efforts will be made to seduce and mislead the citizens of the several states by holding out to them the deceitful prospect of benefits to be derived from a surplus revenue collected by the general government and annually divided among the states. And if, encouraged by these fallacious hopes, the states should disregard the principles of economy which ought to characterize every republican government and should indulge in lavish expenditures exceeding their resources, they will, before long, find themselves oppressed with debts which they are unable to pay, and the temptation will become irresistible to support high tariff in order to obtain a surplus for distribution.

Do not allow yourselves, my fellow citizens, to be misled on this subject. The federal government cannot collect a surplus for such purposes without violating the principles of the Constitution and assuming powers which have not been granted. It is, moreover, a system of injustice, and, if persisted in, will inevitably lead to corruption and must end in ruin. The surplus revenue will be drawn from the pockets of the people, from the farmer, the mechanic, and the laboring classes of society; but who will receive it when distributed among the states, where it is to be disposed of by leading state politicians who have friends to favor and political partisans to gratify? It will certainly not be returned to those who paid it and who have most need of it and are honestly entitled to it. There is but one safe rule, and that is to confine the general government rigidly within the sphere of its appropriate duties. It has no power to raise a revenue or impose taxes except for the purposes enumerated in the Constitution; and if its income is found to exceed these wants, it should be forthwith reduced, and the burdens of the people so far lightened.

A GOLDEN AGE ECONOMY

In reviewing the conflicts which have taken place between different interests in the United States and the policy pursued since the adoption of our present form of government, we find nothing that has produced such deep-seated evil as the course of legislation in relation to the currency. The Constitution of the United States unquestionably intended to secure to the people a circulating medium of gold and silver. But the establishment of a national bank by Congress with the privilege of issuing paper money receivable in the payment of the public dues, and the unfortunate course of legislation in the several states upon the same subject, drove from general circulation the constitutional currency and substituted one of paper in its place.

It was not easy for men engaged in the ordinary pursuits of business, whose attention had not been particularly drawn to the subject, to foresee all the consequences of a currency exclusively of paper; and we ought not, on that account, to be surprised at the facility with which laws were obtained to carry into effect the paper system. Honest and even enlightened men are sometimes misled by the specious and plausible statements of the designing. But experience has now proved the mischiefs and dangers of a paper currency, and it rests with you to determine whether the proper remedy shall be applied.

The paper system being founded on public confidence and having of itself no intrinsic value, it is liable to great and sudden fluctuations, thereby rendering property insecure and the wages of labor unsteady and uncertain. The corporations which create the paper money cannot be relied upon to keep the circulating medium uniform in amount. In times of prosperity, when confidence is high, they are tempted by the prospect of gain or by the influence of those who hope to profit by it to extend their issues of paper beyond the bounds of discretion and the reasonable demands of business. And when these issues have been pushed on from day to day until the public confidence is at length shaken, then a reaction takes place, and they immediately withdraw the credits they have given; suddenly curtail their issues; and produce an unexpected and ruinous contraction of the circulating medium which is felt by the whole community.

An Excerpt of President Andrew Jackson's Farewell Speech

The banks, by this means, save themselves, and the mischievous consequences of their imprudence or cupidity are visited upon the public. Nor does the evil stop here. These ebbs and flows in the currency and these indiscreet extensions of credit naturally engender a spirit of speculation injurious to the habits and character of the people. We have already seen its effects in the wild spirit of speculation in the public lands and various kinds of stock which, within the last year or two, seized upon such a multitude of our citizens and threatened to pervade all classes of society and to withdraw their attention from the sober pursuits of honest industry. It is not by encouraging this spirit that we shall best preserve public virtue and promote the true interests of our country.

But if your currency continues as exclusively paper as it now is, it will foster this eager desire to amass wealth without labor; it will multiply the number of dependents on bank accommodations and bank favors; the temptation to obtain money at any sacrifice will become stronger and stronger, and inevitably lead to corruption which will find its way into your public councils and destroy, at no distant day, the purity of your government. Some of the evils which arise from this system of paper press, with peculiar hardship, upon the class of society least able to bear it. A portion of this currency frequently becomes depreciated or worthless, and all of it is easily counterfeited in such a manner as to require peculiar skill and much experience to distinguish the counterfeit from the genuine note. These frauds are most generally perpetrated in the smaller notes, which are used in the daily transactions of ordinary business; and the losses occasioned by them are commonly thrown upon the laboring classes of society whose situation and pursuits put it out of their power to guard themselves from these impositions and whose daily wages are necessary for their subsistence.

It is the duty of every government so to regulate its currency as to protect this numerous class as far as practicable from the impositions of avarice and fraud. It is more especially the duty of the United States where the government is emphatically the government of the people, and where this respectable portion of

A GOLDEN AGE ECONOMY

our citizens are so proudly distinguished from the laboring classes of all other nations by their independent spirit, their love of liberty, their intelligence, and their high tone of moral character. Their industry in peace is the source of our wealth, and their bravery in war has covered us with glory; and the government of the United States will but ill discharge its duties if it leaves them a prey to such dishonest impositions. Yet it is evident that their interests cannot be effectually protected unless silver and gold are restored to circulation.

These views alone of the paper currency are sufficient to call for immediate reform; but there is another consideration which should still more strongly press it upon your attention.

Recent events have proved that the paper money system of this country may be used as an engine to undermine your free institutions; and that those who desire to engross all power in the hands of the few and to govern by corruption or force are aware of its power and prepared to employ it. Your banks now furnish your only circulating medium, and money is plenty or scarce according to the quantity of notes issued by them. While they have capitals not greatly disproportioned to each other, they are competitors in business, and no one of them can exercise dominion over the rest. And although, in the present state of the currency, these banks may and do operate injuriously upon the habits of business, the pecuniary concerns, and the moral tone of society, yet, from their number and dispersed situation, they cannot combine for the purpose of political influence; and whatever may be the dispositions of some of them their power of mischief must necessarily be confined to a narrow space and felt only in their immediate neighborhoods.

But when the charter of the Bank of the United States was obtained from Congress, it perfected the schemes of the paper system and gave its advocates the position they have struggled to obtain from the commencement of the federal government down to the present hour. The immense capital and peculiar privileges bestowed upon it enabled it to exercise despotic sway over the other banks in every part of the country. From its superior strength it could seriously injure, if not destroy, the business of any one of

An Excerpt of President Andrew Jackson's Farewell Speech

them which might incur its resentment; and it openly claimed for itself the power of regulating the currency throughout the United States. In other words, it asserted (and it undoubtedly possessed) the power to make money plenty or scarce, at its pleasure, at any time, and in any quarter of the Union, by controlling the issues of other banks and permitting an expansion or compelling a general contraction of the circulating medium according to its own will.

The other banking institutions were sensible of its strength, and they soon generally became its obedient instruments, ready at all times to execute its mandates; and with the banks necessarily went, also, that numerous class of persons in our commercial cities who depend altogether on bank credits for their solvency and means of business; and who are, therefore, obliged for their own safety to propitiate the favor of the money power by distinguished zeal and devotion in its service.

The result of the ill-advised legislation which established this great monopoly was to concentrate the whole money power of the Union, with its boundless means of corruption and its numerous dependents, under the direction and command of one acknowledged head; thus organizing this particular interest as one body and securing to it unity and concert of action throughout the United States and enabling it to bring forward, upon any occasion, its entire and undivided strength to support or defeat any measure of the government. In the hands of this formidable power, thus perfectly organized, was also placed unlimited dominion over the amount of the circulating medium, giving it the power to regulate the value of property and the fruits of labor in every quarter of the Union and to bestow prosperity or bring ruin upon any city or section of the country as might best comport with its own interest or policy.

We are not left to conjecture how the moneyed power, thus organized and with such a weapon in its hands, would be likely to use it. The distress and alarm which pervaded and agitated the whole country when the Bank of the United States waged war upon the people in order to compel them to submit to its demands cannot yet be forgotten. The ruthless and unsparing temper with which whole cities and communities were oppressed, individuals impoverished and ruined, and a scene of cheerful prosperity suddenly changed into one of gloom and despondency ought to be indelibly impressed on the memory of the people of the United States.

If such was its power in a time of peace, what would it not have been in a season of war with an enemy at your doors? No nation but the freemen of the United States could have come out victorious from such a contest; yet, if you had not conquered, the government would have passed from the hands of the many to the hands of the few; and this organized money power, from its secret conclave, would have directed the choice of your highest officers and compelled you to make peace or war as best suited their own wishes. The forms of your government might, for a time, have remained; but its living spirit would have departed from it.

The distress and sufferings inflicted on the people by the Bank are some of the fruits of that system of policy which is continually striving to enlarge the authority of the federal government beyond the limits fixed by the Constitution. The powers enumerated in that instrument do not confer on Congress the right to establish such a corporation as the Bank of the United States; and the evil consequences which followed may warn us of the danger of departing from the true rule of construction and of permitting temporary circumstances or the hope of better promoting the public welfare to influence, in any degree, our decisions upon the extent of the authority of the general government. Let us abide by the Constitution as it is written or amend it in the constitutional mode if it is found defective.

The severe lessons of experience will, I doubt not, be sufficient to prevent Congress from again chartering such a monopoly, even if the Constitution did not present an insuperable objection to it. But you must remember, my fellow citizens, that eternal vigilance by the people is the price of liberty; and that you must pay the price if you wish to secure the blessing. It behooves you, therefore, to be watchful in your states as well as in the federal government. The power which the moneyed interest can exercise, when concentrated under a single head, and with our present system of currency, was sufficiently demonstrated in the struggle made by the Bank of the

An Excerpt of President Andrew Jackson's Farewell Speech

United States. Defeated in the general government, the same class of intriguers and politicians will now resort to the states and endeavor to obtain there the same organization which they failed to perpetuate in the Union; and with specious and deceitful plans of public advantages and state interests and state pride they will endeavor to establish, in the different states, one moneyed institution with overgrown capital and exclusive privileges sufficient to enable it to control the operations of the other banks.

Such an institution will be pregnant with the same evils produced by the Bank of the United States, although its sphere of action is more confined; and in the state in which it is chartered the money power will be able to embody its whole strength and to move together with undivided force to accomplish any object it may wish to attain. You have already had abundant evidence of its power to inflict injury upon the agricultural, mechanical, and laboring classes of society, and over whose engagements in trade or speculation render them dependent on bank facilities, the dominion of the state monopoly will be absolute, and their obedience unlimited. With such a bank and a paper currency, the money power would, in a few years, govern the state and control its measures; and if a sufficient number of states can be induced to create such establishments, the time will soon come when it will again take the field against the United States and succeed in perfecting and perpetuating its organization by a charter from Congress.

It is one of the serious evils of our present system of banking that it enables one class of society, and that by no means a numerous one, by its control over the currency to act injuriously upon the interests of all the others and to exercise more than its just proportion of influence in political affairs. The agricultural, the mechanical, and the laboring classes have little or no share in the direction of the great moneyed corporations; and from their habits and the nature of their pursuits, they are incapable of forming extensive combinations to act together with united force. Such concert of action may sometimes be produced in a single city or in a small district of country by means of personal communications with each other; but they have no regular or active correspondence with those who are engaged in similar pursuits in distant places. They have but little patronage to give the press and exercise but a small share of influence over it; they have no crowd of dependents about them who hope to grow rich without labor by their countenance and favor and who are, therefore, always ready to exercise their wishes.

The planter, the farmer, the mechanic, and the laborer all know that their success depends upon their own industry and economy and that they must not expect to become suddenly rich by the fruits of their toil. Yet these classes of society form the great body of the people of the United States; they are the bone and sinew of the country; men who love liberty and desire nothing but equal rights and equal laws and who, moreover, hold the great mass of our national wealth, although it is distributed in moderate amounts among the millions of freemen who possess it. But, with overwhelming numbers and wealth on their side, they are in constant danger of losing their fair influence in the government, and with difficulty maintain their just rights against the incessant efforts daily made to encroach upon them.

The mischief springs from the power which the moneyed interest derives from a paper currency which they are able to control; from the multitude of corporations with exclusive privileges which they have succeeded in obtaining in the different states and which are employed altogether for their benefit; and unless you become more watchful in your states and check this spirit of monopoly and thirst for exclusive privileges, you will, in the end, find that the most important powers of government have been given or bartered away, and the control over your dearest interests has passed into the hands of these corporations.

The paper money system and its natural associates, monopoly and exclusive privileges, have already struck their roots deep in the soil; and it will require all your efforts to check its further growth and to eradicate the evil. The men who profit by the abuses and desire to perpetuate them will continue to besiege the halls of legislation in the general government as well as in the states and will seek, by every artifice, to mislead and deceive the public servants. It is to yourselves that you must look for safety and the

An Excerpt of President Andrew Jackson's Farewell Speech

means of guarding and perpetuating your free institutions. In your hands is rightfully placed the sovereignty of the country and to you everyone placed in authority is ultimately responsible. It is always in your power to see that the wishes of the people are carried into faithful execution, and their will, when once made known, must sooner or later be obeyed. And while the people remain, as I trust they ever will, uncorrupted and incorruptible and continue watchful and jealous of their rights, the government is safe, and the cause of freedom will continue to triumph over all its enemies.

But it will require steady and persevering exertions on your part to rid yourselves of the iniquities and mischiefs of the paper system and to check the spirit of monopoly and other abuses which have sprung up with it and of which it is the main support. So many interests are united to resist all reform on this subject that you must not hope the conflict will be a short one nor success easy. My humble efforts have not been spared during my administration of the government to restore the constitutional currency of gold and silver; and something, I trust, has been done toward the accomplishment of this most desirable object. But enough yet remains to require all your energy and perseverance. The power, however, is in your hands, and the remedy must and will be applied if you determine upon it.

While I am thus endeavoring to press upon your attention the principles which I deem of vital importance in the domestic concerns of the country, I ought not to pass over without notice the important considerations which should govern your policy toward foreign powers. It is unquestionably our true interest to cultivate the most friendly understanding with every nation and to avoid by every honorable means the calamities of war, and we shall best attain this object by frankness and sincerity in our foreign intercourse, by the prompt and faithful execution of treaties, and by justice and impartiality in our conduct to all. But no nation, however desirous of peace, can hope to escape occasional collisions with other powers, and the soundest dictates of policy require that we should place ourselves in a condition to assert our rights if a resort to force should ever become necessary. Our local situation, our long line of seacoast, indented by numerous bays, with deep rivers opening into the interior, as well as our extended and still increasing commerce, point to the Navy as our natural means of defense. It will in the end be found to be the cheapest and most effectual, and now is the time, in a season of peace and with an overflowing revenue, that we can year after year add to its strength without increasing the burdens of the people. It is your true policy, for your Navy will not only protect your rich and flourishing commerce in distant seas, but will enable you to reach and annoy the enemy and will give to defense its greatest efficiency by meeting danger at a distance from home. It is impossible by any line of fortifications to guard every point from attack against a hostile force advancing from the ocean and selecting its object, but they are indispensable to protect cities from bombardment, dockyards and naval arsenals from destruction, to give shelter to merchant vessels in time of war and to single ships or weaker squadrons when pressed by superior force. Fortifications of this description can not be too soon completed and armed and placed in a condition of the most perfect preparation. The abundant means we now possess can not be applied in any manner more useful to the country, and when this is done and our naval force sufficiently strengthened and our militia armed we need not fear that any nation will wantonly insult us or needlessly provoke hostilities. We shall more certainly preserve peace when it is well understood that we are prepared for War.

In presenting to you, my fellow-citizens, these parting counsels, I have brought before you the leading principles upon which I endeavored to administer the Government in the high office with which you twice honored me. Knowing that the path of freedom is continually beset by enemies who often assume the disguise of friends, I have devoted the last hours of my public life to warn you of the dangers. The progress of the United States under our free and happy institutions has surpassed the most sanguine hopes of the founders of the Republic. Our growth has been rapid beyond all former example in numbers, in wealth, in knowledge, and all the useful arts which contribute to the comforts and convenience of man, and from the earliest ages of history to the present day there never have been thirteen millions of people associated in one

An Excerpt of President Andrew Jackson's Farewell Speech

political body who enjoyed so much freedom and happiness as the people of these United States. You have no longer any cause to fear danger from abroad; your strength and power are well known throughout the civilized world, as well as the high and gallant bearing of your sons. It is from within, among yourselves – from cupidity, from corruption, from disappointed ambition and inordinate thirst for power – that factions will be formed and liberty endangered. It is against such designs, whatever disguise the actors may assume, that you have especially to guard yourselves. You have the highest of human trusts committed to your care. Providence has showered on this favored land blessings without number, and has chosen you as the guardians of freedom, to preserve it for the benefit of the human race. May He who holds in His hands the destinies of nations make you worthy of the favors He has bestowed and enable you, with pure hearts and pure hands and sleepless vigilance, to guard and defend to the end of time the great charge He has committed to your keeping.

My own race is nearly run; advanced age and failing health warn me that before long I must pass beyond the reach of human events and cease to feel the vicissitudes of human affairs. I thank God that my life has been spent in a land of liberty and that He has given me a heart to love my country with the affection of a son. And filled with gratitude for your constant and unwavering kindness, I bid you a last and affectionate farewell."

http://www.presidency.ucsb.edu/ws/print.php?pid=67087

My thanks to Stewart Ogilby of Sarasota, Florida, USA who posted this on the internet for all to share.

"I believe that banking institutions are more dangerous to our liberties than standing armies. If the American people ever allow private banks to control the issue of their currency, first by inflation, then by deflation, the banks and corporations that will grow up around [the banks] will deprive the people of all property until their children wake-up homeless on the continent their fathers conquered. The issuing power should be taken from the banks and restored to the people, to whom it properly belongs."

– Thomas Jefferson
(3rd US President, 1743 – 1826)

EPISODE THREE

Restoration of The LAW

"Seek ye first the kingdom of God and his righteousness and all things shall be added unto you."
– Matthew 6:33

"But he that keepeth the law, happy is he."
– Proverbs 29:18

CONTENTS

Introduction	341
Jade's Story – THE DIVINE PLAN	344
Aemilianus' Story – SAINT GERMAIN'S FREEDOM MESSAGE	354
Boudikka's Story – THE GREAT CRASH OF 2012	358
Harald's Story – SOUND MONEY	373
Li's Story – AMERICA'S ENLIGHTENED FREE ENTERPRISE ECONOMY	389
Wende's Story – THE NEW INDUSTRIAL REVOLUTION	397
Suzanne's Story – ABUNDANCE IN HEALTH	400
Ptolemy's Story – LIBRARY OF TRUE RELIGIONS & ANTIQUITIES	409
Guinevere's Story – THE GOLDEN AGE OF ENERGY	413
The Secret Speaker's Story – THE NEW POPULAR MUSIC	419

ADDENDUM – WHAT CAN I DO?   **441**

Peaceful Non-Cooperation	443
Example Letters	453
LETTERS TO THE PRESS	457
The People's Bank	457
Bankers Perverted the Money System	458
Change Needed to Save the Economy	459
Creation of a New Bank is Called for	459
Government too Big, too Bossy and too Costly	460
Leaders Failing to Act on the Economy	461
God's Economic Policies Needed	462
The Golden Age Begun	464

INTRODUCTION

"What is good for the One is good for the All, for the All is in the One and the One is in the All."
— **Kim Andrew Lincoln**

This last episode is the story of the making of the Golden Age economy that arose from the ruins of the counterfeit kingdom.

In this tale we fast forward exactly one hundred years to January 9th 2112, to the Academy of Saint Germain in the town of Jackson, Jackson Hole, Wyoming, USA.

The students have returned from their Christmas break and are eager to continue their studies in manifesting abundance, which is the main focus of this special school sponsored by the Ascended Master, Saint Germain. In this future time education is the highest priority. It is open and free to all at every level, and no expense is spared in providing students with everything they need to learn new skills and raise their consciousness. Teachers and lecturers have been replaced by Masters, a title that denotes the holder's great wisdom. For as the Golden Age had begun to take shape it was realised that only those with the highest consciousness should be permitted to teach young minds, and thus receive the mantle of Master. For this was one of the highest accolades the people could bestow upon a citizen and thus all Masters were treated with great reverence and respect – as Alexander the Great and the sons of the nobles had treated their Master, Aristotle.

The Masters of this enlightened age were not recruited from teacher training college as young teachers were a century before, but from the 'University of Life' where each candidate was chosen because they had excelled in a particular field of endeavour. And thus, most Masters entered teaching at the end of their primary careers – as Master

A GOLDEN AGE ECONOMY

Prospero had done. He is the Senior Master of Economic History at the Academy and the principal character in this story. I should also mention that 'Prospero' was the Master's chosen name, not his birth name – in fact nobody knew his real name and no-one inquired, for why should they, he was Master Prospero, and that was all they needed to know. As to the Master's appearance, I can only report that it had changed somewhat over the years, as the Master had decided to grow his hair and a beard. Indeed, anyone who had known him before these changes would not have recognised him now. As far as his age was concerned, well no one was sure, although most people would have described him as middle-aged – whatever that means. His nationality was Citizen of the United Kingdom, but he lived almost permanently in America, having two houses, a small one near the Academy, and a much larger residence in the Hollywood Hills where he spent his vacations – when not travelling around the world. There were rumours that he was quite a wealthy man – a multi-millionaire in fact, but no one could say how he had acquired his money. As for his family, well that was yet another mystery.

At the end of the 2111 autumn term Master Prospero had instructed his first year students to prepare a lecture that they were to give to their fellow students at the start of the 2112 term. The theme of the lectures concerned what happened with the economy before, during and after the Great Crash of 2012, with the emphasis on how the economy had been restored. Each student had been given a subject to work on based on their individual interests and abilities. The purpose of the talks was to test the students' knowledge and understanding of the previous year's study and to fill in the gaps that Master Prospero had deliberately left in the syllabus, as he wanted his students to do more than just regurgitate what he had already taught.

So the scene is set for the first day of term and the first student lecture, but before I move on, a few words to the wise.

Although I look back from a future time, the tale that I tell is a projection of events that may or may not happen. In other words, all that I describe is *my* story, my immaculate concept of what I would like the future to be. It is my heart's desire turned into thoughts and ideas

Introduction

that I have envisioned in my mind. For, as Hermes stated, the universe is mental. It is created in the mind and made manifest by the power of the spoken word and the actions we take. We create our own reality and we become what we think about most. In writing this book it is my intention to influence the outcome, in the sense that the trains of the future run on the tracks that I have laid down here. And thus, if I was the only person on Earth, then what I say and what I do is the future because I alone am creating it.

But this is not exclusively my world.

It is **our** world. And although it is my wish to create, I am only one of seven billion souls on Earth – and all of us are intended to add to this great work that our Father/Mother God began.

What I am saying is that I cannot predict exactly what will happen. No one can – not even the Ascended Masters – though they can see into our hearts and our minds and guess what we are likely to do, they cannot be certain, because we all have free will and the right to change our minds, and thus to change the future. So please bear this in mind as you read my story through the characters you are about to meet. And, as you read on, I invite you to contribute your own ideas so that we create this Golden Age together. For on this track many different trains may run.

Jade's Story

THE DIVINE PLAN

"We alter our future by continually raising our consciousness from that of disempowered victim to empowered creator God/Goddess."

– **Unknown Ascended Master**

It is 9.00am on the 9th of January 2112 and the Academy is bristling with excitement as the students make their way to the first lectures of the new term and the New Year. There are nine young men and women in Master Prospero's class and some of them are showing signs of anxiety as the Master has given no prior indication of who will be the first to give their presentation. Some students, however, are more relaxed as they have reasoned that the lectures must be given in some sort of order as all stories must have a beginning, middle and end. But Jade, who is nineteen, a brunette and with the figure of a fashion model, has not realised this, nor that she will be the first speaker, because nothing moves forward without a plan and 'The Divine Plan' is the title of the talk she is about to give.

I should mention that every student had had a tutorial with the Master at the end of the autumn term to discuss what he wanted them to talk about, but this meant that Jade had had to do a lot of work over the holidays, because she had not always paid attention during lectures, preferring instead to engage in telepathic conversations with her boyfriend in San Francisco where she is based. But, of course, the Master knew this, which was one of the reasons for this annual 'revision' exercise.

Master Prospero walked briskly into the lecture theatre and every student immediately stood up – such was their respect for him. After going through the syllabus and study plan for the new term, he turned to Jade and invited her to come down to the lectern.

This is the transcript of Jade's presentation:

"We know from the official scriptures and the akashic records in heaven that the fallen angels were given a limited time to outplay their games on our planet and that by the time the primary elements of the Armageddon had ended (21/12/2012) most of them had been judged by the Court of the Sacred Fire on the God Star Sirius. Not a single fallen angel had been prepared to bend the knee to beloved Alpha and Omega and so when their physical bodies gave out their spiritual beings went straight to the second death. This meant that they were completely wiped out and thus never able to re-embody and cause harm in the physical or astral planes again. Those of the power elite who still had some light in them were given the opportunity to embody on another planet that had been created by the Elohim. This planet was much like Earth, having been designed to accommodate those evolutions who had refused to raise their consciousness and were thus still stuck in duality, with their pride, selfishness and warring ways. For, as we know from our spiritual studies, this is what characterises a third dimensional (3D) tribal society, the workings of which today, we find difficult to comprehend and physically painful to imagine.

As 2012 drew to a close a massive vibrational shift started on Earth and throughout our galaxy that was to continue for the next twenty years. This gradual uplift in vibrational frequency made it increasingly difficult and eventually ultimately physically impossible for 3D souls to remain here. But those who were already operating at the fourth dimensional level were invigorated by the change for they felt that they had been given a new lease of life. And yes, this was the reality, because with the big shift everyone was moving closer to heaven and people rejoiced in that knowledge and in the warmth of the experience. Earth was slowly but surely stepping up a gear into the fast lane that is occupied by fifth dimensional (5D) planets. She was moving faster now and was well on her way to becoming the Freedom Star that she had always been destined to become. For indeed this is what we are all working towards. For it is the ultimate aim of the divine plan for our planet, Earth.

Whereas 5D living is characterised by service to others the signature dish of the 3D world is service to self. So the 'End of Days' period that was portrayed in many movies of the time was extremely 'eventful'. Those of the fallen angels who knew that they would go straight to the second death felt that they had nothing to lose and so they set out to cause as much havoc and destruction as possible. But in many ways this outpouring of wickedness only accelerated their demise as it was the catalyst that brought about 'The Great Awakening' of the people.

This started from about 2002 when legions of Cosmic Beings of the 144,000 who came with Sanat Kumara to assist the people of Earth began to remember their individual missions. They had come to anchor their light in the Earth and with the help of their spirit guides, guardian angels and the Ascended Masters, they began to shine their lights into the dark corners of the Earth exposing the wrongdoing of the power elite. They created 'Truth About' websites and wrote books and made films and gave lectures that explained how the masses were being hoodwinked by the power elite. Gradually people's awareness of the truth increased and within a decade the most spiritual people were ready to lead the majority into a revolution to stop the destruction of the Mother energies on Earth.

THE 10% RULE

There were three distinct groups of people on the planet: the top ten per cent who were the most spiritual; the middle eighty per cent, and the bottom ten per cent – who had the lowest level of consciousness. The significance of these numbers is that the middle eighty per cent would have followed either the top or bottom groups depending on which group demonstrated the greatest leadership. This was the secret to the control of the planet at that time – the way unto heaven or hell.

And so it was that the top ten per cent of the most spiritually enlightened people on Earth began to demand that their countries be governed in accordance with God's Laws and the middle eighty per cent of people started to listen to them and lend their support. Within a decade the clarion calls for change were so loud that the political classes could no longer ignore them. There was an outpouring of peaceful non-cooperation with the power elite and this was a clear signal that there was about to be a change of management on Earth.

The Occupy Movement

Many different protest groups had laid their stakes in the ground and declared that "enough is enough" and one resistance movement was called 'Occupy Wall Street' that began in 2011. This was a peaceful protest against the corruption, criminality and greed of the bankers and speculators who controlled most countries' economies through their perverted monetary and banking system based on enslavement to debt. The Occupy movement spread rapidly around the world aided by the internet and especially social media sites like 'Facebook' to the point where the '99%' of people steadfastly refused to continue participating in the power elite's wicked and dualistic games.

The Credit Crunch & the Great Recession

While this had been happening the Holy Spirit had been active too, as between 2008 and 2012, the towers of Babel that the Luciferians, Laggards and Anunnaki had built, began to fall. As far as the monetary and banking system was concerned the seeds of its destruction had been sown three centuries earlier with the official sanctioning of fractional reserve banking in England, but things really came to a head in 2008 when the first financial volcano, the 'Credit Crunch', erupted. This was a warning shot across the bows of the bankers' sinking money ship. And the message from heaven was that it was time to establish a sound money system that served everyone, and not just the power elite. But the warning went largely unheeded and consequently, four years later, the second financial volcano exploded. But this time the damage done was so great that the towers of Babel could not be rebuilt. For even if it had been possible they would not have been able to function as the people now knew how they had been robbed and enslaved by the power elite. In fact, the 99%, as they came to be known, were so angry with the politicians, bankers and speculators who had allowed the collapse to happen that these fallen ones ran in fear of their lives and many were never seen or heard of again.

Saint Germain's Role

But something else had been happening behind the scenes in which our beloved Saint Germain had had a very large hand.

As all students of this Academy are aware, Saint Germain played a pivotal role in establishing America as the leader of the free world. Indeed in his embodiment as Christopher Columbus he discovered the American Continent. And, three centuries later, as an Ascended Master who had re-embodied, he was present at the signing of the Declaration of Independence. In fact, what the history books of the time did not record was that before the delegates signed their names to the Declaration, Saint Germain had had to persuade them to do so with an inspiring speech about freedom that was the equal of any soliloquy he had written as Shakespeare. Moreover, prior to that he had spent a great deal of time assisting, encouraging and mentoring both George Washington and Benjamin Franklin (two of the Founding Fathers) to get the thirteen States to the point where they were prepared to break their bonds with England. He inspired Thomas Jefferson to write the wonderful words of the Declaration of Independence and was the principal designer of the American flag, the star-spangled banner. But what is less well known, is that he is the spiritual Father of America who was inadvertently brought to life in the fictional poster character of Uncle Sam who implored American males to join the second war against the British in 1812.

But was Uncle Sam a fictional character? No, not really, because his name derives from Saint Germain's past life as the Prophet Samuel – hence the name Uncle Sam.

So we can see that he has been – and still is – the guiding light and helping hand in the rise of our Republic and the other nations of the world who have benefited from his tireless work in assisting them to express the full measure of the freedom flame that he represents as the God of Freedom.

But there is more to tell, for in the decades that preceded the tumultuous events of 2012, a secret plan had been hatched in heaven for the purpose of enabling the people of Earth to make the transition from the Dark Age economy, which they were weary of, to the enlightened one that they dreamed of – and longed to manifest. The Ascended Host knew that if the economy had been allowed to collapse completely, without there being a Plan B in place to aid a recovery, then the devastation and suffering that would ensue would put the building of the New Jerusalem at risk or, at the very least, delay its construction. It was also felt that the people had suffered enough in the Armageddon and in the 500,000 years that the fallen angels had held sway on Earth, and that it was now time to give the people the opportunity to make creative use of the new found freedom that they were about to experience – as the power elite would no longer be holding the reins of power. And, though many were involved in the implementation of this plan, it had largely been the brainchild of our beloved Saint German.

But there was to be no free ride in the sense that people could rest on their laurels and let the angels and Ascended Masters do all the work. As we all know we are blessed because we live in a universe where the Primary Creator has given us free reign and thus the beings in heaven – though there are many more of them above than there are humans here below – cannot interfere by doing the work of creation that God has entrusted to us, his co-creators.

So what happened after the big shift began on 21/12/2012?

Well, I cannot say, for this is a tale that perhaps one or more of you is soon to tell. But before I take my leave there is another aspect of the divine plan that I would like to share, of which our brothers and sisters of a century past were – with the exception of a few – blissfully unaware. And that of course is the story of our 'Space Brothers'.

A GOLDEN AGE ECONOMY

Space Brothers

What people of a hundred and thirty years ago did not realise was that many of the movies and TV shows that featured strange-looking alien races and planets, warp-drive spaceships, wormholes, wars in space and Galactic Federations were all based on reality, albeit a reality of which they were not aware. We have all seen these shows from the media archives. *The Hitchhiker's Guide to the Galaxy, Deep Space Nine*, my favourite, *Star Trek* and the *Star Wars* series of movies that were so popular then. As the technology for deep space travel did not exist and the movements of Anunnaki spaceships to and from Earth and the moon went undetected, some people thought that our planet was the only one inhabited by intelligent life. And, as scientists and governments had said nothing to the contrary, that idea prevailed in the minds of many, but for the rest, the vastness of the Cosmos gave rise to much speculation that we had friends in the Milky Way, and perhaps beyond – and possibly some not so friendly souls too. So, was it pure coincidence that these so called sci-fi TV shows and movies started to appear at that time or were they inspired by the Ascended Masters to prepare us for what was to come? Well, as coincidences cannot occur, that question is answered!

Polarity Integration

Another mystery for the majority of our 3D and 4D ancestors was the name of the game that they had been playing up until the time that Earth ascended and the Golden Age of Saint Germain began. I refer, of course, to the universal game of spiritual evolution called 'Polarity Integration', which is one of many games that have been played in the different universes that make up the infinite totality of the ever expanding 'All that Is'. This was the game chosen by the twelve Elohim (Creator Gods) who founded this universe, and who invited souls from other universes experienced in this game to come and play it here.

I do not intend to recount the history of the 'Three Earths' and the wars between the humans and reptilian races that led to the destruction of the first two Earths, as most students here lived through those times, and anyway, this important part of our Galactic history is well documented at: www.nibiruancouncil.com. But what I am going to talk about is the meaning of polarity integration and its relationship to the teachings given by Jesus and Gautama Buddha who came with Sanat Kumara on the rescue mission to Earth.

In this context, polarity integration means the integration of the two opposites of light and dark. Light corresponds with everything that is imbued with the vibration of love, such as happiness, forgiveness, sharing and service to others. And these in turn correspond to the chakras above the heart. And dark corresponds with all fear-based energies, like anger, hatred, greed, selfishness and lack that are associated with the lower chakras. The light represents the reward and the dark the lesson or challenge that we must overcome. The key is to see the value in both the positive (light) and the negative (dark) in any given situation, as all experience teaches us something that will help us to raise our vibration.

The ultimate aim of the game is to achieve compassion, which is the integration point where enlightenment and therefore balance are found. The greatest challenge of the game is finding value in the dark, because when we are party to unpleasant experiences we naturally want to put them behind us rather than to dwell on those aspects of the lessons that helped us to move forward in spiritual terms. Without new challenges to overcome, we become spiritually stuck, and so to work properly, the process of creation needs the interaction of the positive (expanding, male energies) and negative (contracting, female energies) to both create new life, and to move existing life onwards and upwards.

We are all players on the great stage of life and therefore we are destined to play many roles within the polarity spectrum. And, it is only by doing so that we have a chance of winning the 'Golden Globe' for *compassion* that is the goal of this game.

We evolve spiritually through our experiences in different planetary schools and each one has different degrees of free will. Earth is a school room where souls are given the opportunity to experience the full extent of their choices and so this planet has been designated a 'grand experiment'. There have only ever been two other planets in our universe where free will was unrestricted and both of them were destroyed in the attempts to achieve polarity integration.

In Jesus' teachings the equivalent of the integration point of compassion would be what he called the 'Middle Way', which is that place beyond relative good and evil (duality) where we are able to observe conflicts from a point of absolute detachment and peace, so that what harm is said and done flows over us and passes away. This is why Jesus taught that we should turn the other cheek. It is to stop the endless tit for tat escalation of violence that occurs when each side refuses to forgive the past actions of the other. But with that teaching Jesus did not mean that we should stand idly by and let evil flow, but that we should call to the powers in heaven for its judgement. The same idea is embedded in the teachings of the Lord of the World, Gautama Buddha, who says that we must conquer all desire and become detached from it, so that we are not driven by those thoughts and feelings that prevent the light from flowing through our bodies from above to below and back again. And thus, it is only when we have neutralised these fear-based energies – so that they have nothing in us – that we can attain enlightenment.

When we look back at the polarity integration game from the highest level of consciousness that we can possibly imagine, i.e. from that of the Creator Gods surveying all that they have made, we see life, at the Galactic level, completely differently. For the human and reptilian races had only been playing their designated roles in the game the founders decided they should play – for the ultimate good, which is the spiritual evolution of all life. And when you really think about this from our standpoint, there is no bigger picture than this.

The reptilians that included the Anunnaki were given a creation myth that said that they had the right to conquer and destroy any planet and its inhabitants, and the humans were told that they must strive to live in harmony with all races. To use an ancient colloquialism, the reptilians played the baddies and the humans the goodies. But either race is neither right nor wrong or good nor bad because we are all strutting players on the stage of life.

"Life's but a walking shadow, a poor player that struts and frets his hour upon the stage."

– William Shakespeare
(From his play, *Macbeth*)

Thank you."

Aemilianus' Story

SAINT GERMAIN'S FREEDOM MESSAGE

Master Prospero was mightily pleased with Jade's lecture, as she had surpassed even his expectations of what is possible when we apply ourselves to the task in hand. The other students were impressed too, as Jade had displayed a side of herself that hitherto had been hidden. However, her dissertation had been somewhat longer than the Master had envisaged as he had only allowed three hours for all the presentations with a half-hour contingency for overruns. He looked at his watch intently and then beckoned the next speaker down to the podium.

Aemilianus (Aemil for short) was a dark, athletic-looking young man from Rome, who had a passion for poetry and ancient Greek and Roman history. Aemil was very much a free spirit and had been delighted to have been given this subject for his lecture.

This is what he said:

"Looking back into the mists of our 3D history it is difficult to say when the people of Earth were most free because we can measure freedom in so many different ways. For example, it is easy to relate to the concept of physical freedom because clearly if someone has been confined to a prison cell there can be no argument that their freedom of movement has been severely curtailed. But what about their spiritual freedom – their ability to think, to imagine, to create in the mind? Indeed, one could argue that an incarcerated person, who is provided with accommodation and food and who has immediate access to medical services has been liberated from the chores of daily life that devour the attention of the majority, and thus in purely spiritual terms, prisoners could be considered to have greater freedom because they have the time and energy to focus their thinking on creative pursuits.

I have, on occasions, thought what I might do to occupy my time if I found myself in prison, and I always came to the same conclusion, which was that I would write, as it is one of my greatest loves. But what of the slaves who were forced to toil in the thousand years of the Roman Empire? Were they any more or less free than the young children who were sold by their parents into industrial bondage in the cotton trade in India one hundred years ago? And how free was the family living in a socialist Sweden where almost all of their needs were provided for by the State, funded out of punitive taxation that was levied on the people who barely had to think for themselves. And how does that compare to the poor souls who were subjected to starvation, abuse and all manner of tyranny by the North Korean regime of the 'Kims' during the second half of the twentieth century and early part of the twenty-first century?

So what are the answers to these questions? And what does it really mean to choose freedom? Well, our beloved Saint Germain answers as follows:

"It means to free the electrons in your body and consciousness to flow with freedom's fire. It means to allow the electron to choose the path of freedom and not to subject that electron to the bondage of a limited consciousness, a limited matrix. It means to free your own self-awareness so that you can be aware of the self as having the potential of the Infinite."

We learn from Elizabeth Clare Prophet, who held the spiritual office of the Guru Ma and was a messenger for the Ascended Host during the later part of the twentieth century, that:

"Saint Germain is concerned about freedom and its preservation in every nation. He speaks out about the selling away of America – the giving away of her funds and technology. The American people should not have to bear the burden of the support of all nations. Saint Germain especially deplores the selling of military secrets, arms and weapons to those who turn around and use these against the sons and daughters of God in every nation."

She goes on to say that Saint Germain saw the biggest foe to freedom as our own selfishness and self-indulgence and that if we allowed it to go unchecked it would cause us to lose our freedom.

She said that:

"Saint Germain inspires us to make greater sacrifices for freedom, to not indulge ourselves so much in luxuries, but to realize that the calling and destiny of the American people is to guard freedom and to be the watchmen on the wall of freedom for the world. This involves sacrifice, but Saint Germain says that if we allow America to be the last remaining republic and the last place where full freedom is accorded the individual, we will not stand. Therefore he is for the defence of freedom in every nation and he holds us accountable for allowing the deaths of millions of people, as we have previously supported the totalitarian regimes that have taken over their nations."

During the course of an interview that Elizabeth Clare Prophet gave about Saint Germain's views on freedom, she relayed the message that America should defend Taiwan as an island of people of light and that it should not become a football between East and West. And that American children should receive the "right education and the right understanding of our nation and its peculiar genius".

And that:

"Rather than advocating the blending of all nations into a one-world type of government, Saint Germain teaches us that the individual genius of every nation must be preserved as a crucible for individual self-government and that the types of self-government that people evolve must be unique to their own souls' evolution."

On the form of government that nations should choose, Saint Germain expressed the view that the US system was not necessarily the best for every nation and "that a world-elite body ruling peoples who ought to be ruling themselves and who ought to be taught the way of self-government", was inconsistent with the ideals of freedom.

As the God of Freedom, he reserves his harshest rebuke for World Communism saying that he sees it as the greatest threat to individual freedom, especially the freedom of the soul to walk the path of initiation with the Christ and the Buddha. Where that freedom is denied, the purpose for life and for living is lost and then the very purpose for the perpetuation of Earth itself is lost.

He explains that every soul on Earth is intended to be free to attain reunion with God. Where that freedom is denied, those who deny it must be challenged. He is fervent about this because the people of the world today are in embodiment to inaugurate a new age – two thousand years when the flame of freedom in science, education, art and culture must be extolled.

Saint Germain cautions that, as a people and government, we cannot compromise. We cannot sit at the table with the enemies of freedom and proceed to give away entire territories and nations and actually seal the fate of millions of souls in the hands of those who are the tyrants.

He warns us that these tyrants exist in both the East and West and that we must watch those of our representatives in government who are not actually continuing the purposes for which America was founded. He says that it is important that we realise that it is more than material freedom that must be guarded: it is spiritual freedom.

Saint Germain's message is that America's purpose is to champion free enterprise over Socialism because the free enterprise system affords the maximum opportunity for individuals to develop the Christ-potential within themselves, and that this is compromised when governments and/or large corporations do for the individual what they should be doing for themselves. He warns that under Socialism and Corporatocracy the individual is deprived of their freedom to create. He teaches that without the freedom to create there is no freedom. The opportunity to create is the basic endowment we have with the gift of free will.

He states that when governments do everything for people, so that they do not have to exercise the muscles of the mind or even physically move themselves, then the energies of sloth, self-centeredness and the pleasure cult take hold. And, that if we allow that to happen, then the freedom we cherish so much will surely slip away."

Aemil thanked his audience then quickly returned to his seat.

Boudikka's Story

THE GREAT CRASH OF 2012

The speaker after Aemil had sensed that she would be next and was already gathering up her papers when the Master invited her down to the lecture platform.

Boudikka had flaming-red hair that plunged to her waist, and the fire of her Celtic ancestry burned in her eyes. She was a woman who demanded attention. When she spoke you listened and when she moved, the eyes in the room followed the rhythm of her tune.

This is her speech:

"What was surprising about the Great Crash of 2012 was that no one who understood how the economy worked (or should I say did not work) was surprised. The economic soothsayers and prophets of doom had been forming an orderly queue to pronounce upon its coming many decades before. But nothing that they said had ever found its way into the mainstream media because it had been censored by the power elite.

Any economist of note had denounced fractional reserve banking as a Ponzi scheme and said that it only served the interests of the bankers. Congressman Ron Paul (who was seeking the Republican Party Presidential nomination at the time) advocated its immediate abolition and used the following starkly-worded analogy to describe it:

"It's sort of like a drug. You get some benefits if you keep using it – you know, run up debt, run up inflation, monetize the debt, make a bigger bubble. Just like a drug addiction, the drug addict feels better when he keeps getting drugs. But the high can't last forever and, like so many cases of drug addicts, if you don't do something about it, you kill the patient. And right now the patient is very, very big, and that's the worldwide economy."

In the United Kingdom the Governor of the Bank of England, Mervin King, who had been in office when the Credit Crunch struck, was similarly disparaging in his remarks, saying that: "Of all the ways of organising banking, the worst one is the one we have today."

To pronounce that fractional reserve banking was the heart of the world's economic problems was never in dispute. The issue was that the remedy was never aired in public – even by the world-renowned BBC, which was supposed to be impartial.

So what then was the trigger that set the world economy on this course towards potential oblivion?

Well, many different opinions have been aired on this subject and I believe that all of them have varying degrees of merit. My own view is that this volcano began to rumble in 1971 when President Nixon took America off the Gold Standard. He had been desperate for money to fund the crippling cost of the Vietnam War and rather than raise taxes he chose the politically expedient option of allowing the Federal Reserve to crank up the money-printing presses and counterfeit the dollar. Thus the currency became detached from the value of the gold against which it had been partially backed. By any standards this was a treasonous act, but it was not the first time that an American President had resorted to such criminality. Naturally this action was highly inflationary. It was really from this point onwards that the amount of debt that had been piled upon the people started to build in a noticeable way.

It was in the following two decades that the use of highly-leveraged debt instruments got seriously out of control. During the Clinton years all restrictions on this type of activity had been lifted and the curse of derivative trading was unleashed. Unbeknown to all but the most enlightened, this money madness was sowing the seeds of the future collapse.

The expansion of the City of London that followed the abandonment of credit controls under Margaret Thatcher's government

A GOLDEN AGE ECONOMY

had been another contributory factor. The illuminati regarded the London City State as the world capital of finance. Washington DC was their military hub and Vatican City in Rome their religious centre. These three autonomous jurisdictions were responsible to no one but the elite, and yet their combined power was so great that they exercised significant influence over the planet.

Essentially what the power elite had created was a massive debt-making machine with which to enslave the people, but over which they could not exercise absolute control.

In answer to the question what caused the Great Crash my assessment is that it was two things: debt piled upon more debt.

The first debt was created by the fractional reserve banking system, where money was created out of nothing, as debt. And the second debt was derivative-based debt, where institutions bought insurance (credit default swaps) against the possibility of a debt default by companies and countries who had become indebted. But the important point here is that in the main these financial institutions had no 'insurable interest' in that debt, meaning that if the borrower defaulted they would not be directly affected. What they were doing was betting that there would be a default with the expectation that they would make a profit. This created the possibility that in the event of a default, the insurers (who were the biggest US banks) of the debt would have no chance of paying out on the policies they had underwritten because they did not hold sufficient reserves to meet all claims. And thus, derivatives made the existing tower of debt taller, so that all it would take to bring the tower down was a relatively small default, because with so many people gambling on the same risk, the financial impact would be multiplied many times over. But this type of derivative made up only about 8% of the total market. Two thirds of it ($500 trillion) was concerned with trading related to interest rates. And with all the problems that were about to surface, massive claims on this side of the business would turn out to be much more than the $70 trillion world economy could bear.

The other important link in the chain was the chain itself, as all financial institutions were in some way linked together through this vast cesspool of debt, so that if one of them got their feet dirty the mess would quickly spread to the rest. Indeed, the interconnectedness of all life was never more evident than in the business of creating and increasing debt.

The economic devastation that spewed forth when the expected debt defaults occurred was unprecedented. As Jade suggested in her lecture, the Credit Crunch of 2008 was the hors d'oeuvres, but the main course was the Great Crash, four years later.

Greece was famous as the birthplace of democracy and the home of the Olympic Games, but in 2012 it earned the dubious distinction of becoming the first developed nation to play host to the unravelling of the Dark Age economy. Greece's economic woes - it's over generous welfare system and the relaxed attitude of its people to paying taxes - were legendary; but the good times could not go on forever, without a reality check. And that duly arrived in the decade that preceded the Great Crash. By the time the government had realised that the party was over, it was too late to roll back the overspending without causing great harm to the economy, but with the bailiffs standing at the door it appeared that they had no choice, and so enormous hardships had to be endured by the people if the government was to avoid bankruptcy and ejection from the euro. But it was not to be as the default that they had tried so hard to avoid finally came to pass in 2012.

The illuminati were determined to stop the euro from collapsing, as they needed it to be the springboard for their planned single world currency. But the markets were not fooled by all the debt reshuffling moves by the European Central Bank and International Monetary Fund and so the axe eventually fell. Following Greece's default, the financial vultures appeared overhead waiting to feed off the next national corpse that was about to fall. And they were not to be disappointed. For once the first domino had fallen that put pressure on the next. But as that one was weak too, it also fell, and that exerted even more pressure on the next domino in line. And so, one by one, the economies of the euro zone began to fail, and, in economic terms, mainland Europe became a battlefield full of sick and wounded economies.

Even though the United Kingdom had its own currency, it was not immune from the fallout as British banks had exposure to both

A GOLDEN AGE ECONOMY

sovereign and corporate debt in the euro zone. As the depression deepened default rates soared taking the major banks to the brink of insolvency. Within a short time those 'too big to fail' banks that were not already owned by the State became so.

What happened in one European country was fairly representative of what happened in the others – although the least indebted countries suffered less. Our national archives and history books are full of detailed accounts of what took place during these tumultuous times. However, as the City of London was the headquarters of the Illumunati's worldwide financial empire it seems appropriate to share with you an account of the unfolding events in the United Kingdom. I will then move on to summarise what happened in our country and elsewhere. To make these accounts a little more interesting I have decided to describe the UK scenario through the story of a private citizen, and the US one from the 'free' internet archives.

The UK citizen, Mr Clinnol, was an Independent Financial Adviser, who had predicted the Great Crash eight years earlier and, although the timing of his forecasts had not been precise, the main thrust of what he believed would happen was close to the mark. I collated the information I am about to present from material that Mr Clinnol had made public, as he had been active in his opposition to the way the economy had been manipulated and had gone to great lengths to explain to people how they had been deceived by the power elite and what they could do to put things right.

Mr Clinnol's interest in the workings of the economy had been heightened following his experience of the Dot.Com bubble of 2001. He had come to the conclusion that the entire economic system was inherently flawed and that it was destined to self-destruct sometime after 2006. In 2003 he made some predictions about what he thought might happen in key areas of the economy and devised an investment strategy to protect his clients' wealth from the devastation he foresaw. He had not, however, envisaged a two stage collapse so that when the Credit Crunch arrived in 2008 he had been surprised by the lack of its severity.

In December 2003 he made these predictions:

Boudikka's Story – The Great Crash of 2012

"The Bank of England (BoE) base interest rate is unlikely to exceed 4.5%. If it does it will not stay there for long. It will most likely fall to 1 – 1.5%, but could easily hit zero."

The base rate actually peaked at 5.75% in July 2007 and then tumbled rapidly to 0.5% where it stayed for over three years before falling to zero in 2012.

"The cheapest mortgages will be lifetime trackers. But once it is clear that interest rates are likely to fall significantly, lenders will make them less attractive or withdraw them completely."

This proved to be completely correct and resulted in Mr Clinnol's clients making huge savings, as the interest rate on the re-mortgages he recommended was between a quarter and a half per cent above the BoE base rate.

"There will be a big increase in crime – especially crimes like muggings and burglaries. There will be a resurgence of interest in people growing their own food in order to save money."

There had been one violent riot in 2011, but by the end of the following year they had become a regular occurrence in economically deprived areas as there was extreme poverty with many young children and the elderly not having enough to eat. The number of peaceful protests had also increased with demonstrations organised by different pressure groups. But the biggest single protest rally had been arranged by the Trade Union Congress (TUC) who used the occasion to call for the creation of a sound money system – backed by gold. People of all ages and from all walks of life took to the streets in every major town and city in the country. The police estimated that about ten per cent of the population had taken part. There had been so many protesters in London that traffic in the metropolitan areas had come to a standstill. This was the defining moment for the anti-power elite protest movement because the people had become as one in their opposition to failing government policies. The majority knew that there was a better way to run the economy as 'solution' articles had been published widely on the internet. The illuminati had been exposed and the people had awakened. Those politicians that had supported the dark forces realised that the game was up and that their reign was over. The TUC rally had proved to be a watershed moment, as shortly afterwards things really began to change – as we shall no doubt discover in the lectures that follow mine.

Mr Clinnol's 'home grown food' prophesy had turned out to be accurate too, as most people had needed to save money wherever they could. But something else happened and that was an increasing awareness of the importance of fresh food – as opposed to processed food – in the diet. And, also that it was not necessary to use dangerous chemicals in the food production process.

"Only the strongest banks and insurance companies will survive and several small building societies will fail."

Northern Rock, Halifax and RBS had fallen victim to the Credit Crunch and had to be brought under State control. Some small building societies (savings and loans) had been so weakened that they had to be rescued by their stronger rivals. Taxpayer bailout money and bank recapitalisations had brought some temporary respite, though bank lending had declined, which caused the economy to slow down. All had been relative calm until the waves from the Greek default struck UK shores. This had been no tsunami – and it had been expected – but as I shall now explain this rolling stone had yet to gather moss.

Of all the things that could go wrong with an economy, what politicians of the time feared most was a banking collapse. This is because when banks go down they tend to take the whole economy down with them. Under the fractional reserve banking system the privately owned banks had been both the creators and destroyers of money. They created it when they made loans but destroyed it when those loans were repaid. So in order to maintain the money supply, banks had to keep making new loans otherwise the supply of money would have dried up. And, as we know, when there is not enough money in circulation to exchange goods and services, the economy descends into a deflationary spiral of falling prices and increasing unemployment – as happened in the Great Depression of the 1930s.

Under the banking rules of the time, known as the Basel accords, banks had only been allowed to lend out a fixed multiple of the current value of their capital. And the ratio of loans relative to the value of a bank's capital had been known as the 'capital adequacy ratio'. The rules decreed that government bonds that banks owned had to be valued for capital adequacy purposes on the basis that the issuer of the bond would not default. Banks were deemed insolvent when their capital adequacy fell below the prescribed limits.

At that time, Greek government bonds had been held by many different banks in the euro zone and elsewhere and thus those bonds were part of the bank's capital and, in accordance with the rules, had to be valued at 100% of their face value.

So we can see that if the Greek government defaulted on its bonds then those banks with large holdings would suffer. And this was precisely what happened. There was simply not enough money in the weakened European countries to bail out all of these banks, and even if there had been, the people would not have stood for it because they were still paying for the bailouts that had been forced upon them four years earlier. The most strategically important banks were saved and others were hastily merged together to stave off bankruptcy, but as for the rest, well, they were thrown to the wolves.

The effect of this had been to shrink the money supply by an amount far greater than the value of the bonds. So, for example, if the capital adequacy ratio was 5%, then a default of £5 billion would have led to a reduction in lending of about £100 billion. And with this reduced money supply, loans were harder to repay, and this in turn had increased the number of defaults as the dominoes fell.

The Financial Armageddon had arrived, and it did not end there, because with the shrinking money supply came shrinking prices, not just in consumer goods and services, but also in assets like property and shares.

Whereas fractional reserve banking creates excess money and inflation on the upswing, on the downswing the exact opposite occurs causing a cascade of loan defaults and loss of liquidity so that there is less money to exchange goods and services, and the economy winds down.

"The FTSE 100 will not exceed 6750."

A GOLDEN AGE ECONOMY

It peaked at 6732 in October 2007.

"Stock markets will become increasingly volatile. Daily swings of 10% or more in the FTSE 100 and other share price indices will become common place as markets are driven more and more by an emotional sea of greed, anger and fear."

Volatility is primarily a function of fear and risk and, following the mini crash of 2008, the fear never went away, but was made worse by the sovereign debt crisis that had developed in Europe. Swings of the magnitude predicted did not arise until the dominoes had started to fall and some people used the opportunity to make a lot of money. However, judging from newspaper headlines of the day it is clear that few made a killing, though the streets did run red with blood.

"I see the FTSE 100 index of leading UK Companies falling by 60-65% to 1650 and staying at around that level for many years to come. I do not think it will recover.".

This had been a very good guess and quite close to the mark.

"I do not see a future for speculative investing, as, following falls of the magnitude I envisage, I believe that stock markets will eventually die out through lack of investor support. This is already happening as the number of private investors in the stock market is at an all-time low.".

Again this had been an insightful assessment though it did not happen overnight.

"I expect to see most British household name insurers going down. And I do not think the government will prop them up. As a result of the shortage of insurance underwriting capacity I expect to see general insurance premiums rise substantially."

The British had invented insurance in the seventeenth century and Mr Clinnol had worked as a self-employed agent for the company that started it all – Sun Alliance. Insurance had always had a comforting air of certainty about it and had been considered to be a safe, solid and secure business within the financial services sector. It was a major employer and a big earner for the UK economy. But all that changed when the dominoes started to fall. In fact, by the time the Crash had run its course only a handful of big insurers were left standing. With

Boudikka's Story – The Great Crash of 2012

about three quarters of the industry decimated, those firms that remained did very well, particularly on the general insurance side, where home and motor insurance policies were either a legal requirement or considered essential. The insurers that fared worst were those who had had a large number of eggs in the pension annuities basket – as when the stock market had collapsed they were unable to meet the income guarantees that they had contracted to provide and consequently many retirees were impoverished. Some of the UK's biggest insurers had been taken down in the wave of insolvencies and the financial regulator was once more left aghast by its own lack of foresight. The organisation was subsequently pilloried in the press for its failure to protect pensioners and many senior managers were forced to fall on their swords. Not long afterwards this much derided and unloved organisation was disbanded by a unanimous vote in parliament as the politicians were desperate to push the blame for the crisis as far away from themselves as possible.

"Unemployment could hit 25% or more – that's about 6-7 million."

Sadly, the outcome here was an under-estimate in terms of the actual number of people who wanted to work but could not find employment – and in some European countries like Greece and Spain the percentages were a lot higher.

"I estimate that about three quarters of Independent Financial Advisers and half of mortgage brokers will go bust or leave the industry."

By the end of 2011 the number of registered mortgage brokers had dropped by two thirds, though it was to fall further after the Great Crash. Within three years of the Crash the IFA community had been decimated. Of the few firms that remained, some had merged with accountants and solicitors to offer a one-stop "Professionals" service. These three professions had suffered greatly in the depression that followed the Crash, so by pooling their resources some of them had been able to survive. The top-end IFA firms whose incomes had derived more from tax mitigation advice were less affected, but those who specialised in investments and pensions had a torrid time dealing with all the complaints for 'unsuitable advice' that arose after the markets had collapsed. In the end most had had to throw in the towel because investment business dried up and most clients could not afford to keep on paying the premiums on their life assurance and other protection policies, which reduced adviser incomes further.

In 2005 he said:

"The Pension Protection Fund would be drained of cash from claims."

It was.

"I think that the trigger for the next crash could come from derivatives that are directly linked to interest rates. This is because the banks are heavily exposed to them and the market is so vast that any misconception about the likely future path of interest rates has the potential to collapse the financial system in an instant".

As I have already stated, the stone started to roll (downhill) with the Greek crisis, but it was the effect that this eventually had on derivative markets that caused the most damage and brought the world financial system to its knees.

Clearly much of what Mr Clinnol predicted in 2003 related more to 2012 than 2008, as we are now able to confirm, though in most instances he underplayed the severity of the outcomes. Where there is no dispute is in the accuracy of his investment advice and the superb results he achieved for his clients through his willingness to anticipate rather than react to events.

In January 2010 Mr Clinnol made a number of predictions about the approaching General Election as well as some personal observations concerning the leader of the Conservative Party, David Cameron.

He said:

"I think May 6th is the most likely date."

That was the actual date of the General Election.

"David Cameron will most likely be the next Prime Minister."

He was.

"The size of the Conservative Party majority will depend on the extent to which David Cameron and his team come up with policies that are of benefit to all people."

He did not get an overall majority and was forced into a coalition with the Liberal Democrat Party as not enough voters thought that his policies would benefit them.

"The economic challenges the Prime Minister will face will be greater than any leader before him. He will be torn between loyalty to his peers (the power elite) who helped him into office and by doing right for the country as a whole. If he allows himself to be pulled in the direction of the power elite's agenda the consequences will be dire, meaning that unless there is massive public opposition, the New World Order agenda will stand a chance of gaining further ground, with the result that personal freedoms will be eroded even more, or even lost completely."

Sadly, David Cameron started out on the low road of serving the interests of his peers, as most people had expected he would. Some legislation was passed that inhibited personal freedoms, though nothing like on the scale of President Obama's decimation of the freedoms enshrined in the Constitution and Bill of Rights.

"If David Cameron rises to the challenge he will probably co-opt talent from other parties into his cabinet or, preferably, form a government of national unity from all parties, as Churchill did during World War Two. The economic chaos is likely to be such that in order to properly rectify three centuries of economic wrongs against the people of this country the Prime Minister will have to issue a declaration of war against poverty and the perverted economy."

David Cameron had brought in other ministerial talent, but this had been a condition of the deal done with Nick Clegg (leader of the Liberal Democrat Party), in order to secure his Party's support for a coalition government. David Cameron had not voluntarily declared war on poverty, but initially had increased it with the austerity measures he had approved. These policies, however, were later reversed. To his credit, the Prime Minister did eventually see the light and abandon his allegiance to the power elite. He had been helped in this decision by a realisation that there was really no other option given the devastation that had been wrought, and by his willingness to seek advice from those who had the best interests of the people and country at heart. He later became great friends with the next American President (after Obama) who had integrity and honesty and had been blessed with great wisdom. The two countries forged even closer ties and worked together to rebuild their shattered economies. This relationship was genuinely 'special' as well as being beneficial to the world at large.

"David Cameron has the potential to be a truly great Prime Minister, but, if and only if, he is prepared to represent and fight for the interests of ALL people in this country. To do this it is imperative that he distance himself from his rich and powerful friends in the world of banking and finance – especially the Rothschild and Rockefeller families who, through their vast network of banks, multi-national corporations, trusts, foundations, pressure groups, banking organisations (BIS), charities, media interests and political affiliations, virtually controlled economic life on this planet! I do not exaggerate! But above all, he must be prepared to listen to the advice of those who know how to set the economy on a course of sustainable growth and whose advice is not tainted by a desire for power, position or money. One of the most important skills of leadership is the ability to know who your true allies are by separating the pure in heart from the liars and the lie."

This turned out to be a wholly accurate assessment.

2012 US Presidential Election

The differences between the political systems of the UK and USA were largely cosmetic, as all the main parties were under the control of the power elite. The Conservative and Republican Parties had similar ideology and the Labour and Liberal Democrat Parties were positioned more in the Democrats' camp. Prior to 2012, voters in elections never really had a choice because most candidates for the office of President had been sponsored by the power elite and thus had been committed to implementing the New World Order agenda.

The 2012 election campaign, however, was different, because for the first time the people were presented with a genuine choice. This was between Congressman Ron Paul, who represented the forces of light and freedom and President Obama whose strategy seemed to be to promise something publicly with one hand and then secretly take it

Boudikka's Story – The Great Crash of 2012

away with the other. President Obama acted like a magician in that he employed illusion and trickery to conceal the dark intent and actions of those who had put him in office.

2012 was the election year when the battle for the soul of America was fought. Ron Paul's beliefs were akin to those of the founding fathers and, in particular, Thomas Jefferson, who believed in minimalist government so that citizens would have the maximum opportunity to exercise their creative powers. This was the complete opposite of Obama's vision, which had been for a big brother state run for the benefit of the power elite, with the freedoms of the 99% curtailed to the point of virtual non-existence.

Ron Paul's vision of how the American people should be allowed to out-picture their freedom was the same as Saint Germain's and so you could say that Ron Paul was heaven's choice, as his role had been to show the people the road that would take them to the Golden Age and an enlightened free enterprise economy.

Looking back with the benefit of hindsight it is easy for us here to recognise the glaring differences between the two visions of the future that Ron Paul and Barack Obama offered in their election campaigns. But we must be careful to remember that it was not so easy for people living in those times to sift the wheat from the tares because the media had been anti-Paul from the beginning. It was not until he had come close to winning the Republican nomination that the media manipulators were forced to even acknowledge his existence. Ron Paul won the nomination because his views and policies resonated with real Republican voters who could see the logic and truth in what he said.

The illuminati in the Party could not understand how they had let him slip through their fingers. They had not reckoned with the fact that he was being protected by the greatest power in Heaven, the Prince of Archangels, beloved Archangel Michael, angel of the First Ray of God's Power and Will, and his legions of mighty blue lightning angels.

But on this particular occasion it did not matter that the power elite controlled media were hostile to Ron Paul's campaign because he had the greatest ally that any politician could ever have on his side and that was the *truth*.

A GOLDEN AGE ECONOMY

By the time the election campaign was under way the economic waves sent out by the problems in Europe had amassed the destructive power of a tsunami. When they hit America's east coast all that had been hidden from the people concerning the economy was unearthed and everything that Ron Paul had predicted came to pass. And so, slowly but surely, America began to awaken from its deep sleep.

The impact of the Great Crash launched Ron Paul's election campaign into the stratosphere as voters realised that he was the only candidate with practical solutions to the appalling levels of poverty and deprivation that were rapidly spreading across America. Citizens who had previously dismissed Ron Paul started to listen to his speeches and inwardly digest their content. Traffic to his website soared. Within a few months the economy had deteriorated to such an extent that Democrats stopped caring that Ron Paul was a Republican. All that mattered to them was that they believed that he would end the Great Recession, as it came to be known. Politics with all its division and backbiting came to be regarded as an utter irrelevance. The people demanded solutions, not soundbites, action not promises and Ron Paul was the man they believed they could trust to deliver.

On November 6th 2012, news of Ron Paul's landslide victory reverberated around the world.

Thank you."

Boudikka bowed playfully to her audience and then returned hurriedly to her seat.

Harald's Story

Sound Money
The Rock of the Economy

"Like slavery and apartheid, poverty is not natural. It is manmade and it can be overcome and eradicated by the actions of human beings."
– **Nelson Mandela**

Boudikka's five and a half thousand-word lecture went down well with her fellow students and she knew from the expression on the Master's face that he was pleased with it too.

After the mid-morning break, the first student to come back into the lecture theatre was a tall blonde, blue-eyed Norwegian male of twenty-two years. He was clever, good looking, and possessed a sparkling personality. Harald was the class heart-throb and he wore a grey imitation animal skin cloak across his shoulders. His friends called him 'Greycloak'.

Once everyone had settled into their seats, Master Prospero asked Harald to come down to the stage.

This is Harald's presentation:

"President Paul moved quickly to address America's problems. He was a man on a mission and he knew that the key to the future success of the American economy – and indeed all the economies of the world – lay in establishing a sound monetary base built on the rock of Christ truth. He had envisaged a system where money was no longer created as debt, but where the money used had an inherent value that was

A GOLDEN AGE ECONOMY

equal to the goods and services for which it was being exchanged.

Research the history of money and you will discover that it started out as a barter system where, for example, five sheep were worth one horse, or one camel, or whatever people agreed. The important point is that there was an exchange of equal consideration, whereby the scales were balanced, meaning that no transaction took place unless the intrinsic value of the items being traded was perceived to be equal by the parties. This system worked well in primitive tribal communities, but as society advanced and the demand for consumer goods grew, a new method of exchange was needed to overcome the practical issues of using bulky items for trade. Gold solved this problem because it was universally accepted as a method of payment and small quantities of it were extremely valuable – attributes that make it ideal for use as currency. But what really sets gold apart from other precious metals are its spiritual qualities, as brought to light by the God of Gold, through the Summit Lighthouse, a century and a half ago.

In the West, paper money started out as an IOU for gold. Examine an original pound note issued by the Bank of England and inscribed are the words:

"I promise to pay the bearer the sum of one pound in gold on demand."

When America came off the gold standard in 1971 the Federal Reserve Bank (Fed) was free to counterfeit the currency by issuing more paper dollars than there was gold in Fort Knox. Thus the dollar became disconnected from something of real value. This meant that when the government needed more money the Fed was happy to print it, thereby increasing the disconnection to such an extent that by the time electronic money had become dominant, it was capable of being counterfeited, ad infinitum. This excess money, however, caused inflation, and thus destroyed the dollar's purchasing power.

And so from this brief history we can see how the power elite exacerbated the perversion of the money system by taking America off the Gold Standard. They adulterated the purpose and intent for which money was created, which is as a medium of exchange and store of future value. President Paul understood this and was, therefore, determined that the USA would return to the God standard of the Gold Standard, so that the dollar would once again be fixed in value to gold.

There was, however, the small matter of where the gold would come from to fully back the new 'gold dollar', as this new currency would come to be known. This is a difficult mystery to unravel because no single person in embodiment knows the whole truth of how it came to be that all the gold that was needed materialised, as if by magic. I believe in miracles and some people might say that what happened was a miracle – just like the two loaves and the five fishes that Jesus made feed the five thousand. Yes, with God all things are possible, and I believe that heaven had a very big hand in the events that led to the establishment of the sound money system that we still have today. But there are other more fact-based explanations that I would also like to share with you.

The first fact is that by 2012 all the gold that was needed to back the US dollar and other currencies had already been discovered. It had been dug out of the ground over millennia and was located in various storage areas across the planet.

The second point is that from dictations given by God of Gold via the Summit Lighthouse, we also know that gold grows in the earth and that our spiritual attainment (consciousness) can be measured by the amount of gold that has already been unearthed.

So the gold definitely existed, but who owned it and where was it to be found?

Well, some gold was held by national governments, but those countries who had converted to fiat currencies reasoned that they had little need for gold, so in the years leading up to 2012 they had gradually sold off their bullion reserves to help offset the rising cost of economic failure in their own countries. And so it is logical to conclude that what gold remained was largely in private hands.

Thirdly, we know from the history books that much of the gold that had been discovered in the West had, over many centuries, been transferred to the East because the Indian and Chinese races were shrewd traders who would only accept pure gold in payment for all the exotic goods that the West demanded from them as the wealth of the western nations had grown.

Fourthly, it is safe to assume that there must also have been vast reserves of gold stored in private vaults (other than in those owned by Royal Families) because it had been calculated that the richest family (House of Rothschild) was worth an estimated $300 trillion. It is likely that a significant portion of that amount would have been held in gold and that all of this wealth would not have been known to the tax authorities.

Fifthly, there were stories circulating on the internet that postulated that before China fell under communist rule the last Emperor had transferred all China's gold to Taiwan where it was stored in giant underground caves and that the quantity was so great that it would have been sufficient to provide 100% backing to all the world's currencies.

The most elaborate story, however, described a secret international agreement between 'white knights' in the world's governments to return control of the planet to the people and to introduce key reforms. In the United States these reforms included: removing debt from the economy, abolishing the Fed and replacing it with a US Treasury Bank System and US Treasury currency backed by gold, replacing income tax with a national sales tax on new, non-essential items, restoring Constitutional Law, removing the current administration to allow a fresh start at national level with new elections within 120 days, ceasing all aggressive US military actions and declaring world peace. This story also suggested that Congressman Ron Paul had been one of the prime movers in trying to get this plan announced and that it had the support of Generals and Admirals within the military. My research also revealed that this plan was about to be announced when the Twin Towers in New York were destroyed, which for one reason or another put a spanner in the works and prevented the reforms from being implemented. Needless to say the illuminati opposition to these reforms was absolute, which is why the main elements of the plan did not see the light of day until Ron Paul had been elected President.

Sixthly, we know from the Bible (Revelation) and dictations given by the Ascended Host in the decades leading up to 2012 that God's final judgment was due to fall on the wicked and unrepentant and that:

> "They that hath not multiplied light for good but hath turned it to darkness, from them shall be taken even that light which they hath misqualified."
>
> **– Sanat Kumara**
> (The Ancient of Days)

And from the Law of Karma we know that all karmic debts must be repaid, meaning that those who stole from the people must return what they had taken in part recompense for their crimes. And that the date 21-12-2012 marked the end of a grand cosmic cycle and thus marked a point in time and space when all things had to be balanced.

Saint Germain had said that the eradication of poverty should be the first priority in the Aquarian Age and so it was no surprise when President Paul announced that the military and the forces of law and order had tracked down gold and other valuables worth trillions of dollars that had been secreted away by the power elite; money which the President promised would be used for the good of all.

Good Company

President Paul was in good company with his views on how the new US monetary and banking system should be structured.

Look at a list of the greatest twentieth century economists and you will find that all of them were opposed to fractional reserve banking (FRB), believing instead that banks should be legally required to hold 100% reserves on demand deposits – meaning that if every depositor emptied their accounts at the same time the banks would be able to cover these positions.

The first American economists to advocate this were those of the Chicago School (F. H. Knight, L. W. Mints, Henry Schultz, H. C. Simons, G. V. Cox, Aaron Director, Paul Douglas and A. G. Hart) whose 'Chicago Plan' was dismissed by lawmakers both before and after the Great Depression, even though a comprehensive poll of academic economists confirmed, by a resounding majority, that the plan had great merit.

'A Program for Monetary Reform' was another paper that echoed anti-fractional reserve sentiment. Chief among the six eminent economists who co-wrote it was Irving Fisher, who was famous for his work on the quantity theory of money. Milton Friedman, the founder of 'Monetarism', was influenced significantly by Fisher, calling him "the greatest economist the United States has ever produced".

The libertarian 'Austrian School of Economics' had also concluded that FRB should be abolished and that small government and minimum state intervention in the economy were preferable. Ludwig von Mises of the Austrian School was the first twentieth-century economist to propose the establishment of a banking system with a 100% reserve requirement on demand deposits, as did fellow 'Austrian School' economist Nobel Laureate Friedrich A. Hayek. In 2012 Jesus Huerta de Soto was the leading Austrian school economist who, in his book *Money, Bank Credit and Economic Cycles* proposed reform of the banking system that included the need for a 100% reserve requirement for private banks. His views were also shared by Frenchman Maurice Allais, who had received the Nobel Prize for Economics in 1988.

In 1962 Professor Murray N. Rothbard had proposed a pure gold standard based on a free-banking system with a 100% reserve requirement and had commented that bankers who operate a 'fractional reserve' are, in effect, criminals because they commit the crime of misappropriation.

Another pre-eminent economist who had favoured significant monetary reform was Nobel Prize winner Milton Friedman who, in his 1960 book *A Program For Monetary Stability* implied that governments, rather than private banks should issue the money supply.

In the years leading up to 2012 the clarion calls for sound money grew increasingly loud, reaching a crescendo in the post-Credit Crunch months of 2008. The most damning indictment of all, however, came not from a practising economist, but from Sir Mervyn King, Governor of the Bank of England, who, judging from other profound comments he had made at that time, was pulling his punches when he said:

"Another avenue of reform is some form of functional separation. The Volcker Rule is one example. Another, more fundamental, example would be to divorce the payment system from risky lending activity – that is to prevent fractional reserve banking."

So President Paul had had the most distinguished professional body of opinion behind him, but what of the highest authority; was he in harmony with the immeasurable wisdom of the hierarch of the Aquarian Age, our beloved Saint Germain, who 70,000 years ago led a Golden Age civilisation that occupied what is now the Sahara desert. Well yes, he was; for in dictations that Saint Germain had given to students of the Ascended Masters in the years preceding 2012, our beloved sponsor had outlined the spiritual principles that a Golden Age economy should be based on, which I shall now summarise.

The Money Laws – Key Principles for Sound Money

Money in its pure form should be two things: a medium of exchange and a way to store value for different times when that value is needed and cannot be produced on a short-term basis.

Money, instead of being a means to an end, should not be allowed to be turned into an end in itself – meaning that the money system should not be capable of being perverted beyond its original intent and design into a scheme where the power elite can use money not only to gather privileges for themselves – that they could buy with money that they hoard for themselves – but they could go beyond that and use money to further their never-ending quest for power and control over people.

There must be a direct correspondence between money and things of real value like goods and services. In other words, it should not be possible to counterfeit money by creating more money than is needed to exchange the value of goods and services produced in the economy. Under this principle it would be permissible to use paper money but only as an IOU for pure gold in storage, which is the real money. Electronic money would also have to be backed by gold so that money

A GOLDEN AGE ECONOMY

cannot just be created out of thin air on a computer screen, as used to happen when banks made loans. Ideally, gold should be passed hand-to-hand as currency as advised by the God of Gold for the important spiritual reasons he has given.

People should only be rewarded according to their willingness to multiply their talents:

Through their ingenuity of bringing forth new ideas, new inventions, better ways of doing the same old tasks.

Through their willingness to take risks by taking an initiative by doing something that no one has done before – and therefore they cannot know what the outcome will be.

Or by their willingness to put forth the labour that is needed in order to get the economy to run.

It should not be possible to gain something for nothing or a variant of that, reap the rewards of other people's labour. The derivatives business is a good example of this mindset, as would be all other forms of predatory speculation. Money lending where interest is charged (i.e. usury) would also contravene the money laws as is explained in the Bible and the Qur'an.

The control of the medium of money should not be used to control people – for suppressing them or by stealing their labour without the people understanding what is happening. Taxation by Inflation and enslavement through debt (where money was created as debt) are the main ways this happened before 2013.

There should be no more money in circulation than is needed to exchange the total value of goods and services that are produced by a society. This is because excess money causes inflation, which is a hidden form of taxation that was used by the power elite in most countries to steal the value of people's labour. If the true rate of inflation was 10% and the total impact of direct taxes was 40% then the actual rate of taxation was 50%.

Where money is used as a store of value through saving then it should be put to good use by sharing it (lending it out) so that it helps the economy to grow. The phrase "when money flows the economy grows" illustrates this point.

Harald's Story – Sound Money

Saint Germain's pronouncements on investing are that where the employees of a business are also the shareholders and therefore the sole owners of that business then they would be multiplying their talents as risk and reward is shared and no one can reap the reward of another's labour. However, non-worker shareholders and/or bondholders who receive an income and/or potential capital gain and/or losses when their investment is traded would not be considered to be multiplying their talents. The implications of this were far-reaching when you consider the large number of people that had become totally reliant for their income on privately funded retirement schemes and state paid pensions by the end of the twentieth century. Indeed in some countries – and most notably the UK – the financial services industry that provided these savings and investment schemes had overtaken manufacturing in terms of its contribution to the economic output of the country. The industry and those it served were misqualifying God's energy on a massive scale and thus the Law of Karma demanded that this negative energy be balanced as indeed it was in the Great Crash of 2012.

The creation of money must be under the sole control of the people. In other words private banks must not be allowed to create money, but that this power should only be exercised by the State via a publicly owned and accountable central bank or similar organisation.

Money must be created free of debt.

Saint Germain notes that money itself is not evil, but is merely a form of energy, that if used correctly facilitates the smooth running of the economy whilst allowing it to grow in a sustainable way.

As I shall shortly explain Saint Germain's 'Key Principles' are essentially no different to the teachings given to the Prophet Mohammad, who was instructed in God's Laws by the Archangel Gabriel – though admittedly the financial world then was much less complex. The modern system of Islamic finance, however, had not evolved fully until the latter part of the twentieth century when the strains in the western model (based on fractional reserve lending and creating money as debt) had started to show through. Indeed, I believe that the Sharia law-based approach to finance was the divine antidote to the sick western system that only benefited the bankers, who were allowed to tap the taxpayer for bailout money every time their giant Ponzi scheme ran into trouble.

By the beginning of the twenty-first century the exponential demand for Islamic banking and finance services had attracted the attention of the illuminati who controlled the West's competing, but highly flawed, FRB system. These dark forces realised that if the Islamic monetary system was not brought to heel its success would highlight their failing model, and thus the calls for an end to fractional reserve banking would become deafening.

Illuminati Bankers Eliminate Threats to Their Dominance

At that time the American illuminati showed signs of being in a strong position, though under the surface their structures were crumbling. The US was the world's largest economy and its greatest military power. The dollar was the reserve currency, the White House was a branch office of the Fed and oil was priced and traded in dollars. But all of this power was threatened when the Iraqi dictator, Saddam Hussein, stated his intention to conduct oil sales in euros. The Illuminati reacted, and, as they say, the rest is history. Shortly afterwards another Arab dictator, Libya's Colonel Gaddafi, threw down the gauntlet with his plan for a trans-African currency, based on the gold dinar, and he too found that he was not long for this world. And then there was Iran and its plan to demand gold, instead of dollars, for oil.

Positive Money in the UK

(www.positivemoney.org.uk)

In addition to the Occupy Movement that had set up camp in front of St Paul's Cathedral in the City of London a much more focused protest movement came to prominence in 2011/2012 that had the support of a small group of Members of Parliament (MPs) from the three main political parties. This organisation was mainly funded by modest monthly donations from members of the public who, like the group, were determined to get fractional reserve banking abolished. The group's name was 'Positive Money' and from modest beginnings it built itself up into a major force for change within and outside the British political establishment. This was, I might add, much to the annoyance of the power elite within the coalition government, who were still wedded to the old ways through their close ties to the House of Rothschild and other banking families. However, once the Prime Minister realised that he had been riding the wrong horse, he quickly aligned himself with President Paul and his policies, and assisted him in every way possible to help bring to justice the criminals within the financial power elite. Before becoming President, Congressman Paul had made the decision to call upon the 'white knights' within the military if he won the Presidency as he knew that they too wanted to set America on the right-handed path. In fact, their support was crucial because the President's plan was to redeploy both the military and all the forces of law and order (FBI, CIA, NSA etc) to track down every dollar that had been looted from the American taxpayer by the power elite and to bring those responsible to justice for their crimes and, in particular, their monumental levels of tax evasion, which ran into tens of trillions of dollars. This plan had the wholehearted support of every good person on Earth.

Vatican Supports Islamic Finance

Pressure on the power elite and their monetary system came from other unexpected quarters too. At the height of the Credit Crunch in March 2009, the internet financial newspaper, Bloomberg, reported that the Vatican had said that banks should look at the rules of Islamic finance to restore confidence amongst their clients at a time of global economic crisis and that: "The ethical principles on which Islamic finance is based may bring banks closer to their clients and to the true spirit which should mark every financial service." And so, despite all the negative press that Islamic countries had been getting from the western illuminati-controlled media, the Pope had decided that he could no longer remain silent on the issue of the West's wicked financial system.

So let us now take a look at the Islamic financial model.

ISLAMIC BANKING & FINANCE

The basis for all Islamic finance lies in the principles of the Sharia (Islamic) Law, which is taken from the Qur'an and from the example set by the Prophet Muhammad. Central to Islamic finance is the fact that money itself is not considered important, but is merely a means to an end. Muslims are not allowed to lend money or receive money from someone and expect to benefit, as interest (riba) is prohibited. Making money from money is forbidden, as wealth must only be generated through legitimate trade and/or through investment in assets, such as a business. What is important is that money is used in a productive way.

The principal means of Islamic finance is risk-based trading where the outcome of any trading activity cannot be known. Gains accrued from trade must be shared between the person/s or entity providing the capital and the people providing the expertise.

The term 'Sharia' refers to Islamic law as revealed in the Qur'an and through the Sunnah of the Prophet Muhammad. The authority of Sharia is drawn first and foremost from the specific guidance laid down in the Qur'an.

The second main source is the Sunnah, which is what the Prophet Muhammad said, did, or approved of, and refers to the way in which the Prophet Muhammad lived his life.

The third source is Ijma'a (consensus), which involves the interpretation and analysis of newly arising issues by eminent qualified scholars of Fiqh who will arrive at a consensus or ruling about the issue in question.

The fourth source is Qiyas (analogy), which is the process of analogical reasoning from a known injunction to a new injunction. According to this method, the ruling of the Qur'an and Sunnah may be extended to a new problem provided that the precedent (asil) and the new problem (far'a) share the same operative or effective cause (illah).

The fifth source is Ijtihad, which is the effort of a qualified Islamic jurist to interpret or reinterpret sources of Islamic law in cases where no clear directives exist.

Types of Islamic Financial Arrangements

Ijara

Ijara is a form of leasing. It involves a contract where the lender buys and then leases an item, for example, a consumer durable, to a customer for a specified rental amount over a specific period. The duration of the lease, as well as the basis for rental, are set and agreed in advance. The lender retains ownership of the item throughout the arrangement and takes it back at the end of the rental period.

Ijara-wa-iktana

Ijara-wa-iktana is similar to Ijara, except that included in the contract is a promise from the customer to buy the equipment at the end of the lease period, at a pre-agreed price. Rentals paid during the period of the lease constitute part of the purchase price. Often, as a result, the final sale will be for a token sum.

Musharaka

Musharaka means partnership. It involves a person placing their capital with another person with both sharing the risk and reward. The difference between Musharaka arrangements and normal banking is that the parties can set any kind of profit-sharing ratio, but losses must be proportionate to the amount invested.

Ijara with diminishing Musharaka

The principle of Ijara with diminishing Musharaka can be used for house purchase. Diminishing Musharaka means that the lender reduces their equity in an asset with any additional capital payments made by the purchaser in excess of the rental payments. The borrowers' ownership in the asset increases as the lenders' decreases by a similar amount each time the borrower makes an additional capital payment. Ultimately, the lender transfers ownership of the asset entirely over to the borrower.

Mudaraba

Mudaraba refers to an investment made on behalf of an investor by a more skilled person. It is a contract between two parties where one party provides the funds and the other party provides the expertise, and where both parties agree in advance to the division of any profits made. In other words, if one party is, for example, a bank then the bank would make Sharia compliant investments and share the profits with the investor, in effect charging for the time and effort. But if no profit is made, the loss is borne by the investor and the bank takes no fee.

Mudarib

In a Mudaraba contract, the expert who manages the investment is known as a Mudarib.

Murabaha

Murabaha is a contract for purchase and resale that allows the customer to make purchases without having to borrow money and pay interest. The bank purchases the goods for the customer, and re-sells them to the customer on a deferred basis, adding an agreed profit margin. The customer then pays the sale price for the goods over instalments, effectively obtaining credit without paying interest.

Qard

A qard is a profit-free loan where a customer deposits money in a current account in a bank which is in effect a loan to the bank that then uses that money for investment and other purposes. The loan is repayable in full, on demand.

Wakala

Wakala is an agency contract, which usually includes in its terms a fee for the expertise of the agent. A bank may use this type of arrangement for large deposit accounts where the money deposited belongs to the customer, but where the customer appoints the bank as their agent in return for a fee to cover their expertise.

Adapted from information supplied by the Islamic Bank of Britain.
www.islamic-bank.com

For more in-depth teachings on how the western monetary and banking system was contrary to the teachings in the Qur'an, and therefore God's Money Laws, I recommend the essay 'Islam and the Future of Money', which can be found at the following website

metaexistence.org/dinarbook.pdf

Please note that this essay had proved to be of particular interest to Muslims who were struggling to reconcile their involvement with the Judeo-Christian money system that had enslaved them. The article was a call to Muslims to help restore the gold dinar and silver dirham as the currency for Islamic nations as Colonel Gaddafi had been trying to do before he was killed by forces allied with US, French and UK governments.

ISLAMIC MONEY LAW IS GOD'S LAW

When you compare the tenets of Islamic finance revealed by Archangel

A GOLDEN AGE ECONOMY

Gabriel with Saint Germain's 'Key Principles for Sound Money' you will see that there is no discernible difference between the two because, to use a well-worn phrase from a hundred years ago, these Ascended Masters were both singing from the same hymn sheet, in the sense that they were only recounting what are God's Money Laws.

By the time of Ron Paul's inauguration as President he had built a momentum for change that was so powerful that you could feel its energy in the airwaves. America had awoken; the world had awoken; excitement and expectation were everywhere.

But as the old saying goes, Rome was not built in a day, and the enlightened free enterprise economy that President Paul had promised the American people would take a little longer to establish too. But what did happen on that first day, which was the day that the new President gave his inaugural address, and that was watched by half the world on television, was that the people felt in their hearts that what the President said was possible – that indeed anything was possible – if they adhered to the Universal Laws of Life.

Within two terms in office President Paul's vision of a sound money system built on the rock of Christ truth had come to pass and the Golden Age Economy was well on its way to becoming fully manifest.

Thank you."

Li's Story

AMERICA'S ENLIGHTENED FREE ENTERPRISE ECONOMY

"An economy is a living entity and, like all living things, it must be rooted in firm and fertile soil and have the freedom to grow in the light in accordance with God's Laws."

"Go into any park and find that single tree that is set apart from the rest, the one that has perfect symmetry and that is bigger than the others. Now ask yourself why is this tree so exceptional? Well, it is because it has had the freedom and the space to grow. It has not been inhibited in any way nor has it had to compete with other trees for the life-giving light of the sun and the essential nourishment in the rain. It has received all that it needed to flourish and has done so. Ask me what an enlightened free enterprise economy is like and I shall point to that tree."

– Kim Andrew Lincoln

It will come as no surprise to learn that Li, who was the next student to speak, was Chinese. He was from Xian, formerly called Chang'an – the ancient capital, which, in the seventh century, was the largest, most cosmopolitan city on Earth, with a population of over one million. In the Chinese language the first name you read is the surname, and Li was Li's surname. But because Li sounds the same as Lee in English and Li's 'Christian' name was difficult to pronounce, everyone called

A GOLDEN AGE ECONOMY

him by his surname. Li is a popular Chinese surname and the most famous Li in Chinese history was probably Li Shi Min, who, with his Father and sister, founded the Tang Dynasty and who later ruled as the Emperor Taizong. Li was an expert on the history of the Tang Dynasty, the early part of which was considered to be China's Golden Age.

This is his presentation:

The divine test for any law, regulation, or economic policy, is: does it benefit all people and does it help to raise all life? If there is any chance that what seems right to man might be detrimental to the planet or indeed any part of life then it would not be deemed enlightened. That which is enlightened is imbued with God's light and thus is in harmony with God's Laws. Enlightenment is an absolute state of consciousness that has no points in between. Something is either in harmony with God's Laws or it is not.

For any child of God it is an easy thing to know what is right for the economy, but we must remember that until the Armageddon had ended the forces of darkness – who had controlled much of the material world – were not interested in doing right for the good of all. Their reason for being was to do only that which they believed was right for them and to poison, both in a literal and metaphorical sense, everything else. But what they failed to realize was that in not serving the All, they were not serving themselves, and thus were acting as the architects of their own demise.

"Do unto others as you would have them do unto you" was the guiding principle that the leader of the free world applied to his time in office. This common sense approach had its foundation in his Christian beliefs, as Ron Paul had publicly stated that Jesus Christ was his saviour and this showed through in all the policies and laws that his Administration brought forth.

So let us now look at some of the enlightened changes that Ron Paul made as President:

Li's Story – America's Enlightened

40% Price Cut

Once the sound money system had bedded down and usury had been abolished massive costs were taken out of the economy equivalent to a price cut on all goods and services of about 40%. The impact this had on employment was unprecedented because of the huge and instantaneous increase in people's disposable income. All the extra spending amounted to the biggest boost in job creation in the history of the planet. But this was just the beginning because once the genie of abundance had been let out of the bottle there was no putting it back.

Bureaucracy Shrunk

All western economies had been weighed down with burdensome bureaucracies that did little but cost a lot. And, in the US, it was no different. President Paul's attitude to big brother government was that it should not exist because it is unproductive and restricts people's freedom. But he was also mindful of the fact that you should not cut government jobs faster than you can create private sector ones because of the hardship it causes to the dispossessed. And so policies were instigated to assist those in transition. The President's aim was to reduce the total level of taxation in the US economy to a maximum of 10% of national income, which represented about a 75% drop from the level it had been in 2012.

The President's core belief was that less government would create more wealth and freedom for the people. The following quote was probably a fairly accurate representation of his thoughts on the matter:

> "To reduce the size of central government, do not cut by 25% – or even 50%; be bold, go for a 100% and work back from there."
> **– Kim Andrew Lincoln**

Transforming an economy to one based on the principles of enlightened free enterprise can only be done gradually, as it takes time to implement the necessary changes if economic dislocation is to be minimised.

Compassion is everything, and as a doctor who had delivered over four thousand babies into the world, this was something with which President Paul was copiously endowed. Having said that, he was no easy touch and did not suffer fools gladly.

Among the first of the departments of State to be axed were the terrible twins: Homeland Security and the Transport Security Administration (TSA). The Food & Drug Administration (FDA) was also dismantled as it was considered 'not fit for purpose' and those of its functions that were retained were hived off to other departments, thus ensuring that the potential for corruption to exist between the promoters of chemical solutions in food and healthcare and the regulator was reduced. In fact, this policy was repeated throughout government service, as over the years the cosy relationships that had built up between corporations and regulators had become inimical to the interests of US citizens.

National Tithing

Another of the President's key priorities was the elimination of poverty at home and abroad. He believed this to be the first priority of the developed world and that any political system that actively worked against this aim did not deserve to survive. When we consider that hundreds of billions of dollars had been lavished on the space program and weapons of mass destruction, while two thirds of the world's people had been living under the threat of starvation, then this was a righteous realignment of priorities. Ron Paul was mindful that the leader of the free world had a duty to lead by example, and thus to help elevate those who were less fortunate. He was also shrewd enough to realise that the American people would eventually benefit from this policy, once the virtuous spiral of abundance began to flow. He allocated ten per cent all of tax revenues to this purpose, as Jesus had taught that everyone should give a portion of their income to God, meaning to charity, as when we give we receive more in return and that ten per cent of net income was an appropriate amount to give. The example that President Paul set caused a massive upswing in charitable giving and consequently much good work was done.

WARS ENDED & OVERSEAS AID INCREASED

The President was determined that the world should know that America was a friend to all freedom-loving peoples and governments and that the old days of corporate-sponsored terrorism and exploitation of the less fortunate (globalisation) were over. One of his first acts was to cease all hostilities overseas and to close most foreign military bases. Half the savings made went towards tax reduction and the other half paid for special aid programmes that were designed to help poor countries become self-sufficient that hitherto had been dependent on foreign aid. This proved to be highly advantageous to the USA in the longer term, as once the economies of the aid recipients had grown sufficiently with the help of these programmes, the people were well disposed to trading with America and in this way all parties benefited. Moreover, all 'conditional' overseas aid programmes were discontinued.

MASSIVE TAX REDUCTIONS

On the tax front all income and capital taxes were abolished and replaced with a sales tax levied on non-essential items. This meant that another of America's most hated institutions, the IRS, could be massively downgraded. The rate of the sales tax started out at 20%, but was progressively reduced in line with the vast cost savings in running the government that the President's policies achieved. But what helped most to get the rate down was the mammoth surge in economic growth, which stayed in double figures for every year of the President's term in office. Yes, America's GDP doubled in eight years! In fact, in his last year the President was able to announce that the sales tax would be reduced to six per cent because economic growth had swelled tax receipts so much. There were calls for the President to be allowed to serve for a third term because people did not want the good times to end, but no one could persuade him that that was the right thing to do.

The Rise of the Free Market

The brake that big corporations had put on the wheels of commerce and enterprise had held back economic growth and innovation, constrained employment, and – through the imposition of restrictive practices and monopolies – made goods and services much more expensive than they needed to be. Usury and speculation had also had an exceedingly negative impact on people's discretionary spending.

Globalisation, which in reality had been a short-term cost-cutting exercise for multi-national corporations, had proved hugely expensive to society as a whole, as the social costs of the jobs lost in developed western economies were simply transferred to the taxpayer. Other downsides were the economic exploitation of foreign workers and the pollution caused by insalubrious production practices designed to reduce unit costs. Then, there was the untold damage that all this had done to America's reputation abroad. An audacious plan was needed to restore the free market and America's standing in the world.

The Great Crash of 2012 had dealt a severe blow to illuminati-controlled corporations that had made up a significant part of the economy. The winds of the Holy Spirit had buffeted those businesses that had persistently broken God's Laws and thus whose activities were harmful to society. This left an opportunity for those companies that remained to increase both market share and prices because they had less competition. The President, however, had anticipated that this would happen and was determined that corporations should not be allowed to exploit the situation at the expense of the people. Prior to his election he had formulated a plan to establish a 'Free Trade & Enterprise Commission' for the purpose of reviewing the propriety of all laws related to the regulation of trade and markets. This was to ensure that these laws did not contravene the inalienable rights and liberties that were supposed to be guaranteed in the Constitution and Bill of Rights, but which many former Presidents had trampled over in their contempt for the people and God's Laws. The Commission was established under the Chairmanship of a Supreme Court Judge who had been chosen personally by the President for his good character and non-allegiance to any secret society that had the potential to take him away from the path of truth and justice. In total, thirty-three experts served on the Commission. There were sixteen men and sixteen women, plus the Chairman (male) who had a casting vote on those changes that were put before the President for turning into law. Among the panel were some of the highest ranking officers in the armed forces who were there as silent watchers and guardians of the power of the people to ensure that justice was done and that it was seen to be done. There were experts in constitutional law, commercial law and international law and trade agreements, and, for the first time, there were representatives of all the true religions, whose purpose was to certify that in drafting new rules for the conduct of trade and commerce at home and abroad none of God's Laws were broken. The Commission was primarily concerned with the restoration of God's Laws because only when this happened would abundance be able to flow in the manner and to the extent that God had intended when humankind was charged with the task of taking dominion over the Earth.

The changes that were recommended were on a grand scale and miraculous in every sense of the word. In spiritual terms it was the second coming of Jesus as what Jesus had taught was at last being enshrined in law. The sons and daughters of God had come of age and were laying the foundations for the Golden Age Economy to manifest.

To describe the full extent of these restorations would fill thousands of pages and so the best way I can think of to explain the affect they had would be to imagine that you were in embodiment at that time and that you knew what was wrong with the economy. Well, I can confirm that all those wrongs were righted for the guiding light of Saint Germain and Archangel Zadkiel was there every step of the way in that Commission as it had been there when the founding fathers set America upon the path of righteousness in the drafting of the Declaration of Independence, the Constitution and the Bill of Rights. Saint Germain may not have been there in the physical, but he was most certainly there in spirit, as were many other members of the Ascended Host. For this was a very important time in the evolution of Earth and our Cosmos.

Every effort was made by the Administration to explain to people precisely what was being proposed and the reasons for it and I can tell that there was much celebration for everyone knew in their hearts that these laws were God's Will and that they would bring great prosperity to ALL.

Although President Paul was a libertarian and a believer in many of the ideas of the Austrian school of economics, he did not agree with their belief in the primacy of individual freedom, because it failed to recognise that human beings are social beings, not isolated individuals. Self-interest reigned supreme for libertarians. There was no room for social justice, no care for the good of all people. And there was no room for the Middle Way that Jesus taught – balance in all things, service to others and raising all life. In their worship of self the Austrians justified usury, but this was not something that could be part of the Enlightened Free Enterprise Economy that President Paul envisaged and that eventually came to pass.

Thank you."

Wende's Story

A NEW INDUSTRIAL REVOLUTION

Wende is also Chinese, but her friends pronounce her name in the English way of Wendy. Her family were originally Xianbei, a Mongolian nomadic people residing in Manchuria and other parts of north-east China. Wende is petite with long black hair that flows down to her slim waist. Li and Wende are lovers and during the Christmas break worked together on their presentations. They are so close that everyone thinks they are twin flames.

This is what she said:

"Where it had threatened their profits and control over the people the power elite had suppressed new inventions, innovation and new technologies on a gargantuan scale. Had these creations been launched into the marketplace they would have brought great progress and prosperity to the world but, instead, illuminist businesses and bankers had either bought up and buried what had been invented, or saw to it that the theories and the ideas were never put into practice by starving the inventors of development funds. Let us not forget that the illuminati's New World Order plan was to subjugate, impoverish, enslave, poison and kill the majority of the people on Earth. Probably the most glaring example of suppressed technology was in the motor vehicle and energy industries that were under the total control of power elite families like the Rockefellers (oil) and Ford (motor vehicles). However, when it came to technology that could potentially advance the illuminist agenda, like weapons of mass destruction, surveillance equipment, biological weapons, vaccines and other chemical compounds that could be used to slowly poison the masses, then any amount of money was always available for R&D.

A GOLDEN AGE ECONOMY

The matter of suppressed technology had come to the attention of the Free Trade & Enterprise Commission, and having deliberated on it very thoroughly they had recommended to the President that because this was such an important issue, a small Department of State should be set up called the Department of New Technology. Its function would be to keep track of all new technologies that might be of benefit to humankind, so that the government could use its good offices to assist entrepreneurs – particularly when it was in the national interest to do so. The Commission also proposed that it be made an offence, punishable by an unlimited fine, for any individual, corporate entity or organisation to deliberately suppress any technology or invention for selfish ends. As you can imagine, this was difficult legislation to draft, but the President was determined to resolve this issue and put the best legal minds on the case.

The Act that was passed unleashed a whirlwind of new technology onto the market, some of which was over a hundred years old. And, because the legislation was retrospective, all existing technologies that had been suppressed had to be registered, and, as many of the patents had lapsed, this technology was suddenly available free to anyone who wanted to use it.

The implications of this for the illuminist corporations, who had relied upon suppression to keep their outdated monopolies afloat, was dramatic. These pariah entities who thought they had escaped the buffeting winds of the Holy Spirit during the Great Crash of 2012 were now subject to the laws of the enlightened free market. The restricted markets they had created with the help of corrupt politicians were no more. As was expected, many of these companies went bust, but this was no loss to the economy, as all the redundant staff quickly found work in the new industries that were being created at a rate that was unprecedented in the history of this planet. Full employment had arrived and so much work was available that many people had more than one job.

And, somehow, as though it had all been planned, which of course it had, there was a rapid increase in the population because there was so much money around that nobody gave a second thought to the extra cost of having children.

Wende's Story

And there was yet another benefit that all this new technology brought with it, which was that innovation reduced the need for people to work long hours. Within twenty years the average full-time working week had fallen to twenty hours. There was so much wealth being created that people did not need to work overtime to make ends meet. Young mothers did not need to go to work to put food on the table as the salary of one adult in a marriage was more than enough to provide for the family. Sound money had eliminated inflation and within twenty years living standards had increased tenfold, when wages, taxes and the cost of living were taken into account. In the USA the average full-time wage was $120,000 p.a. and yet goods and services were only about half the price in 2032 that they were in 2012. Plus the rate of the national sales tax was only six per cent.

Thank you."

NB: Wende's presentation had been very short because she had scored the highest marks in the previous year's coursework and so had been rewarded by the Master with a short lecture.

Suzanne's Story

Abundance in Health

Suzanne was a stunningly attractive brunette from London who had been an art student before her change in career. She had also spent a number of years working as a model and had been quite successful. She was very interested in health issues and was therefore pleased to have been given this subject for her lecture.

This is what she had to say:

Mass Poisoners

"As we know from our studies, the power elite prior to 2013 were mass poisoners. They spread spiritual poison through the spoken word with their lies and half truths and pumped physical poison into the air, water and soil. They put toxic chemicals into processed foods and pharmaceuticals – the latter killing more people than illegal drugs like crack cocaine and heroin. And they poisoned people's minds with trash TV, pornography, ultra-violent films and video games and every perverted kind of music imaginable so that the light would be forced from people's chakras.

I find it difficult to understand how wicked these dark ones were, as when I look around me now all I can sense is love, beauty and peace; in nature, and in the hearts and minds of people everywhere.

The Valley of Venus

I am reminded of a song that I heard at a friend's party some years ago that was written in the early 1980's by a young Englishman from North London whose name escapes me. The song he wrote was entitled 'The Valley of Venus' and the English group that performed it was 'First Things First'. It was about a daydream where the writer longed to be in a place of great beauty and tranquillity, where the sun always shone and where there was "no bad news". It was a sentiment expressed by many artists, for at that time the energy veil (evil) was so strong that most people believed it would never be penetrated by God's light.

Gratitude

Those times were indeed horrendous when looked at from our fifth dimensional perspective. And I feel compelled to say that we owe a great debt of gratitude to those brave souls who had volunteered to live through the trials, tribulations and hardships of the Armageddon and the forty-two months of anti-Christ rule, when unspeakable acts of wickedness were perpetrated on the people. And yet despite all the suffering, the spiritual warriors of the hundred and forty four thousand from Venus were still able to anchor their light in the Earth and to win the victory that helped bring us to the place of peace and freedom that we inhabit today.

Increasing Health Awareness

It is true that there had been an increasing awareness of the importance of leading a healthy lifestyle, although this was more heavily focused on the physical aspects of health than the spiritual.

In response to this increasing awareness the power elite tried to eradicate those foods and supplements that were health-giving and that prevented disease. But the top ten per cent of the most spiritual people were not fooled by these strategies – that in almost all cases were flagrant breaches of the law as defined in the Constitution and Bill of Rights. The spiritual warriors in the 'Army of Light' had learned to become as wise as serpents and as harmless as doves, so that whenever the illuminists in the FDA and CDC acted against the people's health

A GOLDEN AGE ECONOMY

interests they were exposed in the 'Truth' media that operated via the internet. Facebook, YouTube and the thousands of 'Truth About' websites were the means by which such news was spread. One of the best known of these websites was www.naturalnews.com. On occasions such events were also commented on by the Ascended Masters through their sponsored organisations. And so in these ways awareness grew.

All of this activity had registered on Ron Paul's radar and he had decided that once he had been voted into the White House he would act to end the tyranny.

Removing The Cancer

By the time Ron Paul had become President, no one in his administration was under any illusion as to the monumental amount of work that needed to be done in order to establish a Golden Age economy and to reignite America's freedom flame.

Over the years the power elite had perverted everything that was good, and so it fell to the President to order his staff to labour under the presumption that everything that had been touched by previous Administrations had been made impure. He told them that they had to review every law, every rule and every regulation because the serpentine thinking had crept into every corner of government and therefore had to be rooted out and dealt with. The requirement was that the whole fabric of government had to be cleansed and made physically and spiritually pure. The medical analogy he used was that the cancer had to be excised and all traces removed from the body of the Federal Government. He made it clear that he would not tolerate wrongdoing in the Whitehouse, as it was the duty of the President and the government to lead by example and thus to only do good works as Jesus had done.

As a result of this policy the laws of restoration were like the great flood that cleansed the earth of all abominations created by the Watchers and the Nephilim.

The line was drawn and woe betide anyone who dared to cross it.

Suzanne's Story – Abundance in Health

Federal Health Commission

In 2013 The Federal Commission on Health was set up on similar lines to the Trade & Enterprise Commission. A summary of the key recommendations that later became the law were:

Vaccines & Prescription Dugs

All immunity from prosecution for vaccine manufacturers was removed so that any individual or group of individuals (class action) were free to sue Big Pharma for any harmful effects that their products caused.

In order to combat compulsory vaccine programmes in states where children were targeted the law was changed to make it an offence for any person to administer a vaccine to a minor without the written consent of their parent or guardian. Offenders could be imprisoned for this crime with lengthy terms imposed if the minor died as a direct result of the vaccine being administered. Any adverse effects that resulted from administering the compound would result in the sentence being increased commensurate with the damage done to the child's health. Moreover, if it could be proved that an employer had ordered an employee to administer a vaccine without due consent, the employer would be considered to be jointly and severally liable and sentenced in an appropriate manner. The sentence could include imprisonment of the responsible officers of the employing entity, plus an unlimited fine, plus the right of the victim to sue the employer and/or the employee for damages. This law was later amended to protect adults as well so that no pharmaceutical company could use vaccines as part of a covert population control programme, which the illuminati had been working towards in the pre-2012 era. As a further precaution to prevent this, all existing vaccines had to be resubmitted for approval by the regulator that replaced the FDA. The onus was placed on the producer to prove that their products were safe and this applied to all chemical substances promoted for medical use by pharmaceutical companies.

Where there had been a death caused by any existing approved

A GOLDEN AGE ECONOMY

prescription drug or vaccine, the manufacturer was required to submit the product for re-approval. This ruling ensured that drugs that were known to be harmful were withdrawn, as in every case where re-approval had been sought it was denied. The withdrawal of so many drugs from the market caused physicians to reappraise their treatment programmes and to look for alternative cures. This created a resurgence in non-chemical remedies and treatments such as natural remedies and other forms of healing that did not use any substance as the basis for the cure. These treatments took up the slack from dwindling pharmaceutical sales. The vaccine business died out because no company could prove that their products were safe and the unsurprising thing was that no one died as a result of the withdrawal of these chemical concoctions. In fact, the opposite was true as the number of deaths declined and the cost of medical insurance fell as fewer costly drugs were prescribed. Psychology as a means of treating the root cause of disease became a massive growth industry when it was realised that all illness begins in the mind and the teachings of Mary Baker Eddy became a compulsory part of the syllabus in medical schools. And the natural remedies and supplements industry went through a renaissance when all restrictions on them were lifted.

These new laws benefitted everyone except the illuminati, whose population control programme was brought to a halt, and whose hugely profitable chemical business suffered death by a thousand cuts so that within fifty years it was a shadow of its former self.

Fluoridation of public water supplies was banned as were all animal experiments.

CHEMICALS IN FOOD

The same strict standards of re-approval that were applied to the pharmaceutical industry were carried over to the food and drink business, so that non-natural ingredients had to be proven safe or be withdrawn. As a result MSG (yeast extract) and all chemically based sweeteners, like aspartame, were withdrawn from sale along with a long list of other rogue substances which the FDA had approved because of its corrupt relationships with the chemical industry that went back to the time of its creation. A cynic might say that FDA policy was to wave through anything that was chemical-based and to ban all natural products that were in competition with their chemical equivalent. However, on the basis of the evidence that view was not so far from the truth.

Other significant changes that were made were to the ingredient labelling regulations so as to stop the practice of manufacturers disguising the levels of unhealthy ingredients like sugar by giving them different names.

Genetically Modified Organisms (GMO)

Despite the massive level of support given to GMO corporations like Monsanto by illuminati-controlled government agencies like the FDA, the public was not convinced that their 'Frankenstein' foods were safe. And they were right to be concerned. Even more disturbing was that the six biggest GMO corporations had bought up most of the world's seed suppliers – virtually eliminating competition in the market.

The patenting of genetically modified seeds was regarded by many as the work of the devil, which, of course, it was, because the strategy of the GMO manufacturers was to engineer a situation where naturally grown seed could be withheld from the market, so that the only seed available to farmers for planting was the genetically modified variety. In this way the GMO suppliers could gain control of the world's food supply, which was a key part of the New World Order plan to own and/or control everything on the planet. However, this was not consistent with the principles of a free market economy, and so with the support of the public behind him, the President determined to find a legal way to outlaw these practices. In the end it was fitting that science provided the solution and the means to rein these corporations in as government-instigated research proved that GMO foods were harmful to human and animal health and the environment. And this was the ammunition that the President needed to regulate these products out of existence. At the same time he also brought in strict laws to prevent monopolies and restrictive practices and put in place oversight measures to ensure they were vigorously enforced.

Agrochemicals

Public pressure for a return to organic methods of farming, where the use of chemicals was not permitted, caused the agrochemical industry to go into rapid decline. Manmade fertilisers were never essential to agriculture as the Bible recommends that a field used for growing crops should be left fallow every seven years so that the soil can regenerate. The Great Recession that followed the Crash of 2012 resulted in many more people growing their own food. And once people had experienced the superior taste of home-grown produce, demand for the chemically raised and treated versions supplied by supermarkets fell away. Nevertheless, strict safety rules were applied to these toxic chemical concoctions, which accelerated the rate of their decline.

The Violet Flame

There is so much I could say about the Golden Age of Health that followed the reformations, but Master Prospero has asked me to be brief. I cannot finish, however, without mentioning the greatest aid to our spiritual and physical health that there is, and ever was, and, that until a century ago, had only been revealed to students of the Ascended Masters – and this, of course, is the violet flame.

The violet flame is the seventh ray aspect of the Holy Spirit. It is the sacred fire that transmutes the cause, effect, record and memory of negative karma. It is the power that can erase our past mistakes, and is also called the flame of transmutation, of freedom and of forgiveness. When we invoke the violet flame into our lives it changes the vibration of our negative energies into positive ones and transforms negative thoughts and feelings. If used properly it has the power to heal and even reverse the aging process.

The colour violet has the highest frequency in the realm of visible light. It is the last colour our eyes can see before moving into the invisible spectrum of light. Thus, it is the transition flame between this world and the next and has the greatest ability to interpenetrate and transform matter. Einstein stated that matter can be converted into energy and energy into matter, but that energy/matter cannot be created or destroyed – only transformed. Focus on an atom and you will see that its nucleus is surrounded by electrons and much empty space. Matter may appear solid, but in reality it is spinning particles widely separated by space. The faster our electrons spin the higher frequency or vibration of light our bodies can carry. When we are ill and/or our bodies are polluted and weighted by impure substances our bodies are denser and our electrons slow down.

If you have felt the presence of the Holy Spirit, your guardian angel or your spirit guide you will know what it is like to experience a higher vibration. Usually these encounters last for a short time, and then our vibration drops back to its former rate. But if each time we could retain some of the experience of this higher vibration, we would start to change. Our bodies would stop aging and we might even start looking younger. We would have more energy, feel lighter, need less sleep and generally be happier and more at peace. This and more can be achieved by using the violet flame. Repeat a specific word cadence or mantra and the vibration of that word affects our auras. God used the power of the spoken word to create when he said, "Let there be Light!" And there was Light. We are made in the image and likeness of God and are co-creators with God. We are the only life-form on Earth given the power to communicate through speech. And it is through the word that we create. Thoughts are unspoken words, and all words are preceded by thought. But in the matter universe, although thoughts are powerful and create in themselves, words carry power when spoken out loud. A simple fiat to the violet flame, repeated several times, can draw this light to us: "I AM a being of violet fire; I AM the purity God desires."

For more information on how to use the violet flame to work miracles for yourself and others please visit: www.theosophiaistheway.com

A GOLDEN AGE ECONOMY

Conclusion

The realisation that the power elite wanted to keep the masses in a constant state of ill health was the catalyst that brought about change in the way the post-2012 world approached the business of healthcare. The emphasis shifted from using chemicals to treat the physical symptoms of disease, to a holistic approach, where the spiritual aspects of illness were considered before anything else. In practice this involved doctors putting psychology before pharmacology and surgery. This is not to say that medication and the knife have no place, but that they should be regarded as a last resort. The medical profession came of age when they accepted, as fact, that disease in the physical body is the effect of a cause in the spiritual being (psychology) that occupies that body, and that what manifests in the physical body is an out-picturing of a problem in the spiritual body (mental body) or mind. For Hermes stated that "the universe is mental".

In the years that followed the reformations, self-healing took off. The economic benefits of divine healthcare brought huge savings in costs as the sick care system promoted for the benefit of Big Pharma suffered a cardiac arrest.

Workers' stress levels went down and their productivity went up. The healthcare sector shrank, which released people to work in the wealth-creating sector and this was better for the economy as a whole. Steadily improving physical and mental health meant that fewer people had to be cared for in homes for the elderly and this released money for other things and helped to reduce taxes. Abundance in health had arrived.

Thank you."

Ptolemy's Story

LIBRARY OF TRUE RELIGIONS & ANTIQUITIES

The next speaker was blonde-haired young man from Macedonia in Greece and although his name means 'warlike', he was a kind and caring person who enjoyed peaceful pursuits like writing poetry and reading books. Master Prospero must have thought he was very spiritual too, given the title of talk he was about to give.

This is what he had to say:

"One of the things the world lacked prior to 2013 was spiritual leadership and purpose. People were disunited through race, colour, class, education, country and, of course, faith. Divide, bind and rule had been the mantra of the power elite and fomenting division through religious conflict was the meat and drink of what they liked to do. Within the Christian Protestant movement were hundreds of denominations, all with a slightly different take on what they thought a Christian should be. Although the Catholics were, generally speaking, closest to what Jesus had taught, the fallen angels at the top of the church hierarchy had been – to their eternal shame – the first to pervert, censor and steal Jesus' core teachings.

Other true religions had their different sects too, and each claimed to be nearer to God than the next. They disagreed on issues of minor importance and never seemed able to see the big picture, meaning that they failed to grasp the reality that there are no religions – there are only God's Laws. If Earth had been one continent with one language, then we may have been united by one faith. But that was not to be. The reality had been different faiths for different lands and different times.

But then something happened. The world got smaller. The age of

A GOLDEN AGE ECONOMY

mass communication arrived. A common language, English became the language of international business and this helped to bring different peoples and cultures together. And then came the greatest invention of them all, the internet. It linked billions of people across the globe without the need for anyone to leave their homes. Hindus could talk to Christians, Muslims could chat with Buddhists and Jews could interact with Taoists. With this global communication network people soon realised that they were not divided at all. Human hearts beat to the same time; they feel the same pain, and are filled with the same love because essentially we are all the same – made in the image and likeness of our Father-Mother God.

In these lectures today, we have heard how the citizens of America and the world gradually awakened to the truth of All That Is. We have learned how eventually they saw through the illusions that the power elite had created with their counterfeit kingdom. We have been reminded how our forefathers reconnected to the truth and wisdom in God's Laws, because in their heart of hearts, they knew that it was the only way to restore the broken economy. We have heard the amazing results that were achieved once God's Laws had replaced man's laws, and specifically, how abundance began to flow and miracles started to happen. But there was more that could be done, for this gentle awakening was only the beginning.

A few years before the fireworks went off in 2012, Jesus had made it known in certain spiritual circles that he wanted to see a central point of focus for those who wished to bring God's Laws back into their lives – a place where people could study the teachings of the world's true religions. Jesus had envisaged that visitors should be able to access information – free of charge – via the internet and also buy books and other enlightening materials that would be published to help fund the cost of providing this service.

The world's first Great Library was in Alexandria, Egypt, but it was deliberately burnt down during the time of Julius Caesar and Queen Cleopatra by dark forces jealous of the power, influence and prestige that it had brought to that country. Moreover, it was the desire of these saboteurs to prevent humans from attaining the empowerment that wisdom and awareness brings, and rather than share power they wanted to wield more. But the greatest power, the most liberating power, is the power that comes from knowing the truth of All That Is – the secret wisdom of ages that is contained in the scriptures and writings of the Ascended Masters and Saints; works that have accumulated into a vast patchwork of wisdom and truth dating back to the time when beloved Sanat Kumara first brought the Word of God to the people after the Great Flood. Jesus' wish was that this reservoir of knowledge be made available to all, so that there would be the potential for a mass raising in consciousness that would burn through the energy veil and free the people. Knowledge is power and to understand how the universe works is to understand how God's Laws can lift us up in our daily lives.

I believe that it was part of the divine plan that a new library be built in Alexandria because that had been the site of the original Great Library that the Pharaoh, Ptolemy I, had begun. And so, after many years of planning, preparation and fundraising by the two people who had agreed to undertake this task, this glorious enterprise began to take shape.

Egypt had been devastated by the effects of the Great Recession. Fewer tourists were able to afford the pleasures of cruising on the Nile, staring in awe at the pyramids of Giza and exploring the Valley of the Kings. Consequently, the government had been keen to co-operate in bringing this potentially lucrative tourist attraction to their country. There had been much debate about whether the library should be located in Cairo or Alexandria, but in the end common sense prevailed and Alexandria won the prize. Another suggestion that the government had considered was the rebuilding of the Pharos, but when they looked into the costs the idea was quietly dropped – though not forgotten.

Apart from books, the intention was always that the Library should exhibit religious relics, artefacts and antiquities as these would be the items that would help to draw in the crowds. Can you imagine the interest if, for example, it had been possible to exhibit the spear of destiny, the crown of thorns and the shroud of Turin all in one place and at one time?

A GOLDEN AGE ECONOMY

We are all familiar with the Library of True Religions & Antiquities (LTRA), as it was named, as it is where some of us did our research for today's talks. I have visited the LTRA in Alexandria and cannot recommend it highly enough. Using advanced carbon dating techniques it has been confirmed that some of the exhibits go back to the time of the Great Flood. And there are other amazing items on display that had formerly been hidden away in the Vatican's secret vaults.

So what else is there to say on this subject? Well, the LTRA did raise awareness of God's Laws. It did help to bring people closer together, but most importantly, it made a significant contribution towards putting spiritual teachings back into the heart of the school curriculums and thus into people's lives. Children (and adults) had access to an amazing resource, so that instead of just learning about Christianity or Islam or Judaism, they had the opportunity to learn about all the true religions and how they all converge into the ONE TRUTH that is God's Laws.

Thank you."

Guinevere's Story

The Golden Age of Energy

"Gold is divine currency and crystalline energy is divine energy."

– Kim Andrew Lincoln

Guinevere was born in Anglesey, a small island in North Wales, off the north-west coast of mainland Britain. It was there, two thousand years earlier, that the Roman army had wiped out the Welsh druids, who were the pagan spiritual leaders of the Celtic people. And, it was during this massacre that Queen Boudicca went to war with the Romans and nearly succeeded in kicking them out of Britain. Guinevere, however, was a peace-loving lady; a child of nature who was happiest in the great outdoors: running in the sun, walking in the woods and swimming in the sea.

This is what she had to say:

"My friends, you know that I am no scientist, and so to talk to you about a subject rooted in the deep soil of science is not an easy thing for me to do. Perhaps, in his infinite wisdom, our beloved Master has asked me to present this subject to you precisely because I do not have a scientific mind, and thus will convey to you the essence of what is important to know about the most enlightened form of energy that came to power the world in the post-2012 world without sending you to sleep with explanations that frankly are beyond my understanding. Ah, I see that the Master is smiling, so perhaps I have struck the right chord here.

So, where to begin?

A GOLDEN AGE ECONOMY

Beginning at the End

Well, just to be different, let's break with the accepted conventions of storytelling and start at the end of the story. For in this tale the end is now, because today the type of energy to which I refer is not an idea or an expectation, it is an established fact. The building we occupy is heated and lit by it. But if someone from a hundred years ago were to be teleported to the present day, and was sitting here with us in this lecture theatre, they would be looking around the room and comparing it to the buildings from their own time. And one of the questions they might ask is: what type of energy do you use to power this building? And we would answer: "Crystalline energy". But when they asked: "What is that, and where does it come from, and how is it delivered to homes and factories?" what would our answers be?

Well, when I asked myself these questions I realised that I could not answer them with any degree of scientific authority, but then, on reflection, I do not think it is actually necessary for me to do so. What I consider to be more important is to explain how we changed from the Dark Age fuels to this enlightened one, which I suggest is the gold standard of all energy sources.

From the perspective of nations held to ransom by over-priced fossil fuels and deadly nuclear power, crystalline energy was the perfect solution to the power needs of our twenty-first century friends. It was relatively inexpensive, clean and there is an inexhaustible supply. This was exceedingly good news as prior to 2013 the main energy sources of oil, coal, natural gas and nuclear power were unsafe, polluting and highly toxic. Moreover, these fuels had become so expensive through supplier manipulation and predatory speculation in the financial markets that they acted like a giant ball and chain on the leg of the economy. In many cases people were spending as much as 20% of their disposable income to power their houses and cars, and in winter many elderly people died from hypothermia because they could not afford to heat their homes. Then there was the indirect costs related to these Dark Age fuels, such as impaired health and environmental pollution. The people and the planet desperately needed a solution to the energy problem, but all that came forth from the politicians was ever more costly and less effective alternatives like solar and wind power that were developed solely to line the pockets of the power elite.

THE SOLUTION

What most people did not know in 2012 was that it had been claimed by a number of sources (Edgar Cayce and James Tyberonn being two) that a tried and tested solution had been used tens of thousands of years earlier on Atlantis, but that much of the evidence of it had either been hidden for safekeeping or lost under the sea. And yet, in the twentieth century, our forefathers utilised crystals to power radios and watches, and the 'new age community' used them to heal and enhance health. So the fact that crystals were actually being employed as a power source lends a great deal of credibility to the proposition that a society far more technically and spiritually advanced than the one of 2012 might have used them too – albeit on a much grander scale.

A cynic might say that crystalline energy had been suppressed by the power elite, but I am inclined to think that the powers in heaven were not prepared to release the knowledge needed to make this energy viable until the people of Earth were ready to receive it. In other words, the technology would not be made available until they had made a concerted effort to dispense with the satanic science of nuclear fission, and stopped the suppression of the cheap and clean energy technologies that Tesla and others had attempted to bring to market – only to be thwarted by the power elite.

This is an extremely important point because what was said to have happened on Atlantis was that dark forces took control of the crystalline energy power grid and misused it for military purposes – as twentieth century man and the Laggards from Maldek had done with nuclear power. This activated the Laws of Disintegration and Karma, and thus, within a short time, the complex apparatus that supported the grid was destroyed along with some, but not all, of the giant crystals that were the power source. This set off a chain reaction of tsunamis, flooding and earthquakes that eventually caused Atlantis to sink into the sea. Other

A GOLDEN AGE ECONOMY

sources say that some of the crystals were saved, deactivated and hidden so that they could be used again at a future time.

So now we can understand why the Ascended Masters were resolved not to allow this tragedy to be repeated in the Aquarian Age. I believe that they decided to keep the technology under wraps until humankind had convinced them that it would be safe in our hands – meaning that our consciousness had risen to the point where we had become as harmless as doves.

Benefits

Crystalline energy is similar to gold in that it is imbued with powers capable of elevating human consciousness, and consequently the measure of its worth is incalculable. Crystals transmute negative energy and function as amplifiers and transformers of various energies into biological energies that rebalance and re-energise our bodies at the cellular, emotional, mental and spiritual level. The famous mystic and clairvoyant Edgar Cayce claimed that the Atlanteans understood that crystals could heal the aura and, through healing the aura, the healing of the physical body could be accomplished. The Temples of Healing on Atlantis helped people live extremely long lives in the same body. Indeed, some sources say that the 'Alta Ra', who were the scientist-priests who managed and operated the crystalline power grid, lived up to 12,000 years, and that some of the famous scientists we know today, such as Einstein, Da Vinci and Tesla were among them.

But what is so amazing about crystalline energy is that the above benefits are *in addition* to the primary functions that crystals perform as a power source and medium for data storage and communications.

Not Free Energy

But let us be clear, crystalline energy was never free then or now. Indeed, the infrastructure it requires is complex and costly – as with water, where considerable expense is incurred supplying it to homes and businesses.

Guinevere's Story – The Golden Age of Energy

THE BIG SWITCH

What happened in the years after 2012 when the suppressed energy technologies were released was a rush to bring new cleaner and cheaper power sources on stream. These took market share from the old fuels, which were gradually phased out. But it took time, for as we know, it takes decades to safely decommission a nuclear power plant. And, with the oil-based fuels, huge infrastructure had been created that employed lots of people, plus there was little financial incentive to dismantle it as in 2011 there was $200 trillion in oil reserves. Having said that, consumers have real power, and they wanted clean and cheap energy and the newly created energy companies wanted to satisfy that latent demand, and so steady progress was made. As more and more of the power elite were permanently removed from Earth the process accelerated, until one day some bright spark came up with the idea of using giant crystals as a primary energy source, and, as they say, the rest is history.

GOLDEN AGES

The Ascended Masters tell us that Atlantis' Golden Age lasted from 40,000 BC to 18,000 BC, though the civilisation spanned 200,000 years in all. At its peak it was a utopian society that achieved the highest level of light consciousness in the history of Earth, although here in the Academy we hold the immaculate concept that we shall do greater works during this Golden Age of Saint Germain. The dark era of Atlantis occurred during the last 7,000 years that ended with the Great Flood around 10,500 BC. And, as I have said, the events that led to the sinking of Atlantis began when crystalline energy started to be used for offensive (war-making) purposes. And in the forefront of this wicked work were the life-streams who later embodied as Hitler and Himmler in the first half of the twentieth century. The negative karma created by the dark forces on Atlantis was such that only the destruction of this civilisation could repay the karmic debt amassed. From these dark days, however, humankind learnt many lessons. Apparently about 70%

of all people on the planet Earth in 2010 had at some point incarnated on Atlantis.

It was the end, but it was also the beginning, because in the 12,500 years that elapsed between then and 2012, those who had re-embodied on Earth, and who had lived on Atlantis before, were given another opportunity to know again what a struggle life can be when we do not live in accordance with God's Laws. After the Great Flood the lights literally and metaphorically went out on this planet. There was not a single soul that had the Christic light in them. Men lived like beasts, for civilisation had effectively become extinct. In every sense these times were dark times. Had beloved Sanat Kumara not volunteered to mount a rescue mission to anchor his light, and the light of the 144,000 cosmic beings who came with him, then Earth would have been abandoned by the spiritual hierarchy as a school room for evolving souls. Twelve thousand five hundred years later, and despite the best efforts of the fallen angels to keep us in darkness, the light has broken through the energy veil and it becomes much stronger and more intense with each passing day.

But what the people of 2012 did not realise was that it has been claimed by some that the most advanced civilisations in the Milky Way (Arcturian and Sirian) used crystalline energy as a power source and thus it was appropriate that it should be reinstated in the Aquarian Age that was destined to be the next Golden Age on Earth. This did not happen immediately, but once the people had been made ready spiritually and the governments of the world had agreed to the restoration of crystalline energy, then the gates of knowledge in heaven opened, and all that the scientists needed to know became known, and all that had been lost was found.

Thank you."

The Secret Speaker's Story

THE NEW POPULAR MUSIC

After Guinevere had sat down Master Prospero reclaimed his place behind the lectern. He looked around the room into the eyes of all his students and then addressed them with the following words:

"I am deeply touched and humbled by the great honour you have done me here this day. You have all given your best and the outcome has exceeded my expectations. I am immensely pleased with what you have achieved, so thank you. In your desire to excel you have expanded each other's knowledge, and thus the great tapestry of economic history that resides within the heart of this Academy is more than it was three hours ago. With that thought I suggest we all go to lunch, but please be back here for 2 pm to welcome our mystery guest speaker. He is a very dear friend of mine, whom I have known all my adult life and is one of the greatest composers of his generation in the new music that I know you all love. Moreover, I can assure you that you will be entertained, as no doubt he will regale you with stories of his band's touring experiences and try to embarrass me into the bargain with tales of our past. His lecture will focus on the new popular music that started to be played in the years following the Armageddon as well as the old music that was left behind. So, please enjoy your lunch and I will see you all later."

The Master was speaking on his personal communicator when the students filtered in to the lecture theatre after their lunch break. He looked very worried as he put the device back into his pocket.

He spoke to the class, saying:

"Can I have your attention please? I have an important announcement to make concerning this afternoon's speaker. I have been just been informed that my friend has been taken ill on his way here from his home in LA and therefore will not be able to join us, so rather than cancel this session I will speak in his place. Please forgive me if my words are not so polished and rehearsed as yours, but I have had no time to prepare and thus shall be speaking straight from the heart."

The Master was clearly shaken by the news he had received, but as he started to talk about the life of his friend and his music his mood changed. He became more confident and the smiles returned, for clearly these two were very, very close.

This is what he said:

The Power of Music

"Music contains within itself the invisible hand of spirit that, when it is imbued with the vibration of love, can reach into our hearts and touch our souls. Music can lift us up; it can inspire us, soothe our ruffled brows and even make us laugh. Music is pure emotion, but it is much more than this, for it can do so many things that there are not the words to convey the totality of all that music is and all that music can do. Music is the sound of creation; for it was the power of God's spoken words that issued the command: "Let there be light" and there was light; and thus it could be said that we owe our very existence to the illimitable power of music.

Music can be a force for great good, for the beloved Goddess of Music has said that: "Every discordant condition on this planet could be dissolved and consumed by the right kind of music." Note, however, that she said "the right kind of music", for the wrong kind of music can do immeasurable harm.

Beloved Sanat Kumara teaches a path of sacrifice, service, selflessness and surrender and his presence can be felt while playing the music Finlandia by Sibelius. This magnificent composition is his keynote and anchors such a flame of freedom that it was banned by the Nazis in World War II.

In the Dark Age the fallen ones understood the power that music is, and that it can be perverted for dark purposes as crystalline energy was used for evil on Atlantis. They knew the secret damage that could be done to the Children of the Sun because music that is not in alignment with God's Laws can be used as a tool for draining the light from the human chakras and thus can drag souls down into degradation – and even to death.

ANCIENT BELIEFS

Some philosophers from ancient times believed that good music disposes us to virtue, whereas bad music disposes us to vice. They held music to be the most important of the sciences and the most powerful path to religious enlightenment. Moreover, they believed that it provided the basis for stable and harmonious government.

The Chinese Emperor, Shun, monitored the music played in his realm to ensure that it was correct. He tested the exact pitches of the current notes of music and had various musicians and instruments play the local folk songs and check that all this music was in perfect correspondence with the five tones (notes) of the ancient Chinese musical scale. In this way he was able to judge if there had been a breakdown in the culture of his kingdom.

In the sixth century, the Roman philosopher Anicius Boethius, wrote:

"Music can both establish and destroy morality. For no path is more open to the soul for the formation thereof than through the ears. Therefore when the rhythms and modes have penetrated even to the soul through these organs, it cannot be doubted that they affect the soul with their own character and conform it to themselves."

He also wrote that:

"Music is so naturally united with us that we cannot be free from it even if we so desired."

In a Greek city state a teacher was exiled because he had added another string to one of the traditional instruments. The American philosopher Henry David Thoreau wrote: "Music can be intoxicating. Such apparently slight causes destroyed Greece and Rome, and will destroy England and America."

Some people think that music is a reflection of the society, meaning that the civilisation comes first and the music it produces afterwards; but when we look into the annals of history the evidence tends to support the opposite view, as in Egypt and Greece, it was the decline in their music that caused their fall.

The Fallen Angel Plan

As with every other aspect of life on this planet the dark forces had a plan for perverting music, which the Ascended Masters had known for centuries would be implemented when the fallen angels were released from the pit after World War II. So, in order to help humankind resist the temptations that this dark music would present, the Ascended Masters inspired the introduction of Classical music as an example of what the proper mode and rhythm and expression of harmony should be so that we might be able discern the difference between what was the right kind of music and what was not. The Ascended Host held the immaculate concept that we would reject rock music when it finally arrived, once the fallen angels had come of age. This 'devil's music', however, proved to be very popular with the younger generation. They were attracted to it by its syncopated beat that they could dance to, and thus the plan to subvert young people and bring society down met with early success.

Elvis

In America Elvis Presley became the leading performer of the new style of R&B music that had its roots in the jazz and blues that mainly black musicians had performed. What Elvis had been able to do to further the illuminati plan was to bring this new music to the mass market. He was the perfect delivery system because of his superlative talent as a singer, exceptional goods looks and incomparable ability to move on stage in a manner that women found irresistible. But the jewel in his crown was his status as an alpha white male that made him and the songs that he sang acceptable to all audiences, but especially white audiences.

The Beatles

But Elvis was only the warm up act in comparison to what the biggest group of all time, The Beatles, had been able to achieve in advancing the illuminist agenda. The Beatles were a musical phenomenon. In addition to employing the rock beat, they added strong melody and meaningful lyrics with subliminal messages about their use of drugs, which informed much of their later music – especially on the groundbreaking *Sergeant Pepper* album. In 1964 they began using marijuana and moved onto LSD a year later. Their song 'Lucy in the Sky with Diamonds' explicitly references LSD. With the guiding hand of their manager, Brian Epstein, the Beatles' influence extended into the fashion industry where their male fans copied the hair and clothes styles of their heroes. They also transformed the music industry in terms of helping to improve the financial rewards for artists and revolutionised touring with their concerts in massive venues like the Shea Stadium in New York. They also introduced what we know today as 'The Music Video' to promote their record sales.

But what is little known is that wholesale abortion followed as The Beatles introduced the drug culture into America and the "if it feels good, do it" philosophy that had been promoted by the occultist and agnostic Aleister Crowley and his student Aldous Huxley. Huxley was famous for his dystopian work of fiction *Brave New World* that imagined a future world where people found solace in promiscuous sex and habitual drug taking. In his personal life Huxley was well known for advocating and taking psychedelic drugs like LSD. The group The Doors was apparently named after another of Huxley's novels *The Doors of Perception*. Pictures of both these social revolutionaries and the fallen angel founder of communism, Karl Marx, appeared on the *Sergeant Pepper* album cover (along with many others) as they were all heroes of The Beatles.

Satanic Music

The history of the music that followed The Beatles and other sixties bands became progressively darker and more openly Satanic. Lyrics were filled with death, murder, rape and all manner of perverse behaviour, though invariably you could not make out the words for the noise. Rock music sub-divided into classic rock, acid rock, hard rock, techno rock, punk rock, rap and metal – to name but a few. It has been a continual downhill journey into sounds that have no relationship to harmony, love, beauty and God, but mostly to death, drugs, hell, Satan and sexual perversions – just as the illuminati had envisioned.

So let us now take a more detailed look at the main components of this perverted music.

SYNCOPATION

At the top of the list is the syncopated beat or rock beat that originated from African voodoo rhythms as described in the song: The Ballad of Voodoo Rock.

Music is held together through rhythm or beat, in metres or measures. In conventional music, like classical music, the beats are naturally grouped into groups of two, three, four and are called measures. The metre of a piece of music is the arrangement of its rhythms in a repetitive pattern of strong and weak beats. Typical metres include 2/4, 3/4, 4/4 and 6/8 (two, three, four and six beats in a measure). The first beat in each measure is always accented, so that it is played more loudly than the other beats. The strong beat is the first beat in the measure as in a waltz, where the heavy beat is followed by two lighter beats. A waltz is in triple metre – one strong beat followed by two weak beats, then repeated.

In a military march, however, you have a heavy beat followed by a light beat, then another heavy beat followed by another light beat. This is duple metre – as one would march in left-right-left-right patterns.

Syncopation, on the other hand, is a disturbance or interruption of the regular flow of rhythm, where the accent is placed on the 'wrong' beat. This technique is used for variety, and is an effective and versatile tool that composers can utilise to create rhythmic interest. In syncopated rhythm it is the weak beat or an in-between beat that is stressed. Weak beats and in-between beats are known collectively as 'off beats', and so syncopated rhythm may also be called 'offbeat rhythm'.

Another inharmonious technique is the simultaneous use of two or more rhythmic patterns, such as 'two against three'. This is called polyrhythm (multi-rhythms) and is used most frequently in African cultures and to a lesser extent in jazz and rock that came out of African voodoo music.

What distinguishes syncopation – used for variety – in jazz and ragtime, and the rock music that followed it, is that with the latter the syncopated beat is used continuously, so that you get the constant offbeat pounded out by the drums. This literally rocks the chakras and the cells, atoms and electrons in our bodies from their natural flow. It draws the life force out of our bodies so that we have no strength or will to be. Indeed, it is the antithesis of Be-in-g.

I personally know this to be true because I have known many drummers who have confirmed to me that prolonged exposure to syncopation caused them to experience dark moods and to act out of character. They would leave the stage after doing a ninety-minute gig on a negative high. They stated that they felt as though they had been drained like the victim of a vampire would feel and needed a fix to replace what they had lost, which was their life's blood, meaning their light. But that light could not be so easily replaced and so they took in whatever else came to hand at the time such as drugs, alcohol, excessive sex or the venting of their aggression on the hotel's furniture and TV sets. And yes, we have all heard those stories of rock groups like Led Zeppelin who participated in the most bizarre acts after gigs, and by all accounts I have no reason to doubt that these reports were true as a consequence of the deleterious effects that their impure music had upon them. But joking aside, musicians cannot subject themselves to this continuous level of abuse without paying a very high price in terms of damage to their physical health and peace of mind, and thus the list of rock stars that paid the ultimate price is a very long one indeed. The movie *Rock Star*, made in 2000, is a fair representation of that lifestyle, but we must not forget that even though they may not have been consciously aware of it, the audiences suffered just as much from the negative impact of syncopation as the groups they came to hear, which, of course, was the intention.

Discordance

A good example of discordant music was the rebellious 'punk rock' that crashed onto the scene like a juggernaut in the mid 1970s with groups like the Sex Pistols. This music was full of youthful energy, though not positive energy, but energy packed with violence and aggression that frequently transferred itself into the audience, causing fights to break out. One particular song from the Sex Pistols that I have studied contained the constantly repeated line "I am the anti-Christ" – a statement with which many adults at that time agreed. The Sex Pistols were not accomplished musicians and regarded their lack of ability as a badge of honour. Moreover, they often played out of tune, as they believed that it added to the overall effect they were trying to create, which was shock, awe and destruction.

Punk rock later morphed into various other styles including the satanic sounds of death metal where the music was characterised by full-blown discordance, meaning a complete absence of melody, harmony and colour. When combined with a wall of syncopated sound the audience's senses were assaulted into a state of submission. The result was that the listener became weakened and will-less from the draining of their light.

Discordance can be discerned by the human ear, but the science of cymatics has proved that it can be seen too. This was achieved with experiments conducted in the late twentieth century that demonstrated the effect that different types of music had on the physical structure of a snowflake. If you have ever seen what a snowflake looks like under a microscope you will know that it is incredibly beautiful in its design, being comprised of elaborate patterns and shapes that are based on sacred geometry. Now when the vibration of classical music was applied to the snowflake there was no noticeable difference to its composition, but when rock music was played the exquisite patterns disintegrated into a distorted and unrecognisable mess. In his book *The Secret Power of Music*, David Thame impresses upon us the importance of music to our physical and mental wellbeing. I recommend it to those who want to know more.

Negative Lyrics

The spoken word carries great power but when sung it is even more powerful.

A common device that the fallen ones used to keep people down, and thus under their control, was to reinforce the idea in song lyrics that people are unworthy and unimportant and thus cannot rise up in consciousness. For example, in a so-called 'love' song the protagonists are portrayed as unfaithful and untrustworthy. Love is never spiritual, but always physical and conditional, expressing the idea that "I will love you only if you do what I want". Human relationships are made to look shallow and people are depicted as mean-spirited and vengeful. This is a form of mental programming, because if you keep repeating a lie often enough there is a good chance that people will eventually accept the lie as truth. Hitler employed this technique to great effect. It was also used in the TV soap operas of the time. The storylines were rarely uplifting, but rather focused on people's weaknesses, never their strengths. The aim was to create a new reality, or should I say, unreality, because we become what we think about most, so if people can be continually persuaded to think that they are unworthy then that is their new reality – that is what they become. Thus popular songs can be a powerful medium for controlling the population.

Hooks

To be hooked is to be addicted. A fish caught on a hook is under the control of the fisherman. And so, as fishers of men, the power elite's reason for inserting a hook in a song was to control the listener through their addiction.

In the Dark Age music business hooks were embedded in songs to sell them, and in so doing get as many people as possible addicted. Once they had bought the record the idea was that they would keep playing it to satisfy the addiction. The second reason for implanting a hook in a song was for the purpose of mind control, as once the listener was attracted by the hook, they could then be spoon-fed any message/s that the writer and/or record company wanted to convey – thus making it possible for the listener to be influenced and controlled.

Now, I am not saying that there was conspiracy behind every song released, because that was clearly not the case. My point is that by virtue of their structure popular songs can easily be manipulated for nefarious purposes – as happened increasingly in the years leading up to 2013.

In musical terms we might define a hook as a musical idea, often a short riff, passage, or phrase used mainly in rock, pop, hip hop and dance music – to catch the ear of the listener. In popular songs the hook can be the whole chorus or part of it; it can be melodic or rhythmic and may incorporate the main motif for a piece of music. For example, the melody to the lyric "And I will always love you" in the song 'I Will Always Love You'.

One definition of a hook is a musical or lyrical phrase that stands out and is easily remembered. Other definitions describe the hook as repetitive, attention-grabbing, memorable, easy to dance to and the part of the song – sometimes the title or key lyric line – that keeps repeating. The hook itself may vary in length from the repetition of one note or a series of notes or a lyric phrase, full line, or an entire verse. Essentially, the hook is what sells the song and some songwriters have stated that to create a hit song you need to incorporate at least five different hooks. A hook may also be a vocal timbre or a specially-created sound effect.

Symbolism & Hypnotism

The advent of the music video presented the dark hierarchy with innumerable opportunities to plant negative thoughts into people's minds using imagery that worked, both at a conscious and subliminal level. As destructive words enter into the mental body via the ears, so

The Secret Speaker's Story – The New Popular Music

downbeat images can be transported via the eyes. If, as I have done, you have ever studied any of the old music videos put out by artists known for promoting the illuminist agenda, then you will have noticed that they are full of symbolism and striking imagery that is wholly satanic in nature. The purpose here is to hypnotise the audience into believing that Satan/Lucifer is the real God and therefore the one they should be worshipping. This was dressed up in what many young people would have considered to have been 'cool' imagery, in terms of set designs, costumes, make-up, dance steps and sensuality, so as to downplay the seriousness. In most, but not all, cases the satanic symbols and imagery used were so subtle that it was barely noticeable to anyone but the sub-conscious mind. Flashing such images on and off, rapidly and repeatedly, created a hypnotic effect that was designed to brain-wash the weak-willed and impressionable – mechanised man being the obvious targets.

HORNED BEAST HAND SIGN

The most conspicuous of these symbols was the horned beast hand sign that many young people used at rock concerts to identify with each other, and which most mistakenly believed was the symbol for rock music. The truth, however, is that the meaning is: I am a Satanist, I worship Satan and I am proud of it. This sign was used by many rock stars of the period, because they were either ardent Satanists or because they had sold their souls to the devil (record company) in return for fame and fortune. As you will recall from the Bible, Satan offered Jesus the whole world if he would but follow him.

Indeed, there were stories circulating the internet then that suggested that some artists had been required to sign their recording contracts in their own blood, as a demonstration of their commitment to the ways of evil. Whether these stories are true or not, I do not know, but what was true was that record companies did have a huge hold over their stars, advancing their careers when they were cooperative, but shutting them down when they refused to do as they were told – as was the case with the King of Pop, Michael Jackson, and countless others. Look in the media archives and you will see that so many of these rock stars died in mysterious circumstances and this raises the question: was it their music and lifestyle that killed them or the music corporations they were signed to?

Politicians

The horned beast hand sign was also used in public by some political leaders (e.g. Presidents Bush and Clinton) who believed they were untouchable and so did not care who knew that they were Satanists. Incidentally, the V for Victory sign that Winston Churchill made famous during World War II is an illuminati hand sign, reversed.

All Seeing Eye

Another common illuminati symbol was the 'All Seeing Eye' that appeared in the top section of the pyramid on a US dollar bill. This single eye is a spiritual one, known as the 'Third Eye' that relates to perception and wisdom. As we know, Lucifer was an Archangel on the wisdom ray before he rebelled against God. In the decade that ended in 2013 big-name pop stars who unashamedly used symbolism connected to the single eye of Horus in their music videos included Lady Gaga, Beyonce and Rihanna – though there were dozens of others who employed one or more of the music perversions I have highlighted. Horus was the Egyptian God who was representative of the fallen Archangel, Lucifer.

The chequered floor design – made up of black and white squares – and the triangle (representing the pyramid) were other commonly used illuminati symbols.

Truth Hard to Accept

What I have given you is not, by any means, an exhaustive list of illuminati symbols, as to go through them all in detail would take more time than we have available today. We have covered a lot of material in

The Secret Speaker's Story – The New Popular Music

this lecture, but what I have disclosed is by no means all new. For a century ago, there were those of the 144,000 who were conscientious in making this information available, but their words of warning did not want to be heard by the youth and some of the older ones who had been snared in these illuminati traps. They did want to admit that those things in which they had invested so much of themselves were impure and had caused them harm from the light they had spilt. They did not realise that light taken away presents an opportunity for low vibrational energies to breed in the space vacated. And they did not want to hear that the ownership of the music industry by the fallen ones was part of a plan to subjugate and control them. And even less did they want to know that these dark forces were intent on keeping them in a low state of consciousness by getting them addicted to malevolent music and the unsavoury practices of drug taking and the like that are its progeny. These reactions, however, were entirely understandable.

I know from my own years as a rebellious young man that formative minds do not like to think that they can be manipulated. We all want to believe that we are beyond the influence of external forces. Such ideas do not play well with the ego that imagines itself to be superior and therefore infallible. But though the ego may judge itself to be perfect, it is not, and the young people who were coming of age at the time of the Armageddon – though they were reluctant to grasp the nettle of these revelations – were not so easily fooled by the executives in the music industry, who thought they were in control. For those young people had been chosen to be on Earth at that time to help bring in the new enlightened age that included in its blueprint 'A Golden Age for Music'.

THE NEW MUSIC

In preparing the ground to describe the new forms of popular music that were brought forth after the Great Crash of 2012, I have had to talk about a lot of negative and unpalatable subjects, but this has been necessary because the purpose of studying history is to learn from the mistakes of the past so that we can make better future choices. The

A GOLDEN AGE ECONOMY

Chinese understood this truth, which is why they were so diligent in their record-keeping. There was nothing that their Emperors said and did that was not written down and yes, you may well raise your eyebrows, because even what happened in the bedroom was recorded so that the Emperor might learn to be a better lover.

The misuses of rhythm and sound energy that destroyed the ancient civilisation of Lemuria and contributed greatly to the fall of Atlantis were very powerful lessons that needed to be learnt. And yet the lesson was repackaged and sent back to us in the way that music was perverted by the fallen angels – as I have described.

So what did these lessons teach us?

Well, my personal view is that they helped us to understand the real power of this wonderful gift of music that our beloved Father-Mother God has bestowed upon us. And we have learnt this through our experimentation with the wrong kinds of music – music that did not serve us as it did not raise all life. But most importantly we have learnt that we must treat this immensely powerful science of music with the greatest of respect because as the beloved Goddess of Music has pointed out there is no condition that cannot be cured by playing the right kind of music. Now that is a definitive statement from one who should know, and it is why I decided that this last lecture today should be about music because it is so important.

When we look back at the Great Crash of 2012 we may look upon it more as a watershed moment in history than a set of economic events. I have this image of the falling of the curtain on an important act in the play of 'Life on Earth'. Symbolically, though, it might be more accurate to say that it was God's Judgement of the Dark Age, and with it the dark music.

What we do know from accounts written at that time was that one of the biggest changes that occurred was in people's expectations – their hopes and their dreams. People had been to hell and a back during the Armageddon and they wanted to see a way through to the light of the new age – they wanted something better but more especially something real.

At this time there were many musicians who had been waiting in the wings for the curtain to go up so that they could release the new music that was in alignment with the Mother energies and the rhythms of life* – for even though people may not have been aware of it – at an inner level, they yearned to be infused with the light that the right kind of music can bring. And so the stage was set for the new groups, the new singers and the new songs...

El-Le-Eye-Em

One such group was called El-Le-Eye-Em and my friend was their composer, keyboard player and musical director. The chief architect and lyricist of the group had begun formulating his ideas for the band from about 2004 onwards and had written a large number of songs that did not have music added to them until 2012/13 when the writing team formally came together.

The trauma of the Armageddon had presented an opportunity for a new style of popular music to emerge that was sensitive to the times, and that offered hope for the future. This would be music that would re-enforce all that was good, righteous and pure about our lives here on Earth and that would give encouragement and vision to the task of building the Golden Age, as well as dealing with the debris of the Dark Age that continued to clog up the arteries of so many people's lives.

The group's name was unusual because it is not of this world, in the sense that it did not derive from any known language on Earth at that time. The lyricist had claimed that he had received the name telepathically from his spiritual advisers, though he said that he did not get the full name initially, but a shorter version. He had no idea what it meant, until one day about five years later, it suddenly came to him and he knew intuitively that what he had received was correct. The meaning is: The Power of Love, Wisdom & Unity, where: El = Power; Le = Love; Eye = Wisdom and Em = Unity.

---

* The rhythms of life are 4/4, 3/4 6/8 2/4, 12/8, 5/4, 7/4 and 12/4

A GOLDEN AGE ECONOMY

Early Musical Influences

The song writing team of El-Le-Eye-Em were heavily influenced by the great classical composers, e.g. Bach, Beethoven and Mozart, plus some of the 'progressive' rock bands of the time like Deep Purple, Focus, Emerson, Lake & Palmer, Yes, Genesis, Camel and Supertramp. Among the lyricist's favourite classical pieces were Mozart's 'Requiem' and Bach's 'Jesu Joy of Man's Desiring' (Josh Groban version). My friend on the other hand particularly liked Beethoven's symphonies.

The duo was also inspired by virtuoso groups like Deep Purple because of their abilities as composers, improvisers and musicians. The lyricist first heard Deep Purple on the radio when they performed the 'Concerto for Group & Orchestra' live at the Royal Albert Hall with the Royal Philharmonic Orchestra conducted by Sir Malcolm Sergeant in 1969. The Concerto was a classical music piece composed by Jon Lord, Deep Purple's keyboard player, which had been written for group and orchestra. He was captivated by the idea of blending these two apparently opposing yet dynamic and powerful styles of music together and inspired by the effect it produced. In fact, he later revealed that it was hearing this concert that inspired him to learn to play the drums and later to take up songwriting.

The pair also loved certain styles of melodic rock/blues as performed by such artists as the guitarists Gary Moore and Joe Satriani. And singer/songwriter, Jon Anderson, who also fronted the group Yes was another. Jon's music was very spiritual and brought messages of love, hope and comfort to that lost world with songs like his hit single 'I'll find my way home'. Satriani's song 'I believe' was also in a similar vein.

Up until 2012 the writing team had never really attempted to write any openly commercial songs until the opportunity presented itself with the occasion of my friend's eldest daughter's wedding. He told me that apparently the lyricist had woken up early one morning and written down the words to a song called 'My Daughter'. When my friend saw the words he added the music and was so pleased with the result that he decided that he would sing it solo to his daughter as part of the Father of the Bride's speech. When the full production version of the song was eventually released it proved to be incredibly popular and is still played at weddings today.

Enlightened Pop

The duo were the beating heart of El-Le-Eye-Em, though it was not long before other musicians had been brought in and the group was ready to start rehearsing their set of 'enlightened pop', as the lyricist called them. He had penned over thirty numbers by the time the pair had become full-time musicians in 2013, with their own studio in which to work and rehearse.

What differentiated El-Le-Eye-Em's enlightened pop from nearly all other types of modern popular music like rock and traditional pop was that it did not have the syncopated beat as its basis. Syncopation was only ever used to add variety here and there, but never as the core part of the rhythm. This did not mean that you could not dance or tap your foot to El-Le-Eye-Em's music. On the contrary, they made a point of performing songs using all the rhythms of life (i.e. 4/4, 3/4, 6/8, 2/4, 12/8, 5/4, 7/4 and 12/4) that corresponded to the chakras. Whereas rock music literally rocks the light out of the listener's energy centres, El-Le-Eye-Em's non-rock rhythms – overlaid with beautiful lyrics and melodies – caused people's chakras to spin more rapidly so they could hold more light. Hence the description 'enlightened pop'. The effect this had on audiences was very positive as they would leave the venue feeling revitalised, energised and happy rather than drained and punch drunk as was usually the case with most rock and pop concerts

During the introduction to their live show the male and female lead vocalists would make the following statement of intent: "Ladies and Gentleman we are El-Le-Eye-Em and tonight we're going to lift the roof off and let the light in." Now on the face of it this was a pretty straightforward statement of intent, but when you analyse these words there was much more to them than is apparent on the surface.

So what were they really saying?

Well, my own view is that they were implying that they were going

A GOLDEN AGE ECONOMY

to (physically and spiritually) raise the audience up to great height with their music so that – in a metaphorical sense – they would be able to touch the ceiling or even break through it, so that the light from the stars and heaven could enter in and fill their chakras. "Lift the roof off" has several layers of meaning: i.e. to uncover, expose or reveal hidden truths, which means raising awareness. But this phrase also implies power and high levels of energy, which was a core characteristic of the band's music. It possessed an underlying strength and intensity, though this was always tempered by passages of exquisite beauty and harmony that carried within them the vibration of love. "Let the light in" means helping abundance to flow by playing the 'right kind of music', which is music that qualifies God's energy. Taken together these two phrases really mean helping to raise consciousness by fanning the threefold flames of Power (El) Love (Le) Wisdom (Eye) that bring people together in Unity (Em).

The wisdom aspect in the group's name (i.e. Eye) corresponds to the lyrics in the songs that undoubtedly played an important role in the overall aim of raising consciousness. We know the immense power that the spoken (or sung) word carries within it. Hindus chant mantras because they are positive affirmations that can change reality and thus change our world. Decrees serve the same purpose and similarly the power of the spoken word (in the lyrics) can be used in popular music for creative as well as destructive purposes.

The following two examples illustrate the point. The first sets of lyrics are overtly sexual in nature where the intent is to encourage perverse sexual activity and to denigrate love in human relationships.

> I want your bad thoughts
> Your uprighted stick
> Want you in my backdoor place
> Lover you're sick
>
> **– Lady HaHa**
> (A verse from the fictional song 'Sick Romance')

The Secret Speaker's Story – The New Popular Music

The words of the second song, however, celebrate the wonders of nature and the love that our Creator has for his Creation. The theme is gratitude as when we are grateful for what we have received we will be given more abundance in return, meaning more light. So we can see that the intent behind the first set of lyrics is to drain light from the chakras whereas with the second it is to draw more light down.

> I am caressed by the Sun's bright rays
> Bringing light and life to the Earth this day
> I feel the warmth by the Father's hand
> And the Mother's love filling all the land
>
> **– El-Le-Eye-Em**
> (A verse from the real song 'Elements of Love')

I do not propose to recount the details of the tremendous international success that my friend's group enjoyed in the years after their first tour of the United Kingdom, nor will I tell about the Foundation that they set up to help fund the Library of True Religions & Antiquities, as I believe that most of you will already be familiar with these events.

Suffice it to say that El-Le-Eye-Em and the other groups like them that came onto the scene in the post-2012 era did have a significant impact, because they provided the traditional rock and pop audiences with a positive listening alternative that they did not perceive to be so vastly different – though in spiritual (vibrational) terms the difference was the chasm between heaven and hell. Once large numbers of people had been introduced to this new style of popular music it grew to be a permanent item on listening menus and the glaring disparity between the old and the new music became increasingly obvious.

Enlightened Pop made people feel good. They were calmer, less fractious, more co-operative, less aggressive, more loving, less selfish, and more compassionate. In fact, in every way you can imagine, people felt better about themselves and their neighbours. Divisions disappeared. The sense of separation that hitherto so many people had felt between themselves and their Creator passed away. People began

A GOLDEN AGE ECONOMY

to enjoy life because the economy was working and everybody was earning more. Abundance was flowing. And the funny thing was that the more people listened to the right kind of music the better life became. It was as if someone had been putting fairy dust in the water. But it was not the fairies who were the bringers of fortune, it was the right kind of music!

And so I want to leave you with this quotation, which I gave you verbally at the beginning of this lecture; but lest you forget I am going to write it on the screen now. I believe that this is one of the most significant quotations ever to be uttered by a member of the Ascended Host for our benefit:

> "Every discordant condition on this planet could be dissolved and consumed by the right kind of music."
> **– Beloved GODDESS of MUSIC**
> (through the Messenger, Edna Ballard, 16/1/1944 Chicago, Illinois, USA)

So with that thought this lecture is concluded, but before you leave I ask if you would send your healing thoughts to my friend who was unable to speak of these things in person with you today.

Thank you and I will see you for our next scheduled lecture here on Wednesday at 10 am."

Postscript

TO THE SECRET SPEAKER'S STORY

DATE: 24-07-2112

Master Prospero's star student, Wende, had been feeling decidedly unwell during the previous two days of her stay at the family's beach house in Malibu. She could not put her finger on what had been causing her such distress until she started to read the morning paper. For on the front page was the story of two men who had been found dead the day before, in adjacent rooms, in the same Beverly Hills hotel. The newspaper story stated that according to police reports both men had apparently died peacefully in their sleep, but that what was unusual was that the doctor who certified the times of death was almost certain that both men had passed away at exactly the same time.

As to their identity, the story mentioned that the bearded gentleman was Master Prospero who taught Economic History at the Academy of Saint Germain in Jackson, Jackson Hole, Wyoming, and that the other man was a world famous musician and composer and one of the founding members of a group called El-Le-Eye-Em. The report went on to say that hotel staff had seen the two men together on several occasions and that they appeared to be very good friends.

On reading this Wende became terribly upset as she had adored the Master and was also a great fan of El-Le-Eye-Em's music, but the most astounding fact in the story, which she could barely read for the tears in her eyes, was that both men were reported to have been a hundred and fifty-seven years old when they passed away.

ADDENDUM

What Can I Do?

"The world will not be destroyed by those who do evil, but by those who watch them without doing anything."

– Albert Einstein

Peaceful Non-Cooperation

"First they ignore you, then they laugh at you, then they fight you, then you win."

– Mahatma Gandhi
(Spiritual leader of India who led his country to Independence from Great Britain in 1947)

Disarming the Beast

One of my avowed aims in writing this book has been to provide an overview of the influence and reach of the power elite – though I have deliberately downplayed the full extent and depth of their wickedness in order that it should not overshadow my primary objective of demonstrating that there is an alternative way of running our economic affairs that can guarantee prosperity for all.

That the power elite are a rampaging beast from whom we need protection is, I hope, no longer a matter for debate. And, if I were to summarise the second episode of this book in a single sentence, it would be to say that the power elite had deployed three key weapons to control us: secrecy, knowledge and theft. Consequently, my immediate intention is to help to disarm them of the first two, so that we can not only stop the third from continuing but also get back everything they have stolen from us. But for my plan to work this book must reach the widest possible audience. Information is power, and thus, for the many to be empowered, the many need to read this book.

Tell Your Family & Friends

In making this book free to read on the internet I have made this possible, but it is a strategy that leaves me without funds to promote my work, so I am asking for your help. Please tell your family and friends about *A Golden Age Economy*. Presently, Facebook and Twitter are probably the easiest ways to inform people quickly and email is another. I take this opportunity to thank you for anything you are able to do to bring this book to people's attention.

Lobby Your MP
(elected representative)

Another action you may wish to consider is to contact your MP to tell them that you have read this book and that it provides solutions to our economic problems that you would like to see implemented. You might ask them to use their influence to persuade the government to introduce a sound money system based on the principles described in this book, and you might also add that you will not support any MP who is not totally committed to establishing an enlightened free enterprise system.

As a former officer of a major political party my experience of politicians is that they do take notice of their constituents' views, as they know that without our continued support they are ultimately unemployed. I have drafted a sample letter that you may wish to use for this purpose, which you will find at the end of this section. If, however, you know your MP you may wish to use a different approach or form of words.

Vote for the Person Not the Party

> "Voting for independent candidates helps to stop the banks from controlling government policy through the party political system that they created."
>
> – Kim Andrew Lincoln

We should not forget that the party political system was encouraged by the bankers as a means of diverting blame away from themselves for the problems that fractional reserve banking causes – as explained

What Can I Do? Peaceful Non-Cooperation

in Episode Two. And thus, whilst it may seem appropriate to remove support from the main parties who seem intent on maintaining the status quo, I believe that we should proceed with caution as there are some MPs in the British Parliament who belong to the three main parties, who I know would like to see a sound money system established – and it is the same in America. My point is that it is no longer appropriate to vote for political parties. Our focus must now be on voting for the right candidate, and if no suitable candidate presents themselves for election we should not vote at all, as second best will not serve us or our country.

> "Now is the time to take an interest in politics because only politics can change the economics."
>
> **– Kim Andrew Lincoln**

Write to Your Newspaper

Another good way to get the attention of large numbers of people quickly is to write a letter/s to the editor of the reader's letters page of your local, regional or national newspaper. I took this approach after the Credit Crunch by writing one letter every week for two months, and all but one of them were published. You will find the unedited versions of these letters in the 'Letters to the Press' section that follows. Please also be aware that when a politician reads a newspaper the first place they are likely to go is the readers' letters page as this is where they discover what the voters are thinking about different issues.

For the benefit of American readers of this book I have drafted a sample letter that can be sent to the readers' letters section of US newspapers which readers are free to use as a template and amend as appropriate. This letter is located at the end of this section just before 'Letters to the Press'.

Don't Feed the Beast

One of the defensive strategies that the Russians used against

A Golden Age Economy

Napoleon's invading army was to deprive it of food by burning all the crops along the route to Moscow and evacuating the area of farm animals and people. Even Moscow itself was abandoned. As the French army advanced further into Russia its supply line from France became so stretched there was not enough food to go round, forcing a hasty retreat during the bitterly cold winter months. The combination of freezing conditions and lack of supplies destroyed the French army as an effective fighting unit and thus forced Napoleon to flee hurriedly back to France leaving his army to perish from cold and starvation.

The moral lesson here is that you do not have to fight the beast in order to neutralise it. What you must do is to stop feeding the beast so it dies of hunger. What keeps the beast of the power elite fed and in business is our money, which they conspire to steal from us and utilise in the ways I have described in Episode Two. They use our money as a weapon against us, as they believe it makes them strong. Without our money they think they are nothing so we must not give them any more and we must withdraw that which they already have.

Starve the Beast

By combining our individual efforts we can starve this beast to death. We do not need to go to extremes, as all it takes is for a lot of people to do a little, which is far more effective than a few doing a lot. Remember that the 99% represents seven billion people. This is real power when measured against an estimated illuminati membership of just thirteen thousand.

Here are some effective actions we can take:

Grow our own food
Where practical we should attempt to grow as much of our own food as possible, and where it cannot be grown, to buy it from local farmers' markets and retailers that are not owned by the power elite, i.e. local 'Mom and Pop' stores. If you are not sure what constitutes a power elite

business do some research on the internet, but usually these companies are quoted on the Stock Exchange – although that does not mean that all quoted businesses are beyond the pale. Not only will this strategy save us money but we can control what goes into our food and avoid it being contaminated by toxic chemicals used in insecticides and crop sprays. We can also guarantee that the foods we grow are free of GMOs. For health reasons choose fresh food over processed wherever possible. If we have to buy, we should try to do so based on ethics rather than price alone otherwise we could be contributing to the economic destruction of our world. The general rule is to shop locally, buy organic (if we can afford it) and avoid packaged foods produced by large corporations that have no concern for our health, and that use every trick to disguise what is really in the food they produce. Sadly, we cannot rely upon government regulators and protection agencies to ensure that the food we buy is safe to eat. For help on this go to: www.naturalnews.com

Avoid products from companies that exploit their workers
Better to buy goods made in our own country, if possible, as this will help to increase local employment and dissuade domestic manufacturers from shipping production and jobs overseas where foreign workers are likely to be exploited.

Favour firms that are owned and run by their employees
This is the business model for a Golden Age economy that is favoured by Saint Germain and the Ascended Host and it explains why businesses like the John Lewis Partnership in the UK and J C Penny in the USA always do well. By supporting good practice we encourage it to spread.

Be discriminating consumers
We should try to spend our money locally and where it will support good business practice and ethical behaviour. We should try to keep the money we spend in the area where we spend it as this promotes local employment. Every time we buy something we should ask the

A GOLDEN AGE ECONOMY

question, "Does this purchase support a corporation that is working against the interests of me and my family?" and act accordingly.

Barter

Barter wherever possible, as this cuts bankers out of the loop and helps to increase the living standards of those with little cash. We can barter surplus food we have grown, goods we have made or skills we have. Remember that our time has value and we all have skills that other people may need from time to time: e.g. a haircut for a car wash or some gardening for some decorating. The other major benefit of bartering is that it is not subject to income tax and thus deprives the big brother state of funds.

Reduce reliance on banks

Whereever possible we should switch to cash transactions using notes and coins as this will help to stop the international banking cartel from introducing the 'mark of the beast' system of electronic money trading. This is the single world currency operated via RFID chips that the Rockefellers want people to have implanted in their right hand or forehead as described in Revelation and Episode Two of this book. This must be resisted at all costs. In the James Bond movie *Casino Royale* 'M' (Judi Dench) insists that James Bond (Daniel Craig) has one of these RFID chips implanted in his right arm so that she will always know where he is. The suggestion here is that if it is acceptable for James Bond to be 'chipped' then why shouldn't everyone else? The power elite attempt to brainwash us via the movies just as much as they do in the music business.

Pay off credit cards and loans

Although they are convenient, credit cards are the most visible manifestation of money created as debt. Moreover, they are expensive to use, both in terms of charges and fees, and the rate of interest is generally a lot higher than conventional bank loans. So, for these reasons, we should make a determined effort to rid ourselves of credit cards completely. Indeed, we should try to pay off all bank debt.

Support ethical banking

The most obvious way to stop feeding the banking beast is to withdraw our money from the illuminati-controlled banks and put it into places where it can do some good, such as local credit unions and mutually owned building societies. Better still would be to support banks that operate the Islamic finance model, based on Sharia law. We can also support ethical lending banks like the Triodos Bank.

> "As the creation and distribution of money should be the sole preserve of the state, I can see no reason for private banks to exist – other than to offer a savings and loans service where the bank cannot lend out more than it takes in and where fees instead of interest are charged. In the UK the Post Office could be affiliated to a State-run 'People's Bank' to provide banking services, and this would have the added benefit of breathing new life into those communities that, as a result of profit-driven rationalisation programmes, have had these services removed."
> – Kim Andrew Lincoln

Remember that when we deposit £1,000 in a bank the fractional reserve 'multiplier' will turn that into at least £9,000 on which the bank earns interest. But when we withdraw £1,000 we deny them the ability to make £9,000 in loans, which shrinks their profits and reduces their ability to steal the value of our money through the inflation this excess money created causes.

In the USA most credit unions are not permitted to bet on derivatives, which at the time of writing (March 2012) have a financial exposure measured in hundreds of trillions of dollars, which is more than enough to collapse the world economy.

> "A sound bank is one where depositors' longer term savings are reinvested in order to help the economy grow. It is, by and large, a pretty boring business. But that's all right, because an exciting bank is not a place where you would want to put your money."
> – Kim Andrew Lincoln

A GOLDEN AGE ECONOMY

Reduce our dependence on oil
Next to the monetary and banking system, oil is the second most powerful means by which the power elite exercise their control over us. Finding ever more ways to use less oil weakens their hold.

Operate a personal gold standard
The God of Gold recommends that we re-establish our personal economies on the gold standard by transferring the equivalent of between 0.5 – 1.0% of our monthly incomes into gold as a matrix and focal point, and that what gold we do not adorn ourselves with should be stored securely. He says that our bodies and those of our children need to become adjusted to the vibration of gold as this will help us to manifest the Christ consciousness that is our earthly aim.

> "As for the future of the speculation (investment) business I do not see one because I think that these parts of the financial services industry will self-destruct soon."
> – Kim Andrew Lincoln

Stop supporting the power elite by working for them
Yes it's easy to say, but with high levels of unemployment in the West it's not so easy to do. But if we think about it logically, if we all stopped working for the power elite tomorrow we would put them out of business. Without employees to prop up their evil system it cannot function and continue to bring us down.

The solution is simple and strategically sound: we stop working for the bad guys – the forces of darkness within government and industry – and choose instead to only work for the good guys, meaning ourselves on a self-employed basis, or if that is not appropriate, for businesses that do not cause harm to society. If, at the same time, we only spend our money with good firms then the jobs will be there so that we can make the switch. The power to do this lies in our own hands.

Vote for Ron Paul in 2012
As I stated in episode three Ron Paul is the only candidate (of

What Can I Do? Peaceful Non-Cooperation

significance) who will fan the freedom flame and thus do what is right for Americans and the rest of the world. It is through his leadership that America can regain its dominant economic position as China (a communist country where Chairman Mao is still widely worshipped) is now the strongest economy in terms of international trade and equal in Gross Domestic Product (GDP) to the USA. www.RonPaul2012.com

If you are not eligible to vote in the US elections please urge any friends and family you have in American to vote not Republican or Democrat but to vote for RON PAUL!

> "To serve the people well politicians do not have to be perfect, just pure in heart".
> – **Kim Andrew Lincoln**

> "The care of human life and happiness and not their destruction, is the first and only object of good government."
> – **Thomas Jefferson**

Further Reading

> "To manifest a Golden Age economy we must first manifest a Golden Age consciousness."
> – **Kim Andrew Lincoln**

In strategic terms the list of actions described above will help to curtail the negative activities of the power elite, and the Laws of Disintegration will bring their towers of Babel down. This will stop the New World Order from materialising, but these actions alone will not bring a Golden Age economy about. For that to happen we have to make it happen, by raising our game, by being more of the divine spiritual beings that we truly are. This means engaging in activities that will take us above the level of the duality consciousness that prevails on this planet and that is directly responsible for creating the dire conditions we are experiencing now. In short we need to work on developing a Golden Age Consciousness. For the spiritual tools and teachings that

A GOLDEN AGE ECONOMY

will help us to do this I recommend: www.theosophiaistheway.com. This website is sponsored by the Ascended Masters and contains their most recent teachings.

> "If you want to awaken all of humanity, then awaken all of yourself; if you want to eliminate the suffering of the world, then eliminate all that is dark and negative in yourself. Truly the greatest gift you have to give is that of your own self-transformation."
>
> — **Lao Tzu**

LETTERS YOU CAN USE TO LOBBY YOUR MP AND WRITE TO YOUR NEWSPAPER

LETTER ONE – FOR UNITED KINGDOM VOTERS TO LOBBY THEIR MP

Dear ...

THE SOLUTION TO OUR ECONOMIC PROBLEMS

Two centuries ago a great injustice was voted out of existence when slavery was abolished in the British Empire. Now I call upon you as my MP to follow in the footsteps of William Wilberforce and support the abolition of another form of slavery, the fractional reserve banking system (FRBS), which has denied the people of this country the abundance that our Creator wants us to have.

I am inspired to write to you after reading an extraordinary book that sets out in simple terms precisely how we can create unparalleled prosperity, by taking back control of our economy from the privately owned banks. This book is entitled *A Golden Age Economy* and it provides credible solutions to all our economic problems that the author, Kim Andrew Lincoln, claims are easily solved if we follow the Universal Laws of Life that relate to the economy, and on which the enlightened free enterprise system he espouses are based. If you are not familiar with how the FRBS steals our wealth and destroys the economy I refer you to the chapter 'The Biggest Crime of All Time' in Episode Two, which describes how this giant Ponzi scheme works – or should I say does not work!

I shall not be voting for any candidate at the next election unless I am convinced that they are fully behind the abolition of the FRBS and

A GOLDEN AGE ECONOMY

the establishment of an enlightened free enterprise system. MPs that I know want the FRBS outlawed include Michael Meacher, Steve Baker and Douglas Carswell. They also support the 'Positive Money' campaign www.positivemoney.org.uk, which I consider a possible first step on the road to fundamental change. I personally will not be satisfied until every vestige of our corrupt and counterproductive monetary and banking system has been dismantled and I ask for your support in helping to bring this about.

A Golden Age Economy is a book for our times and it can be read for free at: www.agoldenageeconomy.com

Yours faithfully,

(Your Name)

PS: I have informed my Facebook friends about the *A Golden Age Economy* book.

NB

To email the above letter to your MP go to: www.writetothem.com and type in your postcode to obtain your MP's contact details. You can then from the website version of this book www.agoldenageeconomy.com copy and paste this letter into the text box provided and then click to send the email. The whole process takes about a minute or so to complete and I promise you that it will achieve positive results.

LETTER TWO – FOR USE BY UK CITIZENS TO SEND TO THE READERS' LETTERS PAGES OF NEWSPAPERS IN THE UNITED KINGDOM

THE SOLUTIONS TO OUR ECONOMIC PROBLEMS

Two centuries ago a great injustice was voted out of existence when slavery was abolished throughout the British Empire. Now there is another beast that needs defeating and that is the beast of debt and fractional reserve banking that has enslaved us all, stolen our money and destroyed our economy.

I am inspired to write this letter having just finished reading an extraordinary book entitled *A Golden Age Economy* that explains precisely how we can create unparalleled prosperity, simply by taking back control of our economy from the private banking network. This book provides credible solutions to our economic problems that the author, Kim Andrew Lincoln, claims can all be solved if we follow the Universal Laws of Life that relate to the economy.

Kim is calling for the establishment of an 'enlightened free enterprise system' that he says would work for the benefit of all people – not just the power elite. He claims that this system is based on the teachings given by Ascended Masters like Jesus, St Joseph and Mother Mary and that unless it is introduced there is absolutely no chance of a sustainable economic recovery as he claims that the fractional reserve banking system that is used here and in most countries is the root cause of all our financial problems.

A Golden Age Economy is a book for our times that can be read for free at: www.agoldenageeconomy.com

Letter Three – For Use by American Citizens to Send to the Readers' Letters Pages of Newspapers in the USA

THE SOLUTIONS TO OUR ECONOMIC PROBLEMS

One hundred and fifty years ago our countrymen went to war to end the injustice of slavery. Now there is another beast that we must defeat that has enslaved us with debt, stolen our money and destroyed our economy. I am talking about the 'fractional reserve banking system' (FRBS) that is controlled and managed by the privately owned banks that make up the Federal Reserve.

A GOLDEN AGE ECONOMY

I am inspired to write this letter having just read an extraordinary book entitled *A Golden Age Economy* that explains precisely how we can create unparalleled prosperity, simply by taking back control of our economy from the Fed. This book provides credible solutions to our economic problems that the author, Kim Andrew Lincoln, claims can be solved if we follow the Universal Laws of Life that relate to the economy.

The author is an English financial adviser who, like Congressman Ron Paul, wants to end the Fed and abolish the FRBS. He also calls for the establishment of an enlightened free enterprise system that works for the benefit of all people being based on the teachings of Ascended Masters like Jesus, St Joseph and Mother Mary.

In the last episode of his book Kim tells the story of what happened on Earth from 2012 onwards looking back in time from the year 2112. The story is set in the Academy of Saint Germain in the town of Jackson, Jackson Hole, Wyoming, and told through lectures given by a class of economic history students. They speak about what was done to rebuild the economies of America and Europe after the 'Great Crash'.

A Golden Age Economy is a book for our times that can be read for free at: www.agoldenageeconomy.com

Letters to the Press

Writing letters to local, regional and national newspapers is an effective way of getting the attention of politicians, and it encourages others to join in the debate so that a powerful momentum for change can be built.

The People's Bank

The solution to the 'credit crunch' is strict control of the money supply – not more borrowing. Our economy is like an engine, with a badly designed carburettor that is incapable of delivering the correct amount of fuel so that the engine can run smoothly. When too much fuel flows to the engine, it races dangerously out of control (boom). And when there is not enough, it slows down and eventually stops (bust).

And so it is with our monetary system.

When there is too much money in circulation it causes the inflation that devalues our labour, and when there is insufficient money to buy what is produced, deflation and mass unemployment result. These two conditions can only be addressed by ensuring that the amount of money available to spend in the economy is always equal to the value of goods and services produced. When this happens prosperity is assured because everything is in balance, and thus the economy can grow in a sustainable way and boom and bust is avoided.

The lesson of this economic crisis is that banks should no longer be allowed to create excess money through lending. Oversight and control of the money system is the job of government – not the private sector. We must take back control of our economy by stopping the banks from running the system and robbing us blind. The faulty carburettor is their 'fractional reserve banking system', which must be thrown on the scrap heap. And ownership and control of the money system must be handed to the people.

A GOLDEN AGE ECONOMY

This crisis presents us with a wonderful opportunity to establish a 'Golden Age' money system where we are all served by just one bank – the People's Bank. Now that would be bail-out money well spent.

Published in the *Shropshire Star* daily evening newspaper in 2008.

BANKERS PERVERTED THE MONEY SYSTEM

Our economy is collapsing because the private banks that create most of the money in circulation have perverted the money system beyond its original intent and design. Instead of money being a means to an end – as a medium of exchange and a store of future value – they have turned it into an end in itself. Whereas money was our servant, it is now our master as we have become debt slaves to the banking elite, who designed the present system for the purpose of stealing our wealth and exercising power and control over us.

Governments have acquiesced by allowing banks to create excess money by issuing credit (debt). About 97% of the money supplied is created in this way. And banks earn interest on every penny they lend. The only money that banks do not profit from is notes and coins issued by the Royal Mint.

As Banks are allowed to lend ten to thirty times the value of their reserves, there is usually more money in circulation than is needed to buy the goods and services produced. This has caused the inflation that devalues our labour. And, as the price of things like houses has increased, we have been forced to spend a greater share of our income on interest, thus increasing bank profits.

The cumulative effect of the creation of all this excess money is that we are up to our necks in debt and can no longer afford to pay the interest. The banks have run out of people to lend to, so the banking system is collapsing under its own weight.

If we had had a money system run in service of the people, for the people and by the people we would not be facing any of these problems today.

Published in the *Shrophire Star* daily evening newspaper in 2008.

Letters to the Press

CHANGE NEEDED TO SAVE THE ECONOMY

The idea that you can fix the economy and create sustainable economic growth without first dealing with the underlying causes of the problem is completely insane and yet that is what the government is doing and opposition parties are proposing. They serve a bitter soup, but with different spoons when, in fact, a new course is needed. No amount of policy tinkering will have the desired effect because all economic systems in use today are fundamentally flawed. None serve all the people all of the time, as wealth, privilege and political control are inevitably conferred on the few at the expense of the many.

In this country wealth is concentrated in the hands of the top 1% and our personal freedoms and democracy are continually being eroded. In accordance with the second law of thermodynamics, which states that all imperfect forms will eventually be broken down to their base state, our economy and society is on the verge of collapse.

Our salvation lies in the words of the great spiritual teachers like Jesus, Mohammed, Buddha and Krishna whose basic message was that we are individualisations of God and that we cannot raise ourselves up without first raising all life.

For our economy this means that we must embrace and enfranchise *ALL* members of society so that everyone has an equal opportunity to 'multiply their talents' without being exploited, oppressed or enslaved by any individual or organisation or by any imperfect mechanism built into the model. It is a philosophy which states that personal freedom and abundance are our divine right but we cannot receive them at someone else's expense. I call this economic model 'Enlightened Free Enterprise' and believe that if it were adopted planet Earth would immediately enter into a new 'Golden Age'.

Published in the *Shropshire Star* daily evening newspaper in 2009.

CREATION OF A NEW BANK IS CALLED FOR

The Governor of the Bank of England is to be congratulated for criticising the Government and Financial Services Authority (FSA) for their lack of control over the banks, but he does not go far enough.

As an industry insider, I despair at the way the FSA – an unaccountable quango staffed mainly by ex-bankers – fails to provide any meaningful protection to the public. This is due in part to its cosy relationship with the banks. It over-regulates firms that are in competition with the banks, but pose little risk, while giving free rein to investment bankers whose massive bets would have crashed the financial system had we not bailed them out. These bankers have decimated our economy with their recklessness and greed and in so doing have forfeited their right to exist as privately owned and run businesses. If they are too big to fail then the taxpayer should own and control them.

I am sure I speak for most voters when I say to Gordon Brown that we have had enough of your 'New World Order' agenda of boom, bust and bureaucracy. We are fed up with high prices, high taxes and mass unemployment. We want a money system that is capable of delivering sustainable economic growth and that can cure our present financial ills, as well as end world poverty. We want these things because they are our divine right and because we know that they can easily be achieved. We demand that the tables be turned on the money changers and 'fractional reserve banking'. We desire a debt free, money system that serves everyone and releases the people from financial slavery. We call for the abolition of usury and the creation of a publicly owned 'Peoples' Bank.

Published in the *Shropshire Star* daily evening newspaper in 2009.

Government Too Big, Too Bossy & Too Costly

Do not be alarmed by government scare stories concerning swine flu because a really serious pandemic is about to break out – an insidious disease called busybodyitus. This condition is caused by governments who lavish increasing amounts of taxpayer money on trying to control every aspect of our lives and in so doing reduce our rights and standard of living. It is a complaint that will undoubtedly lead to a Great Depression.

Yes, Alistair Darling is at it again with an increase in the tax on flights, but this time he admits that it's not meant to be green – though it certainly is greedy. Not content to take over 40% of our income in taxes he wants even more money to balance his books. Having blown over a trillion pounds on the banking bailout, he is introducing more wealth-sapping schemes to subsidise our floundering economy – including a 50% income tax rate, starting next April.

Every day we get poorer as this government mammoth grows fatter. As the number of quangoes increases, more busybodies are taken on to boss us around and drain our freedoms and wealth away. If we are to claw back our rights and riches, the operation and reach of government must be reined in. Government certainly has a role – as a regulator of the private sector and provider of essential services – but the simple truth is that it has become too big, too bossy and too costly.

We must stand together and halt the legions of state bureaucrats before we are overrun. Governments do not diet easily, but for all our sakes this one needs to massively slim down.

I urge readers to write their own prescriptions for less government, more freedom and lower taxes before the next general election.

Published in the *Shropshire Star* daily evening newspaper in 2009.

Leaders Failing to Act on the Economy

Following the end of the political conference season we are left wondering what the point of it all was as no party leader has announced a workable plan to fix our failing economy.

With all the expertise available to them Brown, Cameron and Clegg have not said how they would run the economy without creating inflation and deflation and making bankers rich at our expense. Yet it can be done and they know it.

It seems to me that there is a conspiracy of silence between the banks

– who created the system – and the politicians who allow it to continue. They refuse to reveal how their 'fractional reserve banking system' drains the life blood out of the economy by transferring wealth from the people to the banks, through the device of debt and interest.

The reality is that this three-hundred-year-old system has reached its mathematical limits because we can no longer afford to pay the interest on the cumulative debt created. It is a 'pyramid' scheme that has collapsed and cannot be revived.

A new system must be established where the State working through a 'People's Bank' creates the money needed to get the economy going again but links it to something of real value, like gold, so that unemployment and this boom and bust regime are eliminated. If the three main political parties are not prepared to act, then we must elect a new and enlightened breed of independent politicians who are not slaves to the party machine and the vested interest of the private banks that control the world.

Published in the *Shropshire Star* daily evening newspaper in 2009.

GOD'S ECONOMIC POLICIES NEEDED

The financial system is too important to our physical and spiritual well-being to be controlled by deluded bankers like Lloyd Blankfein, boss of Goldman Sachs, who in a recent press report claimed that his firm was doing 'God's work'. I suggest the evidence is to the contrary and that banks like Goldman Sachs are working for the other guy – the one whom Archangel Michael kicked out of heaven because he had become so filled with pride that he was no longer prepared to serve humankind.

Spiritual pride and the corrupting influence of absolute power have wrought the downfall of many who thought they were too big to fall and is one of the reasons why our economy has been brought to the brink of ruin. These 'Masters of the Universe' have become so mired in the illusory world of mammon that they have lost touch with reality and forgotten how to serve the greater good.

By destabilising the financial system with 'derivatives', they have shrunk the economy and stolen our jobs. That is not doing God's work.

By manipulating the money supply they have engineered rises and falls in asset prices that have brought about massive transfers of wealth from private investors to the banks. This is not doing God's work.

By enslaving the good people of this land with an ever-increasing burden of interest payments they have created poverty and prevented sustainable economic growth. Again, this is not doing God's work.

But if the government were to set aside self-interest and place the power to create money in the hands of the people via a People's Bank then this would be doing God's work. And, if they made the charging of interest illegal, as Archangel Gabriel told the Prophet Mohammed to do, then I am sure that God would say that his work was being done and there would be much rejoicing in Heaven as there would be on Earth.

Published in the *Shropshire Star* daily evening newspaper in 2009.

The Golden Age Begun

So many voices here do sing
Christ Victory is won
For in our hearts he is alive
Our Golden Age begun.

Dear Saint Germain this time is yours
Your highest vision comes
Duality is on the wane
The dark from Earth have gone.

Our Will and Power is reclaimed
And love that is divine
And wisdom takes us to the truth
The One in All we find.

The Golden Age, the Golden Age
Begun because we say
And all the hurt of ages past
Our love consumes today.

Forgiven all who have us wronged
As they forgive this day
Mistakes we made were learning
To find the Middle Way.

Freedom we seek unlimited
The banner that we wave
Abundance our God given right
No more shall we be slaves.

© COPYRIGHT 2009 **KIM ANDREW LINCOLN**

SOURCES

BIBLIOGRAPHY

BROWN, E. H., *The Web of Debt* (Third Millennium Press, Baton Rouge, USA, 2007).

CAWTHORNE, N., *Daughter of Heaven* (Oneworld Publications, Oxford, 2007).

HERMES, MERCURIUS TRISMEGISTUS, *The Divine Pymander* (Translation by John Averred, London, 1650).

GOLD, C., *Queen, Empress, Concubine* (Quercus, London, 2008).

ICKE, D., *The Biggest Secret* – updated second edition (David Icke Books, Ryde, Isle of Wight, 1999).

MICHAELS, L., *The Unseen Power In I Am* (Shangra-La Mission, USA, 2009).

MICHAELS, L., *The Way of Being* (More to Life Publishing, USA, 2009).

PROPHET, E. C., *Fallen Angels and the Origins of Evil* (Summit University Press, Montana, USA, 2000).

PROPHET, E. C., *Predict Your Future: Understand the Cycles of the Cosmic Clock* (Summit University Press, Montana, USA, 2004).

PROPHET, M. L & E. C., *The Science of the Spoken Word* (Summit University Press, Montana, USA, 2004).

RYAN-COLLINS, J. /**GREENHAM**, T. /**WERNER** R. / **JACKSON**, A., *Where Does Money Come FROM?* (New Economics Foundation, London, 2011).

SPROTT, D., *THE HOUSE OF THE EAGLE* – Book One of the Ptolemy's Quartet (Faber and Faber, London, 2004).

THAME, D., *The Secret Power of Music* (Destiny Books, Rochester, Vermont, USA, 1984).

A GOLDEN AGE ECONOMY

WEBSITES

www.ascension-research.org, 2011.
www.askrealjesus.com*, 2007.
www.askjesustruth.com , 2011.
www.bigeye.com, 2011.
www.burzynskimovie.com, 2011.
http://canadianawareness.org , 2011.
www.divinecosmos.com, 2012
www.educate-yourself.org, 2010
www.flixxy.com , 2011
www.financialsense.com, 2009.
www.financialsensearchive.com, 2009.
www.fool.com, 2011.
www.globalresearch.ca, 2011.
www.heraldtribune.com, 2010.
www.illuminati-news.com, 2011.
www.islamic-bank.com, 2012.
www.johnperkins.org, 2011.
www.kybalion.org, 2010.
www.larryhannigan.com, 2009.
http://metaexistence.org/dinarbook.pdf, 2012.
www.monetary.org, 2010.
http://moneyreform.wordpress.com, 2010.
www.moveyourmoney.org.uk, 2012.
www.nesara.us, 2011.
www.neweconomics.org, 2010.
http://www.nibiruancouncil.com, 2006.
www.organicauthority.com, 2011.
www.pesn.com, 2012.

*Relates to certain material relating to a divine economy published on this website prior to Kim Michaels losing his position as a messenger for Jesus and other Ascended Masters of the Great White Brotherhood. Jesus has now passed judgement on this website for the false teachings it promotes.

Sources

www.phoenixmasonary.org, 2010.
www.positivemoney.org.uk, 2011.
www.prisonplanet.com, 2011.
www.pureinsight.org, 2006.
www.pymander.com, 2009.
www.relfe.com, 2008.
www.reluctant-messenger.com, 2010.
www.sacred-texts.com/eso/pym/index.htm, 2009.
www.shangrala.org, 2010.
www.seri-worldwide.org/id435.html , 2010.
www.squidoo.com/Illuminati, 2011.
www.tentmaker.org/biographies/origen.htm, 2010.
www.tsl.org, 2009, 2010, 2011, 2012.
http://theenergylie.weebly.com, 2011
www.theecologist.org, 2011
www.thehealthyhomeeconomist.com, 2011
www.theosophiaistheway.com, 2011, 2012
www.themoneymasters.com/monetary-reform-act, 2011
http://wakeup-world.com, 2011
www.webofdebt.com, 2009
www.wikipedia.org, 2009, 2010, 2011. 2012
www.youtube.com/watch?v=sDjcVrZnemM&feature=youtube_gdata_player, 2012

Films/Tv

ALEXANDER – *Director's Cut*, Director, Oliver Stone, Warner Bros. 2004.
CLEOPATRA, Director, Franc Roddam. Based on the book *Memoirs of Cleopatra* by Margaret George. Universal Studios, 1999.
CASINO ROYALE, Director, Martin Cambell. Based on Ian Fleming's book. United Artists, 2006.
GANDHI, Director, Richard Attenborough, Columbia Pictures, 1982.
JESUS OF NAZARETH, Director, Franco Zeffirelli, ITC Entertainment Ltd & RAI, 1977.

A GOLDEN AGE ECONOMY

JOHN ADAMS, Director, Tom Hooper. Based on David McCullough's Pulitzer Prize winning book, HBO, 2007.

WAR AND PEACE, Director, Sergei Bondarchuk. Based on Leo Tolstoy's novel, Mosfilm, 1965-67.

WALL STREET – MONEY NEVER SLEEPS, Director, Oliver Stone, Twentieth Century Fox Film Corporation and Dune Entertainment III, 2010.

Articles

Recreational Drug Use in America by Lorraine Michaels, published on www.theosohiaistheway.com , 2011. This article was first published in 2005.

The Flow of Energy in the City Foursquare (The Reestablishment of the Gold Standard) Pearls of Wisdom Vol. 53 No.23, The Beloved God of Gold with the God Tabor, published by the Summit Lighthouse, Montana, USA, 2010.

Here's How We Messed Up Our Financial System by Morgan Housel published on www.themoneytimes.com/node/72401, 2009.

Modern Money Mechanics. Published and Distributed by the Federal Reserve Bank of Chicago. The original booklet was by Dorothy M. Nichols and published 1961. The latest revised version was by Anne Marie L. Goncy and published in 1992. It is available to read online.

The Retreat of the Shadow Lenders, Why Deflation and not Inflation is the Order of the Day by Ellen Brown published on www.webofdebt.com, 2009.

The Marginal Productivity of Debt by Antal E. Fekete, published on www.financialsensearchive.com, 2009.

The Key to Abundance by Lucia Sweetland published in the Utica New Age Examiner on www.examiner.com/article/the-key-to-abundance, 2011.

The Aquarian Age Gospel of Jesus, the Christ of the Piscean Age, transcribed by Levi H. Dowling, published on www.reluctant-messanger.com, 2011. The web– link is www.reluctant-messenger.com/aquarian_gospel.htm

Bilderberg 2011 Discussion Leaked via Moles Inside by Daniel Estulin published on www.danielestulin.com, 2011.

Author's Acknowledgements

Elizabeth Lincoln
To my dearest wife, Elizabeth, for her support and generosity in allowing me the time to devote to this project. Darling, I could not have done it without you and that is the absolute truth. You are my rock and I thank you from the bottom of my heart xxx.

Anni Law
To my dear friend and spiritual sister, Anni, who suggested I undertake this work and whose encouragement, words of wisdom and messengership has been of immense assistance. Anni, I am indebted to you.

Lorraine Michaels
To Lorraine, who in her spiritual office as the Guru Ma and messenger for the Ascended Masters has been the source of much of the material for this book. Lorraine you are an inspiration.

Tom Watkins
My thanks to Elizabeth and Tom for their input on the design of the front book cover.

Manuel Greenwood
And lastly, special thanks to Manuel Greenwood of Dawley Web Design for his graphic design work and technical wizardry. www.dawleywebdesign.co.uk